PRACTICAL INTELLIGENCE

Roger Peters

PRACTICAL INTELLIGENCE

working smarter in business and everyday life

1817 **Harper & Row, Publishers**
New York, Cambridge, Philadelphia, San Francisco, Washington,
London, Mexico City, São Paulo, Singapore, Sydney

FOR ARDEN

PRACTICAL INTELLIGENCE. Copyright © 1987 by Roger Peters. All rights reserved. Printed in the United States of America. No part of this book may be
used or reproduced in any manner whatsoever without written permission
except in the case of brief quotations embodied in critical articles and reviews.
For information address Harper & Row, Publishers, Inc., 10 East 53rd Street,
New York, N.Y. 10022. Published simultaneously in Canada by Fitzhenry &
Whiteside Limited, Toronto.

FIRST EDITION

Designer: Ruth Bornschlegel

Copyeditor: Marjorie Horvitz

Library of Congress Cataloging-in-Publication Data
Peters, Roger.
  Practical intelligence.
  Bibliography: p.
  Includes index.
  1. Executive ability. 2. Personality and
intelligence. 3. Practical judgment. 4. Success in
business. I. Title.
HD38.2.P47   1987   650.1   86-46096
ISBN 0-06-015681-3

87 88 89 90 91 RRD 10 9 8 7 6 5 4 3 2 1

I hear and I forget.
I see and I remember.
I do and I understand.

Contents

Preface

This book gives practical advice about practical abilities. I hope it will help you work smarter through a better understanding of the diversity and development of practical intelligences.

As my use of "intelligences" suggests, describing diversity entails making distinctions among various kinds of intelligence: practical versus academic, personal versus mathematical, spatial versus verbal, and so on. Distinctions among abstractions like intelligences allow me to write about each of these many ways of being smart. These distinctions are, however, artificial even if they are useful. Connections among intelligences are as important as the intelligences themselves. Thus, as you read each of the interviews and case studies that illustrate a particular form of intelligence, note all the others at work beside it.

Artificial distinctions are only the most obvious of several simplifications that I use to expand your notions of how intelligences work. In many cases I gloss over theoretical complexities and empirical contradictions. If you are interested in pursuing the deeper intricacies of practical intelligences, they are well documented in the references at the end of the book.

Books, like all human enterprises, are products of nature and nurture. I must acknowledge my debt to the grandparents of this book, the researchers whose work I cite. I also thank the father, Daniel Goleman, whose *New York Times* article first brought the phrase "practical intelligence" to my attention. The godfather was Glenn Cowley, who convinced me that there was a book in Goleman's article, and managed the practical details of bringing it to term. George Klemp of Charles River Consulting provided an avuncular trust fund of methodology and encouragement. Between bouts of morning sickness, I was nurtured by my extended family at Fort Lewis College in Durango, Colorado: Norman Linton, Hal

Mansfield, Gloria Manucia, and Steve Roderick. A shower of reviews, amendments, and horse laughs from friends and colleagues elsewhere, especially Claudia Blair and Sharon Landesman, made my labor more productive than painful. Hugh Van Dusen of Harper & Row was the obstetrician; he gave me better care than a writer a month past the due date deserves. My midwife/coach was editor Cynthia Merman, who got me to the delivery room, and once there, told me how to breathe and when to push. Thanks to all these people, my delicate condition yielded robust issue. Nevertheless, when it comes to bad manners or more serious errors, I am the first to admit that this book is my baby.

PART ONE

PRACTICAL INTELLIGENCES, STYLES, AND SKILLS

1.
Working Smarter:
The Context of Practical Intelligence

There is nothing as practical as a good theory.

—KURT LEWIN

Top performers "work smart." They think well about the practical problems of their jobs, including those that have to do with getting ahead. Take my friend Bob, an executive in what used to be *the* phone company. He claims that when he was in charge of the pay phones in his state, they all worked. I believe him. He can fix anything, but he never has to because everything he uses is meticulously maintained. The clocks he builds as recreation all strike at once. Bob is good at what he does because he knows how to keep an eye on the right ball—and how to manage someone who can watch it when he can't. Psychologists call this sort of know-how "practical intelligence."

Practical intelligence is much more than the "school smarts" measured by IQ. As Emory University psychologist Ulrich Neisser puts it, "There are many ways for people to be smart. The ones IQ tests measure are just a few of hundreds." It takes different kinds of intelligence to back up a semi, negotiate a raise, calm a child, or find your way in a new city. Practical intelligence (let's be practical and call it "PI") includes abilities such as dexterity, sensitivity, and a sense of direction. Some ways of being smart are as much a matter of style as of ability, of "how" as well as "how well." It takes different styles to buy a used car, design an ad, or manage a portfolio of investments. PI is skeptical, intuitive, action oriented, flexible, and creative.

This book explains all the varieties of practical intelligence, using examples from business, law, medicine, teaching, selling, shopping, investing, driving, and other everyday activities. In this chapter, I show you why PI matters, and explain how much richer and more diverse it is than conceptions of intelligence based on school learning. Chapter 2 explains how conceptions of intelligence have evolved into what psychologists call the "new look" in intelligence, and Chapter 3 outlines my approach to PI. The subsequent chapters concentrate on these ways of being smart and help you to identify, understand, and learn particular kinds of practical intelligence. The payoff is that you may be smart in ways you do not suspect, and that you can learn new ways to work smarter.

PRACTICAL INTELLIGENCE IN ACTION

Here's a case of practical intelligence in action. Alan Morton is a successful real estate developer in New York and Florida. One muggy Saturday morning in July, Morton's top salesman, whom I'll call Bernie, sat on the corner of his desk, looking out the window at the other salesmen swarming around customers touring a model home. Morton came out of his office and saw Bernie. "We're not paying you to stay in here," he growled.

"None of those people are buyers," Bernie replied, sliding off the desk and into his chair.

You're in Morton's shoes. What do you do? Are you going to be assertive, or are you going to trust Bernie's judgment?

Al didn't press the point. Sure enough, within a few minutes the lot was empty and the salesmen, soaked with sweat, were back in the air-conditioned office. A minute or so later, while the other salesmen were still milling around the water cooler, grousing about "mooches" and "tourists," a young couple in a Dodge station wagon pulled in. Bernie sat up as the driver opened the car door for his wife. By the time they were both out of the car, Bernie was out the door. Ten minutes later, he and the couple were in the office, signing a contract.

Webster's tells us that "intelligence" comes from a Latin word meaning "to make distinctions," and defines intelligence as "the ability to apprehend the . . . facts in such a way as to guide action towards a desired goal." Bernie's sale depended on his ability to choose between the "hot prospects" and the "sightseers," to apprehend the facts about potential customers in order to make a sale. He identified the prospects by gathering and combining several kinds of information and ignoring others. He noticed that the couple was young, that they drove a station wagon, and that the man helped the woman out. These facts were combined with sociological information about the kinds of people who drive station wagons and psychological information about solicitous husbands who go shopping with their wives on hot Saturday mornings. All of these facts were processed in the few seconds it took the couple to disembark. Because he had carefully weighed similar kinds of information about the previous visitors, he was fresh and cool when he did go out. As for Morton, he had known enough about Bernie to keep his mouth shut.

Bernie's uncanny ability to sniff out prospects is unusual, but all successful salespeople have it to some extent. Consider a study done for a large retailer by Dr. George Klemp, senior partner of Charles River Consulting in Boston. Klemp studied the differences between excellent and less effective salespeople. He found that, contrary to what many experts, managers, and salespeople themselves believe, excellent salespeople are not aggressive. They do not hustle all prospective customers. It is the less successful salespeople who, "by contrast, tend to hustle people—all potential customers, regardless of the customers' level of interest." Sensitivity to "level of interest" is an important part of the practical intelligence of the successful seller.

Persistence, ambition, and in Bernie's case, the courage to remain in air-conditioned comfort in spite of the desires of his boss are extremely important. But ambition and drive are not enough. Bernie's courage, ambition, and persistence, which he shared with the other salesmen, were not decisive in making the sale. His practical intelligence was.

Here's another case, which you can use to test your own PI. First, I'll give you the problem and ask you to come up with a solution. Then I'll tell you what happened.

This case comes from an interview with the chief executive officer (CEO) of Zoetrope Studios. Zoetrope is the creation of director-producer Francis Coppola, who made *The Conversation, The Godfather, Apocalypse Now, The Outsiders,* and many other films. Located in the shadow of San Francisco's Transamerica Pyramid, Zoetrope is housed in a Victorian survivor of the great earthquake. Small by Hollywood standards, Zoetrope has survived a few earthquakes of its own. Like Coppola himself, the studio has a reputation for placing artistic integrity ahead of financial solvency.

The day-to-day operation of Zoetrope is in the hands of Coppola's *consigliere,* CEO John Peters, a graduate of New College in Sarasota, Florida, Oxford University, and Yale Law. Coppola's penchant for making beautiful movies that lose lots of money places a special burden on Peters, a burden that becomes a crisis whenever a film is in production. During shooting and editing, minimum expenses, even if no film is rolling, run between fifty and one hundred thousand dollars a day. With that sort of meter running, there is tremendous pressure to get things done quickly, even if they will need to be redone later.

Coppola's *The Cotton Club* was a success, but it was shot under circumstances that were inauspicious, to say the least. The script was rewritten day by day, and cost overruns were so large that at one point the producer and Coppola nearly dueled. While Coppola was shooting in New York, Peters was in San Francisco bailing Zoetrope out of one of its chronic fiscal crises—he was negotiating the sale of a major asset, the venerable Hollywood General Studios. The financial backers of *Cotton Club,* concerned about costs and sensing opportunity in Zoetrope's crisis, attempted to renegotiate Coppola's directing contract, tacitly threatening to withdraw support. Needless to say, the proposed new terms were not to Coppola's and Peters's liking. Peters caught the red-eye to New York.

In the morning, he attended a meeting in the law offices of a firm not involved in the negotiation. His opponents were tough-minded "money men" from Las Vegas, and they would not give an inch.

That's the case. Now take the test. As a consultant to Zoetrope Studios, what do you recommend? Do you give in quickly and get back to work? Do you call what you hope is their bluff? Or do you stall, hoping for a miracle?

In the midst of the wrangling, an employee of the law firm appeared, announcing a call from Coppola. There was no time to return the call, so Peters had the message read aloud. It said that Coppola was at the British Airways VIP lounge at JFK airport, about to board the Concorde for London. If the money men wanted him to stay in town to direct *Cotton Club,* they had ten minutes to call him. Otherwise they could reach him in London, where he would be investigating another film. The money men went bananas.

In Peters's words, Coppola's threat was "a masterstroke." Transmitted via a disinterested source, and verifiable by a phone call, the message that Coppola was willing to drop *Cotton Club* was emphatic and uncontestable. Staying in New York would have meant that he was willing to listen to the new offer. Going back to California would have been a weak rejection. Going to London, which by Concorde takes less time than most cross-country flights, was exactly the right message in exactly the right medium—actions speak louder than words. Playing on his own eccentric reputation, he had made exactly the statement necessary to convince the money men that he meant business, so there was little risk and no bluffing involved. Within forty-eight hours, Coppola was back on the set, working under the original contract. He had made the money men an offer they couldn't refuse.

Coppola's ploy is an example of a canniness very different from conventional academic conceptions of intelligence, but it is intelligence nonetheless. Psychology textbooks define "intelligence" as "the ability to acquire and use knowledge." Coppola used his ability to acquire and use information to apprehend the facts of the money men's concerns, international travel, and the state of the negotiations to distinguish among his options in order achieve the goal of keeping the original contract. PI is often a matter of style. Coppola's intelligence was not so much in what he said as in how he said it.

KNOWLEDGE IS CAPITAL

Over forty years ago, Winston Churchill predicted that "the empires of the future are the empires of the mind." Churchill's prediction has come true. According to an article in *Business Week,* we are in a period of "historic transition" in which organizations are coming to be valued "in terms of intangible assets such as knowledge and information processing." In the age of information, knowledge is capital, and the ability to get and use knowledge is the key to productivity. The importance of intelligence in modern work is emphasized in "People and Productivity: A Challenge to Corporate America," a report by the New York Stock Exchange (NYSE) Office of Economic Research. Researchers found that up to one half of the productivity gains of the past came from the intelligent use of knowledge, from "human capital." According to this report, investing in human capital, or "working smarter," is our best hope for increasing productivity. Working smarter means developing PI.

Nowadays, most work is not producing goods but processing information. According to a recent article in *Scientific American,* managers in business devote more than 80 percent of their time to "preparing for and attending meetings and 'presentations,' to collecting information, or to making decisions based on analysis of alternatives." Management consultant Peter Drucker, writing in the *Wall Street Journal,* says, "Information is the manager's main tool, indeed the manager's 'capital.'"

Managers aren't the only "knowledge workers." So are lawyers, doctors, teachers, technicians, engineers, bureaucrats, and more than half of all employees. There are several reasons why the ability to handle information is more important for all workers every day.

Making things continues to be important, but as robots move from science fiction to factory floor, the primarily clerical and service jobs that remain require the kinds of practical intelligence that only humans have.

Furthermore, the more we try to design robots to do manual labor, the more we realize that even the "simplest" manual tasks are far more complicated than we think. It is considered an accomplishment to get a robot to select the correct part from a bin. Even jobs classified as "unskilled manual labor" often require considerable intelligence. Psychologist Sylvia Scribner studied the mental strategies used by warehouse workers in assembling mixed orders of various kinds of products. She found that expert workers assembled cases with far fewer moves than novices used. To take a simple example, an expert with an order for a case and three quarters would *remove* a quarter case, whereas a novice would typically *add* three quarters of a case to an empty carton. A manager who took the time to select and train workers who could quickly learn the shortcuts used by the experts would quickly recover the time.

Finally, people who excel at menial tasks risk promotion to jobs that depend more heavily on higher-level thinking.

As individuals, organizations, and societies advance, working becomes more and more a matter of thinking. Therefore, no matter what work you do, developing your practical intelligence is your best shot at advancing yourself and your organization.

THEORY AND PRACTICE

We have not allied ourselves with Churchill's empires of the mind. We still think of intelligence as somehow separate from "real" affairs. We remain victims of the ancient and artificial segregation of thinking from doing, of theory from practice. Theory and practice *are* different. Each has its own peculiar intellectual requirements. Thinking is creating information, and has no direct consequences other than surprise. Doing creates information too, but it also has real consequences—money spent or saved, cases settled or appealed, lives saved or lost. The value of thinking lies in this difference: Thinking allows us to anticipate ill consequences without suffering them.

Plato separated the intellect and its pure ideas from the body with its practical skills. This distinction laid the foundation for Aristotle's separation of theoretical from practical thinking and his view that theoretical intelligence is superior to practical intelligence. These opinions may have made sense when the philosopher was master and the artisan was slave, but they are now obsolete. They were perpetuated by the dichotomy between mind and body, which crippled psychological thinking about practical intelligence for two thousand years. In the Middle Ages, scholastics distinguished between the "liberal" arts, so called because they were suitable for free men, and the fine and mechanical arts, suitable for artisans and others who handled material things.

Psychologist Rudolph Arnheim, an ardent defender of the intellectual value of making and doing, wrote: "The middle class handles chiefly symbols . . . the working class handles chiefly things." As a result, "a pathological detachment . . . is equated with the highest form of human intelligence," and this intelligence is seen as "a privilege of the middle class." Nowadays, academicians and those in their thrall like to think of themselves as unconcerned with the bottom line.

John Raven, an educational consultant, points out that educators, psychologists, and to some extent people in general do not value bureaucratic competencies. Today, however, what doesn't get administered well doesn't get done well, no matter how brilliant and diligent the people in the trenches are. We will never measure, much less foster, practical intelligence until we value it enough to look for it. One goal of this book is to expand conceptions of intelligence to include and validate administrative and other nonacademic ways of being smart.

A reaction to the view that theory is somehow superior to practice is the disdain that practical people have for theoretical intelligence. The stories they tell about theoreticians show that this reaction is as old as Plato's segregation; the prototype of the genre is a tale about the Greek mathematician/astronomer Thales, who allegedly stumbled into a ditch while contemplating the stars. Yet Thales proves that the practical reaction is just as silly as the theoretical snobbery that elicits it. Thales was a theoretician, but he gave us such practical lore as the number of days in a year and ways of surveying impassable distances.

The practical reaction got a boost from the industrial revolution, which made practical technology the master of theoretical science. Today, Harold Geneen, former CEO of ITT, expresses a contempt for theory that is all too common among people of affairs. In reaction to his colleagues' subjection to management theories "X, Y, and Z," he proposed his own "theory G: You cannot run a business, or anything else, on a theory." Another practical man, a management consultant who advises college administrators, likes to say that when he demonstrated a management information system to an audience of deans, one of them, concerned about selling the system to the faculty, asked, "It may work fine in practice, but how does it sound in theory?"

Another probably apocryphal tale, told by applied mathematicians, concerns the well-known German mathematician Zassen-haus, who was looking for a laundromat in an unfamiliar city. He gathered his clothes into a bundle and walked up and down the streets, but couldn't find one. Eventually it occurred to him to use the Yellow Pages. Entering a nearby phone booth, he found an entire page of laundromats. He left his clothes in the phone booth and returned to his hotel room, smiling to himself. "Did you take your clothes to the laundry?" asked the doorman. "No," replied Zassenhaus, "but the problem is essentially solved."

The legitimate distinction between theory and practice is now an obsolete discrimination. Though as different as locating a laun-dromat and actually doing the laundry, theory and practice are logically inseparable. Avoiding practice is a practical consequence. "The only thing necessary for the triumph of evil," wrote Edmund Burke, "is for good men to do nothing." Similarly, belief in the uselessness of theory is itself a theory. As economist John Maynard Keynes wrote at the end of his *General Theory,* "Practical men, who believe themselves to be quite exempt from any intellectual influ-ences, are usually the slaves of some defunct economist." Although he would probably be among the last to agree with Keynes about anything, Harold Geneen himself acknowledges this point when he refers to his disavowal of theories X, Y, and Z as "theory G."

Though as different as male and female, theory and practice are likewise at their best when they cooperate, as is illustrated by an-other parable: A thinker and a doer stood on a riverbank. They noticed a drowning man being swept downstream. The doer jumped in and saved him, but no sooner had he reached the bank when a woman was swept by, and then another man, and another. The doer jumped back in and was able to save the woman, but not the men. Meanwhile, the thinker climbed a nearby hill. From the top he could see that upstream, a bridge was out. One by one, cars were falling into the river, and some of their occupants were escap-ing, only to be swept downstream. He called the doer and together they blocked the road. The thinker had a good theory; the doer put it into practice.

The moral of the parable, that both theory and practice are essential, is a dominant theme of several recent analyses of contem-porary society. For example, in *The Coming of Post-Industrial Soci-ety,* sociologist Daniel Bell wrote that the "axial principle" of our new age is the "dominance of theoretical knowledge as the main-spring of innovation and policy."

Both the ivory-tower academic and the bottom-line businessper-son are victims of their respective prejudices against doing and thinking. Until recently they have received little assistance from psychologists, who, in their preoccupation with academic intelligence, have promulgated a view of intelligence that is just that, academic. With good cause, many real-world workers have denied the relevance of psychological theory to their affairs. The rest of us are victims too: In the age of information more than ever before, our personal and national productivity have suffered because of a widespread denial of the interdependence of thinking and doing.

STREET SMARTS VERSUS SCHOOL SMARTS

This denial and other misconceptions about intelligence are products of the major institutions for training people to get and use knowledge: schools. In order to expand your awareness of the varieties of intelligence, then, I need to spend a few moments on the many important differences between school and the real world.

Schools are supposed to prepare us for everyday life, and once upon a time, when working was mainly manufacturing, they did a good job for the small fraction of the population who needed basic skills. Today, we need not only the basics but advanced skills as well: innovation, delegation, negotiation, discretion, sensitivity, skepticism, and other managerial competences. Schools are not even trying to teach these skills. Ivan Illich and Jonathan Kozol, Albert Shanker and John Raven argue that schools are not preparing us as citizens and workers. Recently, management scientists have joined the chorus of psychologists and other critics. Whether or not you agree with these critics, it is clear that schools do whatever they do in contexts very different from the workplace.

One important difference between the problems of school and IQ tests, on the one hand, and those of the real world, on the other, is complexity: The problems we learn to solve in school are those that someone has already solved. In other words, they are problems that *can* be solved, problems with one "correct" answer and one "correct" route to that answer. They naturally tend to be simpler than problems that haven't been solved. In school there is no time for problems that take days, weeks, or years to solve, or that have no solution at all.

A second difference between school and work is that school skills come neatly packaged and labeled. As a result, when we solve a physics problem, we know that the solution depends on physics and nothing else. In the real world, the most important problem is often to recognize that there is a problem, and then to decide what kind of problem it is. Medical, economic, political, and technological problems typically have different kinds of solutions. In the real world, such reconceptualizations often emerge in the process of finding a solution. A physician called upon to treat an air traffic controller who hates his boss, smokes three packs a day, and has borderline high blood pressure must decide whether the problem is a medical one in the first place. The doctor might decide that the real problem is a stressful job where co-workers encourage smoking. If the patient is willing and able to leave his job, convincing him to do so may be an effective nonmedical means of reducing stress. On the other hand, if the patient is unable to find other work, the solution may be sought medically, in terms of blood pressure regulation designed to reduce the risk of heart attack.

Third, practical problems often involve skills that most schools don't teach and IQ tests don't measure. None of the kinds of thinking Bernie the real estate salesman did had much to do with academic knowledge. We don't teach sensitivity, intuition, and creativity in school, not because we don't value them but because we don't know how.

Fourth, unlike textbook and IQ problems, practical problems often have several solutions. In such cases, solution depends on generating a large number of solutions, then deciding which ones are best, or at least good enough. The pioneering cognitive psychologist Frederick Bartlett pointed out that in practical problems, the range of alternative solutions is generally not known in advance, the list of alternatives changes as solution progresses, and other alternatives and problems emerge as work goes on. For example, consider the problem of getting a group of busy people together for a meeting. Initially, you have to find out what times are available, so you get everyone's schedule. As you go about scheduling your meeting, other meetings are called, so your list of available times changes. When you've finally found a time slot acceptable to everyone, you find you won't have the information you were planning to present.

Fifth, the criteria by which we judge multiple solutions are often incommensurable. For example, in designing a cam profile, we might find that some designs are good because they are cheap to make, others because they will last longer. There is no generally accepted way to compare these alternatives.

As many educators have pointed out, in the real world one seldom works alone. Unlike exams, term papers, and other academic projects where collaboration is cheating, most practical enterprises require teamwork.

Finally, since school problems are used to evaluate, they are supposed to be fair—i.e., the student is provided with enough information to solve the problem. With real-world problems, this is seldom the case. You often need to do extensive research before you really understand what the problem is. Promised or not, we never get rose gardens; decisions are almost always made under conditions of incomplete information.

We can see all these differences between school and work in our two cases: Bernie didn't learn how to identify buyers in high school, and Coppola did not learn how to handle Las Vegas money men in college.

Given the important differences between school and work, we should not expect grade point average or IQ tests, which were developed to predict success in the classroom, to tell us much about what abilities will make us successful in sales lots and on movie sets. Indeed, there is no relation between grade point average at any level and occupational status or salary. Even very low IQs are poor predictors of ability to function. Psychologists who study mental retardation speak of "six-hour" retardates, whose intelligence is labeled "subnormal" during school hours but who function normally outside school.

In order to develop our own PI, we need to find out how sensitivity, intuition, creativity, verbal ability, critical thinking, and other forms of practical intelligence work in practical settings.

We all may be smarter than we think, in ways we do not expect. If you are like most people, you have only the vaguest idea of your intellectual abilities. Much of this ignorance is the result of the mystification surrounding IQ: the secret scores; the misconceptions that IQ equals intelligence and that it doesn't change; and the denial, defensiveness, and confusion these misconceptions promote. By understanding PI, we can better understand our own intellectual strengths and weaknesses.

But before we can understand PI—the broader conception of intelligence developed by psychologists interested in real-world thinking—we need to understand what their predecessors meant by "intelligence."

2.
The Politics of Intelligence

A good theory is one that holds together long enough to get you to a better theory.

—DONALD HEBB

Plato's *Republic* proposed an aristocracy of intellect led by a philosopher-king. Three hundred years later, the word that gave us "intelligence" was employed for the first time, in an oration by the Roman statesman Cicero, who used it to refer to the ability to discriminate. And ever since then, discrimination is exactly what intelligence has been about. Today, psychologist Daniel Keating, a spokesman for what he calls the "new look in intelligence research," challenges the presumption that "we who study [intelligence] formally have the primary right to define it, and hence usually end up having more of it than other groups that differ on the basis of education, social class, race, sex, or a combination of these." This chapter will show how, thanks to psychologists like Keating, we have moved to a more democratic view of what it means to be smart.

In the twentieth century, a "monarchic" view of intelligence as a single ability has vied with views of it as a federation of various abilities. These latter "oligarchic" and "democratic" views represent the old tradition of "faculty psychology," according to which there are a few or many independent intellectual abilities, called "faculties": memory, perception, creativity, and so on. Faculty psychology is behind the old joke that old deans never die—they just lose their faculties.

With the rise of scientific psychology around the turn of the century, European psychologists took what seemed to be a reasonable first step in applying scientific methods to intelligence: They tried to measure it. A Frenchman, Alfred Binet, developed the first practical test of intelligence, as a means to a completely practical end—to identify and above all to help children who might benefit from what we now call "special education." As a citizen of the land of liberty, equality, and fraternity, Binet embraced a pluralistic view of intelligence: "the mental faculties of each subject are independent and unequal."

It was too much to ask the educators he served to assign children to classes by using a whole set of "independent and unequal" scores, so Binet used the concept of "mental age" as a measure of overall performance on tests of many different abilities. As Binet put it, "One might almost say, 'It matters very little what the tests are so long as they are numerous.'" Binet arranged a variety of school-type questions in order of increasing difficulty on the basis of percentage correct obtained by children of various ages. A question that about 65 percent of the children of a certain age got right was called a test for that age. Any child who could do most of the "seven-year-old" questions, for example, was said to have a "mental age" of seven, whatever his or her age in years.

Binet suppressed his theoretical inclinations, and eschewed speculation about the nature of what it was he was measuring. His disavowal of theory established a tradition of measuring intelligence without defining it, which dominated thinking about intelligence until recently.

Binet constructed his potpourri of tests only to identify and help retarded children in school. But he was barely cold in his grave when Louis M. Terman, a psychologist at Stanford University, began to adapt Binet's questions to different ends. It was Terman who popularized the test known as "Stanford-Binet," which became the standard for most later tests of intelligence. Terman advocated universal testing of schoolchildren to the end of "curtailing the reproduction of feeble-mindedness." The tool he used to discriminate (against) the "feeble-minded" was IQ.

IQ stands for "intelligence quotient." Once upon a time, the numerator of the quotient was Binet's "mental age." The denominator of the quotient was the testee's age in years. The result was then multiplied by 100 to yield a whole number. In algebraic notation,

$$IQ = \frac{\text{Mental Age}}{\text{Age in Years}} \times 100$$

Thus, a ten-year-old who scored like the average twelve-year-old would have an IQ of 120 ($12/10 \times 100 = 120$).

This formula for the "ratio IQ" worked pretty well for the children for whom it was originally designed. By carefully weeding out questions that younger ones did better on than older ones, psychometricians (those who use tests to measure personal characteristics) constructed tests with an average IQ of 100 at every age. (There's a problem with adult testees, which I'll get to shortly.)

Impressed with psychologists' success in measuring intelligence (which they had yet to define), people in business, government, and especially the armed services asked for a scale that could compare an individual's performances throughout his or her lifetime. David Wechsler constructed such a scale, the "standardized" and still the most commonly used adult IQ test, the Wechsler Adult Intelligence Scale (WAIS).

ANARCHY

By the 1920s, IQ, as measured by the Army Alpha and Beta tests (the latter for illiterate testees), was considered the only practical measure of intelligence. However, the legacy of Binet's and Terman's atheoretical approaches remained. There was still confusion and disagreement about what it was these tests were supposed to measure. At about this time, the *Journal of Educational Psychology* published an article with fourteen different definitions of intelligence. Here are a few of them:

- The ability to carry on abstract thinking. —*L. M. Terman*
- Ability to adapt oneself to relatively new situations in life. —*R. Pintner*
- The capacity to learn or to profit by experience. —*W. F. Dearborn*
- The capacity for knowledge and knowledge possessed. —*V. A. C. Henmon*
- Having learned or the ability to learn to adjust oneself to the environment. —*S. S. Colvin*

What is most interesting about these definitions is that they reflect no agreement about the most basic characteristics of intelligence, disagreements that remain unresolved today. Pintner's and Colvin's definitions explicitly involve practical application, but Terman's and Henmon's seem almost perversely abstract. The first three definitions refer to intelligence in the sense of potential; the last two include intelligence as potential plus some degree of achievement ("having learned," "knowledge possessed").

Underlying this distinction between capacity versus achievement is a metaphor of the mind as a bucket. We each have a bucket of a size determined early in life, possibly at conception. Some of us have large buckets but only a little knowledge sloshing around on the bottom. Others have smaller buckets that are full to the brim. And some of us ("geniuses") have huge buckets with lots of knowledge and room for more. This distinction allows us to admit that there are people who are intelligent but poorly educated, just as many people know a lot but don't seem to be able to use what they know anywhere but in academia, where one can get paid for reciting lists of facts. The distinction between capacity and contents has practical implications: If intellectual capacity is innate, we cannot expect to do much to enhance intelligence, practical or otherwise. We will return to the capacity-versus-contents issue shortly.

Many psychologists were understandably dismayed at the absence of any generally accepted definition of intelligence. The great experimental psychologist E. G. Boring attempted to resolve the issue with his notorious nondefinition of intelligence: "Intelligence as a measurable capacity must at the start be defined as the capacity to do well in an intelligence test. Intelligence is what the tests test." Since it abrogated all responsibility for telling us what intelligence *really* is, Boring's suggestion might be described as anarchic—it left the throne of intellect vacant.

Boring's irony was intentional, but he was serious in his suggestion that psychologists rely, at least temporarily, on the testers to tell them what intelligence is. Boring's suggestion was taken all too seriously. Terman, Wechsler, and others quickly succeeded in promoting IQ not only as a measure of academic intelligence but as a definition of what it means to be smart in general.

Anarchy still reigns. The most influential groups of psychometricians are those who have rejected theories of intelligence altogether. As Harvard psychologist Richard Hernnstein put it, Binet "finessed the weighty problem of defining intelligence itself. He had measured it without saying what it was." To the layperson who needs to know what intelligence is in order to use it better, this might seem to be a cop-out. No matter, says IQ defender Arthur Jensen, for "probably the most important fact about intelligence is that we can measure it. Intelligence, like electricity, is easier to measure than to define. . . . There is no point in arguing the question to which there is no answer, the question of what intelligence *is.*"

This view *is* a cop-out; it does not help us to understand and use our intelligences. Useful measurements are impossible without a theory that tells you what you're measuring and why your measurements work. Jensen's analogy makes my point far better than it makes his. As philosopher Hilary Putnam points out, electricity is easy to define precisely because we have a good theory of what electricity is—the flow of charged particles. We know that ammeters measure electricity, not because we have agreed that electricity is "what ammeters measure," but because we have a practical theory that tells us what electricity is and *why* ammeters measure it.

The "operationalist" attitude, which says that intelligence is whatever it is that tests test, is satirized by F. Adler's Cn Test, which "measures C and C is what the tests measure."

Adler's Cn Test

1. How many hours did you sleep last night? _____
2. Estimate the length of your nose in inches and multiply it by two. _____
3. Do you like fried liver? (Mark 1 for yes and −1 for no.) _____
4. How many feet are there in a yard? _____
5. Estimate the number of glasses of ginger ale the inventor of this test drank before inventing it. _____

Add the above items. The sum is your crude Cn-score.

The Cn Test notwithstanding, psychometricians share the attitude toward measurement expressed by Lord Kelvin: "When you cannot measure, your knowledge is of a meager and unsatisfactory kind." Psychologist George Miller has an appropriate reply: "If your knowledge is meager and unsatisfactory, the last thing in the world you should do is make measurements." Our knowledge of intelligence, especially practical intelligence, is indeed meager and unsatisfactory. It's appropriate, therefore, to include a cautionary quote from another expert on measurement, the survey researcher Daniel Yankelovitch:

> The first step is to measure what can easily be measured. This is O.K. as far as it goes. The second step is to disregard that which can't be measured or to give it an arbitrary quantitative value. This is artificial and misleading. The third step is to presume that what can't be measured isn't very important. This is blindness. The fourth step is to say that what can't be measured doesn't really exist. This is suicide.

MONARCHY

In the late 1920s, an English psychometrician named Charles Spearman stepped into the power vacuum left by those who insisted on measuring intelligence as the only way to find out what it was. Intelligence, Spearman said, had become "a mere vocal sound, a word with so many meanings that finally it had none." Spearman was nothing if not consistent. After this proclamation, in all his many writings about intellectual ability he never again used the word "intelligence." Spearman was no kinder to IQ, which he called a "gallimaufry of tests" that had been "picked up and put together without rhyme or reason." His contempt did not, however, prevent Spearman from using the results of IQ tests. Noticing that people who did well on one kind of question were likely to do well on others, Spearman argued for what he called the "monarchic" view that there is one general intellectual capacity, which he called *g*, and defined as the capacity to "educe [discover] relations and correlates." For example, to complete the analogy "Courage is to bravery as humor is to ————," you must educe the relationship between courage and bravery, then apply this relationship to humor in order to determine the correlate that completes the analogy. Spearman installed *g* in the throne as a single, monarchic intellectual power; *g* is a measure of a unitary, general intellectual power that supposedly works in all sorts of situations.

As we approach the turn of a new century, many noted defenders of IQ, including Hans Eysenck, Richard Hernnstein, and Arthur Jensen, accept the divine right of King *g*. This monarchic view is pervasive; whenever we use "intelligence" in the singular, we are unconsciously adopting it. Perhaps this is why people who take experimental tests are called "subjects."

According to the monarchic view, we don't need a separate concept of practical intelligence—PI is just general intelligence applied to practical matters. This view leaves us with IQ as the measure of a general intelligence that works in school and on the job.

Many psychometricians, impressed by the variety of the questions on IQ tests, regard IQ tests as a sort of intellectual decathlon: To get a high IQ is to be an "all-round intellectual." And indeed there are many different kinds of questions. (To see this variety, take a look at some of the problems in Chapters 8 and 9 of this book; and to get a better idea, and a good estimate of your own IQ, use Eysenck's *Know Your Own IQ*.) However, as the differences between the problems of school and the real world described earlier demonstrate, compared to the range of practical problems, those of IQ are quite narrow. IQ tests are more like the biathlon, the Olympic event requiring the combination of small-bore riflery with Nordic skiing. Real-world competence and success in life are much more complicated and more varied than success in school.

For Hernnstein, Jensen, and other monarchists, the power behind the throne is Queen IQ. They continue to defend the utility of

IQ by employers because they believe that IQ tests measure general intelligence, which they regard as a fundamental biological trait. Charles Spearman, who gave us g, had no doubt that he was measuring something real. He proposed that a "material energy" corresponding to g would someday be discovered. Similarly, Richard Hernnstein says, "Many biological traits display normal [bell-shaped] distributions, so that the construction of IQ tests has been guided by the expectation of normality. However, if the expectation were far wrong, IQs would not show the useful statistical properties of normal distributions to the considerable extent that they do." Note that Hernnstein's logic is circular. IQ shows a normal distribution because it has "useful statistical properties." But those properties are themselves the result of the fact that questions are selected and scores are "transformed" with normality in mind. This is not to say that there is nothing biological about intelligence. Some of the most interesting research on intelligence has to do with its biological bases.

On the other hand, in the absence of a physiological description of intelligence, both IQ and g are only statistical abstractions, examples of what John Stuart Mill had in mind when he wrote about the false belief that "whatever has received a name must be an entity or being, having an independent existence of its own. And if no real entity answering to the name could be found, men did not for that reason suppose that none existed, but imagined that it was something peculiarly abstruse and mysterious." Intelligence is a biologically relevant characteristic, but there is more to biologically adaptive intelligence than IQ.

MEASURE FOR MEASURE: TESTING IQ TESTS

Because school smarts are an important part of "street smarts" and "office smarts," and because IQ is a part of most popular and psychological conceptions of intelligence, we need to spend a little time demystifying IQ. There are three criteria by which psychometricians judge measurements like IQ.

The first characteristic of a good test is reliability. You should, over a period of weeks or months, get consistent scores on different forms of the same intelligence test—scores shouldn't depend on your mood, the season, or other extraneous factors. IQ tests are in fact fairly reliable. When scores do change significantly, there's generally a good reason: Experience, maturation, illness, or some other factor has changed the abilities the test is supposed to measure.

The second characteristic of a good test is precision. IQ scores have two or three digits, and thus seem quite precise. Their precision is, however, illusory. Truly precise measurements of quantities like time, weight, length, energy, and money are what scientists call "ratio scales." Both differences and ratios of ratio measurements are meaningful. The difference between one hundred ten dollars and one hundred dollars is the same as the difference between one thousand ten dollars and one thousand dollars: ten dollars. And two hours is twice as long as one hour, two pounds are twice as heavy as one pound, and so on.

A less precise type of measurement is the "interval scale," in which differences between scores (but not ratios) are meaningful. When we use the Julian calendar to measure time, we are using an interval scale. A.D. 2000 doesn't stand for "twice as much time" as A.D. 1000, but the ten-year difference between 2010 and 2000 is the same amount of time as the difference between 1010 and 1000. Temperature is also customarily measured on an interval scale. It takes the same amount of energy to move a thermometer from 60 degrees to 80 as from 40 to 60, but 80 is not "twice as hot" as forty. Interval scales also display additivity: Intervals can be meaningfully added throughout the range of measurement. Four score and seven years refers to the same length of time whether they are years in the 1800s or the 1900s.

The least precise form of numerical measurement is the ordinal scale, where numbers refer to relative ranks, like first and second place. Ordinal scales are imprecise because, as happens in many races, first and second place might be separated by hundredths of a second while third and fourth are minutes behind. Another ordinal scale is the Duncan scale, used to rank various occupations in terms of prestige from 0 to about 100. On this scale, doctors are rated about 90, and police are at 40, which is about the average. Interval and ordinal scales can be useful, but neither is as precise as the ratio scales used to measure length and money.

No one claims that IQs constitute the ratio scale most of us have in mind when we think of scientific measurement. No one claims that someone with an IQ of 150 is "twice as smart" as someone with an IQ of 75.

There is considerable disagreement about whether IQ constitutes an interval or merely an ordinal scale. British psychometrician Hans Eysenck, for example, likes to compare IQ to thermometer readings, which are interval measurements. On the other hand, many psychologists argue that IQ is not even an interval scale, that transformations of raw scores preserve only order, not differences. Stanford psychologist J. P. Guilford says that the IQ scale is best viewed as an ordinal scale. Experimental psychologist Robert Plutchik points out that some psychometricians *assume* additivity of equal intervals but that "No one has seriously tried to show that . . . number of errors . . . are based on an equal interval scale or show the property of additivity."

IQ ranks people in ways that psychometricians may find useful, but the difference in intelligence between an IQ of 130 and one of 125 may not be the same as the difference between a 120 and a 115 IQ. Nor is it possible to say (for example) that training that raises IQ by an average of five points plus diet that raises it by five points will produce a ten-point IQ change. Since IQ satisfies the requirement for neither equality of intervals nor additivity, it seems clear IQ is not measured on an interval scale.

Therefore, IQ flunks the precision criterion of a good test, and what is worse, it masquerades as more precise than it really is. Disagreement about whether IQs are interval or ordinal measurements is a symptom of the fundamental problem: Psychologists cannot agree about what it is they're measuring.

The third and most important property of a good test is validity, the degree to which it measures what it's supposed to measure. A test, like any other measuring instrument, can be precise and reliable without being valid: One of the CEOs I interviewed has a very precise and reliable Omega watch, but he keeps it five minutes fast, so it's never valid.

The consensus among psychometricians is that IQ tests are valid as measures of school smarts in children. Validity does not imply fairness—to say that IQ tests are valid measures of academic aptitude may simply mean that schools and IQ tests are unfair in the same ways.

Problems arise, however, when we equate IQ with intelligence in general, especially in adults. As I have said, abilities measured by IQ are an important part of intelligence, but they are only a part. The special problem that arises when IQ scores are used to measure school or other intelligence in adults is the result of standardization. IQ is mental age divided by chronological age times 100. The problem is that mental age levels off somewhere around twenty, while chronological age keeps increasing. Thus, someone whose score at age twenty yields a "superior" IQ of 120 would, by the ratio formula, get an IQ of 60 if he or she does just as well on the test at age forty. Nowadays, therefore, IQs are no longer computed by formula. Instead, in the elegant euphemism of statistics, scores are "transformed": They are looked up in a table that, for each chronological age from three to seventy, gives what is called the "deviation IQ."

Though "Intelligence Quotient" has a nice mathematical ring, IQs are not really quotients at all.

Hans Eysenck, a defender of IQ as a measure of children's school smarts, says of this standardization: "Giving an adult an IQ, therefore, is a kind of make-believe operation." Raymond Cattell, another supporter of IQ in schools, says, "To continue to regard the traditional intelligence tests as a general intelligence measure when applied after the age of 20 is pure illusion."

The IQ in your personnel file is standardized not only by age but by region, sex, and generation. Every year, any questions on which males, females, or this year's testees do better than females, males, or testees of previous years are weeded out. Even if exposure to video games drastically reduced the school smarts of most males who took the test, their IQ would, by fiat, remain the same as the previous year's males: 100. Even if there are ways in which fifty-year-olds are smarter (or dumber) than twenty-year-olds, the average IQs for both groups are the same: 100.

Thus, the ways IQ scores are determined raise serious questions about their validity as measures of adult intelligence out of school.

IQ and Competence

Nonpsychologists' skepticism about the practicality of IQ and school smarts is captured in the old quip "If you're so smart, why ain't you rich?" How much *does* IQ tell us about someone's chances for success? Not much. Psychologists measure associations between variables like IQ and success with numbers called "correlation coefficients." A correlation of zero means no association whatsoever, a correlation of 1 means a perfect association.

There are so many ways of being good at many occupations that some readers may wonder whether real-world competence and success are quantifiable at all. Nevertheless, we must do the best we can, and measure success in terms of income, ratings by peers and supervisors, and so forth. Correlations between IQ and income or occupational status run about .5. This correlation is about the same as correlations between the heights of fathers and their sons. The average IQ of professional workers, for example, is 120 or higher, while that of clerical workers is around 108. However, each group's scores overlap those of the other, so there are many clerical workers whose IQ is above the professional average. This means that if I know your IQ I can guess your income, but I wouldn't want to bet much of *my* income on my guess.

So much for monetary success. What about performance on the job? Here the correlations are even weaker. Correlations between

IQ and proficiency at various kinds of jobs (as rated by supervisors and co-workers) run between .2 and .5. The average and most commonly cited correlation between measures of general academic intelligence and real-world competence is about .3. All these figures are modest correlations. However, since they are based on large numbers of cases, they are "highly significant" in the statistical sense. That means they are unlikely to occur by chance. However, if we interpret these correlations in terms of how much of the variability in real-world competence we can attribute to academic intelligence, we find that the correlations are not significant in the usual sense. A correlation of .3 means that one variable (IQ) explains less than 10 percent of the variation in the other (real-world competence). That means that conventional conceptions of intelligence ignore 90 percent of the individual differences in PI. Even the correlation of .7 (based on data published in 1947) cited by Hernnstein and other defenders of IQ as a measure of real intelligence accounts for less than half the variance in competence.

Are the modest correlations between IQ and various measures of success evidence that IQ *causes* success? The fact that two quantities are correlated doesn't mean that one causes the other. (My favorite example is the supposed high correlation between birth rates and stork populations.)

No one denies that the skills measured by IQ are essential for schoolwork. The problem is that there are many "confounding" factors, like status, which are correlated with both IQ and success. Arthur Jensen and other defenders of IQ cite studies that show that "high-I.Q. children in later adulthood markedly excelled the general population on every indicator of achievement that was examined: . . . higher occupational status; higher income; production of more articles, books, patents, and other signs of creativity; more entries in *Who's Who;* a lower mortality rate; better physical and mental health; and a lower divorce rate."

On the other hand, Harvard psychologist and management consultant David McClelland argues that such studies *"may* show only that the rich and powerful have more opportunities, and therefore do better in life." In other words, the studies cited by Jensen show too much: If high- and low-IQ people differ in so many ways, how can we be sure that IQ, and not, say, physical or mental health, is the key to their greater success? One way in which this might work is described by psychologist Robert Rosenthal. In a book on what he calls "the Pygmalion effect," Rosenthal raised the possibility that IQ might operate through a kind of self-fulfilling prophecy: Teachers who know students' IQs treat the ones with high IQs preferentially.

The failure of IQ to describe PI is in part due to the empirical approach adopted by psychometricians. Traditionally, they define "success" as income or rank in an organization. They contrast a group of highly successful executives with a group of executives who are less successful. They then identify the intellectual abilities that the successful executives have and the less successful ones don't have. These abilities are called "predictors of success." At first glance, this seems like a reasonable approach to PI, but in fact it has serious shortcomings.

The first difficulty is inherent in the use of correlational data. Remember the lesson of the stork populations and birth rates: The fact that something (IQ) is correlated with something else (success) doesn't mean that the first thing *caused* the other. The fact that successful presidential candidates have been taller than their unsuccessful opponents doesn't prove that height makes a successful campaign.

Second, by limiting their study to what has already happened, empirically oriented psychologists may be closing the door on important abilities that are not now associated with monetary success but that could increase performance if they were allowed to. Creative or critical people in large organizations usually don't get promoted to positions where their creativity or criticism could have some effect. Creativity, criticism, or other abilities incongruent with the organization slip through the cracks of an empirically based description of PI.

Consider the case of a vice-president of General Motors who never made it to the top because he quit out of frustration. Speaking of the hierarchy that prevented him from exercising his talent for long-range planning, he said: "This is totally inconsistent with any thoughtful and creative originality. . . . You couldn't be a planner. . . . It was like standing in the boiler room and tending a machine and you were just watching it instead of running it." We will never know what this VP might have done for GM if the organization had let him apply his intelligence. He is not alone in his alienation. Irving Janis of Yale University uses the term "groupthink" to describe the general tendency of organizations to censor dissent. He makes a strong case that organizational rigidity was an important factor in such examples of practical unintelligence as Watergate and the Bay of Pigs confrontations. That's why Robert Townsend, Thomas Peters and Robert Waterman, and others tell us not only to keep our "mavericks" but to encourage them—even when it hurts. Like the narrowly empirical definition of intelligence as "what the tests measure," narrow definitions of success can blind us to abilities that have important practical uses.

Yet a third problem with psychometric approaches is a fixation on invisible, immutable "traits." Psychological traits are defined as personal patterns of consistency that people carry with them from situation to situation. Behaviorists are fond of pointing out that traits are ghostly entities—very few important ones have ever been connected to anything real. Moreover, cross-situational consistencies in behavior are elusive: A woman in a library reads, and when she goes to a swimming pool she swims, and there may be no relationship between the styles with which she reads and swims. Such low levels of cross-situational consistency make many psychologists skeptical about the utility of traits in predicting and controlling behavior. Traits are by definition insensitive to change. If we are interested not only in identifying but in enhancing PI, we need to consider more than the traits measured by psychometricians; we need to look at the processes investigated by cognitive psychologists.

A final problem with rigidly empirical approaches is pointed out by psychometrician Hans Eysenck and educational consultant John Raven: Before you try to find out whether someone can complete an IQ test question or delegate authority effectively, you need to know whether that person cares enough to try. My favorite example is from the fourth grade, when we were learning long division. Kids who couldn't reduce simple fractions in class were calculating batting averages to three places during recess. Empirical psychologists try to measure value without introducing values. That works fine when what you're measuring is a physical system, but as Raven points out, when what you're measuring depends on motivation, attitudes, and values, values come first.

Values also enter into the success side of the correlation. Money, status, and proficiency are easily measured, but they are only part of success. Today, many workers define success in terms of intangibles like meaning and quality of life as well as in more traditional terms. Any description of the relationship between ability and success must take these new meanings of success into account.

The differences between school and work, problems with the determination, validity, and precision of IQ, the low to modest correlations between IQ and success, the confounding of IQ and success with status, the immutability of traits, and the problems of value all suggest that there is much more to PI than IQ. Reservations about these issues lead some of the staunchest supporters of IQ in schools (like Hans Eysenck) to challenge the utility of IQ at work. These practical issues must be resolved by anyone interested in understanding or using PI.

HIERARCHICAL REFORM

By the 1930s, Spearman's g (backed by Queen IQ) was secure in the throne, where in the minds of many psychologists it remains today. In the 1940s, however, g's power was modified by constitutional reforms. Like g itself, these "hierarchical" reforms are still influential.

The simplest hierarchical variation was proposed by Spearman's student Raymond Cattell. Cattell distinguished two kinds of g, "fluid" and "crystallized." Fluid intelligence is a general intellectual ability, independent of special forms of learning, expressed in perceptual speed, in spatial tasks like those requiring mental rotation of abstract shapes, and in inductive reasoning about arbitrary geometric figures (for example, choosing the next shape in a sequence containing a triangle, a square, a pentagon, and a hexagon). Crystallized intelligence, unlike fluid intelligence, depends on particular kinds of knowledge: vocabulary and other verbal knowledge, arithmetic, "common sense," mechanical knowledge, and other skills acquired through particular kinds of experience.

According to Cattell, people tend to be high in both fluid and crystallized intelligence, or low in both. There are, of course, occasional exceptions: illiterates who "will astonish you in a game of chess, or by solving a wire puzzle with which you have struggled in vain," and Sheridan's Mrs. Malaprop, whose vocabulary outstripped her judgment.

Cattell believed that success in both school and the real world depends on a combination of fluid and crystallized intelligence. In the two environments, the necessary fluid abilities are comparable, but the particular crystallized abilities needed in real-world occupations are different from those of school and IQ. Thus, Cattell regards IQ as useless as a measure of practical intelligence.

Instead, he proposes a "dual IQ." Fluid intelligence scores would be used to predict how people will do when moving from school to work or from one job to a very different one, or to the same job in a different culture. For predictions about how people are likely to do in the same job or similar ones, crystallized intelligence would be far more useful. To Cattell, neither kind of g is superior to the other. For predicting how well someone is likely to do at a job, you may need measures of both fluid and crystallized intelligence.

Crystallized intelligence, to a much greater extent than fluid, can be taught. Logical-mathematical and verbal intelligences are mainly crystallized; they depend on special forms of learning that are taught in school. Intra- and interpersonal intelligences depend on socialization by family and peers, so they, too, are heavily crystallized. Spatial and body intelligences, on the other hand, do not depend so much on "a well-stocked memory," and seem to be mainly a matter of fluid abilities like perception and performance. Thus, we would expect greater success in enhancing academic and personal intelligences than spatial and body intelligences. We do not yet know enough about how spatial and body intelligences develop to presume that the role of learning is insignificant, so we ought to try to enhance them, too, while preparing ourselves for more modest success than in other realms.

The situation becomes especially complicated when we get to cognitive style, the way a person prefers to handle information. Successful executives and teachers, for example, depend on intellectual speed, an important aspect of fluid intelligence. They also rely on strategic planning and managing information as well as on analysis and criticism, all more a matter of crystallized verbal and logical reasoning. Flexibility, activism, and intuition, each a matter of handling novelty, should rely heavily on fluid intelligence. As you'll see in the chapters on cognitive styles and creativity, particular kinds of knowledge play a major role. Given the complex relationship between the fluid-crystallized distinction and complexity, criticism, analysis, activism, intuition, and creativity, we are again advised to try to enhance these patterns, even without a guarantee of success.

Cattell noted that unlike other crystallized abilities, mechanical knowledge, a form of crystallized intelligence associated with competence in many jobs, is *negatively* correlated with fluid intelligence. In the late 1940s, this paradoxical relationship was incorporated into another influential hierarchical model. The then eminent British psychometrician Cyril Burt (now notorious for his fudged data on the inheritance of IQ) separated "intellectual abilities" from "practical" ones. Into "intellectual abilities," which he identified with *g*, Burt placed all those academic competences that matter at Oxford and Cambridge. Into the "practical" group he put mechanical, spatial, manual, and other such working-class abilities.

As a classically educated member of the upper class, Burt was a good Aristotelian. He not only divided "the human mind" into two major groups of abilities, but used the distinction to perpetuate the belief in the superiority of the intellectual over the practical. The distinction outlived Burt's own. Today, the distinction between purely intellectual and more practical abilities is accepted even by those who reject the notion that one is superior to the other.

A more detailed hierarchical theory was proposed in 1950 and developed through the '60s and early '70s by psychometrician Phillip E. Vernon. Like Burt, Vernon distinguished two kinds of *g*. The first intelligence he called "verbal-educational ability," which includes reading, spelling, linguistics, and creativity. His second form was "practical-mechanical," and it includes perceptual speed, mechanical information, scientific and technical skills, and the ability to handle spatial relationships. According to Vernon, some skills, like mathematical and clerical abilities, appear in both the educational and the practical subgroups of *g*.

If the maps of intelligence provided by Cattell, Burt, and Vernon are valid, people who are smart at school should generally be good at practical trades, and people who aren't very good at school should not in general be very good at work. However, there should also be some people who are smart at school but not at work, and vice versa.

Hierarchical theories are only minor reforms: Although they talk about subordinate dukes and earls of intellect, King *g* remains at the top of the organizational chart. These theories leave plenty of room for debate, but because they highlight differences between academic and practical intelligences, they are more useful for our purposes than the purely monarchic one. Hierarchical views of intelligence are a big step toward a view of intelligence that will be useful to those of us who are more interested in practice than in theory.

Oligarchic Reform and Democratic Revolution

Though hierarchical theories were minor reforms that left king *g* on the throne, ruling a retinue of second-order factors, they admitted diversity in the form of different groups of abilities. They thus offered aid and comfort to advocates of theories that Spearman called "oligarchic," referring to rule by several autonomous powers. Oligarchic theories grant autonomy to independent intelligences, each of which varies from person to person. Some of us are much better with numbers than with words, some of us are much better with tools than with people, and some very articulate and sensitive people can't find their way across town without instructions.

Oligarchic conceptions are a big step toward a practical theory of intelligence. The first of these pluralistic notions was, appropriately enough, proposed by someone from the world of work, a former electrical engineer who left Edison's laboratory to study intelligence. While working with Edison, L. L. Thurstone was impressed by the extent to which people could be smart in some ways and not so smart in others. Thurstone's reform dethroned king g and installed in his place seven dukes, the Primary Mental Abilities (PMAs): spatial visualization, perceptual ability, verbal comprehension, numerical ability, memory, word fluency, and reasoning.

Today, the oligarchic tradition is represented by Harvard psychologist Howard Gardner's theory of Multiple Intelligences (MIs), which provides the framework for Chapters 4 to 9. Gardner has carefully and strictly specified the criteria according to which a kind of ability can be considered a separate intelligence. It has to have (1) its own independent neural basis in the brain, (2) prodigies displaying that form of intelligence alone, (3) a set of distinctive core operations, separate (4) developmental and (5) evolutionary histories, (6) well-developed tests by which it can be assessed in isolation from other abilities, and (7) its own system of symbols, like words, mathematical signs, or emotional expressions. On the basis of these criteria, Gardner distinguishes seven Multiple Intelligences: logical-mathematical, verbal, spatial, musical, bodily, interpersonal, and intrapersonal. As you will see, several of his Multiple Intelligences correspond neatly to forms of practical intelligence described by psychologists, management consultants, and other students of real-world intellectual functioning.

Once Thurstone had deposed general intelligence, the castle gates were open to revolutionary throngs of intelligences, like those of Joy Paul Guilford's "structure of intellect" model. Using statistical methods similar to Thurstone's, Guilford proposed 150 independent kinds of intelligence. The figure 150 came from applying five kinds of operations (cognition, memory, divergent production, convergent production, and evaluation) to five kinds of contents (visual, auditory, symbolic, semantic, and behavioral), to create six kinds of products (units, classes, relations, systems, transformations, and implications). A person may have any level of each of the 150 kinds of intelligence, so to specify a person's intelligence completely requires 150 different numbers, not just one, as in the IQ.

By the early 1960s, experts on intelligence had earned a crack made by John F. Kennedy, who said that the first part of the word "expert" is an unknown quantity and the second part is a drip under pressure. His comment is still valid. Psychologists cannot, for example, even agree about what *kind* of measurement IQ is, because they have not decided what it is they're measuring. If we psychologists were doctors, we would be arguing about whether there's more than one kind of disease, or whether there's a "general" sickness common to all. Some of us would define "disease" as "what the thermometer measures." A few of us would be using CAT scans and artificial organs, but most of us would be using leeches and black magic. However, thanks to the rise of a new way of thinking about intelligence, all this is changing. The cognitive revolution in psychology is now bringing us new insights into practical intelligence at an accelerating pace. The story of scientific research on intelligence began at the beginning of the twentieth century. The climax comes, appropriately enough, at the end.

ANOTHER NATION

In the 1960s, experimental psychologists interested in learning, memory, and problem solving found themselves in many of the realms claimed by psychometricians. Interested less in abstract abilities and differences among people than in understanding how humans receive, store, and use information, cognitive psychologists developed detailed theories of human information processing, often using digital computers as working models of mental processes.

Today, intelligent information processing in all its forms (including artificial ones) is the subject matter of "cognitive science," a new field that combines the methods and results of cognitive psychology, computer science, and neurophysiology. Cognitive scientists tend to take a broad view of intelligence. Most embrace an understanding of human intelligence based on what people do in everyday settings. Cognitive scientists studying problem solving, decisionmaking, memory, and other complex mental processes are well on the way to a sophisticated information-processing theory of practical intelligence. Such a theory, like other cognitive theories, will rely heavily on "schemes" or "representations," mental processes that "re- present" objects, ideas, and events. Schemes come in several varieties. Some are images, like the mental "pictures" you use when you tell someone how to get downtown. Others are abstract and verbal or mathematical, like the concept of "information."

Cognitive psychologists began by investigating intelligence in artificial, well-defined problem areas, the sorts that can be studied in schools and laboratories: solving algebra word problems, doing "brainteasers," proving theorems, or playing chess. They attempted to understand such intelligence in generic, "power-based" terms: Intelligence equals "computational power," the ability to explore many alternatives quickly. Intelligence was viewed in terms of the "rational model," in which goals are specified, a complete list of alternative strategies and consequences is constructed, and a choice is made only on the basis of quantifiable payoffs.

In the 1970s, however, psychologists took a new look at intellectual abilities untapped by conventional laboratory problem-solving tasks. Studies of expert problem solving in natural contexts like those of medicine, business, and warfare contributed to a point of view that emphasizes "knowledge-based" intelligence. Experts, it turns out (to the surprise of no one but the rational modelers), know a lot. Experts solve problems not by brute force or sheer computational power but by applying all kinds of highly organized information.

Moreover, real-world decisions rarely follow the rational model. In decisions made by doctors, lawyers, executives, and other workers, goals are tacit, data incomplete, and choices risky. Decisionmakers make use of "heuristics," nonrational methods of simplifying problems, which work most of the time. For example, Steven Jobs, then CEO of Apple Computer, relied on his vision of a small, powerful, friendly machine that would somehow create another revolution like the one sparked by the Apple II. To do this, he had to recreate, in the context of a major corporation, the kind of excitement and dedication he and Stephen Wozniak had shared when they began Apple in a garage. Jobs decided to set up a separate division to develop the Macintosh microcomputer. This was a case where a popular simplifying organizational heuristic (a small, tight-knit "skunk works") that works most of the time, and had worked before for Jobs, proved risky indeed. In part as a result of the problems engendered by this project, Jobs was deposed by the man he had hired to free him to direct such visionary projects.

Or take an example where the rational model has a home-field advantage. Chess masters don't explore every possible combination of moves. To do that would take billions of years, even at a rate of billions of moves per second. Instead, they see the board in terms of previous configurations, and on the basis of experience with these configurations they develop heuristic hunches about what possibilities to explore.

Our new theoretical understanding of complex problem solving has, in turn, fed back into practical and personal understanding. From both theoretical and practical points of view, we understand an ability pretty well if we can build a machine that exhibits it. Today, there are scores of commercially successful "expert systems," computer programs that embody the knowledge and heuristics of experts in accounting, medical diagnosis, organic chemistry, household plumbing, computer programming, cleaning up chemical spills, and other specialized domains. The design of an expert system begins with an expert thinking aloud about his or her personal approaches to a particular problem. The transcripts or "protocols" generated by such sessions become the basis for a theoretical description of how the expert's mind works, which is then embodied in a computer program that can be used by others who deal with that sort of problem. The expert system DENDRAL, which analyzes organic chemicals, outperforms the postdoctoral chemists whose expertise it embodies, and at a lower cost. Expert systems are so popular and trendy that software expert Alan Kay calls them "the designer jeans of computer science." Expert systems show how the practical and the theoretical payoffs of PI reinforce each other.

One of the most comprehensive and sophisticated information-processing theories of intelligence is the "triarchic" or "governmental" model developed by Yale psychologist Robert Sternberg. Sternberg is a professor with a list of publications longer than a commencement address, but he manages to come across as an appealing *enfant terrible*. His theory describes intelligence in terms of three "archies," or ways of thinking about intelligence.

The first "archy" consists of mental processes called "components." There are three kinds of components. "Metacomponents" include processes like deciding what the problem is, choosing ways to think about the problem (e.g., by drawing a picture or making a list), and keeping track of progress toward solution. "Performance" components are operations like combining and comparing information. The third group of components all have to do with learning: selecting relevant from irrelevant information, combining information in new ways, relating new information to old.

The second "archy" is experiential. It describes intelligence as handling novelty and "automation," developing automatic "subroutines" that can be executed without effort. Intelligent driving, for example, is being able to adapt to unexpected situations and being able to run on "autopilot" in routine ones.

Context, the third "archy," refers to the demands of the situations in which thinking actually takes place. Intellectual activity does not take place in a vacuum, and to describe how it works is in part to describe what it does, what it's good for. Chapter 1 of this book was in part an attempt to describe the modern context within which PI operates.

When it comes to the unitary versus the multiple nature of intelligence, Sternberg sides with both monarchists and democrats. Although he states that "There seems to be a factor of 'general intelligence,'" he also admits that "Occasionally, people are quite good at one aspect of intellectual functioning, but quite poor at another." Sternberg's attention to experience and context makes his theory especially appealing to students of practical intelligence.

The triarchic theory approaches the traditional concerns of intelligence research with the tools of cognitive science. Cognitive scientists define intelligence in terms of information-processing capacities. Because "information" (unlike "intelligence") is well understood in theoretical terms, it is eminently quantifiable. Information comes in many different forms (verbal, pictorial, numerical, etc.), so information-processing theories of intelligence can accommodate many different information-processing systems, or intelligences. Thus, the information-processing approach allows the mental processes we call "intelligence" to be described precisely and practically because it provides the necessary foundation—a theoretical definition.

Sternberg's theory is an example of the "new look" in intelligence research, which sees intelligence as information processing rather than as disembodied "abilities." The new look is just that, a new way of seeing the old practical issue raised by Binet, expressed in the title of a book edited by Sternberg and Douglas Detterman: *How and How Much Can Intelligence Be Increased?*

One way to approach Detterman and Sternberg's question is by examining the IQs of identical twins who have been reared separately. Since identical twins have identical genes, any differences between members of a pair must be environmental. The IQs of identical twins sometimes vary by twenty points or more. A twenty-point increase would move a person of average IQ from the fiftieth percentile (IQ higher than half) to the ninetieth (IQ higher than 90 percent).

Of course, some of the twenty-point difference may represent a *decrease* rather than an *increase* in the IQ of one member of a pair of twins. Nevertheless, twenty points is a conservative estimate of the amount of influence the environment can have, and from a practical point of view, preventing a twenty-point decrease is just as important as promoting a twenty-point increase. Moreover, even twins separated shortly after birth have shared at least a year of pre- and postnatal environment, and adoptees' environments tend to be similar in many ways; therefore, twenty points is a conservative estimate of potential environmental influence. Indeed, enrichment of children's environments is sometimes followed by IQ increases of over thirty points.

If intelligence is processing (getting and using) information, and if, as many cognitive scientists believe, these learning or information-processing skills can themselves be learned, we have returned to Binet's optimistic view of intelligence as a system of acquired skills. This view was expressed in one of the definitions of intelligence published in the *Journal of Educational Psychology* in the 1920s: "the capacity to acquire capacity." A practical consequence of such a view was spelled out in the 1930s by philosopher of education John Dewey, who described one of the main aims of education as learning how to learn. The great comparative psychologist Harry Harlow went a step farther when he said that all learning is learning to learn.

Increasing intelligence by learning to learn blurs the traditional distinction between innate capacity and learned contents described at the beginning of the chapter. As you may remember, early definers of intelligence argued about whether intelligence is the capacity of an intellectual bucket (capacity to learn), the volume of the contents (knowledge learned), or some combination of capacity and achievement. Research on memory shows that the distinction between capacity and contents is an oversimplification. When knowledge is processed correctly, it makes room for new knowledge and it gets easier to learn more. We should abandon the bucket. A better analogy for the new-look approach would focus on the informational contents rather than the container. When I stuff my shoes into my carry-on bag, I find that there's more room—I can cram my socks into the toes and put my razor and aftershave in the spaces in front of the heels. Well-organized knowledge is like a well-packed suitcase, or a box of boxes, in which small items nest neatly inside larger ones.

In learning by rote, people who know a lot develop richly structured schemes of associated items that provide niches for new ones. For example, the woman at the service counter of the local Nissan dealership has memorized the codes of hundreds of frequently ordered parts. When you go in and ask for a throttle pump plunger set screw lock nut, she loves to say something like, "Oh, a GF37689/234Q, huh? I just got some in." She claims that it was hard to learn the codes at first, but now that she knows the prefixes for different automotive systems, she learns new parts codes without even trying. She doesn't have a particularly good memory—she never remembers my name.

As you'll see in the chapter on verbal and logical intelligence, you can learn mnemonic devices that increase your memory capacity by providing artificial structures that hold new knowledge, like the "organizers" in attaché cases.

Don't confuse the new look with the naive environmentalism of the radical behaviorists who once claimed to be able to train anyone to become anything: "doctor, lawyer, artist, merchant chief . . . regardless of his talents, penchants, tendencies, abilities and race of his ancestors." Most of us agree with developmental psychologist Sandra Scarr: "I do not believe that any child can be made into any adult." We acknowledge congenital constraints on what people can achieve, but as a practical matter, we don't know where those limits are. "Reality," as Wallace Stevens wrote, "is an activity of the most august imagination."

Individual differences are real. Much as I would like to, I will never slam dunk a basketball on this planet. However, as new-look psychologists point out, we do not know enough about intellectual development to rule out social and other environmental differences as sources of (often irreversible) individual differences. The methodological issues surrounding the modifiability of intelligence are like Matthew Arnold's "darkling plain . . . Where ignorant armies clash by night." Estimates of the proportion of variations in IQ (which we have no reason to believe are less modifiable than other forms of intelligence) controlled by hereditary factors range from 16 to 80 percent. Even if we accept the high end of this range, the remaining variance over which we have some environmental control is substantial. Adoption and other environmental changes can move people from subnormal IQs to superior ones.

Thus, though we must accept biological constraints, it makes sense to adopt as a practical working hypothesis educational psychologist Benjamin Bloom's optimistic claim that "What any person in the world can learn, almost all persons can learn if provided with appropriate prior and current conditions of learning."

RECENT RESEARCH ON PI

For reasons that should now be clear, psychologists with an interest in PI have, to use the title of Robert Sternberg's recent book, gone "beyond IQ." Educational Testing Service (ETS), the company that develops and administers the tests used for admissions to undergraduate, graduate, and professional programs, uses the Basic Skills Test to measure practical skills at the secondary level. It tests rudimentary real-world skills like reading newspapers, signs, labels, and maps. As might be expected given this test's emphasis on verbal skills, correlations with IQ are high. Since the skills tested are so rudimentary, however, no one has seriously proposed it as a measure of success in businesses or professions requiring knowledge beyond the high school level.

For such occupations, a more appropriate measure is the self-report. Psychometrician E. E. Ghiselli developed a checklist of thirteen traits, which included supervisory ability, intelligence, and decisiveness and ten nonintellectual personality traits, such as the need for security. Ghiselli's checklist is easy to administer and is valid to the extent that workers understand their own competences. Sometimes, however, as the next approach shows, this extent is limited.

The "ethological" approach is based on the assumption that much of the behavior we see in real-world settings is well adapted to the demand of those settings. Part of the ethologist's job, then, is to discover the intelligence of everyday, commonsense approaches to real problems, especially those that don't look particularly intelligent to the observer.

I once used an ethological approach as a systems analyst charged with designing an automated credit reporting system for the Credit Bureau of Cook County. My first task was to understand the system. I immediately noted that the clerks who read the reports did not "go by the book." Sometimes they read files chronologically, sometimes with the bankruptcies and liens first, and sometimes in what appeared to be a random order. When I asked the clerks about this, I couldn't get a straight answer. Many denied having a consistent plan—they just did "what seemed right at the time." By tapping into their telephone conversations with clients, I discovered that they read information in a particular order for each kind of client. Evidently, over the years, they had learned to identify callers' voices and, without realizing it (probably through vocal cues to impatience), picked up the order that each kind of client preferred: For instance, oil companies, which were far more lenient in granting credit than department stores, were more interested in recent credit history than in the big picture. (This was in the days when a tank of gas cost a lot less than a bedroom suite.)

The classic ethological study is Henry Mintzberg's massive examination of managerial behavior. Mintzberg followed executives around, recording everything they did and said. The results were full of surprises about the enormous variety, rapid tempo, and disconcerting fragmentation of managerial work. For example, they typically enjoy no more than nine minutes without an interruption.

A really "psychological" psychometric approach was made famous by David McClelland. His Thematic Apperception Test presents a picture and asks you to make up a story about it. One picture shows a young man working at something like a lathe, with an older man standing behind him. Presumably the story you tell reveals your concerns. People's stories turn out to be highly predictive of real-world success, but as with Ghiselli's checklist, the traits that emerge, like "need for achievement," are mainly motivational rather than intellectual.

A more promising approach is simulation, in which subjects or job candidates are presented with make-believe situations that closely resemble the real thing.

Norman Fredericksen of ETS has developed the Formulating Hypotheses test, which simulates the diagnosis stage of problem solving by presenting graphs or tables and asking subjects to account for patterns in the data. One table, for instance, showed that workers more often strike in the summer than in the winter. Explanations included contracts' terminating in the summer, the importance of income during winter holidays, etc.

The most famous example of simulation is Fredericksen's "in-basket" technique, in which an executive is presented with memos, letters, phone call slips, files, etc. Subjects are asked to deal with this material as they would on the job. Their actions are sorted into sixty-eight categories, including "recognizes good work," "asks supervisor for advice," "takes terminal action," and "delegates completely." Specific actions are scored for novelty, imagination, and other values.

Fredericksen performed a complex statistical analysis of the results of his simulations and found patterns that included "acting in compliance with suggestions, preparing for action, concern with public relations, procrastination, concern with superiors, informality, directing subordinates, discussing, . . . amount of work accomplished, [and] preparing for action versus taking final action." Some of these patterns predicted success or failure. People who prepare for actions, who have high work outputs, and who frequently seek help tend to be more successful than people who act impulsively, slowly, and alone.

Today, even more realistic simulations are being used by psychologists like Siegfried Streufert, professor of behavioral science at Penn State's College of Medicine. He has worked on human information processing in practical settings for twenty years. As a postdoctoral student at the Personality-Social Laboratory at Princeton, he worked with two other cognitive psychologists, Harold Schroder and Michael Driver. Their book, *Human Information Processing,* was one of the first applications of modern cognitive theory to real-world problem solving, especially in warfare and business. Streufert studies decisionmaking by real executives under controlled laboratory conditions. He presents them with computerized simulations of real problems dealing with, for example, international investments during a monetary crisis. The simulations are highly realistic: relevant and irrelevant information comes in by phone, computer, and VCR. All behavior (including such physiological measures of stress as heart rate) is recorded. Streufert has found that PI is more a matter of style than of IQ. He calls the style "cognitive complexity," and describes it as the ability to handle many different kinds of information from many different sources without getting overloaded.

Robert Sternberg attributes psychometricians' neglect of PI to "a sense that it is not clear that there is any generalized construct of practical intelligence that extends beyond particular tasks or situations." Sternberg and his then colleague Richard Wagner (now at Florida State University) attempted to develop such a construct, the "tacit knowledge" that "leads to real-world occupational success in many fields." By "tacit knowledge" they mean tricks of the trade, the occupational ins and outs that are never taught and rarely discussed. In other words, they believe that PI is not only innate capacity but also knowledge already gained.

Wagner and Sternberg developed questionnaires that presented real-world problems, like rating various strategies for "rapid promotion to the top." These strategies included such options as getting rid of "dead wood," getting more involved in local service organizations, working on problems outside one's department, joining a country club, asking superiors for comments, and adjusting work habits. The questionnaires also asked for ratings of strategies for doing day-to-day work, like having "many irons in the fire," avoiding distasteful tasks, listing daily goals, avoiding trivial tasks, delegating authority, and doing strategic planning.

They sent these questionnaires to several groups of people in business and academe, chosen to represent a wide range of success. Among those from the business group who responded were highly successful executives from the "top 20" *Fortune* 500 corporations, moderately successful executives from businesses not included in the *Fortune* 500, twenty-eight graduate students from the nation's top business schools, fifteen from average business schools, and seven from "modestly rated" business schools. As a kind of anchor, presumably at the bottom end of business success, was a group of Yale undergraduates. In a follow-up study, questionnaires were administered to twenty-nine managers at a bank in New Haven.

The academic group consisted of highly successful professors from the nation's top fifteen departments of psychology, moderately successful professors from psychology departments at less prestigious schools, graduate students from the same top fifteen departments and less prestigious departments, and an anchor group of Yale undergraduates.

Sternberg claims that the results of these studies supported the tacit-knowledge hypothesis. Scores were based on responses that correlated with level of expertise. In other words, the "right" answers were the ones given by the most successful subjects. Scores showed modest but significant (unlikely to be chance) correlations with level of company (.34) or school (.40). Correlations with salary were .46 for the executives and .48 for the bank managers. Correlations with rate of publications, the academic equivalent of salary, were in the same range (.32). Scores did not correlate with measures of g or with years on the job. Sternberg concludes that "tacit knowledge is, in fact, a useful measure of practical intelligence."

Sternberg has come closer than anyone else to a complete theory of practical intelligence (and, as you'll see in the next chapter, of intelligence in general). In his focus on context, process, and experience, he is on the money. He is correct in emphasizing the role of tacit knowledge in promoting competence and success. He is also right in identifying lack of a good theory of PI as the major reason for the scarcity of good measures of PI. To identify and enhance our practical thinking abilities, we need such measures and such a theory. But unfortunately, as Sternberg would be the first to admit, tacit knowledge isn't the whole story. It would be nice if all there was to PI were tacit knowledge. We could compile a handbook of the "ins and outs" of any occupation and we could all become competent overnight. As Sternberg himself points out elsewhere, identifying differences in tacit knowledge leaves unanswered the question of how these differences came about. In work as in sailing, there is more to success than knowing the ropes.

3.
A Practical Approach
to Practical Intelligence

Everything should be made as simple as possible, but not
simpler.

—ALBERT EINSTEIN

We've all seen the commercials on late night TV for "all-purpose
tools," the ones that "glue, screw, and renew." We've all seen the
recipes at the supermarket magazine rack: "Six Simple Steps to
Instant Success." IQ and general intelligence are "all-purpose tools"
that are supposed to work in schools, offices, courtrooms, and operating theaters. Many self-help books of the "Think for Success" variety
offer untested, simplistic solutions to complex practical problems.
There is a good reason why "all-purpose" gizmos are not sold in
stores and oversimplified self-help books are not sold in bookstores.
In the next few pages, I explain my attempt to apply the prescrip-
tion in the epigraph to this chapter.

My approach to PI is simple and practical. Each chapter is built
around descriptions of PI provided by highly competent practitioners obtained through Behavioral Event Interviews. In a Behavioral
Event Interview, the interviewer (in these cases, me) asks subjects
to "walk through" several occasions when decisions they made
turned out well. One or more of these events are chosen for a
detailed analysis, in which subjects are asked to describe their
thoughts, feelings, and actions at each step. (I am indebted to
George Klemp for instruction in this effective technique.) A second
source of data is the autobiographies of successful executives, lawyers, doctors, teachers, technicians, and other workers. Both these
methods have their pitfalls. Autobiographical and, to a lesser extent,
Behavioral Event accounts are subject to the fallibility and construction inherent in human memory, the biases due to introspectors' pet
theories, and the self-serving tendency to forget, minimize, or ratio-

nalize one's mistakes. For this reason, objective results are essential, and I rely heavily on published accounts of intellectual functioning in real-world contexts.

In keeping with my pragmatic approach, my working hypothesis is that some of the abilities we use at work are different from the ones we use at school, and that these skills are different from one another. I begin with the assumption that multiple intelligences is by far the most useful conception, because jobs are different and people are complex. If all the intellectual skills of different jobs are really aspects of one general ability, that fact will become clear once we describe them in their particularity. If, on the other hand, there really are many different forms of PI, trying to make them fit one conception will be worse than useless.

As soon as we begin to explore intelligence in real-world contexts, we find that psychologists, managers, and other students of practical affairs in real-world settings agree on the important characteristics of successful workers. What emerges from an analysis of these descriptions is a view of PI as a combination of intelligences and styles based on knowledge and applied to the skills of particular occupations.

MULTIPLE PRACTICAL INTELLIGENCES

I divide PI into six clusters of abilities, each cluster corresponding to one of Howard Gardner's multiple intelligences (MIs). Gardner sees intelligence not as a single general ability but as several more or less independent abilities, six of which play a major role in real-world thinking. I adopt his point of view, but qualify it in two ways. I am more concerned with connections among MIs than Gardner is, and I divide several of his abilities into two or more subabilities.

The first of Gardner's multiple intelligences is what he calls intrapersonal intelligence—knowing oneself, the ability to acquire and use information about one's own abilities and faults, likes and dislikes, sensitivities, and blind spots. We have all heard the injunction "Know thyself," but until recently, few of us realized that self-knowledge is a task sufficiently complex to require a special form of intelligence. Psychoanalysts have known this all along—that's why they are themselves analyzed, often for years, before they practice on their own. Today, a whole industry (SAGE, est, Esalen, etc.) works to get us in touch with our feelings, while the testing industry continues to tell us about our aptitudes and weaknesses. To the extent that they work, these industries perform a real service; research reveals that intrapersonal intelligence is a major factor in success, especially in business, law, medicine, and teaching.

*Inter*personal intelligence refers to sensitivity—the ability to acquire and use "vibes," nonverbal information about the emotions, motivations, and attitudes of others. Because vibes are nonverbal, some animals, especially dogs and horses, have considerable amounts of interpersonal intelligence. In some people, especially good salespersons and psychotherapists, this form of intelligence is developed to an uncanny degree. Some people use their sensitivity not to sell or to heal but to lead. In *Leadership,* political scientist James MacGregor Burns describes great leaders as people who often know their followers better than the followers know themselves. Of Mao Tse-tung, Burns wrote, "His true genius was in understanding the emotions of others."

Linguistic or verbal intelligence includes vocabulary and grammatical skills, fluency, and the ability to say just the right thing in just the right way. Linguistic intelligence is expressed in reading, writing, listening, and speaking, and is used to understand, to enlighten, and to persuade. In his autobiography, Lee Iacocca claims that among his most important assets are verbal skills: "reading, writing, and public speaking. With good teachers and the ability to concentrate, you can go pretty far with those skills." Linguistic intelligence is essential to success in school, and it is tapped by IQ tests. In fact, the correlation between IQ and vocabulary size is around .9.

Logical-mathematical intelligence is the pure rationality embodied in Mr. Spock, the science officer of the starship *Enterprise.* Its languages are mathematics and symbolic logic, but its applications go far beyond science and math. Anyone who formulates a plan, whether it's a marketing strategy or an ignition analysis, is using this form of intelligence. Like verbal intelligence, logical intelligence plays a major role in school, and it, too, is measured quite nicely by IQ tests.

Logical-mathematical intelligence seems to depend heavily on spatial intelligence, the ability to acquire and use knowledge about spatial relationships. It's what you use when you take a new shortcut or detour. Mechanics, engineers, surgeons, and dentists apply this form of intelligence every day, and executives use it when they draw a cash flow graph or an organizational chart. Some ideas are far more easily expressed in pictures than in words, and anytime you draw or study a map, picture, or diagram in order to express or understand an idea you are using spatial intelligence. Spatial intelligence is tapped by subtests of some widely used IQ tests.

Not so with coordination and dexterity, which Gardner calls body intelligence. We use it when we learn a sensorimotor skill, like how to filet a fish, park a car, or use a computer keyboard. Surgeons, mechanics, commercial artists, or any others who work with their hands are applying this form of intelligence. It is what is lacking in those of us whose sensorimotor styles emulate that of Chevy Chase. As that comedian's imitation of a recent President of the United States demonstrates, however, in some occupations body intelligence is not all that important.

COGNITIVE STYLES

PI is more than multiple intelligences; it is also a matter of style. Descriptions of practical intelligence by psychologists and management consultants emphasize such qualities as skepticism, "a bias for action," cognitive complexity, intuition, and creativity. People of similar ability often use different styles of thinking, or cognitive styles. These styles are not separate intelligences. Rather, cognitive styles are ways of using multiple intelligences. An impulsive, critical, or creative person may exhibit any of these styles in verbal, mathematical, or interpersonal problem solving.

Ernest Hemingway once said that the single most important characteristic for a writer is a crap detector. Crap detectors are essential to anyone who must evaluate information that is liable to be biased, incomplete, or even intentionally misleading. That includes executives, doctors, teachers, and especially lawyers. To be critical isn't to be negative—it's to be discerning. One can be much more positive about ideas that passed the crap detector. Successful executives and lawyers are among the most skeptical people on earth, but they are enthusiastic about any idea supported by facts and logic.

Cognitive styles are usually described in terms of polar continua. For example, psychologist Jerome Kagan describes a continuum from impulsive to reflective. The impulsive-reflective distinction is essential to an understanding of the practical cognitive style. Practical thinkers tend toward the impulsive, action-oriented pole, a style described by FDR when he said, "But above all try something." It was also illustrated by a photographer's formula for success in getting good combat shots. His secret was to set his aperture at "f-8—and be there."

"Cognitive complexity" is a style directly linked to success in real-world situations. Cognitive complexity refers to the amount of different kinds of information a person processes within a short period of time. Siegfried Streufert and his colleagues, who studied cognitive complexity in war games and investment simulations, describe cognitive complexity in terms of "integration," the use of "self-generated information in a decision." They measure quantities like the number of integrations per decision and per period, the number of sources of information going into each decision, and similar quantities. Their results show that cognitively complex people handle large amounts of diverse information by seeing relationships and implications that others don't. Cognitively complex executives use detailed, long-term plans, but they use them flexibly. They are ready to postpone their plans when unexpected problems or opportunities arise. Flexibility came up again and again in my interviews with successful executives, lawyers, and teachers. All spoke of the importance of the ability to put aside one task and take up another without missing a beat—and without forgetting about the first task. Cognitive complexity is being able to juggle while bicycling on a bumpy road.

A growing body of research shows that people who deal successfully with complex, rapidly changing environments do so with a variety of nonrational, intuitive techniques. As a result, intuition, the ability to use hunches and what "feels right," is no longer regarded as a sign of "soft-mindedness." The study of intuition is a rapidly growing area in practical intelligence.

Creativity has yet to attain the respectability only recently accorded intuition, but especially in teaching, marketing, and engineering, workers are beginning to pay attention to "lateral thinking," "conceptual blockbusting," "synectics," and other practical approaches to cultivating creative cognitive styles. Psychometricians describe creativity in terms of "divergent production," the ability to generate a lot of different ideas from a single starting point, like "List all the things you could do with a rock." The practical validity of this task is nicely illustrated by the successful entrepreneurs whose divergent production included selling rocks as pets. Cognitive psychologists have a complementary perspective—they see creativity as redefining problems, seeing things in new ways, making new connections.

There is no particular cognitive style associated with a high level of any one of the multiple intelligences. Intelligences and styles occur in every possible combination. All these independently varying qualities are important in most practical pursuits, but their relative importance varies within and between occupations.

Knowledge and Skills

Mark Twain's formula for financial success was "ignorance plus confidence." The formula is appealing but misleading. When he blissfully applied it to an untested automatic typesetter and confidently invested his life savings, Twain lost his shirt. Today, three quarters of us are knowledge workers, not ignorance workers, yet many of us continue to labor under misconceptions about intelligence at work that are similar to Twain's.

Each of the abilities and styles that go into PI requires extensive knowledge. This view of ability based on knowledge intentionally blurs the textbook distinction between intellectual capacity and intellectual contents, between potential for future learning and what has already been learned. Multiple intelligences are abilities to acquire and use various kinds of knowledge, which as it turns out depend on a richly connected network of prior knowledge. For example, interpersonal intelligence involves tacit knowledge of a universal "body language," and the ability to relate this knowledge to new information, such as the tics and other idiosyncrasies of your boss.

A skill is the well-learned application of knowledge-based abilities and styles to particular tasks. Reading, driving, designing, and negotiating are examples of skills.

Though their relative importance varies from skill to skill, all six multiple intelligences and styles described here are important in work. In particular, intrapersonal intelligence is most important in jobs like managing and the law, where there are many possible careers. Verbal and logical intelligences have the widest range of applications—nowadays, they are prerequisites for success in all professions and many nonprofessional occupations. Next in generality of application is interpersonal intelligence—only the very best surgeons and mechanics can afford to be without it. Spatial and body skills have the narrowest range of application, but they appear indirectly in many technical tasks.

PI Is Learnable

This brings us to *the* practical issue in intelligence today: How does PI develop? Is it fixed at birth by race, sex, and other hereditary factors, or can it be modified by education? My answer is pragmatic: PI, like all forms of intelligence, depends on complex interactions between hereditary potential and environmental opportunity. We know that at any age, changes in environment cause changes in intelligence, and that the earlier and more drastic the environmental changes are, the more dramatic the results.

As a practical matter, therefore, those intelligences that depend on fluid abilities can be affected by experience in general ways, and those that depend on crystallized abilities can be learned. PI is in large part a matter of knowledge, tacit or explicit, and other learnable skills. This is an optimistic point of view, but an eminently practical one. I once worked with a young West African entrepreneur named Albert, who wore on his sneakers a message relevant to all who approach PI from a practical point of view. On the toe of Albert's left shoe appeared the words "never try." On the right, "never know."

Many of us avoid the challenge of intellectual excellence with the talent cop-out. "I'm no good at math"—or drawing, or grammar, or whatever," we say, as though that were an excuse. It's not an excuse. It's the problem. The solution is working smarter: using sound techniques to develop practical intelligences. What we call talent is not so much a gift as an opportunity. What is required to excel is recognition of what those opportunities are and the dedication to capitalize on them. Let's begin, then, with the one of the many ways to be smart that tells you where your opportunities are.

Most people have only the vaguest notions of their real intellectual abilities. Much of this ignorance is the result of the misconceptions that IQ equals intelligence in general and the conventional wisdom that intelligence is an immutable trait, fixed at birth by a kind of psychometric predestination. The concept of PI challenges these pessimistic misconceptions. In addition to the personal promise of PI—that you can learn to work smarter—there are economic and theoretical promises as well. The economic promise of practical intelligence is that working smarter can enhance productivity of individuals and organizations. The theoretical promise of practical intelligence is a more complete conception of how minds work in the real world. Psychologists have come to realize that they have at least as much to learn from practical workers as practical workers have to learn from them. Practical intelligence is on the agenda for managers in search of excellence, and psychologists in search of mind. In Part II, we begin at the beginning, with your understanding of your own values and abilities.

PART TWO

PERSONAL
INTELLIGENCES

4.
Self-Understanding

What am I doing in an office, making a contemptuous, begging fool of myself, when all I want is out there waiting for me the minute I say I know who I am!
                                        —ARTHUR MILLER

Who in the world am I? Ah, *that's* the great puzzle!
                                        —LEWIS CARROLL

Inscribed at Delphi is the oldest and tersest piece of practical wisdom: "Know thyself." Tragedies from *Oedipus Rex* to *Death of a Salesman* show us that we ignore the Delphic oracle's advice only at our peril. But doesn't *Hamlet* show that self-analysis leads to paralysis, madness, and suicide? Practical people waste no time contemplating their navels, or so we believe. The heroes of *our* dramas shoot first and never ask questions. Thus, in order to explain the special kind of intelligence you need to know yourself, I must first convince you that this intelligence is practical. In an appropriately oracular style, I will begin with a parable.

As a member of a family with deep roots in its old-world culture, Lido grew up with a strong sense of who he was. His sense of self was reinforced by the bigotry he faced every day. Like many boys, Lido dreamed of a career in major league baseball, but his sense of self included personal priorities—he always did his homework before going out to the field. When rheumatic fever took him off the field for good, he was able to relinquish his dream. Lido the athlete became Lido the reader.

He graduated near the top of his high school class, and was accepted by a liberal arts college with more than its share of ivy. As he was about to go off to college, war was declared, and his classmates lined up to enlist. He tried to join them, but twice was declared 4-F, and left for college in disgrace. He knew he was good with both numbers and people, so he decided to flesh out his engineering major with courses in psychology. He roared through his last year with straight A's.

After graduation, Lido was recruited by a large corporation, where for the first time in his life he was bored. By then, he knew he was more than an athlete, a soldier, or an engineer, so he went into sales. The postwar recession kept him out of the fast lane, but he enjoyed his job, and threaded his way through the traffic of marketing management. After twenty years, he arrived at the top of a corporation sputtering in the energy crisis of the 1970s. As president, he staked his job on the marketing intuition he had developed over the years, and developed several new and more efficient products. Lido's successes threatened the chairman of the board, who first demoted, then fired him.

Burning with humiliation but confident in his abilities, Lido took a job with a bankrupt rival company just in time for the biggest recession in fifty years. He knew he was at his best as a salesman, so he did what no CEO in the industry had ever done: He appeared on TV to sell his product. He hadn't lost his touch; within two years, his company was the only one in the industry to show a profit and its sales surpassed those of the company he'd been fired from. Today, he is mentioned as a contender for the biggest sales job of all: President of the United States.

This story is a parable, and it also happens to be true. Lido Iacocca has always been sustained by a sense of self that transcends his job: Iacocca knows what he wants. As a child, he loved to read, so he set priorities and succeeded as a student. As an adult, he loved cars, especially cars with long hoods, but he knew that what he loved most about cars is selling them. This realization put him on the road to the presidency of Ford, and when Henry Ford fired him, his sense of self helped him sell Chrysler products as they had never been sold before. The British statesman William Aitken might have had Iacocca in mind when he wrote: "The man who gets ahead in business is the man who knows what he wants—and what he is willing to give up to get it."

THE VALUE OF KNOWING YOUR VALUES

People like Lee Iacocca excel at calculating trade-offs among their wants and needs; they have a clear sense of their values, or priorities among conflicting wants and needs. Howard Gardner (whose theory of multiple intelligences I discussed in the previous chapter) ascribes this ability to a special "intrapersonal intelligence," a "sensitivity to our own wants and fears, our own personal histories," that culminates in a sense of self.

Gardner cites several kinds of evidence supporting his view that intrapersonal intelligence develops independently of IQ and other multiple intelligences. He describes autistic children whose intrapersonal intelligence is so low that they don't say "I" or "me," but who have normal or superior levels of other intelligences. Similarly, there are psychopaths who have a pathological blindness to their own motives combined with uncanny sensitivity to the motives of others. Conversely, Gardner lists people extremely high in intrapersonal intelligence without corresponding levels of other intelligences: Jesus Christ, Mahatma Gandhi, and Eleanor Roosevelt. This short list shouldn't daunt anyone interested in enhancing intrapersonal intelligence. Gardner's contention that intrapersonal intelligence is independent of other forms of intelligence raises the prospect that even those of us who are not oversupplied with school smarts can develop our own sense of self.

Though all cultures influence the development of intrapersonal intelligence, some cultures value it more than others. Americans, for example, have traditionally not valued intrapersonal intelligence to the same extent as the Japanese, who revere those tuned to their *jikkan,* or "real and direct" feelings. However, America's new generation of young professionals emulates the Japanese emphasis on self-understanding. A recent article in the *Chronicle of Higher Education* documents an increase in the proportion of best-sellers with titles related to self-awareness and improvement. Pollster Daniel Yankelovitch reports that, even in the supposedly materialistic 1980s, a majority of Americans still define success in terms of self-actualization rather than income or status. It is not surprising, then, that in a recent study of AT&T management, only 30 percent of young managers expressed a desire for advancement.

Though our traditionally unreflective culture still labels such concerns "narcissistic," the young professionals may be on to something: Sensitivity to one's values and feelings is an important asset in business. This is the conclusion of Yale psychologists Richard Wagner and Robert Sternberg (of the triarchic theory discussed in the previous chapter). They sent questionnaires to bank managers, asking them to rank working strategies (work habits, organizing time, and personal deadlines and rewards) and motivations (incentives like freedom, recognition, and enjoyment). Wagner and Sternberg found that successful executives know their own motives, and use them to maximize their performance. It turns out that successful managers don't have a "nose to the grindstone" attitude. Rather, they choose enjoyable tasks and figure out ways to enjoy the ones they have to do. For example, they think in terms of goals achieved, not time spent. Wagner and Sternberg call this ability "managing self." Their description of managing self is remarkably similar to Gardner's intrapersonal intelligence. The major difference is Sternberg's stress on tacit knowledge: Managing self is mainly a matter of unspoken lore "about the relative importances of the tasks one faces, knowledge about more or less efficient ways of approaching tasks, and knowledge about how to motivate oneself." The importance of tacit knowledge in managing self has a practical application: Unlike innate "hardwired" abilities, tacit knowledge can be learned.

One way to motivate oneself is by finding work that provides the kinds of rewards one values. In his book *Peak Performers,* Charles Garfield, a psychologist at the University of California, describes people who excel at jobs from Bay Bridge toll taker to Nobel Prize chemist. Like the Yale psychologists, Garfield found a focus on goals rather than on activity: "Workaholics are addicted to activity; peak performers are committed to results." Peak performers share several other characteristics, all of which can be learned, though not easily. The central characteristic is a habit of self-analysis, which results in well-defined goals based on a sense of mission. Their missions transcend their jobs, which become avenues to personal development. The Bay Bridge toll taker, for example, wants to be a dancer. He learned to incorporate his dances into his duties, so that he was, in effect, being paid to practice. He told Garfield: "I have a corner office. . . . I can see the Golden Gate, San Francisco, the Berkeley Hills; half the Western world vacations here, and I just stroll in and practice dancing."

Garfield's study provides many practical applications of intrapersonal intelligence. Like Lee Iacocca, successful workers know their priorities, so they are able to work hard without becoming workaholics. For such people there is no clear division between work and play.

Good teachers share the sense of mission of Garfield's peak performers. They are enthusiastic about their methods and their subjects, and they care about their students enough to listen to them and to see problems from their point of view. Because the rewards of teaching are primarily in acting on this sense of mission, not in salary or prestige, for teachers, understanding one's needs and values is not an elective but a prerequisite. Teachers' knowledge of their motives and abilities is tested daily in the classroom. Like wolves spotting the caribou that falters ever so slightly, students have an uncanny instinct (also bred by the imperatives of survival) for indifference, insincerity, defensiveness, and poor preparation. Only teachers who know that they want the satisfactions of teaching more than money and that they have mastered their material can pass this daily test.

Knowledge of one's values is as important in the law as it is in business and teaching. Plato reminds the lawyer that "the trial is never about some indifferent matter, but always concerns himself; and often the race is for his life." There are many kinds of careers in the law, and they can satisfy motives from idealism to avarice; doing well depends on matching one's values to the job. The importance of self-understanding was described by an experienced divorce lawyer who said, "I think it would help if young lawyers were psychoanalyzed."

THE ABILITY TO KNOW YOUR ABILITIES

Knowing what he wanted most was only half of Iacocca's sense of self. The other half was knowing what he could do. Iacocca was good at engineering, but he knew that he was better at marketing. Iacocca exemplifies the person he describes in his autobiography as "The guy with the strong ego [who] knows his own strengths. . . . There's a world of difference," he continues, "between a strong ego, which is essential, and a large ego—which can be destructive. . . . the guy with the large ego is always looking for recognition."

As an example of the large ego, Iacocca might have had John Z. DeLorean in mind. Like Iacocca's, DeLorean's story is a parable— the parallels between the two men are almost too tidy to be true. Both were engineers who drove to the top in a muscle car. While Iacocca was developing the Mustang at Ford, DeLorean was designing the GTO at GM. Like Iacocca, DeLorean left a major automaker to run his own shop: the DeLorean Motor Company (DMC). There he built his dream car, a sleek, stainless-steel-bodied GT designed to combine high performance, durability, and safety. In a biography that, like Iacocca's, has his surname as title, DeLorean relates his attempts to save his spluttering company.

Here DeLorean's story diverges from Iacocca's, and becomes a cautionary fable. DeLorean's misadventures were front-page material for months. His dream is yet to be realized. He was acquitted of criminal charges, but meanwhile he was indicted for diverting almost nine million dollars from DMC. DeLorean's own account makes it clear that he overestimated his abilities. DeLorean's crash is an object lesson in what Daniel Goleman calls the "dark side of the entrepreneur," where "extreme self-confidence becomes an egotistical sense of infallibility." John DeLorean shared the tragic flaw of Willy Loman, antihero of *Death of a Salesman.* "He didn't know who he was." DeLorean got off easy; Willy Loman failed as a father and as a salesman, and succeeded only at suicide.

Inaccurate assessment of one's abilities is costly even when it doesn't lead to collisions with reality like DeLorean's. According to Harold Geneen, such blindness is "worse than alcoholism" in its effects on productivity. He estimates that managers' "arrogant, all-knowing" disregard of their own failings annually costs the average corporation 40 percent of its earnings. Geneen does not use numbers casually. His point is made by the bankruptcy of Braniff, where a "We're number one" attitude inflated some employees' egos to the point that they thought they were better than their customers. When executives who mistakenly think they are master wheeler-dealers attempt to wheel and deal, or when ticket agents think they are better than their customers, disaster is not far away.

It is easy for us to patronize DeLorean's blindness, but a recent study of self-perception described by David Myers shows that most of us are in no position to smirk. *All* of Myers's adult male subjects ranked themselves in the top half of the population in "ability to get along with others." Like Willy Loman, we all deceive ourselves about being well liked. Only 2 percent of Myers's subjects said that they were below average in leadership and only 6 percent saw themselves as below average in athletic ability. Obviously, many of these people's self-assessments had to be wildly inaccurate. Overestimation of one's desirable features is common enough to be given a name: Psychologists call this phenomenon the "illusory glow."

Unlike DeLorean, the Braniff employees, and most other people, highly successful people know enough about their strengths and shortcomings to select a working environment that fits fairly well. Richard Boyatzis, CEO of McBer and Company, one of the country's most prestigious management consulting firms, finds that successful managers have "accurate self-assessment," the ability to "see their strengths and weaknesses and know their limitations." For example, the highly successful entrepreneur and sports marketing consultant Mark McCormack, in *What They Don't Teach You at Harvard Business School,* ascribes his success in part to his ability to combine his passion for golf with the realization that he would never be good enough to be a pro.

Managers with accurate self-assessment readily admit ignorance and mistakes, but they are rarely humble: They accurately assess their performance, good as well as bad, and they take credit where credit is due.

There are several other ways in which knowledge of one's abilities gives one an edge in business. Successful entrepreneurs create environments that provide scope for their abilities; such creativity depends on accurate assessment of those abilities. Management consultant Lyle Spencer of McBer and Company offers this piece of advice to prospective entrepreneurs: "The trick is to build a team, recruit other people who can offer the skills you lack." Following this suggestion requires knowing what you don't know. Managers who are already part of an organization also need to know their abilities in order to delegate the tasks that others may be better equipped to perform.

Psychologist Bill McKeachie finds that teachers can do better by knowing themselves better, and that "they don't need complete psychoanalysis" to do so. They do, however, need to be self-critical: Feedback about teaching performance, minute by minute and year by year, is essential. Good teachers must be willing to incorporate this feedback into their teaching, to try new methods. McKeachie reminds his students that a teacher who is wrong too often doesn't belong in the classroom, but neither does one who is never wrong. The teacher who is never wrong, he says, belongs "not in a classroom but in heaven." Accurate self-assessment is equally important in teaching older students. A study of adult education programs conducted by Carol Schneider, George Klemp, and Susan Kastendiek at the University of Chicago focused on faculty members rated by their peers as "exceptionally effective." Excellent teachers are "flexible" and "self-critical," willing to learn from their mistakes.

SELF-INTELLIGENCE

The lesson of Iacocca's parable is backed by research by psychologists and consultants: In business, teaching, and the law, knowing your own values is an essential asset. The moral of the cautionary tales of DeLorean and Braniff is supported by the testimony of Geneen and other research: Not knowing your abilities is almost always a liability. Getting and using information about your values requires Howard Gardner's "intrapersonal intelligence," which is similar to Wagner and Sternberg's "managing self." Getting and using information about your abilities (Boyatzis's "accurate self-assessment") require a critical capacity to examine one's practical intelligences. Together, knowing your needs and being able to assess your abilities constitute what I call "self-intelligence" ("SI," for short). My working hypothesis is that you can learn both components of SI. The chapters that follow explain ways to know and, in most cases, enhance your abilities. This chapter is primarily an effort to teach you how to know your values and needs.

TEACHING SELF-UNDERSTANDING

Like managers, lawyers, and teachers, psychotherapists must know their values and abilities well: They have to be able to handle their emotional and ethical responses to abnormality, and they have to be able to refer those they can't treat. Moreover, many psychotherapists regard their job as teaching self-understanding. Because self-understanding is doubly important in the practice of psychotherapy, as part of my research for this chapter I talked with several psychotherapists. One interview so vividly conveys the gravity, difficulty, and feasibility of self-understanding that I quote it at length. I'll call the therapist "Dr. Donne."

Dr. Donne's Ph.D. is from the University of California, and he has chaired the psychology department at a midwestern college. In his late thirties, he is licensed as a clinical psychologist in several midwestern states. I interviewed him on campus, on the first warm day of the year. We talked outside, so Dr. Donne's gothic tale was told against a background of Frisbees and softballs, pastel shorts and Hawaiian shirts. Early in our conversation, Dr. Donne talked about how his knowledge of his own attitudes and values influences his decision to take a case. "Sometimes," he said, "I'll get a client whom I know I can't work with, someone whose values and religious beliefs are too different from mine and too rigid to change. Those I just have to refer to someone else."

I asked him to tell me about a high point in his work. Here is his reply, with minor alterations to conceal the identity of the real "Nelda."

"One of my best cases was a woman, Nelda, whose complaints were all physical: numbness, insomnia, headaches. There was lots of neurological information, all negative. She denied that there were any psychological problems. She was seeing me on the advice of a physician, and only wanted to work on the physical stuff.

"Well, five seconds with this woman would tell anybody that there were more than just physical problems. This was one of the most depressed people I ever met. I mean, when she came into the room I felt like I was dying. I diagnosed her as in a major depressive episode, with conversion [of psychological symptoms into hysterical ones], and I suspected the possibility of sexual abuse, even though there weren't any signs when I talked to her. . . . I thought that suicide was imminent. There was complete denial: If I asked how she was, she'd say 'Fine' in a flat monotone. . . . Sure enough, at one point I had to hospitalize her because of suicidal thoughts, and hospitalization is something you never do unless you're *really* worried. . . .

"I knew right away this would take a long time, so I worked up a one-and-a-half-year treatment plan. My hypothesis was some kind of trauma at an early age. I'm very proud of that diagnosis. The audiotape would puzzle you—any psychologist would have looked at the case and said, 'What? This isn't psychosomatic!' My treatment plan was to make some changes at the psychodynamic level, but I didn't tell her my plan. If I had done that, she would have been out of there. I decided to test Freud to the max. . . . I wanted to help her find out what her unconscious conflicts were, hopefully to have some kind of catharsis [i.e., work out a trauma by reliving it], but to acknowledge them at least. I knew the treatment would be long-run deep stuff. . . .

"In order to give her some relief and to reduce her anxiety about treatment, I began with the psychosomatic stuff. I started with the insomnia, using a strictly behavioral approach—progressive relaxation, using the bed as a conditioned stimulus for sleep, not letting her go to bed unless she was exhausted, drinking warm milk. . . . I won her confidence. She was thinking, 'Hey, this isn't psychotherapy—this guy is just helping me sleep.' By the end of two months, we had the headaches and numbness way down. And the insomnia went away a little later.

"At the same time I began sneaking in psychotherapy—working on her adjustment using learning techniques. After about six weeks (I saw her often because of the suicide possibility), I had her discussing her divorce and her anxiety about sex. She hadn't had sex for over a year."

"Could you give me a decisive event in the therapy?"

"One day, she began talking about sex and her husband and how anxiety about environmental events affected the insomnia. She related it to a psychological event: Her husband tried to get her to sleep with him. She was usually way too anxious to talk about this kind of stuff, but *she* brought it up, so I thought: Here's my chance. You practically smile when it goes according to plan. She made the connection that psychological problems were leading to her physical problems. I was now really trying to get her to deal with her feelings, especially anxiety and fear. Dealing with her feelings was the last thing she had ever done. I would push toward her responses —you know, the standard stuff: 'How did that make you feel?'

"In the second year, she could bring up things that earlier she had been too anxious to describe. By now, she could at least talk about her depressed feelings, but she was far from cured; the depression lasted for years. I gave her homework on psychological intimacy.

"Eventually we talked about dreams, fantasies, her relationship with her mother. Turns out she was abused by relatives and friends, and was sometimes practically imprisoned. I went back to the notes I'd made after our first session. There it was: 'possible sex abuse.' She hadn't mentioned anything remotely like abuse back then, but her fragmented ego created new realities in order to survive. I got her to open up more and more, and one day there it was. She told me that she would sometimes sit in the basement and lose herself in different fantasy realities. One of them was a room with a red floor. She believed that if she ever went into that room, she'd die—it was kind of her ultimate escape hatch.

"She was a textbook case of reaction to abuse, but she was so overcontrolled that she had worked out an adaptation. She didn't let it intrude in her daily life. To get to the root of her problem I needed to get her to open up more. At one and a half years, she brought in some other writing. This stuff was like Sylvia Plath—*The Bell Jar* times ten. . . . But she would have gone insane without the writing and the alternate 'realities.' I tried to get her to use the writing more and the basement less."

"How did it work out?"

"It turned into a fantastic relationship. . . . With her anxiety, physical symptoms, and suicidal thoughts under control, and the closet fading out, she enrolled in school and did very well. She was trying to increase her functioning as a professional. She eventually got a pretty good job. I taught her to learn to do self-knowledge skills. She wasn't cured, but I left her someone who could do her own therapy. . . .

"What made this case especially great was that I had picked up on the abuse so early, before she said anything, and because an eclectic approach really worked. Orthodox psychoanalysts would not work on the psychosomatic symptoms, but would go for underlying causes right away. But if I had done that, she would have left therapy. If an analyst had tried to dig in right away, she would have killed herself. So it wasn't just that I helped her. It was that someone else might have killed her. That happens in this business."

This story shows how dangerous unacknowledged internal conflicts can be. To some extent, we all hide our deepest conflicts from ourselves, and when we do so we risk depression and anxiety. One researcher calls depression the "common cold of psychopathology, at once familiar and mysterious." At one time or another, at least 12 percent of the American population suffers from depression severe enough to warrant clinical help. And who hasn't, for one reason or another, had Hamlet's complaint: "How weary, stale, flat, and unprofitable Seem to me all the uses of this world!"

Depression is a complex group of problems—including normal reactions to misfortune. Such reactions typically heal themselves. More mysterious and dangerous are the depressions that may occur when we would least expect it, when life is good. In fact, Wall Street psychiatrist Jay Rohrlick, author of *Work and Love,* finds that depression is often triggered by success. Psychologists disagree about the causes of these mysterious maladies. Perhaps we expect success to solve *all* our problems and are disappointed when it doesn't. Among the many successful people who have suffered from severe depression are Abraham Lincoln, the utilitarian philosopher John Stuart Mill, composer Robert Schumann, Ernest Hemingway, Marilyn Monroe, and psychologist-philosopher William James, who once wrote his father that "thoughts of the pistol, the dagger, and the bowl began to usurp an unduly large part of my attention."

Nelda was also a victim of anxiety, depression's henchman, which is to a considerable extent a failure of self-understanding. Anxiety, which can be as deadly as depression, is often the result of a mismatch between the job's demands and the worker's abilities. Knowing your abilities can help you avoid such mismatches. Anxiety is at the center of the syndrome called the "Type A" personality, characterized by self-denial, impatience, competition, and ambition. Type A people deny their needs, ignore their feelings, and refuse to adapt their goals to their abilities. They act cool and tough and do not easily express vulnerability, intimacy, or dependency. They are always in a hurry and can't stand to wait. They turn every interaction into a contest. As a result, they overschedule, completing a vicious cycle of self-induced stress that all too often is interrupted by a heart attack. Nevertheless, according to Michael Maccoby's *The Gamesmen,* self-denying, competitive, power-driven (i.e., Type A) executives are the heroes of modern corporate culture. Maccoby applauds the recent appearance of "a new corporate type, the gamesman who develops his heart as well as his head." Given the well-documented effects of Type A personality on cardiac disease, Maccoby's use of "heart" is appropriate in more ways than one.

Depression and anxiety are the industrial diseases of the postindustrial society, occupational hazards in organizations that require us to deny our needs and suppress our shortcomings. To the extent that self-understanding can prevent and cure depression and anxiety, it is the most practical intelligence of all. There may be some jobs in which self-knowledge is of little use, but people who do well in these jobs risk promotion to a position where self-knowledge matters. Thus, for managers, entrepreneurs, lawyers, teachers, psychotherapists, and anyone else who works, the Delphic oracle's advice is well taken.

What happens to those who ignore the oracle's advice has been the stock-in-trade of tragedians from Sophocles to Arthur Miller. We are moved by these tragedies because we are similarly flawed. As Walker Percy points out, "it is possible to learn more in ten minutes about the Crab Nebula . . . than you presently know about yourself." As you will see, we are all experts at deceiving ourselves. Nevertheless, although self-discovery is difficult, even in extreme cases it is possible.

THE SELF IN AND AS THEORY

We take the self so much for granted that you may not have noticed that I have been discussing self-intelligence for some ten pages without defining the self that SI is supposed to know. The self is, after all, the most familiar of phenomena, the most immediate fact of experience. Yet the self is also abstract and inscrutable. More mysterious than cannibal galaxies, black holes, and the edge of the cosmos is the mind that can imagine them. Like faint stars seen only out of the corner of your eye, your self vanishes as soon as you look at it directly. When you try to examine your self by introspection, you watch yourself watching yourself and are quickly lost in an infinite regress of mirrors reflecting only mirrors in an endless tunnel to nowhere. Though familiar and abstract, the self is also transcendentally valuable. The self is more than all you can call your own —it is also the owner.

In order to get on with our business, which is learning ways to understand who we are, we need a working definition of this paradoxical entity. A self is a person, a coherent system of perceptions, feelings, memories, thoughts, and behaviors integrated into a stable pattern of needs and abilities.

For some time now, managers, consultants, psychotherapists, and others who use SI on the job have been successfully applying two practical approaches to self-understanding. The first is the psychodynamic point of view, which sees the self as an energy system. The second is the cognitive approach, which sees the self as a processor of information. Until recently, these two approaches seemed to be saying very different things about who we are. The application of the new methods of cognitive science to the self is, however, making sense of what psychodynamic theorists (as well as novelists and philosophers) have been saying all along.

Because these approaches are so different, it's worth spending a few moments clarifying them before showing where and how they converge.

The first and most influential psychodynamic theory is psychoanalysis, a theory developed during the first three decades of this century by Sigmund Freud. Though Freud himself attempted to put psychoanalysis on a scientific course, his methods were not scientific in the way those of biology or chemistry are. Psychoanalytic and, to some extent, all psychodynamic theories are interpretive. Their goal is particularly practical, rather than generally theoretical: to understand what is going on with a particular person at a particular point in his or her life. Psychodynamic descriptions of the self are more like cultural myths than scientific theories. To call them myths is not to say they are false; it is to say that the standards by which their truth is judged should not be those of science.

Freud's psychoanalytic self was like a factory run on steam, a system of vessels ("psychic structures") filled ("cathected") with sexual energy ("libido") under pressure ("repression"). Freud describes a myth of human development: Early in life, as a result of experiences with pleasure and pain, we develop our first psychic structures, self and not-self. Both these psychic structures differentiate so that by the time an infant is a few days or weeks old, there are psychic structures representing self, mother, and libidinally charged body parts: mouth, breast, and genitals. Traumatic repression of libidinal urges results in the Oedipus or Electra complex: fear of castration combined with hatred of the father in males, or envy of the penis and jealousy of the mother in females.

These stories are myths in the sense that they are not literally true: There is no physiological evidence for energies under pressure in the brain, no objective records of expulsions from the parents' bedroom. But as with all great myths, they accurately describe how we believe and act. Freud's myths of the self are like Cortez's maps of America, sometimes wildly distorted on the larger scale but amazingly accurate about details. The Mississippi is not the Northwest Passage and the brain is not a steam engine, but Freud's maps are still good enough to help us find our way around. For most of this century, we have been correcting, not discarding, his first maps. Recent research in cognitive and physiological psychology shows that what is most amazing is how much Freud got right.

Today, we use Freud's myth whenever we think about ourselves in terms of mental "energies," which get "blocked" or "flow" smoothly. The vocabulary of psychoanalysis is embedded in our daily talk: "ego," "guilt," "repression," "neurotic," "oral," "anal," "sex object." Psychoanalysis and its psychodynamic cousin the Transactional Analysis (TA) of Eric Berne (popularized in his best-selling book *Games People Play*) are the approaches most often used today in law and law enforcement, medicine, and management science, as well as everyday thought.

The steam-powered factory was an appropriate myth for an age when we understood and mastered the forces of nature by thermodynamics. Today's self is automated—computers control the boilers and pipes in the basement. We get "input," engage in various forms of "programming" and "deprogramming," and go into "loops." Views of the self that emphasize information rather than energy are called "cognitive," and they are now beginning to rival psychodynamic theories in practical influence. Cognitive theories are more intellectual than are psychodynamic theories. They view the self as a set of hypotheses or theories that we have about ourselves. These hypotheses are embodied in "schemas," or representations. Schemas are patterns of processes in the brain that stand for objects, people, feelings, and events. Like the files of a computerized data base, schemas have slots for incoming information. Schemas actively transform input in order to relate it to existing data. For example, you perceive and relate to your first teacher or boss in terms of the schemas of your parents. In cognitive jargon, you "assimilate the boss to the parent schema."

From the cognitive perspective, the self is an organization of knowledge, a kind of theory. Anthony Greenwald, a psychologist at Ohio State University, compares the ego to a cataloging system in a library, the "Dewey Decimal System of the mind," as Daniel Goleman calls it. The self is what allows you to access a lifetime of information obtained in different places. In Greenwald's words, the self allows the mind "to allocate its resources to storage and retrieval of information (rather than continual revision of its indexing or coding scheme), thereby permitting access to a large amount of information within a single system."

If the self is a theory, as Greenwald suggests, its deepest need is to make sense. Indeed, everyday life provides many demonstrations of the power of our thirst for meaning. We see patterns in random forms of clouds, hear words in the wind, and find unity in our chaotic consciousness. We cannot create random sequences of numbers even when we try, and we cannot bear randomness when it's forced on us. That's why Chinese water torture *is* torture. Harry Levinson, a psychoanalytically oriented management consultant, finds that for most executives the meaning of money matters more than the money itself: Highly paid managers, who compare themselves to CEOs of *Fortune* 500 companies, are in general less satisfied with their salaries than lower-paid ones, who compare themselves to others in their own organizations. A study at GE showed that workers who were led to believe that they were overpaid boosted their productivity to maintain a sense of fairness. What makes many great leaders great is their ability to provide meaning to their followers. And finally, the willingness to die for a cause shows that meaning is sometimes valued more than life itself.

Cognitive views of the self are usually expressed as scientific theories: testable, objective, general, abstract, and above all, tentative. Like all theories, the self is continually in a state of becoming. Accordingly, cognitive therapists are more like scientists or teachers than like "headshrinkers." Their job is not to fix a broken machine but to help you revise your theory. Albert Ellis, the grandfather of cognitive therapy, described his program as "educative" rather than "curative." Ellis's Rational Emotive Therapy (RET) consists in large part of arguments and exercises designed to get clients to abandon destructive irrational premises like: "One should be thoroughly competent, adequate, and achieving in all possible respects if one is to consider oneself worthwhile."

There are other important differences between the cognitive approach and the psychodynamic, but these differences are matters of emphasis. For example, psychodynamic psychologists view depression and anxiety as the results of internal conflicts, while cognitive psychologists see them as contradictions in our theories of ourselves. From either perspective, however, prevention and cure depend on self-understanding. As Daniel Goleman puts it, "all therapies amount to schema repair." While psychodynamic approaches emphasize the irrational motives, and cognitive the rational conceptions, each approach admits the existence of both rational and irrational components in the self, not one on top of the other but inter-mingled.

Both psychodynamic and cognitive approaches see the self as a system of schemas. In psychodynamic theories these representations are complex, often a lot like persons, but in cognitive theory they are much simpler. Both "psychic structures" and "schemas" are, however, representations that screen, select, organize, and retain incoming information. What the cognitivist calls "assimilation" the psychodynamicist calls "transference." In spite of such differences in terminology, Freud himself diagrammed the flow of "excitation" with the cognitivists' favorite tools, what we today call flowcharts.

Finally, from both psychodynamic and cognitive points of view, the regions we are about to explore are forbidding. Whether you call them conflicts or contradictions, our self-deceptions are not merely frictions or glitches but essential structures in our characters. To penetrate these structures, which psychoanalysts call "defenses," takes years. Furthermore, from the cognitive point of view, like any highly complex program we are full of bugs and always in need of updating. Cognitive therapies are ongoing processes, not a one-shot cure.

Since both theories agree that self-knowledge is difficult, the first step in using psychodynamic and cognitive approaches to know yourself is to realize that it won't be easy.

Guided by the stereoscopic view provided by psychodynamic and cognitive approaches, we will now begin our exploration. It will be rough going: though we begin at the sunny surf-lined coast, we will soon be lost in the dark interior of repressed conflict. Psychological theories can't tell you who you are, but they can show you enough of your internal landscape to let you explore the rest on your own.

P. T. Barnum Through the Looking Glass

Imagine that you are taking a computerized personality test. For an hour and a half, you type in answers to over five hundred true-false questions. When you are finished, you press "return," and inscrutable symbols appear on the screen. Eventually the printer begins to spit. What emerges is the following description:

> You have a need for other people to like and admire you, and yet you tend to be critical of yourself. While you have some personality weaknesses, you are generally able to compensate

for them. You have considerable unused capacity that you have not turned to your advantage. Disciplined and self-controlled on the outside, you tend to be worrisome and insecure on the inside. At times, you have serious doubts as to whether you have made the right decision or done the right thing. You prefer a certain amount of change and variety and become dissatisfied when hemmed in by restrictions and limitations. You also pride yourself as an independent thinker and do not accept others' statements without satisfactory proof. But you have found it unwise to be too frank in revealing yourself to others. At times you are extroverted, affable, and sociable, while at other times you are introverted, wary, and reserved. Some of your aspirations tend to be rather unrealistic.

Is this you? Ninety percent of the experimental subjects who took a personality test and then got exactly this description rated it as "good" or "excellent" in terms of accuracy, even though it was not based on their answers. Some expressed surprise that psychology was such an "exact science." The favorable ratings were not due to vagueness or flattery. When the description was modified to include phrases like "You seem to find it impossible to work out a satisfactory adjustment to your problems," more than a fifth of the subjects still rated the description as "good to excellent." We can see ourselves in this description, as well as in the quite specific descriptions of horoscopes, handwriting analyses, and abnormal-psychology text-books, because all psychological traits are present to some degree in everyone.

Consequently, we are more likely to believe a description that applies to anyone than one that applies uniquely to us. Psychologists call our willingness to believe almost any authoritative description of ourselves the "P. T. Barnum effect," after the circus magnate who said "A good circus has a little something for everybody." (He also said, "There's a sucker born every minute.")

One reason we are so willing to accept descriptions of ourselves made by others is that in a practical sense, we *are* what others see. We see ourselves reflected in others' eyes, and what we see there affects who we are. If, like the phantom of the opera, you are seen and therefore treated as a monster, a monster is what you become. If, like Chauncey the gardener in *Being There,* you are treated as a sage, soon a sage is what you will be. What others see of us affects how they respond to us, which in turn affects how we act and who we become.

Around the turn of the century, the social psychologist Charles Horton Cooley took this idea one step farther. He argued that the *only* way to know yourself is through the eyes of others. His view of the "looking glass self" says that we need others not only to *be* ourselves but to *know* ourselves.

Most psychodynamic theorists agree that the self is largely a social construction, but they regard a healthy sense of personal identity as a balance between autonomy and dependence. For example, psychoanalyst Erik Erikson has described the development of the sense of self throughout the life span as a series of conflicts between the existing organizations of the person and the demands of various culturally defined roles: schoolchild, teenager, young adult, parent. Successful resolution of these conflicts results in an ego with well-defined boundaries but capable of intimate melding with others. Psychoanalysts follow Cooley's directions to explore oneself by interacting with others. They explore personal conflicts by getting the patient to transfer them to the therapist, who becomes a surrogate parent to help the patient work out the conflicts.

The looking glass self directly opposes our commonsense notion that there is an inner true self distinct from the personality (from *persona,* Latin for "mask") we present to the world. Of course, we do play roles, but the roles we play affect who we really are. Our faces mold themselves to our masks. Our commonsense notion of an inner autonomous self comes from our culture's doctrine of individualism, the notion that we shouldn't depend on one another for anything, least of all our identities. According to the individualistic myth of the autonomous self, we are self-made men and women; the true self is something separate from and in competition with others. To some extent it is. But it is also part of a process of mutual social construction.

The pragmatic philosopher and cognitive psychologist William James said that the boundaries of the physical self are fuzzy. What James called the "material me" includes not only my body but my clothes, my home, and other personal possessions. I react to a tiny spot on my best suit as though it were a painful wound. My body, grooming, dress, car, and home affect others' images of me, which in turn affect my image of myself. The images others have form what James, anticipating Cooley's looking glass self by a decade, called the "social me." The social me is as much a part of my self as the material me; I am easily hurt by injuries to and pleased by glorification of these images.

Further insight into the extent to which our inner selves are socially determined comes from experiments on emotion. Cognitive social psychologist Stanley Schachter's labeling theory of emotion says that what you feel in a situation and how strongly you feel it depend much more on social context than on either the events themselves or the resulting physiological changes in your body. What you feel depends on how you construe the situation, and how you construe the situation depends on social context.

Schachter and others have amassed plenty of data supporting the cognitive labeling theory of emotion. Some of the strongest evidence comes from experiments in which injections of adrenaline (a hormone released by the body in emotional situations) induce the physiological component (arousal) of an emotion, while social cues are provided to give the emotion its peculiar feel. Physicians often use adrenaline injections to relieve the symptoms of asthma. Typically, the asthma sufferer then feels aroused but not in any particular way. The characteristic feeling of an emotion is absent. Cognitive labeling theory says that the absence of emotional "feel" is due to the patient's attributing the arousal to the drug. If, however, subjects are unaware of the arousing effects of adrenaline and are exposed to cues that allow them to label their arousal, they report feeling the appropriate emotion.

In one classic experiment, subjects were injected with adrenaline. Some of the subjects were informed about the drug's arousing effects but others were told that the injection was "suproxin" and that it would improve their vision. All subjects then filled out a questionnaire containing insulting questions. One question was "With how many men (other than your father) has your mother had extramarital relations? 4 and under; 5–9; 10 and over." While the subjects worked on their questionnaires, a stooge angrily crumpled up his questionnaire and stalked out of the room. Like asthma patients, subjects who were informed about the effects of the drug generally reported that they felt no particular emotion. The misinformed subjects, on the other hand, with the stooge as a model, reported that they felt angry and attributed their anger to the questionnaire. Similar results were obtained under conditions designed to elicit euphoria.

In another experimental test of labeling theory, an attractive female interviewed male subjects either on a swaying suspension bridge 230 feet above a canyon floor or on a sturdy bridge at the bottom of the same canyon. Half the subjects interviewed on the high bridge attempted to contact the interviewer later on, while only 13 percent of those interviewed on the low bridge did so. Apparently, subjects on the high bridge attributed some of their physiological arousal to the presence of the interviewer. This result suggests that labeling theory may explain the popular belief that bullfights, revivals, disasters, and other arousing but nonerotic events make people more open to sexual encounters. Evidently, feelings as different as fear and lust, anger and euphoria, are determined by social context, not by autonomous physiological processes.

It is therefore not surprising that children who for one reason or another are raised in isolation never develop even the rudimentary intrapersonal intelligence necessary to distinguish pleasure from pain. A common result of isolation in early childhood is a nearly complete anesthesia. These children routinely suffer bruises and burns without apparent distress. They also display severe disturbances of self-image. As Howard Gardner puts it, they have had no opportunity to "discover that they are 'persons.' " Their plight is a special case of a general principle that our knowledge of our own emotions depends on social context.

The labeling of emotions is only one of many ways in which our conceptions of our selves are molded by language. Language is at the core of most of our thinking about ourselves and is the purest form of social construction. Thus, although the body may be the bastion of the autonomous self, its gates are open to the influence of others.

Psychodynamic myths from Freud's Oedipus complex to Berne's internal Parent, and cognitive theories from James's material and social selves to Schachter's labeling, have similar implications: A mature sense of self is dialectical. That is, one sees oneself as distinct from others, yet relies on others for that very sense of distinctness.

The realization that the self is inherently social has several practical implications. First of all, one way to find out who you are is to explore your perceptions of the images others have of you. Get someone to ask you "Who are you?" several times, but always when you don't expect it. Chances are you will answer with a reference to a group, with a family name, occupation, or nationality. Then imagine how other members of the group see you.

Second, the social character of the self implies that our needs for community and connectedness are deep and fundamental, not luxuries to be enjoyed after other needs, like the need for achievement, have been satisfied. Thus, rather than deny our needs for approval and support, we should embrace them. A recent article by Daniel Goleman suggests that many successful entrepreneurs have done just that. Goleman reported research showing that many entrepreneurs have an "insatiable need for applause," which they turn into an asset by becoming heroes in their own organizations.

A third suggestion is that you use others' impressions to explore your abilities. A study that compared how people rated themselves in social situations with ratings by observers produced an "illusory glow": We generally rate ourselves higher than others rate us. When these discrepancies are marked, we may want to take a closer look at our performance. You can use others as gadflies: People who don't like you can often tell you more about yourself than those who do. You can also learn about yourself by knowing your friends. What do they value about you? What do you value in each of them? Characters in novels by Jane Austen, Feodor Dostoevsky, Henry James, and other great writers may resonate with you. Such novels allow you to explore your reactions to people you cannot experience firsthand.

Fourth, even if we are in part others' images of us, we can nevertheless choose these others. As William James said of the "potential social me," "I am always inwardly strengthened against the loss of my actual social self by the thought of other and better *possible* social judges than those whose verdict goes against me now. . . . All progress in the social self is the substitution of higher tribunals for lower."

YOU-ALL

James's concept of social selves has one further implication: "Properly speaking," said James, one has "as many social selves as there are individuals" or "distinct groups of persons about whose opinion" one cares. Let's explore this novel and far-reaching implication.

Multiple social selves provide a second explanation for the P. T. Barnum effect. We accept diverse descriptions of ourselves not only because they come from people who help us define ourselves, but also because they are true.

Here again, psychological research contradicts common sense and cultural convention. Only if you are a monarch, a pope, or an editor do you refer to yourself as "we." In Western culture, the self is seen not only as autonomous but as monolithic. Conventional wisdom considers a stable, unified sense of self normal and good, while its opposite, what Erik Erikson calls "identity diffusion," or the extreme and rare cases of multiple personalities, is considered abnormal and bad. Most of us believe in the reality of what James called the "spiritual me," which he placed at the top of a hierarchy, above the multiple social selves. The spiritual me is "the entire collection of my states of consciousness, my psychic faculties and dispositions taken concretely. . . . [It is the] very core and nucleus of our self, the very sanctuary of our life." Yet even for James the spiritual me is only the first among, if not equals, subordinates with at least some degree of independence.

The strongest of the many modern psychological formulations of the commonsense view of a unitary self is Anthony Greenwald's monolithic "Dewey Decimal System" described earlier. I will return to Greenwald's theory shortly, but for now I would like to review the evidence that each of us is in fact many different persons.

Psychologist Kenneth Gergen was "first surprised, then alarmed" when he read several letters he had just written, and found that he "came across as a completely different person in each one." But after years of study, Gergen has concluded that we are "made of soft plastic," and we become the selves we present. Thus, the real mystery is not the extremely rare multiple personality but the normal ability to direct the cast of characters that lives within your skin. "I know who I *was* when I got up this morning," said Lewis Carroll's Alice, "but I think I must have been changed several times since then."

To say that you are many different persons is not just to say your moods change or that you play different roles. You can do that while maintaining the sense that you are the same person. Rather, by our working definition of "self" or "person," there are several separate systems of perceptions, feelings, memories, thoughts, and behaviors, each of which is integrated into a more or less stable pattern of needs and abilities, and each of which operates independently of or conflicts with the others.

Let's list some of your social selves. One of them is the "Parent" of TA. According to Eric Berne, when Parent "is directly active, the person responds as his own father (or mother) actually responded. When it is an indirect influence, he responds the way they wanted him to respond." Parent allows you to function as your real parents did and to do so automatically, saving time and energy. In this, Berne is echoed by modern cognitive research, which shows that we learn to automate almost any mental process, including the commands of our parents. Automation is a common topographical feature of our inner selves: We regard our spontaneous, automatic reactions as most genuine. Freud's version of Parent was the "superego," which he conceived as an internal model of a parent, roughly synonymous with "conscience." Cognitive theorists have arrived at similar conceptions: Seymour Epstein, a psychologist who describes the self as theory, says, "People with high self-esteem, in effect, carry within them a loving parent."

In transactional terms, one of Parent's main jobs is to control the often opposing non- or even antisocial demands of Child. When Child is on stage, according to Berne, "The manner and intent of your reaction is the same as it would have been when you were a very little boy or girl." Child is often selfish and rebellious, but is also creative, spontaneous, and playful. The main function of Freud's superego is control of the animal urges of the "id" (Latin for "it"). Freud endowed the id with both beastly and constructive urges, but most psychologists emphasize what one animal behaviorist calls the four "F's": fight, flight, food, and sex. Cognitive theorists have less to say about the instinctive animal motives of the id than about more cerebral characters like Parent. However, William James's material me, with its "Bodily Appetites and Instincts," including "Love of Adornment, Foppery, Acquisitiveness, and Constructiveness," is analogous to Child and id.

The third transactional self is Adult, who "processes data and computes the probabilities" that are "necessary for survival." Adult is analogous to Freud's "reality-testing" ego and William James's "spiritual me." Adult, or ego, is the character studied by cognitive psychologists, though they prefer names like "executive" or "meta-schema."

In a very real sense, then, you are at least three different persons —Child, id, or material me, who says "I want"; Parent, or superego, the social me who says "I should"; and Adult, ego, spiritual me, or executive, who says "I can."

In Transactional Analysis, Parent, Child, and Adult are called "ego states." Compare what Berne says about ego states to my working definition of a person as a coherent system of perceptions, feelings, memories, thoughts, and behaviors integrated into a stable pattern of needs and abilities. An ego state is a "coherent system of feelings related to a given subject, . . . which motivates a related set of behavior patterns." Ego states are expressed as inner conversations—distinctive words, tones of voice, facial expressions, and dreams. The voice of Parent is "the voice of an actual person." "Parent, Child and Adult represent real people who now exist or once existed, who have legal names and civic identities." They "are not concepts . . . but phenomenological realities."

They are physiological realities as well. Paul MacLean, head of the Laboratory for Brain Evolution and Behavior at the National Institute of Mental Health, describes the vertical organization of the brain: "we might imagine that when a psychiatrist bids the patient to lie on the couch, he is asking him to stretch out alongside a horse and crocodile." The patient, of course, is the ego or Adult, who lives in the cortex, the outermost layer of the brain, responsible for calculation and planning; the horse is the superego, who dwells in the limbic system, a distinct structure that passes on rewards and punishments, and controls automatic responses. The crocodile is the id, who slithers around in the basement of the brain, awash in primal urges. Each of these layers of the brain has not only its own structures and functions but its own chemical messengers and patterns of neural connections.

The trinity of selves is not an integrated whole. Norman Geschwind, professor of neurology at Harvard Medical School, describes these selves as at best a "loose federation." "Even a normal human is not a unity," he says, and "it may be precisely this fact which produces the distinctive character of consciousness. We are most likely to be fully conscious when we are aware that there are multiple tendencies pulling in different directions, and that very complicated decisions have to be made." As an example of the ubiquity of conflict among the levels of the brain, Geschwind describes how hard it is for the cortex to order a natural limbic smile or laugh. As a result, our family albums are full of grotesque grimaces, and boardrooms echo with the hollow imitations of laughter at the chairman's jokes. Psychologically we are divided ego from superego from id, and neurologically, top from middle from bottom.

We are divided left from right as well. About the same time Cooley was developing his notion of the looking glass self, the neurologist Kurt Goldstein handled a curious case: a woman who, like Dr. Strangelove, attempted to strangle herself with one hand while the other hand attempted to block the assault. Goldstein was a champion of the unified self, but ironically, his research culminated in the well known finding that we have two distinct personalities, one in each hemisphere of our brain. Normally, of course, these two personalities keep in touch and only under unusual circumstances do their separate identities emerge, but they are there in all of us.

Whether or not they embody psychological forces in inner selves, all psychodynamic theories regard conflicts between such forces not only as inevitable but as essential. From the psychodynamic point of view, who you are depends on how you resolve, deny, or act out such conflicts.

RET's irrational beliefs (like the one quoted above) are similar to TA's "injunctions" and "directives," commands (usually from Parent) to behave or feel in various ways that are often impossible. (Do not covet thy neighbor's wife.) From the cognitive perspective, our conflicts are contradictions between needs expressed as irrational premises and our limited capacities to fill these needs. William

James described these conflicts as well as anyone. He wrote that he would, if he could, be

> well dressed, and a great athlete, and make a million a year, be a wit, a *bon vivant,* and a lady-killer as well as a philosopher; a philanthropist, statesman, warrior, and African explorer, as well as a "tone-poet" and saint. But the . . . millionaire's work would run counter to the saint's; the *bon vivant* and the philanthropist would trip each other up; the philosopher and the lady-killer could not well keep house in the same tenement of clay.

Saith a sage: "Every commitment is the death of a thousand alternative selves." Knowing what we want is easy, but because so many things we want are mutually exclusive, knowing what we want most is difficult.

However, accepting the inevitability of conflict prepares you to look for practical compromises. William James described one such compromise when he pointed out that self-esteem is the quotient of "success" divided by "pretensions" (or, reduced to the lower terms of SI, abilities over needs). Using this quotient, James proposed a novel way to increase one's sense of success. By expanding one's definition of success to include "the good fortunes of the Vanderbilts," one's self is expanded so that "no wind can blow except to fill its sails." This strategy is adopted by those whose sense of self includes triumphs of their business, football team, or nation.

Ever the pragmatist, James points out to those who want more than this somewhat psychedelic method of boosting self-esteem that there is another way: Instead of increasing the numerator, you can reduce the denominator by lowering your aspirations. He quotes Thomas Carlyle: "Make thy claim of wages a zero, then has thou the world under thy feet. . . . it is only with *renunciation* that life, properly speaking, can be said to begin." This is the strategy of the beatitudes.

Is, then, the commonsense view that each of us is a single self only an illusion? Berne, Freud, Gergen, and Geschwind would answer "Yes," while Erik Erikson, Kurt Goldstein, and Anthony Greenwald would say "No." They would argue that our sense of continuity, our knowledge of our previous states, supports the idea of the unitary ego. Anthony Greenwald uses the phrase "totalitarian ego" to describe his theory of the self as a master filing system. Like totalitarian regimes, Greenwald's self preserves its identity by engaging in various forms of thought control, which I will soon discuss. We can regard the commonsense Erikson-Greenwald view as the goal of the ego; the self strives for totalitarian control but falls far short. Each of our multiple selves is a petty tyrant with its own authoritarian tendencies. We really are the "loose federations" of selves described by Geschwind. We are not totalitarian states but banana republics, with juntas ruling more or less effectively, constantly threatened with revolution by strong opposing factions: more like Argentina than Russia. Multiple personalities are only an extreme version of a general human condition. The real phenomenon is the limited degree of unity we aspire to and sometimes enjoy.

Moreover, we typically cannot, as Greenwald's unitary filing system says we should, access all the information we know. We often get into "tip-of-the-tongue" states in which we know the information is there but cannot get to it. I discuss some practical applications of this phenomenon in a later chapter, but for now, all I need to say is that these states are real, and they cast doubt on the unity of our master filing system. Real libraries have several filing systems, because looking only under author, title, or subject doesn't always work.

Unlike most computers, which typically do one thing at a time, we are parallel multiprocessors: We perform many independent operations simultaneously. To extend the computer metaphor, we are like computers with more than one operating system. Each of our selves can call up the same subroutines, and we can pass information among our various types of files, but not easily.

Then which operating system is the real one? They all are. Even if there is a master command-level system, it, like James's spiritual self, is only the first among equals: just another program.

Though powerful, the aspiration for unity is expendable. Kenneth Gergen notes that "We are burdened by the code of coherence, which demands that we ask, *How can I be X if I am really Y, its opposite?* We should ask instead, *What is causing me to be X at this time?* . . . If a man can see himself only as powerful, he will feel pain when he recognizes moments of weakness. If a woman thinks of herself as active and lively, moments of quiet will be unbearable." Gergen recommends that we emulate the poet Walt Whitman, who wrote: "Do I contradict myself? Very well then I contradict myself, (I am large, I contain multitudes.)"

Because we venerate the cool, tough A type, it's worth stating clearly the major implication of the idea of multiple selves: You have opposite and mutually exclusive needs and abilities. Just because you are strong and competitive doesn't mean you aren't also tender and supportive when the situation demands it. My own model is Balzac, who wrote: "In my five feet three inches I contain every possible inconsistency and contrast."

In *The Androgynous Manager,* Alice G. Sargent argues that we need to cultivate the ability to transcend personal polarities, to move from masculine to feminine, autonomous to dependent, as the situation requires. In particular, men who deny their needs for support, community, and connectedness have much to learn from their female colleagues. Indeed, according to a recent article in the *New York Times,* recognition of a need for social support is especially high in female managers, who are often asked to adapt to traditionally male roles, often highly competitive ones. One female bank manager said, "I know I'm more effective being myself than I am at aping my male peers. But my company would rather see me become a mediocre male clone than let me succeed as a woman."

The need for community is not confined to females. David Riesman and other sociologists have written of executives' deep and often unacknowledged hunger for fraternity. This hunger is a major factor in the demise of the dream of the "electronic cottage" office. People need colleagues, not just a "workstation." In *Beyond Human Scale: The Large Corporation at Risk,* Eli Ginzberg and George Vojta argue that there is a mismatch between the values of large corporations and the needs of young managers, especially their need to share responsibility and decisions. As a result of this mismatch, young managers often leave for smaller organizations with more collegiality. How well have *you* integrated your needs for community and autonomy? Are you willing to accept praise, sympathy, and other forms of support?

Acknowledging previously unexpressed needs is not easy. Psychodynamic psychologists have long noted that it is often easier to turn a need into its opposite than to deal with it directly. Suggestions that cool, tough A types have secret needs for support are often greeted with angry denials. Social critic Phillip Slater notes that "Those issues about which members of a given society seem to feel strongly all reveal a conflict one side of which is strongly emphasized, the other side as strongly (but not quite successfully) suppressed." Conversion thus requires "only a very small shift in the balance of a focal and persistent conflict." (Personality profiles of police match those of some criminal types.) Among the issues about which members of our society feel most strongly are masculinity versus femininity and autonomy versus dependence. Kenneth Gergen notes that these pairs are among the few stable consistent patterns that run through our multiple selves: No matter who we are at the moment, we tend to present ourselves as either masculine or feminine, as providing or needing help.

Other obstacles to acknowledging needs are the demands made

by our institutions. In the interest of productivity, organizations usually ask us not only to defer gratification but to deny our needs. And even when they do acknowledge our needs, according to Peters and Waterman, most businesses provide for one member of contradictory pairs while suppressing its opposite. As managers, we ought to provide challenge as well as security, support as well as independence, and kindness as well as fairness.

In the next leg of our journey, we explore these secret conflicts and their consequences. In psychodynamic terms, our goal is discovery of the conflicts that block your energies. A cognitive psychologist would translate that into debugging your programs. However we phrase the task, the next step is to find some of these bugs or blocks. Unfortunately, the most serious ones are well hidden.

HOW TO DEFEND YOURSELF WITHOUT REALLY KNOWING

Freud wrote that the goal of psychoanalysis is "to make the unconscious conscious." He once compared the conscious mind to the small part of an island above water, the unconscious to the mass below. To modify this metaphor, we might say that no man is an island. Rather, we are archipelagos of multiple selves. Some archipelagos form broken circles, while others are in chains. Just as a geographer who wishes to understand the forms of islands must look beneath the surface of the sea to inspect the volcanic calderas and submarine ranges that give the archipelagos their shape, so the egographer who wishes to understand the conscious mind must submerge into the unconscious.

The charting of the unconscious was the most innovative achievement of psychoanalytic interpretation, and now we take unconscious mental processes for granted. Consider the role of unconscious, automatic subroutines in driving a car. I have one for each of several routes to work, and often arrive with no recollection of which one I used. Moreover, if I am not careful, one of these unconscious programs will take me to work when I started out for the grocery store. Cognitive scientist Donald Norman calls such errors "post-Freudian slips." They are compelling evidence of the role of unconscious mental processes in everyday life.

Freud's unconscious was not just a bank of automatic abilities, but a benthic trench where repressed urges lurked like coelacanths. The automation of mental processes is, however, the cognitive key to the dynamics of repression. The first step in automating repression is to find an appropriate defense. For example, in Lee Iacocca's candid analysis of his firing by Henry Ford III, he wrote: "I never expected a showdown. . . . I wanted that $1 million a year so much that I wouldn't face reality. . . . In my naiveté, I held out the hope that . . . the better man would win." Iacocca fantasized that "Henry would come to his senses. Or the board would get its back up." Psychodynamic psychologists call this defense against anxiety "denial," or wishful thinking.

The next step is to repeat the defense until it becomes automatic. Like the subroutines that let us drive without thinking about it, the defense mechanisms work automatically without our care. Iacocca reassured every member of his staff that the situation was A-OK.

Denial served Lee Iacocca well. He was able to pull down his million dollars a year for much longer than someone who would have appraised the situation more realistically. But he regrets that he didn't get out of Ford earlier.

"Reaction formation," or "reversal," is like denial, only more so. Instead of simply engaging in wishful thinking, you can actively cultivate opposite feelings. When cleverly applied, this mechanism allows you to indulge the very impulses you fear. The textbook example is the censor who handles his erotic impulses by turning them into disgust at the pornography he collects.

In rationalization, or "sour grapes," you find some nonthreatening cover story for your unacknowledged urges. "I'm firing you for your own good—you'll do better elsewhere." Or: "Actually, I'm glad I got fired. Now I can do what I really enjoy."

Displacement through sublimation is the transfer of a disturbing urge to an acceptable object. Showoffs who sublimate their need for applause by becoming entrepreneurs use this one. So do potential hoods who sublimate their aggressive urges and become police.

Projection is transferring an internal conflict to someone else: The teacher anxious about his expertise accuses his students of impertinence.

Cognitive psychologist Matthew Erdelyi has studied the extent to which we use these defenses. In an informal study, he found that rationalization was the most common, used by 96 percent of those he polled, followed by displacement (86 percent), and projection (72 percent). Reaction formation is for connoisseurs, used by only 46 percent. However, a recent study suggests that this number may be higher in large corporations, where many hail fellows well met seem to be reacting against their own shyness.

Precisely because defense mechanisms are so effective, we use them at our peril. The point is to be able to identify them so you'll know when you're using them. They are, in Freud's term, "neurotic"; they distort reality. Moreover, such defenses soon cease to be mere moves we can control and use at will; eventually they pervade one's character. Some of us become perpetual projectors, whining at others' weaknesses and fuming at their hostility. Some of us characteristically react: Fear of laziness gets us out of bed before dawn, and anxiety about physical attractiveness chases us as we jog. Wilhelm Reich forged the phrase "character armor" to describe the defenses we wear.

What is most dangerous about defenses is that they eventually become invisible. In the final stage, defenses are so automatic that one forgets the fear-provoking situation. Then, to paraphrase psychiatrist R. D. Laing, one forgets that one has forgotten. To his credit, Iacocca stopped short of this step. When news of his firing finally came in the form of an elliptical remark by a reporter, Iacocca "had no doubt what he meant."

According to Daniel Goleman, such successful repression results in a condition much like blind spots, areas in the eye that cannot receive visual input. You can detect your blind spots by drawing two dots about three inches apart on a blank piece of paper. Close your left eye and look at the left dot from a distance of about a foot. By moving the page closer and farther away, you will eventually place the right dot over your blind spot, and it will disappear. Only under such special circumstances are you aware of your blind spots, but they are always there, like the parts of reality we ignore. Can you love, hate, or fear someone without knowing it? You bet your blind spots.

Freud's daughter Anna wrote, "All the defense mechanisms of the ego against the id are carried out silently and invisibly. . . . The ego knows nothing of it." Goleman puts it more succinctly: "the sound of repression is a thought evaporating."

How, then, do we know when we're using one of these neurotic defenses? Sometimes we can catch ourselves in an act of repression. Just the other day, when one of my articles was rejected by a minor journal, I was relieved. I realized that it was really more appropriate for *Harvard Educational Review*. More commonly, as Anna Freud wrote, "we are aware only subsequently, when it becomes apparent that something is missing." One way to detect what is missing is through "free association." Using this technique developed by Freud, psychoanalysts often ask their patients to say whatever comes to mind, and look for "resistance," places where the patient refuses to make an association. In the absence of an analyst, perceptive friends and colleagues can sometimes catch a defense under construction. One of mine listened to my rationalization about my article and suggested I send it to *Boys' Life.*

We need to be aware of our defenses, not so that we can eliminate them but so that we can be in control of them. To some extent they are essential if we are to function in the real world. A study by a British psychologist found that both within and across individuals, there is a correlation between neurosis and economic success. The finding that we are most successful when most neurotic would come as no surprise to Freud, who argued in *Civilization and Its Discontents* that neurotic repression is the price of civilization. More recently, in *Vital Lies, Simple Truths,* Daniel Goleman argued that a modicum of self-deception is not only unavoidable but adaptive. To the advice of the oracle to know thyself, Goleman would add another piece of ancient practical wisdom: "Nothing too much."

Without committing myself to the questionable proposition that it is better to be happy than wise, I must admit that Freud and Goleman have a point. In any case, whether our dependence on illusion is alimentary or addictive, it appears that like Willy Loman, we all need a shot of self-deception to face the day.

Self-deception is, in fact, not just a bad habit but an essential feature of the self. In "The Totalitarian Ego," Anthony Greenwald argues persuasively that three "cognitive biases" are essential to our functioning as normal human beings and to our sense of integration and worth.

The first bias is "egocentricity," which refers to our tendency to remember the past "as if it were a drama in which self was the leading player." Egocentricity pervades our thinking about everyday events. Whether we are arguing in court or studying for a test, we are far more likely to remember information that we generate ourselves than what we learn passively. Egocentricity operates in the realm of international politics, where decisionmakers tend to see the behavior of other nations as responses to or directed at their own countries, even when there is no reason for this belief.

"Beneffectance," as Greenwald labels the second cognitive bias, is a portmanteau word, a melding of "beneficence," or doing good, and "effectance," or doing well. Like politicians, we all take credit for good times and blame bad times on forces beyond our control. Greenwald quotes an example from police files on automobile accidents: "The telephone pole was approaching. I was attempting to swerve out of its way when it struck my front end." Drawing on his experience as a teacher, Greenwald notes that those students who get good grades on an exam are much more likely to think it was fair than students who get poor grades. My own experience suggests that teachers are just as subject to beneffectance bias as students. I have noted that when students do poorly on one of my exams it's because they haven't studied, not because it's too hard. Greenwald's point is further illustrated by another classroom phenomenon, which Robert Cialdini at Arizona State University calls "basking in reflected glory." Cialdini and his colleagues found that sweatshirts and other signs of allegiance to the alma mater are more common on Mondays after an athletic victory ("we won") than after a defeat ("they lost").

Beneffectance bias contributes to self-esteem. Depressed people's self-perceptions and evaluations of their abilities to control events are much closer to the ratings they get from others. The finding that when we are depressed we see ourselves more realistically may be one more bit of self-knowledge we are better off without, but it may also help us understand why it's so hard to act when we're depressed. Greenwald proposes that it is the absence of beneffectance bias that makes it so hard to get out of bed. In other words, normal self-deception in the form of the illusory glow mentioned above is not only a cosmetic that helps us feel better about ourselves. It is also a prosthesis that helps us act.

The third of Greenwald's biases is "cognitive conservativism," a tendency to "rewrite history" in order to avoid changing one's beliefs. This tendency is so powerful that the best predictor of the persuasive impact of an advertisement, legal brief, or business letter is not the content of the message but the prior opinions of the reader. We see this bias in our reluctance to accept the metric system, to learn foreign languages, and to adopt new computers and software. Cognitive conservativism is especially powerful in one's self-concept: When we do change our opinions, we are likely to say we "knew it all along," like a politician who claims to have "always favored" a recently vindicated policy.

The three cognitive biases—egocentricism, beneffectance, and conservativism—perform important functions in Greenwald's "Dewey Decimal System" self, which, as you will remember, is a kind of theory. Greenwald points out that like any theory, the self necessarily distorts reality in order to make sense of it. The cognitive biases allow us to access a lifetime of information obtained in different places (and perhaps by different selves). The liabilities of these distortions of reality are more than outweighed by the "asset of allowing the cognitive system to allocate its resources to storage and retrieval of information (rather than continual revision of its indexing or coding scheme), thereby permitting access to a large amount of information within a single system." This point of view makes sense to me. As one who uses computers with different operating systems, I often wonder if I wouldn't be better off sticking with the one computer I know best, even if it is practically a brass instrument.

The cognitive biases and defense mechanisms provide a more or less stable sense of self, but it is an illusion, and a dangerous one at that. These biases can be deadly, but if they are so subtle, powerful, and pervasive, how can we ever know ourselves? First of all, by knowing what forms these biases are likely to take, and vigilantly watching for them. That's why I have described them at such length. Second, by actively taking charge, learning who we are by changing who we are. Here are some ways to do it:

- To the extent that you are a looking glass self, you can choose who you are by choosing those who see you. You are who you meet.

- Often, the confidence that you *can* solve a problem is the key to its solution. If you think you're no good at math, you'll probably approach problems that you label "mathematical" with a self-defeating negativism. Thus, you can improve your performance on a variety of problems if you can relate them to positive parts of your self-concept. For example, if you think of yourself as better with people than with numbers, you can do better on mathematical problems if you relate them to the interpersonal problems you think you're good at, as by saying to yourself: "This is the kind of problem Susan would like. What would she do?"

- Identify situations that make you unconsciously anxious or depressed. Play "statues" with yourself. Periodically (use a watch with an hourly chime) freeze and take note of your posture and expression. Are you slumped? Fighting yourself with unconscious isometrics? If possible, avoid these situations. As the karate *sensei* says, "Best defense not be there." If you can't avoid these situations, apply the principles described in Friedman and Rosenman's *Type A Behavior and Your Heart.*

- The best way to learn the times of day when you feel and perform your best (and your worst) is by trying to change your daily biorhythms. Give your "morning self" a chance. It may take weeks of going to bed early to discover that you are at your best in the morning (many successful people say they are), but it's worth it: traffic-free freeways, freedom from interruption, no waiting for the copy machine, etc.

As one psychoanalyst put it, "Insight isn't . . . simply learning something mildly interesting about yourself. It is *becoming* yourself."

This chapter has mainly been about knowing your values. The following chapters are about the other side of SI: abilities. As we resume our journey, I'd like to pass on a final piece of advice from my favorite oracle, Harvard cognitive psychologist Jerome Bruner: "have faith in where your nose leads you and don't expect to be forever traveling down arrow-straight highways. And above all, race your own race."

5.
Social Intelligence

Two thirds of what we see is behind our eyes.
—CHINESE PROVERB

Lyndon Johnson was a master of all the skills of social intelligence. Historians describe him as "crafty," "shrewd," and "guileful." No one ever accused him of being an intellectual, but he could read people—intellectuals included—as they say, like a book. Historian Arthur Schlesinger, who interviewed Johnson when he was Senate majority leader, sat "hypnotized" as LBJ ran through the entire list of forty-eight Democratic senators, detailing their abilities, weaknesses, values, and susceptibilities to persuasion. At the end of an hour and a half of what Schlesinger called "the Johnson treatment," the historian found not only that the majority leader had anticipated every point he had in mind but that Johnson was much more likable and impressive than he had expected.

I got the Johnson treatment in 1961, and was struck above all by the contrast between the cornball phoniness of his public manner and the folksy sincerity of his private style. What seemed a parody of the Texas courthouse lawyer when seen on TV turned out to be far more appealing in person. Johnson knew how to strike a responsive chord even in a young Yankee with Ivy League pretensions. Discovering my association with John Brademas, then a senior member of the House Committee on Education, he regaled me with stories of his efforts to secure money for school construction.

If Johnson could read a person as an intellectual reads a book, he could read an audience as a librarian scans a card catalog. Johnson's cornball humor, split-second timing, and mobile face were well adapted to small-town southern audiences, and if they didn't work as well in the North, Johnson knew that, too, and tried to tone them down. Johnson's real virtuosity, though, was in the not-so-gentle arts of coalition building, argument, and persuasion. As Brademas later put it, "When Lyndon says, 'Come, let us reason together,' you know it's already over. He knows what you want better than you do." Even before he conducted the Great Society programs as President, Johnson was recognized as a master of legislative orchestration. Today, thanks largely to LBJ, it is almost impossible to imagine how difficult it was to get Congress to listen to, much less approve, civil rights legislation. The Civil Rights Act of 1964 was only the final movement in a symphony of cajolery, bargaining, and threat that Johnson used to move the legislation through committee to open debate on the Senate floor.

Johnson's cunning did, of course, have its dark side. Because it was not combined with similarly high levels of critical thinking, it allowed him to conduct his own undoing, escalating the Vietnam war. It is ironic that, when combined with the power of the presidency, the same social intelligence that made him an effective negotiator in the Senate became a tragic flaw.

In this chapter, I describe how to recognize social intelligence in others and develop it in yourself. After outlining some practical applications and distinguishing features of this valuable ability, I analyze social intelligence in terms of three underlying sensitivities: assessing others' abilities, empathizing with their values and feelings, and understanding group processes. Finally, I describe how effective managers, teachers, and other social agents combine these three kinds of information to build coalitions, defend themselves, and persuade others.

SOCIAL INTELLIGENCE AT WORK

LBJ's cunning is one expression of social intelligence. Another is Ronald Reagan's mastery of body language. There is little doubt that the former actor's stage presence was a factor in his victory over an opponent whose style was far less sincere, natural, and appealing. The same factor worked for the other party twenty years before, during John Kennedy's televised debates with Richard Nixon.

Social intelligence is as important to managers as it is to politicians. In his classic *The Nature of Managerial Work,* Henry Mintzberg of McGill University reported results from one of the few modern time-and-motion studies of managers. Mintzberg found that managers spent between 50 and 90 percent of their time communicating—10 percent with bosses, 40 percent with subordinates, and 50 percent outside the organization. Three interpersonal roles head his list of essential duties: "leader, liaison, and disturbance handler." All three of these roles require the ability to process social information.

Thomas Peters and Robert Waterman, management consultants who work with McKinsey and Company and the Stanford University Business School, devote large sections of their best-selling *In Search of Excellence* to "people sense," the ability to listen carefully, to build coalitions, to provide the rewards that matter, and, especially, to lead. In another best-seller, entitled *A Passion for Excellence,* Peters and Nancy Austin emphasize the importance of interpersonal skills even more. What was one chapter on staying "Close to the Customer" has become five chapters, describing such empathic skills as "the art of naive listening," "uncommon courtesy," and using "raw impressions."

Richard Wagner and Robert Sternberg, whose work on practical intelligence figured so prominently in previous chapters, describe a critical skill they call "managing others": knowing "how to assign and tailor tasks to take advantage of individuals' strengths and to minimize the effects of their weaknesses, how to reward in such a way as to maximize both job performance and job satisfaction, and how to get along with others in general." Wagner and Sternberg found that successful managers delegate as much as possible—even important tasks, if there is someone else who can do them. As every manager knows, that's a big "if"—deciding whether or not someone can or wants to do the job requires considerable interpersonal intelligence. Successful executives were honest in evaluating both good and poor performance, and worked hard to promote their subordinates' careers, even if it meant eventually losing good people.

Given all this, it is no surprise that among the factors of failure in business are fatal flaws in interpersonal abilities. Morgan McCall and Michael Lombardo interviewed top executives and personnel managers at several *Fortune* 500 corporations to learn about executives "who had failed to live up to their apparent potential." The two factors they found most often were "insensitivity: picked wrong people, or were abrasive" and "inability to delegate." No one familiar with the degree to which these qualities were combined in Steven Jobs, the founder and former CEO of Apple Computer, was surprised at his recent ouster by John Sculley, whom Jobs had hired only two years before. Though Jobs was a charismatic advocate of projects, like the Macintosh, that captured his imagination, he reportedly addressed the marketing division of the Apple II series as the "dull and boring product division." On this and similar occasions, Jobs acted as though he were oblivious of normal human reactions. He engaged in attacks on Sculley that others perceived as backbiting and he misinterpreted Sculley's reaction as only a "lover's quarrel." Evidently, it was Jobs's overestimation of the extent to which his board would support him that led to the backfire of his attempt to depose Sculley. To Lee Iacocca, " 'He has trouble getting along with people' " is the "kiss of death." And John D. Rockefeller once said of interpersonal ability, "I pay more for that ability than for any other under the sun."

In terms of the interpersonal abilities they require, teaching and managing are more similar than most teachers and managers realize. Managing requires delegation of authority, which more often than not involves teaching. Conversely, teaching requires supervision of learning, which involves managing. All teachers must lead and delegate as well as explain and instruct. This is as true for college professors as it is for kindergarten teachers. The excellent teacher of adults, according to a University of Chicago study, "exhibits empathy," "learns from student feedback," and shows other interpersonal skills.

Interpersonal skills also figure prominently in descriptions of successful lawyers. Plato described the importance of using and retaliating against flattery and deception. Recent descriptions of lawyering suggest that the intellectual requirements of the legal profession haven't changed much since Plato's time. Interpersonal skills, especially sympathy, sensitivity, and "understanding people," are those mentioned most frequently in Martin Mayer's *The Lawyers.* For example, Mayer describes the importance of sympathy in personal injury and divorce cases, and of leadership in community service.

Attorney Louis Nizer's sympathy for Quentin Reynolds, who was defamed by columnist Westbrook Pegler, caused him to take the case and to argue it with vigor. Nizer knew that the chances of winning were slim, but he took the case with a vengeance that rivaled his client's. The trial's climax came when, incensed by Pegler's failure to appear, Nizer addressed his angry summation to Pegler's empty chair. Nizer's sympathetic indignation reached such heights that at times, as he put it, "The chair seemed to be embarrassed." The result was an unprecedented award of $200,000.

A story told by Appellate Court Judge Harold Medina shows sensitivity's dark side. When Medina was a young trial lawyer, one of his opponents had a reputation as a master of courtroom tactics. During the trial, Medina noticed that this opponent, who often argued in a dramatic whisper, tended to stay on Medina's left side. Realizing that he was missing key points of his adversary's arguments, Medina consulted a physician, who detected a 10 percent deficiency in Medina's left ear. Somehow Medina's adversary had sensed a problem of which Medina himself was unaware.

Each component of social intelligence is important in a variety of practical jobs, and each is critical in some situations. The ability to assess others' abilities is essential to those who build teams of people whose skills complement their own. Like some political leaders, successful entrepreneurs use charisma to enthuse their workers and investors. Empathy for the values of both employees and customers characterizes managers in outstanding service organizations, public and private. Detecting alliances is critical in the foreign service. Lyle Spencer of McBer and Company describes an outstanding officer who "had been able to go to a new assignment in a foreign capital, and very quickly figure out that it was the Prime Minister's mistress' nephew who really called the shots on oil policy —and how to get to this nephew." Building coalitions and managing group processes are essential in matrix management organizations, with their ever-changing task forces. Members of task forces and other committees need self-defense techniques to protect themselves from pressures generated by these group processes. Finally, persuasiveness is the stock-in-trade of the salesperson, the trial attorney, and the politician.

As a case study in the value of social intelligence at work, consider J. L. Foutz. Mutt, as his friends call him, quit school after the third grade. He worked as a sheepherder, ran a trading post on the Navajo reservation, and got into the construction business. Mutt made his first fortune in uranium, and a second in natural gas. He is known throughout the Four Corners area as a philanthropist, two-term mayor of Farmington, New Mexico, chairman of the board of Foutz and Bursum, a highly successful construction and pipeline company, and a breeder of thoroughbreds that don't often lose.

I interviewed Mutt as we drove from his ranch near Mesa Verde in southwestern Colorado to his home in Farmington. Mutt attributes his success mainly to his ability to "analyze the people I work with and find out what their abilities are, to use other people's skills. I think I'm pretty good at that. I've had fantastic people work for me."

Mutt's career in energy exploitation began with a personal judgment: "I had a guy working for me in my construction company. I found out he knew uranium mining, so I bought a test rig and sent him out." After months of trial and error, Mutt and his partner started their first mine, in Monument Valley. Their first truckload of ore regained their investment. After that, Mutt said, "it was all gravy."

As the uranium boom faded, Mutt moved into natural gas pipelines. Again, his timing was perfect—he swung into action just in time for the energy boom of the 1960s. However, Mutt attributes his success less to his own business sense than to his president, Harold Horner. Recalling the day he hired Horner, Mutt said, "He interviewed me as much as I interviewed him. Right off, he asked me, 'Is your company solvent?' I knew he was the man I needed. I knew I had to make it interesting to keep him, so I offered him a thousand dollars a month as a base plus whatever he deserved because of his performance. Then I bought a pipe-testing company and set it up so he owned a quarter of it. That did it. Today, Harold makes a lot more than that, and he's not overpaid."

As we drove from one of Mutt's enterprises to another, I learned that indeed he does have fantastic people working for him, but to me what was even more fantastic is how Mutt deals with them. Whether talking accountantese with his president, mathematics with the engineers, or Navajo with the roughnecks, Mutt's manner was the same: warm and relaxed. Though I didn't always get the jokes, especially when they were in Navajo, it was obvious that they were appreciated. And so was the man who told them.

J. L. Foutz exhibits two basic skills of social intelligence: He knows a good man when he sees one, and what is more, he knows how to interest him and keep him interested. Walter Wriston, who as CEO of Citicorp doubled his organization's earnings in five years, attributes his success to exactly these qualities. In an interview with management consultants Harry Levinson and Stuart Rosenthal, Wriston said, "The finding and the training and the motivating of people is the whole ballgame."

Even in occupations where interpersonal skills are not in the job description, they are often in the job. In the next few pages, I explain how to get and use the kinds of information you need to identify others' practical abilities and put them to work.

SOCIAL INTELLIGENCE

As long ago as 1920, Edward Thorndike defined social intelligence as "the ability to understand and manage men and women, boys and girls—to act wisely in human relationships." In 1933, the psychometrician Phillip Vernon elaborated this definition, adding such skills as getting along and being at ease with others, knowing social matters, being sensitive to stimuli from others, and having insight into the traits and moods of others. Nowadays, Howard Gardner describes interpersonal intelligence as "the ability to notice and make distinctions among other individuals and in particular, among their moods, temperaments, motivations, and intentions. . . . interpersonal knowledge permits a skilled adult to read the intentions and desires—even when they have remained hidden—of many other individuals and, potentially, to act upon this knowledge—for example by influencing a group of disparate individuals to behave along desired lines." Gardner mentions Mahatma Gandhi, Lyndon Johnson, and Eleanor Roosevelt as examples of people with high interpersonal intelligence. To Gardner, social intelligence is the flip side of self-intelligence.

Social intelligence also depends heavily on nonverbal signs, the postures, expressions, and tones of voice that constitute what is popularly called "body language." Because of their sensitivity to these signals, dogs, horses, elephants, and other mammals who work in close association with people often exhibit human or superhuman levels of social intelligence. In my book *Mammalian Communication,* I argue that this is no accident: Not only do all mammals share a repertory of scores of signals, but these signals convey a relatively small number (about twenty-five) of common meanings. Mutual understanding of mammalian messages has allowed us to domesticate those animals with which we can communicate best. As any dog-owner knows, man's best friend is good not only at reading moods but at manipulating human behavior with wags, whines, mewls, groans, scratches, runnings back and forth (with their threat of imminent micturation or worse), and the dog's own lash, the bark. Such displays, which operate deep in the primitive mammalian layers of our brain, are even more persuasive than that most nagging of human importunities, the telephone.

Because social intelligence processes nonverbal information, sensitivity to individuals and groups is often considered a matter of intuition rather than intellect. However, as the ability to acquire and use knowledge from others, social intelligence fits our working definition of intelligence. As you will see, even empathy, the softest of this set of warm and fuzzy-sounding skills, has a hard ratiocinative component.

Several standardized tests measure social intelligence. The George Washington Social Intelligence Test assesses social judgment, identification of speakers' mental states, memory for faces and names, powers of observation, and sense of humor (!). The Social Insight Test requires testees to select the best interpretation of fictitious cases in which people try to get some satisfaction or avoid embarrassment.

Three tests devised by J. P. Guilford relate social intelligence to other intellectual abilities in the Structure of Intellect cube. "Faces" tests the ability to match several faces displaying similar emotions; "Inflections" assesses the ability to match facial expressions with tones of voice; and "Missing Cartoons" measures skill in completing sequences of social acts.

The best-known test of sensitivity to body language is probably the Profile of Nonverbal Sensitivity (PONS) test, which shows a woman in various poses and asks the testee to choose the better of verbal descriptions. The Social Interpretations Test (SIT) is similar. Like the PONS test, it presents information in both visual and auditory form.

Results of such tests and other kinds of investigations show that social intelligence is independent of IQ and other forms of intelligence. Howard Gardner points out that although victims of Down's syndrome characteristically display low levels of verbal and logical intelligence, they are often very good at dealing with people. Similarly, people who suffer damage to the right hemisphere of the brain often retain high levels of verbal intelligence, while showing marked disturbances in their social relationships. Conversely, some victims of Alzheimer's disease lose spatial, linguistic, and logical skills, while retaining considerable social sensitivity.

Psychometrician Norman Fredericksen and two colleagues at Educational Testing Service have argued that social intelligence is a system of abilities quite separate from other intellectual skills. These psychologists studied how well medical students performed on a task requiring considerable social skill: In a realistic simulated interview, they were to inform the "patient" of possible breast cancer, advise her to get a biopsy, and prepare her for the possibility that a breast would have to be removed. The most striking piece of evidence was that the medical students who did best on a test of scientific knowledge were rated *worst* in warmth in interviewing.

A variety of tests and other measures show that in two key components of social intelligence, women generally outperform men. On the input side, seventy-five research studies of sensitivity to nonverbal cues to emotion showed women clearly superior, especially when it comes to judging intentions. On the output side, studies of how social smarts develop show that the key skill is the ability to negotiate; here, too, women generally do better than men.

Do individual and gender differences mean, as some researchers claim, that social intelligence is innate and therefore unlearnable?

No. Richard Wagner and Robert Sternberg consider the ability they call "managing others" to be largely a matter of tacit knowledge, not inborn capacity. And to the extent that we can render such knowledge explicit, we raise the chances of our being able to teach it.

ASSESSING ABILITIES

The first lesson is that there are many independent ways to be smart. People who are high in one kind of intelligence may be high, low, or average in others, so just because your colleague has a way with words, don't assume an ability to navigate in a new city. People who excel at social, verbal, or logical tasks are often hilariously inept at spatial problems. Since multiple intelligences vary independently, it is equally wrong to assume the opposite: that the computer wizard *must* lack social skills, or that the supersalesman must be blind to his own motives. Whatever competences (or deficits) someone shows, stay open to the possibility of others. Your next marketing manager may right now be under a truck in the motor pool.

A corollary to this lesson is to match your mode of communication to the abilities of your audience: For some people pictures are worth much more than a thousand words, but for others they are only confusing.

A third practical lesson follows from the working hypothesis that practical intelligences are learnable: If someone lacks only one of the several abilities necessary to perform a job, consider investing in developing the missing competence, especially if the combination of other abilities is rare. That lesson is easier to assign than to accomplish, because it requires that you be able to judge others' multiple intelligences, a task that daunts most psychologists. This section is not intended to teach you how to be an amateur psychometrician, but it will improve your ability to make practical assessments of the abilities of others by showing you how to recognize and avoid some common errors.

Sociobiologists believe that millions of years of natural selection have made us all into con artists when it comes to displaying our abilities. Whether or not this is so, researchers in social cognition find that the P. T. Barnum effect is not confined to self-perception. We are all "pigeons" subject to a variety of biases.

We see one another with egocentric schemas like the self-deceptive ones described in the preceding chapter. When we first meet a person, whether it's face to face, over the phone, or by reading a résumé, we file incoming information according to *our* values: How will this person do? What would it be like to work with her day after day? Should I take the case? We organize all later information in terms of this schema, which accounts for the overwhelming influence of first impressions. If a Ph.D. on someone's résumé leads you to label her intelligent, when you later learn that she is a skydiver you are likely to file her skydiving under "courageous" rather than "reckless." Negative first impressions are even more powerful: Having heard that a prospective client is manipulative, you are likely to interpret charm as a snow job.

Once we have formed a schema, it becomes fixed; we change new information to fit it into the schema. Social psychologist Lee Ross and his colleagues performed an experiment in which one group of subjects was shown a daring firefighter doing well at his job and a cautious one being less successful. Another group was shown the opposite: daring unsuccessful and cautious successful firefighters. Even after it was explained that the demonstrations were contrived and that there is no relation between risk taking and firefighting ability, the subjects adhered to their first impressions.

Such judgments about abilities or other reasons for actions are called "attributions." First impressions bias our attributions not because they are wrong (they may well turn out to be correct) but because we unconsciously give them more weight than they deserve. A second source of attribution bias is so powerful that it has been called "the fundamental attribution error": In understanding others' actions, we overestimate the importance of the person and underestimate the importance of the situation. The fundamental attribution error is highlighted by the contrast with our attributions of our own behavior. When I see my chairman working on weekends, I attribute it to his compulsive ambition. When *I* work weekends, it's because I've got a deadline. In a case related by Richard Boyatzis, a manager received a complaint that a data entry clerk had been sleeping on the job. The manager checked, and found that the clerk was engaged in a complex and frustrating piece of programming and relaxed for a few seconds every hour or so by resting her head on her arms. She wasn't sleeping—she was decompressing, but her supervisor had walked by at the wrong time. In both cases, the other persons' actions were attributed to a disposition (compulsiveness or laziness) rather than to the situation (working under pressure).

Attribution errors can also be positive. We attribute the expertise of doctors to their wisdom, not to their training, and accordingly assume that they are qualified to speak in areas outside their specialties: international politics and beverages. Similarly, teachers attribute their own classroom performance to their preparation (or lack thereof) but attribute the performance of their students to brilliance or laziness. Attribution error explains the famous Peter Principle, which says that people get promoted to their levels of incompetence. We would expect managers to attribute subordinates' performance to their ability, and to ignore the special situations that may have been responsible for their success or failure.

Since the power of stereotypes and attribution errors in judgments about abilities depend on schemas that are fundamental processes in perception, such biases are inescapable. In Chapters 8 and 9, I discuss some defenses against such biases. For now, the best defense is awareness that no matter how enlightened and sophisticated you are, you are biased in your assessments of others' abilities. As you decide whether to hire, transfer, or take a case, remember that people and jobs are never as simple as your schemas make them seem. Practical assessment requires a kind of open-mindedness, an empirical attitude that says "let's see." There are many ways to be a good firefighter, teacher, or executive. Don't let your schemas keep you from trying out new people.

EMPATHY

As J. L. Foutz's success shows, in applying social intelligence, assessments of others' abilities must be combined with empathy, a sensitivity to others' feelings and values that enables one to put those abilities to work. From a practical perspective, we may regard empathy as the ability to describe others' conflicting points of view in ways they would agree with, or to predict what they will do.

Empathy has two dimensions: emotional sensitivity and intellectual objectivity. Charles Manucia, a clinical psychologist in La Jolla, surveyed counseling psychologists' conceptions of "empathy." The number of psychologists who regarded empathy as either "predominantly intellectual" or "equally intellectual and emotional" was roughly equal to the number who believed that it is "predominantly emotional but may in part be intellectual." The most frequent synonyms used by respondents were "understanding" and "sensitivity," with their respectively intellectual and emotional connotations. Intellectual tasks like predicting behavior as well as emotional responses like sharing feelings (sympathy) have figured in the Kerr-Speroff Test of Empathy, the Thematic Apperception Test, and other attempts to measure empathy.

Richard Boyatzis of McBer and Company found that in managing, the intellectual component of empathy is far more important than the emotional. Boyatzis includes a trait he calls "perceptual objectivity" as part of his "focus on others" cluster of competencies. Perceptual objectivity is the "disposition to view an event from multiple perspectives simultaneously." According to Boyatzis, it resembles Harry Levinson's "sensitivity to others" and is responsible for successful managers' ability "to accurately describe each subordinate's 'side' or view of the issue" and thereby to mediate disputes, to "balance the many perspectives—of subordinates, other managers within the organization, or the various groups in the external environment." Perceptual objectivity requires "affective distancing skills," which Boyatzis's colleague Lyle Spencer describes as an ability to "see clearly the other person's feelings without your own getting in the way." Spencer's final phrase suggests that perceptual objectivity may sometimes suppress the emotional component of empathy. Boyatzis found that perceptual objectivity was related to superior managerial performance, but emotional traits like "positive regard" and "concern with close relationships" were not.

In other occupations, however, the emotional component is important. For example, caring and positive regard consistently head the list of traits of successful teachers. Charles Manucia's survey of counselors showed that Freud's belief that empathy is the basis of effective psychotherapy is widely shared. Ninety percent of Manucia's respondents considered empathy an "important or indispensable element of counseling."

Social psychologists find that both emotional and intellectual components of empathy are important in successful interviewing. This generalization applies particularly to one well-studied type of interview: consultations between patient and physician. In a study of patients' satisfaction with their physicians, three quarters of the patients surveyed considered "caring" more important than "curing." Another study showed that many patients regard these two functions as inseparable, but researchers at the University of North Carolina medical center were able tease apart cognitive and emotional factors. Their analysis of verbal exchanges in medical consultations showed that patients are most satisfied with the emotional tone of a consultation when they are allowed to tell the stories of their illnesses in their own words while getting feedback that tells them the physician is following. Oddly, feedback in the form "mm-hm," was associated with satisfying storytelling, while "right" and "O.K." were not. Patients are most likely to be satisfied with the cognitive (informational) quality of a consultation when, at the conclusion, the physician provides objective factual information about the illness and his or her treatment plan.

Though some theorists believe that empathy is an innate ability, the majority of the psychologists surveyed by Manucia believe that it can be learned. Disputes about the learnability of empathy may be due to a failure to distinguish cognitive from emotional skills. The intellectual component of empathy is certainly learnable. And from that often follows the emotional component.

In some cases, you may be able to cultivate empathy simply by forcing yourself to listen, to pay attention, and to respond with the signals that let others know you are tuning in. Many people are more interesting and comprehensible than they seem, so if you are able to play the role, you may soon find that you are no longer acting.

Another way to learn empathy is by exposing the biases that prevent you from understanding others' points of view. Egocentric schemas block empathy with others' values even more than they skew appraisal of their abilities. Your perception of others' values, beliefs, and feelings is a function of your own. We tend to underestimate the extent to which friends' values differ from our own, and overestimate the differences in people we don't like. Because schemas operate unconsciously, increased clarity in communication often does no good: The clearer your partner expresses his gripe, the more defensive you get. Defensive bias may be responsible for managers' failure to distinguish between major and minor complaints, even when they are clearly expressed. Unconscious wishful thinking also allows us to escape unpleasant follow-throughs when we misconstrue subordinates' nods as agreement rather than mere understanding.

Managers, lawyers, teachers, physicians, and other supervisors must be aware of two values that are far more important for those who must follow directions than for those who give them. The first is equity, the demand not just for good treatment but for treatment that is fair relative to what others get. Teachers who grade generously are often caught unawares by students who receive good but different grades for test answers the students consider similar in quality. The second value of particular interest to subordinates is autonomy. Harry Levinson points out that employees expect managers to help them develop independence and responsibility. The alternative, which he calls the "buying off" psychology, fosters dependency and irresponsibility by an implicit contract that says: "Do as you are told and leave the responsibility to us." The buying off psychology, he writes, "is inherently self-defeating" because it "fosters dependency by arrogating to itself the responsibility for the success of the organization." He points out that when production employees are given responsibility for setting quotas, results are better than when the quotas are set by engineers. Ignoring workers' need for autonomy has resulted in a time-serving alienation from employers and a corresponding allegiance to unions.

In their book *CEO,* Levinson and Stuart Rosenthal describe how Reg Jones, chairman of General Electric, handled requests that he solve problems for his vice-chairmen: "When they asked me what I was going to do about a problem, I asked, 'What are you going to do about it? You are responsible for the operation. Do it.' " Similarly, Walter Wriston described Citicorp as open and participative. "The guy in the gray flannel suit never came to work for the Citibank." Wriston allowed subordinates to carry out projects he did not approve of, like the development of Citibank's own credit card terminal.

Medical patients increasingly look to doctors not merely for cures but for guidance in maintaining their health. Physicians who by explaining the rationale for a treatment plan convey their demand that the patient take responsibility for it are much more likely to get patients to follow that plan. Obstetricians and dentists who allow their patients to signal when pain gets too strong find that the resulting sense of control allows the patients to endure significantly higher levels of pain than when the doctor is in control.

The same pattern can be seen in mature students, who expect teachers to do more than impart wisdom; they expect to be taught how to learn on their own. Programmed instruction, which removes all responsibility for learning from the student, satisfies students' need for structure and security but ignores their need for choice and challenge. Like employees who turned to unions to satisfy their need for responsibility and control, the "teaching machines" of the 1960s were soon abandoned in favor of learning environments like "free universities," which acknowledged the need for autonomy. Carol Schneider, George Klemp, and Susan Kastendiek found that teachers who were perceived as "particularly effective, both by students and by other faculty members or administrators, saw themselves as facilitators of the students' own active learning, rather than as experts, or scholars, or transmitters of significant information."

NONVERBAL COMMUNICATION

There is a third route to increased empathy: reading nonverbal communication. The meanings of each of the approximately 150 nonverbal signals known as "body language" vary from person to person and context to context, so "dictionaries" of signals are useless. Dr. Albert Scheflen, a large, white-bearded psychiatrist who has directed the Albert Einstein College of Medicine Project on Human

Communication, points out in *Body Language and the Social Order* that simplistic views that assign a single meaning to leg crossings, arm foldings, and smiles fly in the face of decades of research.

However, if you are willing to take responsibility for learning the meanings of the signals sent in the contexts you work in, there's plenty to learn—psychologists' estimates of the percentage of information transmitted nonverbally in everyday conversations vary from 70 to 90 percent.

Your first task is to determine how well you read body language. There are a number of tests designed to assess sensitivity to nonverbal communication. The test best adapted to working contexts was developed by R. J. Sternberg and C. Smith, and is described in detail in Sternberg's *Intelligence Applied.* One task is to examine a set of pictures, each of which shows a man and a woman interacting, and decide whether they are closely related or strangers posing together. A second set of pictures shows pairs of individuals at work, and the task is to decide which one is the supervisor. You can test yourself by making similar judgments at parties, meetings, offices, and in other real-life contexts and checking your conclusions by watching long enough to determine the relationship or by asking the people or someone who knows them. Alternatively, you can make and test predictions about where people will sit, whom they will address, or who will introduce the speaker. Such exercises provide valuable practice, especially if you get feedback. Also watch for signals—anxiety, anger, etc.—when you know what's going on. Much nonverbal communication is idiosyncratic, so learn the mannerisms of those you work with. Remember that most of us are not fundamentally insensitive to the subtleties of body language—we just don't pay attention.

Detecting Lies

The belief that failure to make eye contact is a sign of untrustworthiness is one of those simplistic notions Scheflen warns us about. But are there reliable ways to detect deception? Not really. There are ways to detect the distress, uneasiness, and anxiety that often accompany lying, but many people can lie without sending these signals, and sometimes telling the truth is stressful. Psychologists who use personality tests to measure the willingness to employ deceit find that such "Machiavellianism" abounds among normal people. Social psychologist Ralph Exline tricked Machiavellian and non-Machiavellian subjects into lying by assigning a project on which a stooge "cheated" in the subjects' presence. When questioned about the cheating, both kinds of subjects lied, but non-Machiavellians looked away, while Machiavellians looked Exline right in the eye. Thus, like misnamed "lie detectors," we do not detect lies but only nervousness, and are at the mercy of those who can lie without exhibiting anxiety, especially those who have read books on nonverbal communication.

Nevertheless, signs of nervousness often do betray deception or guilt. A decade of research on deception shows that gaze and other facial cues are under conscious control and therefore often quite secure. The body, too, has a fairly high security clearance, so Freud was guilty of an overstatement when he wrote, "If his lips are silent, he chatters with his fingertips, betrayal oozes out of him at every pore." Nevertheless, sometimes shifting position, licking lips, scratching itches, grooming hair, or rubbing fingertips can blow a liar's cover. As the growing use of voice stress analyzers in "lie detection" testifies, the voice has an even lower clearance. Pauses, throatiness, and rises in pitch frequently uncloak a secret. The real security risks, though, are discrepancies among these agents. Because it is hard to control several of them at once, a wry smile or a clenched fist may belie a cheerful voice.

Detecting Affiliations

In real-world situations, it is often imperative to make accurate judgments about how close people are to each other, who potential leaders are, and when someone is lying. In making such judgments, you may be able to use some of the cues to affiliation found by Sternberg and other investigators, but remember that these cues may have different meanings, depending on the people and the situation.

John P. Kotter, author of *The General Manager,* describes building and maintaining an informal network of personal relationships as one of the critical activities common to all general managers. In order to "read" and manage informal networks, you must become sensitive to the subtle displays that express and create bonds of affiliation.

Cues to affiliation include side-by-side body orientations that Albert Scheflen calls "withs." Withs are congruent postures and rhythms, like walking in step, shown by pairs or small groups when entering a room or approaching someone else. Because we tend to control our postures and gaits less than our faces, and because we are more careful about all our expressions, withs, which occur before meetings are officially under way, are often especially revealing.

Once a meeting or other interaction has begun, what Scheflen calls "frames" provide additional information about actual or potential coalitions. When two or more people form a frame, they lean toward each other, turn their sides or backs toward those they wish to exclude, ward off interlopers with elbows or knees, or otherwise create a small zone between them that others cannot penetrate without considerable awkwardness.

Relaxation is another important cue to likes and dislikes. Albert Mehrabian, a pioneer in the study of nonverbal communication, finds that moderate levels of relaxation are associated with liking, and that very tense and very relaxed postures are both associated with dislike and rejection. Mehrabian finds that the more people like each other, the more time they spend making eye contact. Gaze time is easy to misconstrue, however. Extroverts and women tend to look everyone in the eye; introverts and men do not. Such individual differences mean that your judgments of liking must be relative: You can tell that George likes Sam more than he likes Suzy, but you can't tell whether Suzy likes Sam more than George does. Moreover, since the relationship between gazing and liking is not exactly news, close allies often deliberately avoid looking at each other, in order to avoid giving their relationship away.

Allies are, however, far less likely to monitor a display called "congruence," when two or more people in a group share a distinctive posture. Scheflen finds that when people share postures, they are likely to share attitudes as well. Conversely, breaking a consonant posture can signify disagreement or loss of interest. Thus, you can use congruence to detect coalitions and to sniff out potential allies. Family therapists sometimes use congruence as a sign that, say, a child has begun to transfer feelings about his or her parents to the psychologist. Psychoanalyst Frieda Fromm-Reichmann used congruence to enhance her emotional empathy: By imitating a client's posture, she was able to get a feel for her client's moods.

The most reliable sign of liking is so subtle that it can be observed only at very close range. When one perceives an attractive person, picture, or other stimulus, one's pupils dilate measurably. This involuntary response is so sensitive and accurate that it is a major means of testing advertisements, and may account for the popularity of eyeshades among poker players, who are anxious to conceal their reactions to their hands.

In judging who likes whom or what, beware of that most deceptive of signals, the smile. Research shows that like facial expressions in general, smiles are subject to a degree of conscious control. Because most of us are unable to produce a natural winning smile at will, we are at the mercy of those who can. Smiles often function not as automatic expressions of liking but as metasignals, comments on other (usually verbal) messages. For example, a smile may be used playfully, to show that a statement is not meant seriously, or manipulatively, to avoid a counterattack. Anthropologist Ray Birdwhistell notes that smiles' meanings vary geographically. In areas like the South, where people smile a lot, failure to smile may signify anger, while in New York, a smiling Southerner may be asked what's so funny.

Identifying Potential Leaders

A third application of sensitivity to nonverbal communication is identifying potential leaders. The greetings exchanged at the beginning of a party or a meeting can often provide clues to dominance, that mysterious ability to get one's way without threat or other overt sanction. Investigators have found human dominance displays remarkably similar to those of our primate relatives. In greeting, for example, the dominant male—chimpanzee or human—moves forward with neck extended and arms lifted out away from the body. In my book *Mammalian Communication,* I describe many of these parallels, which are especially striking among more distant animal-kingdom relatives, including wolves. In both wolves and humans, signs of who is dominant may be extremely subtle. While studying the social behavior of the wolves at the Brookfield Zoo near Chicago, I was often amused at visitors' conjectures about dominance. They invariably picked a large, active wolf who swaggered as he strode back and forth in front of a large mound. The real leader of the pack was usually lying peacefully atop the mound, but he could freeze the swaggerer in his tracks by opening one eye. As this case shows, in wolves, relaxation is one of the many privileges of dominants. In humans, the most influential members of a group may not be the loudest talkers or the ones at the head of the table. They may be the ones who can afford to relax.

In wolves, humans, and most other animals, the most obvious signs of dominance are displays that increase apparent size. Standing with chest expanded and muscles tense, sitting with hands clenched behind the head, and taking elevated positions, as by perching on the edge of a desk, all have this somewhat intimidating effect.

Touching is another obvious prerogative of dominance in people and other mammals. Social psychologists have discovered a tacit rule that allows high-status people to touch those of lower rank, but prohibits the reverse. When this rule is broken, as when someone attempts to express affection for a higher-status person by touching, people become uneasy, and may even regard the touching as a ploy to acquire higher status.

One of the most subtle signs of dominance is unique to humans because it involves speech. Dominant members of a group control the duration of others' utterances: When high-ranking participants in a discussion nod their heads, show other signs of agreement, or talk longer themselves, subordinates talk longer. When dominants shorten their utterances, others follow suit. Albert Mehrabian suggests that failure to follow these tacit rules may be responsible for managers' intuitions of insubordination. He suggests that the next time you feel you're not getting the respect you deserve, see if your intuition is based on the subordinate's failure to obey these tacit rules.

By the same token, we can use nonverbal signals to avoid rudeness and communicate interest.

Doctors and lawyers are increasingly concerned about charges that they are insensitive to the personal needs of their patients and clients. Recent articles in medical and legal journals recommend common courtesy as a proactive defense against perceived insensitivity. From one such article, published in *Family Practice Journal*, we may infer the following prescriptions for physicians who wish to appear empathic: Offer lots of interpretations, confront the client with contradictions in his report and questions about them, and in general appear relaxed and interested; don't get involved with note-taking, instrument preparation, or other tasks, and don't ask leading questions.

A similar article in *Law and Human Behavior* contains the following counsel to attorneys who wish to appear attractive and trustworthy, and to be recommended and retained in the future: Introduce yourself, being sure to include your first name, shake hands, make small talk, let your client talk, lean forward, look at your client, reflect the content and emotion of your client's remarks, and generally appear warm, reactive, and animated. That such behaviors cause clients to perceive their attorneys as empathic comes as no surprise. The news is that such perceptions are more important in clients' evaluations of their attorneys than judgments of competence.

One of the trickiest situations for those who wish to comment, confront, question, or otherwise contribute to a discussion is how to break in without appearing rude. Some of my worst moments have occurred at meetings when I have waited patiently to get a word in edgewise, then finally interjected a comment, only to have it ignored. Even worse is when my comment is acknowledged but it's made clear that it was out of place and the person I barged in on was only being polite before getting back to the (far more germane) thread of his argument. The only way I know to avoid these gaffes is to watch carefully for what Scheflen calls "terminal markers," cues that a unit of discourse is coming to an end. The most obvious terminal marker is a brushing together of the palms as though to say "That's that." Another terminal marker is breaking a "frame" or "with," and a third is gazing at a listener to look for signs of comprehension. Many terminal markers are peculiar to individuals, so if you often find yourself in my predicament, you ought to learn the idiosyncrasies of those you unintentionally interrupt.

Another tricky situation is when you must contradict what someone else has said. If possible, do this by presenting your view not as opposing but as new, perhaps with the aid of a little smoke: Rephrase the original point of view to minimize conflict, or engage in irrelevant chatter.

At a time when many people seem predisposed to perceive professionals and public servants as uncaring, the best defense is to give no offense.

Understanding Group Processes

Reading nonverbal signals is not only an essential empathic skill; it provides valuable insight into group process. Conversely, since the meaning of any nonverbal signal depends on its context, understanding group process is an essential part of understanding nonverbal communication. In this section, I focus on this vital component of social intelligence, the ability to read and use group processes.

The most important schemas you need to learn in order to understand a group are in the group's culture. Recently, Harvard University professor Terence Deal and McKinsey and Company management consultant Allan Kennedy wrote *Corporate Cultures* to provide managers with ways of tuning into social networks and shared schemas. These two forms of tacit knowledge, according to one study, account for "90 percent of the real business of a large corporation."

Networks

Richard Boyatzis focuses on the first type of tacit knowledge in what he calls "managing group process," using social networks to get people to collaborate. To do this, you must first of all be able to construct schemas for formal and informal networks of interpersonal relationships. Boyatzis shows that competent managers have a "model, theory, or framework" for "line-staff conflict," "informal influence network," and other social phenomena. When they don't have a relevant schema, they seek one, not inductively, by examining the situation, but deductively, by asking for a "road map."

One conceptual tool for handling informal networks is the "socio-gram," a model of important affiliations, antagonisms, power rela-tionships, and information channels. With the aid of the cues to affiliation and dominance described above, you can construct a socio-gram of your organization. If the organization is simple, you may be able to do it on a single piece of paper, using different-colored pencils and single- or double-headed arrows to represent the kind and direction of various relationships. For larger groups, you may need a separate piece of paper for each kind of relationship, and in some cases you may need a three-dimensional model built of styro-foam balls (people) and colored straws (relationships).

In building your sociogram, don't forget to include yourself—sociograms can provide you with the framework for your own inde-pendent power bases. And don't forget to include relations outside the organization, like memberships in professional societies and other groups. As Harry Levinson points out, such groups can serve the same function as adolescent peer groups: They provide indepen-dent sources of power and status by their standards, awards, and cultural conventions.

There are several other ways to use such a diagram. One is diagnostic, to compare it to the formal organizational chart, looking for places where informal networks contradict or fail to support the functions of the organization. Another application is in planning: Sometimes a glance at the informal network will save you big hassles down the road, as when you realize that your streamlined reorgani-zation plan will tear apart some tightly connected informal groups. Finally, in personnel decisions, the sociogram shows you who your key people are: the ones who look like porcupines, with lots of information, affiliation, and influence relationships. Don't be de-ceived by the rigidity of your straws, though—a network is a com-plex dynamic system; some sociologists prefer a model in which balls representing people are suspended from a more or less rigid frame-work (the organizational environment) and connected to one an-other by elastic bands. In this model, shifting the position of any one ball changes the position of every other ball in the system.

The expert manager, negotiator, or leader knows not only how to read such networks but how to resolve conflicts between sub-groups within them: management versus labor, line versus staff, etc. According to Harvard social psychologist Roger Brown, conflicts are resolved and cohesiveness created by "equal status contact in the cooperative pursuit of a superordinate goal." Brown's analysis of successful and unsuccessful resolutions shows that these conditions are not easily met, and when they are not, intergroup conflicts are not resolved. He calls this a "pessimistic" result, but there is a practical lesson, if only a negative one: If you can find ways to meet these conditions, fine; if not, don't waste your time trying.

Shared Schemas

The second basic skill needed to read and use group processes is sensitivity to the shared schemas of the organizational culture.

In *The Search for Signs of Intelligent Life in the Universe,* Lily Tomlin says that reality is "a collective hunch." The same view has been expressed with greater seriousness and at greater length by philosophers and sociologists like Peter Berger and Thomas Luckman, who argue that the commonsense "realities" of everyday life are no more real than a play to which we respond with real emotions. The only difference between the play and everyday life, say such "social constructionists," is that in everyday life the curtain never goes down.

Whether or not one considers all the world a stage in a literal sense, to understand a group at a practical level you must understand the group's shared schemas, and must understand that to members of the group these schemas *are* reality, whether you share them or not. As a manager, teacher, or consultant, you may consider a group's religious beliefs or political ideologies sheer superstition, but you will never mobilize the group if you do not take them into account.

I learned this lesson while teaching the theory of evolution to a class of fundamentalist Christian teachers. After nearly a month of fruitless debate about biological and geological evidence, I took my cue from their leader, a gentle but unbending man who had committed much of the Bible to memory. Rather than building my argument on *my* schemas, I used the schemas the class already shared. By having him recite Genesis I: 24, in which God commands the *land* to produce living creatures, I was able to convince my students that by studying natural selection they were studying God's work, and get on with the course.

Many groups have their shared schemas codified and written in a literal or figurative bible. In most working groups, however, many important shared schemas are not written, explicit, or even conscious. Clinical practice has convinced Erik Erikson, R. D. Laing, Harry Levinson, and other psychologists that defense mechanisms such as the ones described in the preceding chapter are shared by families and by professional organizations like unions and by corporations. Levinson argues that groups have ids, egos, and superegos.

Members thus transfer feelings about their parents to their organizations. The group in turn imposes various kinds of repression, including an "organizational incest taboo" which denies the boss's affair with a secretary, and the corporate Oedipus complex, in which a strong leader refuses to let his "sons" assume control.

Some of the most important tacitly shared schemas are in the form of "games," interactions with ulterior motives. Eric Berne's *Games People Play* is a veritable atlas of such games. For example, in the game he calls "Why Don't You?—Yes But," the opening player presents a problem. Other players suggest solutions, but the opening player shoots each of them down until someone presents what the opener really wanted, which was not a solution but reassurance. Abe Wagner's *The Transactional Manager* provides practical suggestions for dealing with social processes once they have been analyzed in terms of Berne's schemas. On a grander scale, *The Game of Business* by John McDonald uses schemas from mathematical game theory to organize conflict and cooperation among large organizations. All these books are excellent sources of rich schemas that will help you make sense of the serious games of the workplace.

As these notions suggest, psychoanalytically and transactionally oriented psychologists see the family as the key to understanding processes in groups of workers. Presumably such theories will be adapted to handle the fact that the once typical nuclear family, with a working father and caretaker mother at the core of the psychoanalytic model, today occurs in only about 15 percent of American households. Meanwhile, schemas based on the conventional nuclear family have allowed Levinson and other consultants to diagnose and treat organizational neuroses.

We all know one such neurotic distortion from personal experience. Even in emergencies, groups are liable to immerse the main issue in a porridge of nit-picking. The emotional climax of a faculty meeting is the fleeting moment of titillating uncertainty before a major motion gets tabled. However, in some cases, instead of denying imperatives for immediate action, groups distort reality in the opposite direction: They take greater risks than most members would hazard on their own. This phenomenon, which violates the common sense that committees always compromise, is called the "risky shift." Risky shifts have been documented in numerous real-world policy decisions. For example, unanimous miscalculations by a group consisting of President John Kennedy, Secretary of State Dean Rusk, Secretary of Defense Robert McNamara, and several others resulted in the Bay of Pigs fiasco: the death or capture of virtually every member of an expeditionary force of fourteen hundred Cuban exiles sent to invade their homeland. With the benefit of hindsight, every member of the group silently echoed Kennedy's anguished question: "How could I have been so stupid to let them go ahead?"

Recent research suggests that both group indecisiveness and the risky shift are special cases of a more general phenomenon: the tendency of group discussion to exaggerate perceptions, to polarize opinion in the direction of the average. For example, posttrial interviews with jurors show that in 90 percent of the trials, initial ballots are less extreme than, but in the same direction as, the final unanimous verdict. It appears that jurors begin their deliberations with a weak bias favoring one side or the other. As a result of discussion, everyone shifts in the direction of the majority.

In order to use polarization, you need to know why it happens. One reason is that discussants are exposed to more arguments supporting the preferred decision than opposing it, which suggests that you can get a shift away from the original majority opinion if you can come up with enough good arguments. The second reason is that in discussion, people modify their opinions in order to be seen favorably. Thus, after sensing which way the group is going, each member tends to get into the vanguard. For example, in the Bay of Pigs decision, there were early indications of a "get tough" attitude. As a result, as one observer wrote, "doubts were entertained but never pressed, partly out of a fear of being labeled 'soft' or undaring in the eyes of their colleagues." This suggests that you can manipulate a group decision by providing or withholding early returns.

Whether a group shifts decisions in the direction of greater risk or caution thus depends not only on the original disposition of group members but on how others' opinions are disclosed. A similar situation occurs with another opposing pair of phenomena, social facilitation and social loafing.

Social facilitation is an increase in performance of well-learned actions as a result of the presence of others. On tasks like bicycle racing, simple multiplication, winding line onto a reel, and putting on familiar clothes, people make fewer errors when they know they're being watched. However, on more difficult tasks, like running a maze, doing complex math problems, memorizing new subject matter, or putting on unfamiliar clothes, the opposite occurs: People who know they're being watched make more mistakes.

Social loafing is a decrease in performance that occurs when workers think their contribution to a group effort is unnoticeable. In studies of tug-of-war, applauding, and generating electrical power by pedaling, subjects' output was lower when they were part of a team. Social loafing has been proposed as an explanation for lower per-acre crop production on collectively versus privately worked lands in the Soviet Union and Hungary, and the low quality of teamed pickle packing in the U.S. The practical lesson is that for simple, well-learned tasks, individual effort with an audience produces maximum performance. For more complex tasks, it may be better to work alone. In general, people do better when there is direct evidence of their personal contribution. For this reason, in an attempt to improve the quality of their products, some corporations have moved away from assembly lines to the "Saab Model," in which small teams of workers are responsible for, say, assembling an engine. Much of the resulting decline in per capita production is regained through lower rates of rejection by quality-control units.

Indecision, risky shifts, and social loafing can be seen as special cases of another general group phenomenon, the diffusion of responsibility. The unresponsiveness of the bystanders who watched the murder of Kitty Genovese and the results of naturalistic experiments on helping behavior show that when many people are around, none of them is likely to offer assistance. Especially when we are uncertain about how to interpret a situation, we look to others for cues to appropriate action. Evidently, we view responsibility as something like a load: The more people there are around to share it, the less there is for each of us to bear.

Consequently, anything that reduces the diffuseness of an appeal for aid makes a helping response more likely. For example, hitchhikers who make eye contact are more than twice as likely to be picked up than those who don't. Social psychologist Robert Cialdini draws an eminently practical conclusion for dealing with injuries, heart attacks, or other emergencies in public: Address your appeal for help to one particular person.

The deadliest of group neuroses is the syndrome that Yale psychologist Irving Janis calls "groupthink." In a book by that name, Janis describes eight symptoms. The first two are illusions of invulnerability and righteousness, which lead to the risky shift. The second two are closed-minded discountings of warnings or the abilities of competitors. There are two direct suppressions of dissent, either by members at large or, especially, by self-appointed "mindguards"; and two indirect pressures to conform, self-censorship of deviant views and illusions of unanimity. These "subtle constraints . . . prevent a member from fully exercising his critical powers and from openly expressing doubts when most others in the group appear to have reached a consensus." Groupthink obeys a Parkinsonian law: "The more amiability and esprit de corps among the members of a policy-making in-group, the greater is the danger that independent critical thinking will be replaced by groupthink, which is likely to result in irrational and dehumanizing action against outgroups." The result of groupthink is failure to follow the tenets of effective decisionmaking as described in Chapter 7.

The Bay of Pigs debacle is a perfect example of groupthink in action. As Janis describes it, the deliberations that led to this decision had a "we-feeling" of solidarity: " 'We are a strong group of good guys who will win in the end. Our opponents are stupid, weak, bad guys.' "

The tragic explosion of the space shuttle *Challenger* is another example of groupthink in action. NASA officials were so anxious to launch on schedule that they ignored clear warnings about defects in the fuel tank seals, which failed.

As prophylactics against groupthink, Janis prescribes several measures. One is the tactic adopted by Alfred Sloan, who as chairman of General Motors once announced at a meeting: "Gentlemen, I take it we are all in complete agreement on the decision. . . . I propose we postpone further discussion . . . to give ourselves time to develop disagreement." Janis further recommends that independent groups and individual gadflies be explicitly charged with critical analysis of major policy decisions. In Chapter 10, I discuss the tactics of critical analysis in detail.

SELF-DEFENSE

In order to defend yourself and your group against risky shifts, diffusion of responsibility, groupthink, and transactional games, you need some defensive and persuasive techniques.

Sometimes, however, the best of intentions (and behavior) do not deter an attack. In such cases, you are well advised to apply the kinds of verbal judo described in Suzette Elgin's practical guide entitled *The Gentle Art of Verbal Self-Defense*. Elgin teaches us how to recognize various forms of covert verbal attack, and explains how to move along with the overt form of an assault to dodge it or to sweep it away, leaving the covert meaning flat on its back. For example, suppose the attack is of the form: "If you *really* wanted that promotion, you'd spend more time in your office." If you reply to the overt content of the attack in the second phrase with something like: "I do too spend lots of time in my office!" you lose. Most of us could improve our chances for promotion by spending more time in the office. As a counter, Elgin prescribes going after the covert presumption in the first phrase, the implicit accusation that you don't care about promotion, perhaps with something like: "It's ironic that people think I don't care about promotion when my main job is to be in the field [lab, classroom], not my office."

Elgin sees such attacks and counterattacks as based on tacit knowledge that in our culture is much more available to men than to women. As a result, men "learn to admire the skilled verbal infighters, to keep track of the . . . scores . . . and they do not take any of this personally." Her manual makes much of this tacit knowledge explicit and provides plenty of safe paper-and-pencil practice in using an attack's own force against it.

PERSUASION

The tacit knowledge of verbal self-defense is like throws in judo, but the explicit lore of psychological persuasion is more like combinations in boxing. Great persuaders know how to set someone up with a few left jabs before moving in with a right to the chin.

It is a tribute to the effectiveness of such lore that psychologists study persuaders more than persuaders study psychology. In order to learn from some real champions of persuasion, Robert Cialdini posed as a sales trainee at a real estate agency and at a Chevrolet dealership. In his delightful book, *Influence: Science and Practice,* he describes how a prospective buyer, reeling from the impact of a few run-down, overpriced "set-up" houses, becomes an easy target for the sucker punch, the house the realtor really wants to sell. Cialdini points out that automobile dealers are equally adept at making use of such "perceptual contrasts," in a technique they call "low-balling," advertising cars at far lower prices than they will actually cost in the end. After you've committed yourself to spend several thousand dollars for a car, another few hundred for radio, heater, and seats seems insignificant, and to balk seems inconsistent. Yet another application of contrast is the highly effective technique Cialdini calls the door in the face: The trick is to make a big but not outlandish initial request. When the door is slammed, one retreats to what one really wants, which by contrast appears reasonable. Instructions on how to deliver such combinations are codified in books like *The New Psychology of Persuasion and Motivation in Selling:* "when a man enters a clothing store with the express purpose of buying a suit, he will almost always *pay more* for whatever accessories he buys if he buys them after the suit purchase than before."

Much of the knowledge needed to persuade has been rendered explicit by trainers of sales personnel. Among the most effective sales schools are those run by publishers of encyclopedias and, more recently, educational software. As a perennially unemployed undergraduate, I was once recruited into one of these training camps, which every summer turn thousands of mild-mannered college students into door-to-door Muhammad Alis. I quit after a week, not because I wasn't selling encyclopedias but because I was selling more than my bleeding heart could bear. Though my customers were indeed signing up to spend only "a nickel, a dime a day, less than you spend on cigarettes," the total cost (which I never had the courage to calculate) was such that the publisher could afford to pay me a commission of over five hundred dollars a set. Looking back with the perspective of a quarter century and a Ph.D. in psychology, I can see that I was trained in just about every jab, hook, and cross in the book.

The first step in persuasion, as we learned from Bernie the realtor in Chapter 1, is to select someone who is persuadable. In jury selection, this has become a science. For a handsome fee, survey researchers will determine what attitudes are favorable to one side or the other. Then, by asking prospective jurors innocuous questions, counsel can weed out those liable to be opposed to his client. Like selection of sympathetic jurors, choice of encyclopedia customers was deemed too important to be left to chance. Rather, in an artful application of research showing that persuasion about factual matters works better over the phone than in person, prospects were created by telephone "interviews," during which they agreed to homilies about the importance of education to their children. The actual sales pitch was built on this prior factual agreement, but since it required persuading someone to sign a contract, not just agree to a statement, it was conducted *mano a mano*.

The first problem in door-to-door persuasion is to get a foot in the door, to establish some relationship that will allow you to present your appeal. The spiel we were forced to memorize solved this problem for us. I can still recite it: "Hi, ma'am, just stopped by to see your husband. I'd like to step into your living room for a moment because . . ." The request to come in always worked: In spite of my wishy-washy personality, I soon found myself ensconced in suburban sofas, prospectus spread out over the floor. The key to the success of the request was that innocuous little word "because." Social psychologist Ellen Langer demonstrated that people are more likely to accede to a request if you provide a reason, any reason whatsoever. When Langer asked to get ahead of someone in line at a copy machine by saying, "Excuse me. I have five pages. May I use the Xerox machine?" 60 percent of the people she approached complied. But when she added, "because I'm in a rush," the percentage rose to 94. Even if she gave a completely vacuous reason ("because I have to make some copies"), the results were just as good. Evidently, the word "because" operates at a personal, not a rational level, perhaps by making the askee believe that you care enough to explain. Psychologists call this sort of exchange, in which the medium really is the message, phatic communication. Much everyday chatter and most nonverbal communication is phatic. Underlying the banality of meteorological comments and sweet nothings is the important metamessage common to all acts of common courtesy: "I know you are there, and are a person deserving recognition."

Using a blatantly memorized spiel was patronizing to us and the customers, but it worked, in part because I had memorized it and could say it fast. Not only did this prevent the mooch from getting a word in edgewise; it made my message more convincing. Contrary to popular belief, carefully controlled experiments show that listeners consider fast talkers more sincere, knowledgeable, and intelligent than slow talkers.

Though the spiel was recited by rote, there were three places for ad lib remarks. But even here the instructions were precise. At each of these points in the routine, we were to comment on some object in the home and say we had one just like it or that we enjoyed the activity associated with it: "I see you have a copy of *Mein Kampf* [a television, a .38]. I certainly enjoyed the story [soap operas, the feeling of security]." The rationale, I now realize, was that people are more likely to agree with people they like, and next to physical attractiveness, which I could do little about, similarity is the most important factor in liking. For this reason, we were ordered to dress in a suburban middle-class manner: sport coat and slacks, no jeans, no suit.

The spiel also contained several pieces of absolutely transparent flattery. One of them was "Nice house you have here." Once again, my writer knew what he was doing: Research shows that people like flatterers even when they know the flattery is flummery. My script might have been written by Joe Girard, the world's greatest car salesman, according to the *Guinness Book of World Records.* For years, he made annual commissions of over $200,000, selling more than five vehicles every day. One of his techniques was sending greeting cards bearing the simple message "I like you" every month of the year to every one of his more than thirteen thousand customers, many of whom come back year after year.

The spiel used motivation in several other ways. Besides capitalizing on parents' desire to give their kids an edge, it created a sense of obligation by an opening feint: The encyclopedia was offered "free" to carefully selected "test families," who would, however, "in our rapidly changing world," surely wish to purchase the yearbooks needed to update the set. People who feel that you have singled them out to receive a favor have a hard time saying no. Lyndon Johnson was an expert at this trick. As Theodore White points out, Johnson's bids for the presidential nomination were backed by politicians in every state who owed him favors. And in 1960, for good measure, LBJ flew in half a ton of taffy for the Democratic convention.

The feint was followed by a barrage of quick jabs in the form of rhetorical questions based on the telephone warm-up. "Education certainly is essential to success nowadays, isn't it?" You can imagine what came next: "Schools can't possibly teach children all they need to know in our rapidly changing world, can they?" Our instructions clearly stated that we were not to go on until we had secured a verbal commitment to each of these uncontroversial propositions. Eventually you hit the mooches with an uppercut that began below your knees: "So you're willing, then, to participate in our survey?" Since the mooches had already participated in the telephone "interview," and had just spent fifteen minutes agreeing that their kids needed extracurricular assistance, to refuse to participate in our "survey" would have violated the deep need for cognitive consistency that figured so prominently in the discussion of the totalitarian ego at the end of the preceding chapter.

The need for consistency has figured in the triumph of the totalitarian ego over democratic ideology as well as over economic interest. Incremental commitments exploiting the consistency motive were the basis of the brainwashing of American POWs in Korea. Chinese interrogators began by securing agreement with innocuous statements like "The U.S. is not perfect," then assembled and published lists of complaints. In order to remain consistent, those who had agreed to these statements had to see themselves as "collaborators," and were thus easily persuaded to agree to more serious criticisms of the U.S.

Many of the moves we encyclopedia salesmen (we were all male) used were practiced on us. Every day ended with a party at a penthouse swimming pool, with free refreshments designed to create a sense of obligation. We learned to like our supervisors, who presented themselves as being like us: college students who were after the good life. We were required to commit almost a week to training before submitting our principles to the test of manipulating the mooches. We knew what was happening, but the tricks worked anyway. They still do, even after that quarter century and that Ph.D. The other day, I got a questionnaire from the Union of Concerned Scientists. After answering all the questions, I had no choice but to send them a check. Even if you know it's coming, a solid punch can still knock you out.

Robert Cialdini describes some effective defenses against psychological pugilists. Defenses against obligation are tricky because there are some genuinely generous people, so he suggests that you give donors the benefit of the doubt. Accept their gifts, and if they turn out to be ploys, mentally define them as such to avoid feeling guilty when you don't reciprocate. Since we experience our feelings about a message a split second before we intellectualize about it, he encourages us to pay attention to the "stomach signs" that tell us "we are being trapped into complying with a request we *know* we don't want to perform." Finally, notice whether you like a persuader more than you would expect, given the amount of contact you've had. If you do, try to separate the persuader from the message.

LEADERSHIP

When John Kennedy urged young Americans to ask what they could do for their country, thousands volunteered. When Lyndon Johnson cajoled, bribed, and blackmailed his colleagues, he practiced a more rational, business-as-usual sort of leadership. Both Kennedy's charisma and Johnson's cunning depended heavily on social intelligence.

At a time when ideas and information are more powerful than ever, leadership is a practical skill. It comes up again and again in research on successful managing. At AT&T, leadership has been intensively researched for years. Like earlier investigations by Bell System assessment centers, Robert Beck's Management Progress Study found that advancement at AT&T is due in part to "interpersonal skills, especially face-to-face leadership."

Leadership figures prominently in the studies conducted by Richard Boyatzis. In *The Competent Manager,* Boyatzis presents a picture of leadership based on a study of more than two thousand executives. Boyatzis's "leadership cluster" includes the abilities "to get different groups to collaborate well, to use socialized power . . . to build alliances, networks, coalitions, or teams." Boyatzis echoes classic sociological conceptions of charisma when he describes leadership as creating "symbols of group identity, pride and trust."

I have described how rational leaders rely on sensitivity to the needs and abilities of their followers. To this sensitivity charismatic leaders add another: an awareness of where their followers are headed. This "soft path" to leadership is not a new idea. Twenty-five hundred years ago, Lao-Tzu wrote: "To lead the people, walk behind them." Historian James MacGregor Burns describes what he calls "transforming leadership" as depending on the ability to "make conscious what lies unconscious among followers." As a result, as Harvard psychologist David McClelland discovered, audiences "felt more powerful, not less powerful or submissive," in the presence of charismatic leaders.

Besides sensitivity to moods, values, and trends, leaders need expressive and persuasive skills. I have already described mastery of nonverbal signals as an asset of leaders like Johnson and Reagan. Smiles, scowls, and fists are even more important for charismatic leaders, whose expressions and gestures allow them to lead large numbers of people into new enterprises by inspiring powerful emotions in followers.

Persuasive techniques are the rational politician's stock-in-trade, as we saw with Johnson's "reasoning." Charismatic leaders like Kennedy, Gandhi, and De Gaulle also rely heavily on the foot in the door, the low ball, and favors. Suzette Elgin points out that many of charismatic leaders' most effective techniques are standard rhetorical ploys—for example, parallelisms ("Ask not what your country can do for you but what you can do for your country") and metaphors ("New Frontier"). Many leaders are persuasive because they are experts, so not all persuasive tactics are tricks.

The component that seems to distinguish charismatic leaders from rational ones is vision, the ability to imagine alternative futures that provide meaning for followers. The leaders among Charles Garfield's peak performers had this ability; they brought out the best in those they worked with by creating images of achievement. Charismatic leaders, according to sociologists Trudy Heller and Jon Van Til, construe "experience in a way that provides a viable basis for action, e.g. by mobilizing meaning, articulating and defining what has previously remained implicit or unsaid, by inventing images and meanings that provide a focus for new attention, and by consolidating, confronting, or changing prevailing wisdom."

Leaders combine empathy, expressiveness, and sensitivity to changing values with persuasiveness based on academic intelligence. There is, of course, more to leadership, especially charismatic leadership, than intellect: Charismatic leaders have a sense of mission, self-confidence, and at least a willingness, if not a passion, to use power.

The intellectual components of charisma are, according to Suzette Elgin, learnable. This seems to be the case when it comes to social intelligence, which, as I have argued in this chapter, depends on learnable schemas that allow you to assess abilities, develop empathy, and read and use nonverbal communication to manage group process, defend yourself, and persuade others. In the last five chapters of this book, I present ways of learning the verbal, logical, critical, and creative skills that make charismatic leaders.

PART THREE

INTELLIGENCES OF
SPACE AND TIME

6.
Body Intelligence

A moving part of motion, a discovery . . .
Too much like thinking to be less than thought.
—WALLACE STEVENS

When we use the phrase "sixth sense" figuratively, we are selling ourselves short. We do have a sixth sense, called "proprioception," which provides information about our posture and movements. In fact, this body sense is really at least two senses in one. The first of these neglected senses provides the "equilibratory" information about leaning and accelerating that helps us maintain our balance, control vehicles, and know which way is up. Ordinarily we process all this information unconsciously, but we can bring it to awareness by standing on one leg with eyes closed in an open area. The receptors that provide the information for this balancing act are the vestibular organs in the inner ears. Each of these organs consists of three semicircular canals, at right angles to one another, so that they can detect pulls from any direction. The malady called "motion sickness" is due to disturbances in the equilibratory system.

The second neglected sense provides "kinesthetic" information about the movements of body parts relative to each other. Kinesthetic information, which comes from special receptors in joints, skin, and muscles, allows us to go down stairs without watching our feet, shift gears without taking our eyes from the road, and touch-type.

Although they could well be regarded as separate sensory receptors, the vestibular and kinesthetic sensors are generally lumped together and called "proprioceptors." They are among the most refined and sensitive of all sensory organs.

Proprioception and vision are the sensory inputs to a system that Howard Gardner calls "body intelligence," the ability to control the body and manipulate objects. Such control is often called "sensori-motor." The term "motor" refers to movements generated by muscles. The distinction between sensory and motor processes fades when we dissect the nervous system, but it has a practical application. Reaction times are faster when one concentrates on the motor response rather than the sensory stimulus. The next time you need to be the first one through the intersection, focus your attention on your right foot. You can look at the stoplight, but don't think about it—let it serve as a trigger.

Body intelligence is practical, not just for rush-hour drag racers but for anyone who works. Whether we are office workers, medical practitioners, or college teachers, we are all manual laborers some of the time. Body intelligence is intelligence, in spite of the snobbery with which many of us regard physical activity. Body intelligence is learnable, even by klutzes.

Surgeons, dentists, assemblers, technicians, typists, mechanics, weavers, carpenters, potters, drafters, hunters, inventors, and others who work with things combine proprioceptive, tactile, and visual information to control their hands. Much of the thinking that goes into this kind of work is nonverbal, so verbal descriptions of body intelligence at work are rare. However, Dave Bender, an inventor interviewed by Studs Terkel for his book *Working,* is an unusually articulate spokesman. Here's how he describes his work:

> I work with wood, plastic, metal, anything. I work with paper. Even at home.
>
> Sunday I was taking paper and pasting it together and finding a method of how to drop spoons, a fork, a napkin, and a straw into one package. . . . do we blow the bag open? Do we push it open? Do we squeeze it down? So I'm shoving things in and pushing with my wife's hair clips and bobby pins and everything I can get my hands on. I even took the cat's litter, the stuff you pick up the crap with [laughs], even that to shove with the bag, to pull it open. . . . I love making. . . . I don't have neat blueprints. . . . All I have is this. [Taps at his temple.] . . . I can't even make drawings. I'm measuring, taking off three-eighths of an inch or put on two inches here. It's the craziest piece of iron you ever saw. I never saw anything like this in my life. But I saw it working the other day.
>
> When I get it fabricated it'll be a packaging machine. You'll see arms going up and down, gears working, things going, reelers and winders, automatic everything. I know it could be patented. There's nothing like it. It's unique. This is all in my mind, yes sir. And I can't tell you my telephone number. [Laughs.]

A remark made about Peter Hewitt, inventor of the mercury vapor lamp, applies to Dave Bender as well: "Those who knew him, watching him at work, felt that a part, at least, of Hewitt's thinking apparatus was in his hands." Like inventors, engineers, architects, and other designers use working models to think. Similarly, dentists construct models to create novel prostheses as well as to check their fit.

Even managers and other information workers who work "hands on" only in a metaphorical sense need body intelligence in such everyday activities as driving, typing, or sketching. In some of these occupations, computer graphics and word processing programs reduce the need for coordination. Even I can type a perfect copy with Applewriter and make an acceptable figure with MacPaint. Since such prostheses bring complex manual skills within reach of many who would never have considered doing their own typing and drawing, their effect may be to increase the demand for sensorimotor skills: Now that I use a word processor, even I am finally learning to touch-type.

Body intelligence plays such a pervasive role in such mundane activities as driving and repair and maintenance of appliances that we are liable to deprecate what is in fact an ability as intellectual as reading, writing, and arithmetic. Like the mandarins of ancient China, we take a perverse pride in our body stupidity, and revel in the status that goes along with hiring others to do what we consider menial. In order to maintain this status, we must tell ourselves that there is something inferior about work that requires dexterity. Meanwhile, stereotypes of wimpy intellectuals and dumb athletes reinforce the prejudices that segregate body from mind, manual labor from mental work, practical application from theoretical understanding. The obscurity of the sixth sense of proprioception is a symptom of our denial of body intelligence, which depends heavily on this seldom-mentioned sense. To many modern mandarins, the phrase "body intelligence" shares the oxymoronic clang of "fresh frozen," "jumbo shrimp," and "good morning."

We can no longer afford such snobbery. All over the world, people without such hang-ups have boosted their productivity by taking pride in work we too often despise. Here at home, there are some promising signs: Our concern with physical fitness has been around long enough to be more than just a fad, and many of us have learned that the confidence, endurance, and power we feel while running or bicycling do not disappear the moment we return to work. Even in the age of the automatic transmission, some of us prefer to shift for ourselves, and some American cars are beginning to exhibit something alarmingly like road feel.

MIND'S BODY

But is body intelligence really intelligent? It fits our working definition, "the ability to get and use information." One of the most articulate exponents of the view that complex movements of hands and body have just as much intellectual content as lip movements is a remarkable woman named Eleanor Metheny. She expresses the role of body intelligence in knowing:

> To know what a wave is by sharing its motion as you ride its crest on your surfboard. To be speed incarnate. To feel a breathing like the wind as you race the wind for a measured mile. To pivot about your own axis with the earth as it revolves about its pole. To whirl with the whirling stars. To know what force is by becoming a force as you hit and kick and twist and throw your solid body against space—or against another body . . .

Metheny further points out that human symbol-use pervades every movement, and drawing on philosophy, perception, and neurophysiology, she argues that body movements, like all other human acts, are steeped in meaning.

Metheny joins a tradition in cognitive psychology that views sensorimotor skills as the foundation of all mental operations. The Swiss psychologist Jean Piaget and others have shown that infants first conceive the world in terms of sensorimotor schemes, in which objects are represented as actions and their consequences: A nipple is "suck, milk-in-mouth"; a thumb is "suck, tug-on-thumb." After a year of differentiation and refinement, such schemes become the basis for symbolic ones using words. Every adult concept is, according to this view, a cloud of meaning around a nucleus of action. The quintessence of this development is the kind of "muscular images" that Albert Einstein claimed to use in his most creative thinking.

It is difficult for most of us to imagine what a "muscular image" is like, and even harder to imagine how such images could be used to think. However, experiences akin to Einstein's are available to all of us, through the Korean art of finger calculation called Chisanbop. In contrast to traditional Western arithmetic teaching, which discourages use of the fingers, this method teaches children to use kinesthetic information. According to advocates of the system, seven-year-olds who have mastered it can add and subtract columns of four-digit figures faster than adults using calculators. Experts claim that they "feel the answers in their fingers," an experience that sounds a lot like Einstein's "muscular images."

Tracy Kidder's *Soul of a New Machine* provides a glimpse of Piaget's sensorimotor schemas growing and working. As children, several of the brilliant young engineers described by Kidder took apart and reassembled telephones, clocks, and radios. Similarly, books about Steven Jobs and Stephen Wozniak show how important hands-on experience was in the development of the imaginations and intellects of these entrepreneurs. Wozniak built an electronic voltmeter when he was five. Both Jobs and Wozniak were inveterate tinkerers with electronic gizmos, including the "blue box," a small audio oscillator that mimicked the tones that activate long-distance phone lines.

Mathematician Seymour Papert and his colleagues at MIT put Piaget's principle to work in what they call the "LOGO microworld," a system that allows young children to program a device called a "turtle" to perform movements of increasing complexity. Papert claims that the success of "LOGO-land" as a programming environment is due to the fact that it allows children to learn to program the same way they learn to dance, with their bodies.

Following the lead of Frederick Bartlett, modern cognitive scientists, including Jerome Bruner, Howard Gardner, and others, see physical and intellectual skills as involving the same coordination of hierarchically organized control programs. Even at the physiological level, suggest psychologists Charles Solley and Gardner Murphy, the relationship between thought and action may be identity. "The physiological mechanisms of consciousness," they write, "appear to be precisely those required for voluntary actions."

In a similar vein, Howard Gardner quotes Norman Mailer: "There are languages of the body. And prize-fighting is one of them. A prize fighter . . . speaks with a command of the body which is as detached, subtle, and comprehensive in its intelligence as any exercise of the mind . . . with wit, style, and an aesthetic flair for surprise. . . . Boxing is a dialogue between bodies, is a rapid debate between two sets of intelligences." Practical body intelligence (BI) is mainly a matter of the second of these skills, handling objects, so we may define BI as the ability to get information about one's body and its relationship to objects and use this information to make, assemble, dissect, or otherwise manipulate objects, including other bodies.

The philosopher Martin Heidegger described the intellectual content of bodily action this way: "The hand designs and signs. . . . Every motion of the hand in every one of its works carries itself through the elements of thinking, every bearing of the hand bears itself in that element."

Sociologist David Sudnow has written three thoughtful books about the cerebration that goes on when one improvises at the typewriter, the video game, and the piano. He shows how tricks like using peripheral vision and watching a target rather than a paddle dramatically improve performance and learning. Computer recreations may seem a long way from the world of work, but as workers in the electronic office and soldiers on the electronic battlefield come to depend ever more heavily on computerized tools, weapons, and training simulations, contrasts between everyday reality and video games become increasingly academic. In any case, Sudnow's analyses show how sensorimotor skills depend on verbal and spatial knowledge.

Verbal knowledge is an important part of many other sensorimotor skills: Once you are told "the trick," you are well on your way to mastery. In learning to shoot a rifle, instructions to exhale partially, then to balance gradually increasing trigger finger pressure with opposite pressure of the thumb, generally produce an immediate improvement in scores. Similarly, in driving, instructions to maintain the "ten and two" o'clock hand position even during fast sharp turns bring about an immediate gain in sense of control.

BI works in an even more intimate partnership with spatial intelligence. For example, dentists must both visualize the form and position of a bridge or other prosthesis, and install it quickly and precisely. Accordingly, aspiring dentists take tests, like the Form Board and the Finger Maze, that simultaneously assess spatial visualization and manual dexterity. No intelligence works in complete isolation from the others, and BI is not an exception. Its close relationship with other multiple intelligences is a further indication of the intellectual character of body intelligence.

BI's partnership with other intelligences in a variety of practical skills raises the possibility that BI's partners are the brains of the outfit. However, a number of facts (nicely summarized by Howard Gardner) show that BI is an intelligence in its own right.

For one thing, body intelligence may share cortical hardware with intelligences with snootier academic credentials, but it has hardware of its own, the basal ganglia and cerebellum (see Chapter 4). Damage to areas dedicated to motor control can produce apraxias, disorders in which people physically capable of performing all the elements of a motor skill are unable to coordinate or adapt them to act. Conversely, people with damage to linguistic or logical regions of the brain often retain all their sensorimotor skills: One patient, for example, couldn't name common tools, but could use them skillfully. Joey, the autistic "mechanical boy" described by

Bruno Bettelheim, was woefully deficient in other intellectual domains, but had an extraordinary ability to disassemble and assemble machines and to pantomime complex motions, like plugging in and deploying extension cords. Similarly, "H. M.," a neurological patient, was able to learn mirror writing, but was unable to remember that he had learned: Though his performance improved day after day, he was verbally unable to express any recollection.

Just as normal levels of body intelligence often share skulls with low levels of other intelligences, extraordinary levels of body intelligence are often seen in people who are otherwise ordinary. Thus, on the basis of physiology, pathologies, and prodigies, Howard Gardner argues that body intelligence develops independently of other forms of intellectual ability.

Given the independence of body intelligence from other intelligences, it is not surprising that, especially among older subjects, there seems to be little relationship between body intelligence and IQ. Though intelligences vary independently within and among people, no intelligence works independently of the others, and body intelligence is no exception. Body intelligence is closely related to the sensitivity to one's own physiological/emotional states discussed in the chapter on self-knowledge. Body and social intelligences work side by side in acting, mime, and nonverbal communication. And spatial skills are essential if mechanics, inventors, and others are to understand why their manipulations work.

BI SKILLS ARE LEARNABLE

In separating body intelligence into control of the body and control of objects, Howard Gardner may not have gone far enough. Psychologists who study body intelligence, like those who study intelligence in general, disagree about how many fundamentally different abilities are involved in BI, but they have moved generally toward multiplicity. Practically, this means that even if you're a klutz at carpentry, you may have an unsuspected talent for typing. Although early investigators were committed to the notion of a single, general motor ability, by the mid-1940s they had extracted two separate factors, corresponding roughly to Gardner's: one for control of the whole body, the other for control of objects.

More recently, psychologists have divided each of these abilities into subabilities. "Gross motor" control of the whole body has been divided into nine components, and psychomotor manipulation into as many as eleven. A study of the psychomotor skills of pilots found several key abilities, including coordinating large muscle and body parts, especially hands and feet; discriminating directions of motion; tracking moving targets; comparing and describing visual forms; manipulating objects precisely and quickly, and several spatial skills of the sort I'll discuss in the next chapter. J. P. Guilford, whose structure of intellect model was discussed in Chapter 2, proposes a correspondingly refined analysis of body smarts, with four psychological factors associated with each of four body parts: gross body, trunk, limbs, and hands.

Tests of sensorimotor intelligence demolish the claim that there is a general sensorimotor ability. People who do poorly on one kind of sensorimotor task often do quite well on another. "All-round athletes" are people who happen to excel in a large number of independent skills, not people with one generic skill. An individual's rate of improvement varies so much from one task to another that some psychologists suggest we abandon the notion of motor ability entirely and instead focus on the tasks. That lack of coordination on the basketball court does not necessarily slop onto the computer keyboard may be bad news for psychometricians, but it is good news for the rest of us. Another practical implication of the particularity of motor learning is that a program that develops coordination in one skill (say, karate) is unlikely to have much general effect on another (say, driving). What do get transferred from one skill to another are highly specific movements—perhaps a quick jab of the shift lever into third gear, or a lightning jab of the left foot on the clutch.

There is probably no domain of intelligence in which changes not only in performance but in ability are easier to demonstrate than BI. Most of us have learned several complex sensorimotor skills at levels that seemed impossible when we began: Weaving, potting, skiing, writing, typing, and driving are but a few.

Dr. Alan Schafer, an orthodontist I interviewed while writing this chapter, described much of his motor development in dental school as learning to trust his own BI and forgo conscious verbal plans: "You're working upside down and backwards. I had to learn not to think about which way to move the burr and the handpiece but rather just concentrate on the image in the mirror and let my body just automatically take over."

Even after such accomplishments, however, many of us still maintain that we "have no talent" for skills like drawing. Betty Edwards, in *Drawing on the Right Side of the Brain*, refutes such complaints with portraits drawn by her students before and after her program. Because the skills of body intelligence display quick and clear improvement for so many people, BI is a proving ground for the discovery of techniques that enhance skills dependent on other intelligences.

One person who has made his own body and mind such a proving ground is Dolph Kuss. I interviewed Kuss because he is an articulate master teacher of several practical applications of BI. The one we focused on was cross-country skiing. For many people, cross-country, or Nordic, skiing is only recreation, but for fur trappers, timber cruisers, wildlife scientists, and others whose work requires travel over snow, it is practical transportation, under most conditions far more efficient (and enjoyable) than snowshoeing.

Slender, short, and fortyish, Dolph Kuss doesn't look like a coach, but he is a great one. Perhaps it was his physique that fostered his democratic attitude toward coaching. He believes in teaching any skill to anyone who wants to learn it. In the 1950s, as a recreation director in an isolated town in the Rockies, he introduced competitive cross-country skiing to a region where downhill was considered the only way to go. The novelty of the sport and his open admission policy meant that Kuss did not always have the best students to work with. Speaking of his students in those early days, Dolph said:

"These guys had body intelligence, but they didn't participate in any other sport. The coaches at the high school would tease me and say, 'You got the guys who couldn't make it in the band.' These guys were frail, slender, not very well developed. They didn't have the real athletic look—you know, broad shoulders, bulging muscles. They had desire to do it, but they were a pretty motley crew. But out of that came some most unusual people, who became Junior National Champions. We sent people to Olympic teams and other international teams. They were awesome—not because they were so physical but because they were so body smart. They were so technical and efficient in their movements. The results that these boys produced . . . they made me look good."

As a result of his students' success, Kuss was asked to coach the U.S. Ski Team for the 1964 and 1968 Olympic Games, where his skiers became the first Americans to win respectable standings in cross-country skiing events. In 1972, he coached the U.S. Ski Team for their effort at Sapporo, where his student Mike DeVecka took a second place in the Nordic Combined events.

Kuss believes that the method he uses to teach skiing can be applied to any sensorimotor skill. He has used it to teach golf, kayaking, and rock climbing, as well as downhill skiing. Kuss is an expert at making the tacit knowledge of body intelligence explicit. Here is how he does it:

"My approach is to plan every step [of the learning process].

Everything fits together as part of a plan down to every detail. . . . I analyze whatever the skill is. I take it apart so I can verbally create some type of cognition. Demonstration is always a last resort because you can't demonstrate a real movement slow enough to show what to do. Sometimes the words don't make the right picture, so I say it some other way. The method is progressions: step to step to step. You start with the total thing, analyze it into parts, analyze and teach the parts, then put it back together: whole, part, whole.

"I did that for cross-country skiing. Get your body to do this. When your body can do this, add this, and when you can do that, add this. You can't skip a hurdle that leaves a gap. At higher levels you won't have that and it won't be solid.

"In cross-country skiing, your arms control your legs. To glide long and slow, move your arms long and slow. I analyzed arm motion into themes: reach, push, release, follow through. In the push, your hand doesn't clutch the grip. You use the strap. Your hand is free in the back so the pole can continue to push. If you had a grip, the moment your hand passes your hip, the pole would be extracted from the snow. If you don't follow through, you can't ski cross-country.

"After we're sure that everyone has the fundamentals, then you're free to develop your style. Everyone doesn't end up looking alike. But if you're analytical, you work with people and see that they have gone through all these hurdles [the progressions]; you can look at them and see that they do that and that and that. Two people could look different, but they're both doing those things. They look entirely different because they have different styles, some flair: lifting of the foot at the end of the kick is neither good nor bad. It just happens that some people, when they complete their kick, the ski is released from the snow. They relax antagonistic muscles so much that the ski just goes. Someone else might not do it at all, but the essential thing is that they're both kicking.

"If you do it well, at the end you will not exist. Your students won't look to you, because they're better than you."

When I asked Dolph Kuss if anyone could learn a skill by doing this, he replied, "Yes, but they don't." He went on to describe his own learning of a new style of cross-country skiing:

"The Swedes had recently developed a new technique, V-skating [in which one moves the skis in a herringbone-like pattern, even on level terrain]. I had analyzed it, read the literature, developed a progression. First, I tried doing it myself, like Alpine skating. It didn't work. I had to watch somebody who knew how. The difference is, in skating, your feet are in front of you. This technique is much more fun, more elegant, much faster. And you analyze terrain differently. When you ski diagonal [conventionally], it's all vertical, but in V-skating you look at the horizontal side-to-side dimension. If you're on a cambered slope, you do two shorts on the uphill side and a long glide on the downhill side. And you won't believe the acceleration. What made it so great was I was learning a new sport.

"Now, these guys I was racing around here were stronger and fitter and twenty years younger, but they couldn't keep up with me because I had analyzed another technical skill and taught myself. First they said it couldn't work, and I beat 'em. Then they said you can't keep it up for fifty-eight kilometers. So I went to the Birkenbeiner, the largest cross-country ski race in North America. I won my class by over an hour and finished a hundred and second out of seven thousand starters. The point was I could go more efficiently. Then we went on to Lake Placid. I did well there too."

Taking a guess at his age, I asked if the class he raced in was for forty-year-olds. He replied. "My class was fifty-five–fifty-nine. I'm fifty-six."

The method Dolph Kuss uses to teach skiing can be applied to everyday skills like driving, typing, and repairing. This is possible because sensorimotor intelligence is, like other intelligences, to a great extent a matter of knowledge and learning to learn. One of the best demonstrations of the role of knowledge is the fact that people learn motor skills faster if they understand what they are learning: what the goal of each stage is, and how each motion leads to that goal.

Motor skills like skiing, typing, driving, and flying develop in similar sequences of four stages: getting the idea, having the idea, competence, and proficiency. Each stage has its own organization, different from other stages but similar to the corresponding stage of other skills. In the remainder of this chapter, by taking you through the stages of development of a motor skill, I hope to convince you that the intelligence that coordinates the body is just as intellectual as the one that balances equations, and that, like other intellectual abilities, it can be learned.

Stage 1: Getting the Idea

Paul Fitts, a pioneer in information-processing approaches to motor skills, described the first stage of acquiring a new skill as "cognitive": It is largely a matter of understanding instructions and rules. This novice stage in motor skill development has been described variously as "cognitive and exploratory," getting the "idea" or "plan" of the movement, and getting a first approximation that can be shaped.

Although experts disagree on the value of demonstration and explanation at higher levels of skill, studies of the novice stage of typing, flying, archery, and swimming show that explanations are extremely valuable if given in advance, not during actual performance. Simple rules like "Shift at 20 mph" and "Leave one car length for every 10 mph" free novices to pay attention to the processes they need to be working on. Verbal instructions and demonstrations that facilitate understanding of the purpose of such rules help novices translate complex verbal and visual information into first-approximation performance.

An important category of rules conveys the basic postures of various motor skills. Many physical activities are based on a "home" position, which provides a center from which one moves out and to which one returns after each excursion. The "ten- and two-o'clock hand position in driving is one example." Similarly, typing has a "home position": left first finger resting lightly on f, right first finger on j, and the other fingers falling naturally on keys to the left and right. Failure to adopt a relaxed, consistent "home" position requires tense muscles to be untensed and adjusted before they can begin to respond.

In complex motor skills like typing and flying, as in simpler ones like Morse code telegraphy, it usually takes about ten hours of instruction and practice to get through this period. However, Fitts and Mike Posner describe a gifted flying instructor named Alex Williams, who got novice aircraft pilots to solo in three and a half hours. Williams "intellectualized" the motor skills of flying, just as Kuss did with skiing. He analyzed each maneuver into a sequence of cues and movements, and led detailed discussions of each sequence.

Computerized simulations now make it possible to put the rules of the cognitive stage into practice under an instructor's control and observation. Simulations are already used to teach people to drive cars and tanks, fly airplanes and spacecraft, and fire rockets and other weapons. Because they teach motor (and other) skills so effectively, they will be used even more widely in the future. Simulations are not only safer and less expensive than the real thing; they also allow the learner to take advantage of several general principles of sensorimotor learning.

For instance, a general principle of motor learning in this stage is "Pay attention to form and worry about results later." In learning to drive, it is easy to get into bad hand-position habits, and in typing it's easy to fall into bad finger habits, because both bad habits produce acceptable results in the short run. In the long run, however, these habits prevent you from becoming an expert. Though attention to errors of form is crucial at this stage, errors of result should be ignored. At best, attending to bad outcomes is a waste of time. Errors early in the development of a skill, unlike those that occur at higher levels of proficiency, are unsystematic and uninformative. At worst, attending to errors is frustrating and counterproductive. In many kinds of learning, attending to mistakes causes them to be repeated. Simulations allow learners to concentrate on form and ignore errors of result without risk.

Another principle of motor learning states that we learn best in large units. One educational psychologist puts it this way: "Use the largest and most meaningful units you can manage." Simulators permit novice pilots to practice sequences like takeoffs and landings as wholes—the instructor doesn't have to abort a too steep final approach.

Simulators allow novices to learn with all relevant sources of information under control. As one distinguished student of motor learning put it: "All the regulatory stimulus conditions must be provided in the learner's *initial* environment" [italics in original]. Especially in early stages of learning, visual cues, the ones most easily controlled in simulations, are the most important regulatory stimuli. In fact, in some skills, like flying, it is important to learn to ignore vestibular cues, which are often dangerously misleading. Because the vestibular system stops responding when stimulation is constant, as in a banked turn, novice pilots feel that they are no longer turning. In clouds or at night, they are liable to fly what one pilot described as a "perfectly coordinated, [bank-indicator-] ball-centered ever-tightening spiral into the ground."

Mechanics and other technicians may have to learn new skills on the spot. In such cases, they often give themselves a visual self-demonstration. My expert mechanic R. J. Mulheim showed me how he taught himself one new skill: "On these Z cars, see, there's this little hole you have to reach into to install the remote-control mirror. I had to do this [he performed a little twist with thumb and two fingers clasping an imaginary part], but I couldn't learn to do it in the hole. So I practiced it out in the open where I could see what I was doing, reached in the hole, and zoop, one Z car with a mirror."

Stage 2: Intermediate

When, after ten to twenty hours of practice, you have got the "idea of the movement," you are no longer a novice. You are, however, still far from competence. You are still slow and self-conscious. Fitts and Posner call this second stage "intermediate or associative." You are now like the skier who is able to get down most slopes with linked turns, some without stemming, but who is still far from grace. At the intermediate stage, as one researcher put it, "Merely having the right idea of what is required no longer suffices as evidence of learning."

Though your performance is marginal, you now have a repertory of well-learned rules. These rules are like short skis, which are easy to turn but aren't long enough to let you feel your edges bite or slide in snow of different textures. Similarly, verbal rules slow you down and get in the way of better technique.

When you reach this stage, it is time to trade in your "short skis" on better sensorimotor equipment: feedback. The concept of feedback is over twenty-five hundred years old, but the term itself was first used in the 1930s by electrical engineers. Norbert Wiener, a pioneer in the study of control systems, defined feedback as information about the difference between a pattern of action desired and the pattern actually attained.

In typing, skiing, driving, and athletic performance, feedback in its various forms is generally considered the most critical element in skill acquisition. Beginning drivers, for example, don't use feedback much—they pay attention to the speedometer and shift at predetermined speeds. With practice, however, they learn to shift on the basis of the effects of their actions on the car, by the sound and vibrations of the engine.

Feedback can be positive or negative. Positive feedback occurs when the information that is fed back produces a change away from the desired condition, as when frustration at making errors upsets you so much that you make more errors. Positive feedback often results in a vicious circle in which a system goes out of control. This use of positive feedback should not be confused with feedback about positive results. Clearly positive feedback is not ordinarily desirable in any control system, including the one we use to type, ski, or drive. Feedback about success, on the other hand, is valuable, especially at early stages of learning.

Negative feedback occurs when the difference between a pattern of action and that desired produces a change toward the desired condition, as when you compensate for excessive speed by letting up on the accelerator. Thus, whether feedback is positive or negative is a property not of the feedback itself but of the system in which it operates.

Feedback can be intrinsic or extrinsic. Intrinsic feedback arises directly from a movement and its consequences. Both the feeling that you've hit the right typewriter key and the appearance of the desired letter on the paper provide intrinsic feedback, while praise or other rewards (administered by yourself or your coach) provide extrinsic, or "augmented," feedback. Intrinsic feedback is in general more effective than extrinsic, because it is available immediately. But either kind of feedback must be delivered before the learner moves on to the next action; especially in continuous performances like typing and skiing, extrinsic feedback in the middle of the performance often disrupts the smooth flow of movement. Consequently, one text on motor learning advises teachers to use extrinsic feedback only to call attention to intrinsic feedback the student may be ignoring. If used properly, however, extrinsic feedback can be a valuable aid to learning. Not only does it provide a sense of progress, but it can inform you about conditions, like time of day, when you do well or poorly.

Feedback that tells you how you're doing, step by step or day by day, is called knowledge of results (KR). KR can be intrinsic, as when you glance at the page to see the results of your typing, or it can be extrinsic, as when a ski instructor tells you that you are keeping your weight too far back on your skis, or suggests that you look at the tracks you made in the snow. KR can consist of intrinsic visual feedback, as when you see your finger hit the right key (or the wrong one). It also includes tactile, or touch, feedback: the feeling of your finger hitting the key.

Particularly in early stages, intrinsic KR is the most powerful and influential force on the development of a skill. Without it, no learning ever occurs: Imagine typing blindfolded, so that you never knew the results of your performance! Results not only provide information needed to control subsequent movements but, when a movement is performed correctly, also function as rewards.

There are several other ways to increase the efficacy of KR. First of all, KR should be prompt, obtained within one or two seconds at most. KR should also be specific and detailed. If intrinsic, information about the direction and magnitude of the error is extremely useful: When you type *e* for *r,* it helps to know that you were using the correct finger, but that you moved it one space too far to the left. It is easy to get overloaded with extrinsic KR: Both typing and ski instructors tend to provide their students with far more information than they can use. Information overload can be disruptive: You can no more learn to type by checking every letter than you can learn to ski by reviewing every turn. KR works best if you get it intermittently, at a rate that feels right.

By this point in stage 2, you can probably detect many errors by "feel" as you make them, without checking. This feel is the result of proprioceptive feedback about your movements, and now you move from knowledge of results to knowledge of performance (KP), feedback about the form of a movement, as opposed to feedback about its effects (KR). KP tells you how you are doing even before you see the results. An expert shooter, for example, can say whether a shot is high or low, right or left, immediately after squeezing the trigger.

Development of competence in any sensorimotor skill is largely a movement from visual KR to proprioceptive KP. According to Paul Fitts: "As performance becomes habitual, . . . it is likely that such proprioceptive feedback or 'feel' becomes the more important." In later stages of a skill in which, for example, most letters are being typed correctly, or most turns are linked, knowledge of performance is much more important than knowledge of results. Experienced pilots do fly "by the seat of their pants."

There are several reasons why this should be so. First of all, as any skill develops, error rates drop, so you have little to learn by actually watching what you are doing. Second, since the reaction time to a proprioceptive stimulus is just over half the reaction time to a visual stimulus, proprioceptive feedback can be processed much faster than visual information. It is thus possible to move too fast for the visual system to control the movement. At high rates of speed, one must therefore rely on proprioceptive feedback.

Thus, as sensorimotor skills grow more specialized, they move from explicit verbal to tacit proprioceptive knowledge, from knowing that to knowing how. Early in the development of a skill, we can rehearse verbal rules we have learned from our coach: "shift at twenty," "return fingers 'home,'" "use rudder and aileron together." Later, the specialized knowledge is tacit: Few people can express as words the fine points of expert performance. Words are too slow, one-dimensional, linear, and abstract to capture the instant multidimensional cyclic feels that occur as a driver adjusts the line through a turn with the throttle in complete control even at the edge of a skid.

The more you can attend to proprioceptive KP and ignore visual KR, the faster you will learn. Positive approaches to sensitizing you to proprioceptive information are more effective than negative ones designed to break a bad habit.

Speed enhances the shift from visual to proprioceptive feedback. Laboratory experiments show that faster movements are easier to feel than slower ones. Similarly, intermediate skiers find that feeling the snow gets easier when they go faster; forces that are barely detectable at slow speeds become easier to feel at speed. Speed also breaks the "training wheels" habit of saying to yourself what you will do next. If you move fast enough, your body automatically takes over, which in turn makes it easier to go faster. Skiers who press their limits by skiing at higher speeds and on steeper slopes can then return to easier runs with greater grace.

Timothy Gallwey describes the transition from self-conscious, verbal, linear control to automatic, kinesthetic, parallel cooperation in *Inner Skiing* and *The Inner Game of Tennis*. Gallwey describes two selves, one analytic and verbal, the other holistic and intuitive. The verbal self should be allowed to take over at early stages and in times of difficulty, but the rest of the time, the intuitive proprioceptive self should take over.

Gallwey is one of several influential advocates of "mental rehearsal" or "previsualization" as a way of enhancing motor learning. Because feedback is so central in stage 2, the absence of feedback, particularly feedback about errors, is the major limitation of mental rehearsal and other learning techniques based on visualization rather than actual practice. Not only is it nearly impossible for most people to call up kinesthetic imagery, but in mental practice we never catch an edge.

Sometimes feedback isn't enough. In such cases, you have to trick your body with extra input, or as R. J. Mulheim the mechanic puts it, "train your body like a dog, no words, just show it what to do physically." In skiing, instructors do this with instructions like "steer with your knees." In typing, it sometimes helps to have a tactile "crutch." My keyboard, for example, has little pimples on the *d* and *k* keys that help me find home.

In his deeply reflective *Ways of the Hand*, Sudnow eloquently describes the shift from visual to proprioceptive feedback in learning to improvise on the piano: "Looking's workload progressively lightens for finding distances, the gaze at the keyboard progressively diffuses in function. . . . As I reached for chords . . . I was gaining a sense of their location by going to them, experiencing a rate of movement and distance required at various tempos, and developing, thereby, an embodied way of accomplishing distances."

Stage 3: Competence

Fitts and Posner call the competence stage "autonomous," because habits develop a life of their own as they become "less directly subject to cognitive control, and less subject to interference from other ongoing activities or environmental distractions." Even complex movements begin to resemble reflexes: they "run off without much verbalization or conscious content."

Autonomous performance is not simply intermediate performance speeded up. It is a general principle of motor learning, acknowledged since the first quarter of this century, that the swift, smooth movements of competent performance are qualitatively different from the slow, jerky performance of the intermediate stage. The speed and smoothness of stage 3 typing or skiing are signs that a profound reorganization has taken place. Psychologists disagree about their relative importance, but one or more of the following processes are certainly involved:

Overlapping. Overlapping, or "parallel processing," is doing two things at once. Using video recordings, Donald Gentner and Donald Norman of the Cognitive Science Laboratory at the University of California at San Diego found that advanced typists automatically prepare to strike later keys even as they hit earlier ones. For example, when an expert types the common sequence "ion," the right index finger is well on its way to the *n* before the ring finger strikes the *o*.

Feedforward. Whenever you move your head, your eyes automatically compensate for the movement, keeping your eyes aimed properly. You can gain some sense of this automatic correction by interfering with it. By spinning around with your eyes closed, as you may have done when you were a child, you disrupt the vestibular organ that sends the corrective signal. Though children often enjoy the resulting disruption of eye movements (called nystagmus) when they create it themselves, they find it distressing, as adults do, when it is caused by the motion of cars, boats, and airplanes. Ordinarily the compensatory motions are directed by "feedforward," a presetting of the eyes on the basis of the anticipated results of the changes in head (or body) position.

Feedforward explains why drivers don't get carsick: Since they actively produce the changes in speed and direction, they can feed forward information about these anticipated changes in speed or direction to their own eyes. Passengers, on the other hand, can only react passively. During my graduate-student days, when my research required me to spend many hours in light planes, I found a practical application of this principle. When I became unbearably airsick I would take the controls. Five or ten minutes of feedforward generally produced a (partial and temporary) remission of my nystagmus-induced nausea.

Feedforward becomes important only when movements are fast and well-practiced, when an "internal model" of performance has been built into the brain. Thus, some theorists describe later stages of motor learning as a shift from feedback to feedforward. Thanks to feedforward, when well-practiced responses occur too fast for feedback, one need not wait for feedback before initiating the next response.

David Sudnow describes how feedforward makes possible prediction and consequent smooth performance in playing a video game:

> At first it felt like my eyes told my fingers where to go. But in time I knew the smooth rotating hand motions were assisting the look in turn, eyes and fingers in a two way partnership. Walking a rainy street, you identify the dimensions of a puddle in relation to the size and rate of your gait, so the stride itself patterns your style of looking. So too with sight reading music at the piano for instance, where you never look ahead of what you can grasp and your hands' own sense of location therefore instructs the gaze where to regard the score. So too again with typing from a text, where if your eyes move in front of where your fingers are, you'll likely make an error, and thus hands and gaze maintain a delicate rhythmic alignment.

Chaining. Another kind of reorganization is chaining, a process in which each action becomes the cue for the next. Thus, in typing the word "the," the cue for the *h* becomes, not seeing the *h* in the text to be copied or "hearing" it in the text being composed in one's mind, but the proprioceptive feedback from typing the *t*. Since much of this feedback is unconscious, it feels as if the word is being typed as a unit, which, psychologically, it is. The key to chaining is what psychologists call "contiguity": the movements must be near each other in time.

Robert Gagné, an expert on applying the laws of learning to instruction, states that effective chaining occurs when each individual response is well learned, when the intervals between elements are short, when performance of the chain is repeated, and when reinforcement is present at the end of the chain. When driving and ski instructors talk about "rhythm," they refer to the natural rhythms of chaining, not an artificial, metronome-like beat.

Chunking. Chunking is an automatic process of grouping stimuli into perceived units, like the words in this sentence—you don't have to sound them out, because you know them as wholes.

Motor Programs. They operate on output rather than input. You have motor programs for pronouncing familiar words, tying knots, and flipping light switches. In every case, there is a complex automatic sequence of motions that you can execute as a unit. In typing, there are motor programs not only for letters and common combinations, but for operations such as doubling and alternation. Motor programs are often described as "hardwired"; robot-like, they run as units.

David Sudnow describes the intimate clasp of motor program and chunking in learning to play the piano as follows: "As my hands began to form constellations, the scope of my looking correspondingly grasped the chord as a whole, a consistency developed in seeing not its note-for-noteness, but the pattern of its location as a configuration emerging out of the broader visual field of the terrain."

Motor Schemes. Although many motor programs are "hardwired" in early life, and thereafter run as units, some are more flexible and take new information into account. A flexible motor program is a kind of scheme (see Chapter 2) called a TOTE unit (an acronym for Test-Operate-Test-Exit). We can often experience TOTE units in the early stages of learning a skill. As a graduate student, I learned the art of aerial radio tracking, which requires directing a light plane toward a signal from a radio collar worn by an animal (in this case, a wolf). A series of TOTEs began with a test: I compared the strength of the radio signal on each of two directional antennas mounted under the wings of the aircraft. Then I operated by turning the plane in the direction of the stronger signal in an attempt to equalize the strength of the signal on the two antennas. I repeated the test, and if necessary (it always was), performed another turning operation. When the signals were equal, the plane was headed straight toward the animal and I would exit from this unit. Similar TOTEs can be observed as novice pilots and sailors learn to direct their craft on a straight course: Tests of direction alternate with operations that apply negative feedback to correct (or overcorrect) the course, which is then again tested.

In well-practiced actions, TOTE units ordinarily operate unconsciously. We are unaware of the negative feedback and other complex processes involved. Only when we are learning a new skill do we experience TOTE units in the process of becoming automatic.

Hierarchical Organization. Motor programs are organized hierarchically. You have a larger motor program that controls subordinate motor programs.

Automation. The key to progress in the autonomous stage is mainly a matter of making overlapping, chunking, motor programs, and TOTEs automatic. David Sudnow describes what this feels like when one becomes competent at a video game: "You don't so much 'aim' the ball, it seems, as you must somehow allow yourself to let the aiming take place through a private and inaccessible mode of communication between your eye and your hand." A similar process occurs in shooting a shotgun—one learns the art of pointing automatically instead of aiming consciously.

Walter Schneider, a psychologist at the University of Illinois, has studied how simple tasks become automatic, or in the jargon of cognitive science, "hardwired." His work has several practical applications for the automating of typing, skiing, assembly, and other complex skills: consistency and correct execution; several shorter practice sessions instead of one long one; pushing for speed; avoiding distraction; keeping the context as constant as possible; maintaining optimum motivation by setting daily goals, recording your progress, and remembering benefits.

Training simulations are admirably suited to hardwiring skills that would otherwise require enormous expense and effort. For example, on complex tasks, spreading practice out over several short sessions (spaced practice) produces quicker improvements in performance than its opposite, massed practice. Many airplanes require an hour or more of preparation in the form of fueling, preflight checks, routine maintenance, so once one is airborne it makes sense to practice for a long time. Simulators can provide cost-effective spaced practice.

Conversely, however, for rapid automation of simple skills, massed practice is highly effective. Ralph Norman Haber, an expert in visual perception and flight simulation, points out that 95 percent of the time spent in real takeoff and landing practice is wasted on taxiing and circling. Flight simulators allow massed practice of takeoffs and landings in a fraction of the time needed for real ones.

Errors. Since so much processing at competent levels is automatic and unconscious, verbal explanation generally has little effect on advanced stages of complex performance like Nordic skiing or touch-typing. The exception to this rule is the analysis of errors.

So far, we've been concentrating on what's done right, and have not dealt with errors. This is a good policy—errors in early stages of any skill are unsystematic, so there's little to learn from examining them. Errors of competent performers, however, are systematic. Moreover, many are unconscious. When educational psychologist

Leonard West tested 100-word-per-minute typists' ability to detect errors by proprioception alone, half the errors went undetected. Since expert typists catch considerably more than half their errors, they must also be relying on considerable external feedback.

The best way to deal with errors goes against all our previous training. All our lives, we've learned that errors are awful. The wastebasket full of pages with one imperfect lead sentence, bargain prices on factory "seconds," and the crowded dockets of divorce courts are all symptoms of an attitude that we find in learning of all kinds, especially sensorimotor learning: If it's not perfect the first time, give up.

MIT professor Seymour Papert's "debugging philosophy" is an alternative to this destructive perfectionism. Papert regards errors, or "bugs," as an essential part of all learning. Drawing from experience with computer programs, which, like all complex enterprises, *never* work the first time, Papert describes a way to make the most of knowledge of negative results. In a discussion of learning to juggle and walk on stilts (which Papert uses as models for all learning, including mathematical), he writes, "Errors benefit us because they lead us to understand what went wrong, and through understanding, to fix it." Of course, not all errors are equally informative. Some are just plain frustrating: You *know* what's wrong; you just don't know how to fix it. Thus, Papert emphasizes what he calls "constructive bugs," those that can be learned from. Papert's approach is especially appropriate in working with simulations, where constructive bugs that would be risky in real life can be fostered. As Ralph Norman Haber points out, almost all losses in aerial combat occur within the first five missions. Thereafter, the survival rate is over 95 percent. For survivors, the bugs of real combat are constructive; simulation provides a way to make them constructive for pilots who would otherwise be shot down.

Stage 4: Proficiency

Even with diligent application of all the principles described above, expertise requires hundreds or even thousands of hours of practice. Nevertheless, many people do become proficient in one or more motor skills.

Expert typists can converse as they type. Similarly, expert ski racers' skis and expert drivers' cars are extensions of their bodies. Sometimes you can sense an expert's rapport with the medium: When Dolph Kuss skis, every type of terrain bestows its own kind of grace. On the level, he is Plastic Man: His arms and legs seem to bend in places other people's don't. They seem to lengthen as he reaches, stiffen as he pushes and kicks, and liquefy on the follow-through; his skis become skates. On steep downhill sections, he stands planted on his skis in a lithe, centered slouch. If he were any more relaxed he'd be asleep. He goes up hills as easily as he goes down them, and almost as fast. Like other expert skiers, Kuss talks about feeling the snow with the skis, and turning subtle irregularities to advantage. He feels with his skis the way blind people feel and echolocate with their canes. They are unaware of the cane as a sensory medium in the same way we are unaware of the operation of our eyes: We simply see what's out there; they simply feel and hear what's out there. Expert drivers who feel with their wheels, and expert biotechnicians who feel with micromanipulators, report a similar fading from awareness of prosthetic sensors.

But how can this be? Skis don't have sense organs, and yet feeling the snow, the road, and the chip are not metaphors. There are three solutions to this puzzle of sensory extension.

The first solution is that experts see situations in their areas of expertise in a special way. They have a kind of "gestalt" perception that allows them to size up a complex situation as a whole, ignore irrelevant information, relate it to similar situations experienced in the past, and thereby allocate perceptual resources, both conscious and un-, to the features that really matter.

Gestalt-based sensitivity to relevant information allows automatic processing. Expert drivers, for example, have gestalts that let them distinguish impending spins from controlled drifts. Similarly, expert hunters detect game invisible to others, not because of greater acuity, but because they have a gestalt for hillsides without game.

David Sudnow alluded to the second solution when he described how the expert pianist's gaze "diffuses." Experts use what psychologists call the "second visual system," an unconscious movement-and-location processing system that operates at the periphery of vision and is ordinarily in the background. When, while driving, you swerve to avoid an object before you have identified it, your action was informed by this second visual system. A safer way to experience the second visual system in operation is to have someone toss you something when you least expect it. By tossing an apple core to an unsuspecting subject you can demonstrate that this system works unconsciously: Chances are, your unfortunate victim will catch it, then view it with disgust.

When you drive or ski too fast to let your first (pattern-recognizing) visual system work, you are forcing yourself to use your second. Since the second visual system is especially sensitive to movement and location of objects at the periphery of vision (which we usually ignore), you can often enhance speed and automation by looking away from a target you need to deal with quickly. For example, in learning to ski downhill over irregular terrain, you are better off looking downhill, allowing your second visual system to process the bumps under your skis. The unfocused gaze of the expert typist composing at the keyboard suggests that the second visual system may be at work there too.

A third solution to the puzzle of sensory extension lies in what Sir Charles Sherrington, the great British neuroscientist, called a "muscle sense." I learned about this sense in a conversation with Guy Goodwin, a British neurologist who describes himself as working in the tradition of Sherrington. That is, like Sherrington, he maintains that feedback from sense organs is essential to the control of movement. Over ale at a pub in Oxford, he explained the muscle sense in terms of our ability to lift our tankards smoothly to our lips regardless of how full they were and how tired our arms got. The muscle sense provides information about the action of muscles themselves: their work load. It doesn't sense the weight of the tankard as such, or the movement and position of our limbs, but is instead aware of muscle stretch and contraction. We might therefore be justified in calling it a *seventh* sense, but neuroscientists consider it only another form of proprioception.

As a skeptical psychologist, I immediately subjected Goodwin's proposition about our tankard-handling ability to an empirical test. Goodwin meanwhile went on to describe experiments in which he studied the muscle sense by isolating it. He would inflate a blood pressure cuff on a subject's wrist, making one hand numb. With the uncuffed hand, subjects could mimic finger extensions of the numb one. Since the cuff (and a shield) eliminated both visual information about starting position and proprioceptive feedback from the fingers, Goodwin's subjects were presumably using feedback from muscles controlling fingers, which are in the forearm and hence were unaffected by the cuff.

To me, this experiment resembles sensory extension: Just as the muscle sense in your forearms tells you about movements of fingers deprived of proprioception, so the muscle sense in your ankles can tell you about the movements of your equally senseless skis. And so the muscle sense of your fingers can tell you about the movements of your proprioceptionless wheels.

One practical implication of sensory extension is that with practice, people with prosthetic limbs ought to be able to develop the same sort of "feel" that blind people, expert drivers, and proficient skiers have. In the case of "road feel," there are several mechanical links between the driver and the road, so there is in principle no reason why remotely operated devices like robots used for underwater and space exploration could not generate the same sense of being in touch with the materials worked with.

Computerized training simulations often yield a kind of "feel," similar enough to the real feel to sensitize the learner. As a result of this phenomenon, combined with the advantages mentioned above, learning rates with simulators are in general higher than with real practice.

David Sudnow describes the present state of computer art in words that create visions of the potential of computerized prostheses and simulations:

> Now the computer. Our organically perfect tool. Seated upright on behinds just made for that, our hands dangle near the lap at their most relaxed point of balance, while these fingers, capable of such marvelous interdigitation, have a territory for action whose potentials and richness are electronically enhanced beyond the wildest dream.... [In this] word piano ... biotechnical handicraft takes a giant leap forward. The full sequencing, calibrating, caressing potentials of human hands now create sights, sounds, and movements. And the eyes are free to watch, wonder, and direct from above, free to witness the spectacle and help the hands along without looking down.... All the customary boundaries get blurred when you're painting paragraphs, performing etchings, sketching movies, and graphing music.

7.
Spatial Intelligences

We should talk less and draw more.
                    —GOETHE

Nikola Tesla, the "Edison of Colorado Springs," invented, among other things, the fluorescent light, the AC generator, and the high-voltage coil that sparks most automobiles. Tesla claimed that he created his inventions by imagining pictures "more vivid than any blueprint . . . complete in every detail, of every part of the machine." He could, for example, not only visualize a magnetic field but imagine it rotating on its own axis. Vivid as they were, the images that inspired such inventions were less remarkable than those that tested them. According to his biographer, Tesla tested his creations in his imagination, "by having them run for weeks—after which time he would examine them thoroughly for signs of wear."

Tesla's feats of imagination are examples of spatial intelligence at work. Spatial intelligence (SPI) is the ability to get, process, and use information about shapes, sizes, distances, and geometrical relationships. It's what you use when you try to imagine whether you could fit your desk into your car, when you plan a detour around a traffic jam or mentally rearrange your living room furniture.

Many people report that when they solve problems of this sort, they "look at" and "zoom in on," "rotate" or "walk around in," some sort of mental pictures. Others, however, think in words, not in pictures, and cannot imagine what these images are like. We differ so much in our ability to create images that some psychologists call people like Tesla "visualizers," and people like me, who rely more heavily on words, "verbalizers." This chapter shows how spatial intelligence works, how it relates to other intelligences, and how it can work for you. Even if you are a verbalizer like me and think you can't imagine your way out of a new neighborhood, you may have untapped resources of spatial intelligence that you are unaware of. In any case, as in earlier chapters, I provide some suggestions for enhancing your spatial skills.

SPATIAL INTELLIGENCE AT WORK

In Science and Technology

Michael Faraday, who discovered the laws of electromagnetic induction that Tesla applied, also relied on an extraordinary spatial imagination. Faraday imagined magnetic fields as narrow curving tubes that "rose up before him like things." Faraday's theoretical heir, the physicist James Clerk Maxwell, also had a "mental picture of every problem." Though Maxwell's equations that describe the electromagnetic field are models of abstract simplicity, his and other early theories of electromagnetism were so full of imaginary pipes, pulleys, and strings that one commentator peckishly wrote: "We thought we were entering the tranquil and neatly ordered abode of reason, but we find ourselves in a factory."

The climax of the story of spatial intelligence in electromagnetic theory is Einstein's famous thought experiment in which he imagined himself traveling alongside a beam of light at the same speed. Einstein believed that his "particular ability" was not so much mathematical abstraction as visualizing: His "elements of thought" were "more or less clear images which can be voluntarily produced or combined."

The tradition of Faraday, Maxwell, Tesla, and Einstein continues today as physicists explore the abstractions of quantum electrodynamics with the concrete support of Richard Feynman's space-time diagrams.

There are similar stories about spatial intelligence in chemistry: Kekule's image of a snake biting its tail, which led him to deduce the ring structure of benzene, and Watson and Crick's double-helix model for DNA. Images like Kekule's are so common in the creative thinking of scientists that one psychologist wrote: "in the case of every historic scientific discovery which was researched carefully enough, we find that it was imagery, either in dreams or in a waking state, which produced the breakthrough."

Anne Roe, who studied scientists in various fields, found that biologists and physicists tend to think visually, whereas social scientists think in words. Similarly, most of the great mathematicians surveyed by Jacques Hadamard in the 1940s relied on spatial imagery.

In his *Visual Thinking,* Rudolph Arnheim, professor of psychology of art at Harvard and the University of Michigan, shows in detail how spatial intelligence helps us understand the world. "Visual thinking calls, more broadly, for the ability to see visual shapes as images of the patterns of forces that underlie our existence—the functioning of minds, of bodies or machines, the structure of societies and ideas."

From the wheel and the lever of prehistory to the Dymaxion car and geodesic dome of Buckminster Fuller, spatial intelligence has been a powerful force, not only in understanding the world but also in changing it. Arnheim's Harvard colleagues David Perkins and Howard Gardner have argued that spatial intelligence is at the core of creativity, especially in "metaphorical thinking," the ability to translate a situation into a different medium. Donald Schön, in *The Reflective Practitioner,* describes an example of metaphorical creativity performed by product developers who were trying to cure the "gloppy" performance of a paintbrush. One of the researchers noted that a paintbrush is a kind of pump. The "pumpoid" metaphor led to an analysis of the "pumping" action of the bristles, and ultimately to a brush that applied paint more smoothly.

Space as Raw Material

Spatial intelligence is not the exclusive property of creative geniuses, scientists, and inventors. It is a valuable tool for people in several everyday occupations.

J. L. "Mutt" Foutz, the energy magnate whom we met in Chapter 5, relates a more down-to-earth application of spatial intelligence. Early in his career in the gas pipeline business, Mutt bid on a pipeline over Douglas Pass, between Rangely and Grand Junction, Colorado. Today, Douglas Pass has a paved road, but it is still a challenge to get a long truck over it. Conventional wisdom had it that the only way to haul the pipe was around the mountains rather than over the pass. "Those other companies, they looked at that road and said 'no way.' I knew I could have low bid if I could get the pipe over that hill. That would mean hauling twenty-five miles instead of one hundred. I studied that road. I spent a day walking up and down it, imagining how much I'd have to widen the turns. By the end of the day I knew I could get pipe trucks over the pass. My bid was $200,000 under the next lowest. It took me one day with a D-6 [bulldozer] to widen those turns."

Space and objects that occupy space are raw materials for surgeons, dentists, cabdrivers, military strategists, and many others. Because the spatial problems pilots solve are so complex and the consequences of miscalculation so drastic, there has been more research on spatial skills of pilots than in any other field. Pilots navigate using charts, compass and radio bearings, and topographic features. They verify that they have found their destinations by matching the configurations of the runways on charts with the ones they see (typically from a different angle) below. Indeed, a study of the psychological factors promoting effective performance showed that three spatial abilities were essential: interpreting spatial characteristics (shape, size, distance) of stimuli; rapid comparison of visual forms, with attention to similarities and differences; and mental manipulations of visual images.

Mechanic R. J. Mulheim is an expert at all three of those skills. R.J. thinks of himself as an artist as well as a technician. "With machines like this," he said as he filed a new latch for the hood of a venerable but concours 1958 Austin-Healey, "I feel more like Alexander Calder than Mr. Goodwrench."

R.J.'s style is nondirective: He would much rather teach his clients to solve their own problems than handle them himself. As a result, I often attempt simple repairs on my own, and when they fail, I have the opportunity to contrast my spatial and manual skills with his. My most recent failure involved my attempt to set the ignition timing on my car by a standard method: advancing the spark until the engine knocks, then retarding slightly. In order to do this, I had to imagine the rotor spinning around inside my distributor, sending high voltage (from a Tesla-type coil) to each plug lead in turn, then figure out which way to twist the distributor to get each spark sent a little sooner. I stared at my distributor, figured it out, and every day for a week adjusted the timing before leaving for work. At the end of the week, I had used up all the adjustments and my car would barely make it up the hill in front of my office. I stopped at R.J.'s garage on the way home. R.J. popped the hood, examined the firing order, squinted at the timing mark, and gave the distributor a quick tweak. The motor's stumbling idle became a smooth purr.

Fortunately, R.J.'s spatial skill also allows him to explain what he's doing. He drew me a quick sketch that showed I had been moving the distributor in the wrong direction. Smirking, he said, "Hey, Doc, at least it wasn't knocking." I had spent a total of almost an hour on my daily adjustments, including twenty minutes figuring out which direction advanced the spark. In less than a minute, R.J. not only showed me what I'd been doing wrong but timed my car so well that I squealed the tires as I left.

This episode shows what can happen when a verbalizer and a visualizer tackle the same spatial problem. It also shows how effectively a drawing conveys spatial information, when the one doing the drawing has a clear image in mind.

The effectiveness of his sketch suggests that R.J.'s juxtaposition of art and practice is no coincidence. Indeed, as you will see, people high in spatial intelligence frequently excel in both artistic and more conventionally practical activities.

In Design

The artistic and the practical applications of spatial intelligence converge in architecture, urban design, engineering, and other professions that shape our physical environment. A cover article in a recent issue of the exclusive journal *Science* points out that "Pyramids, cathedrals, and rockets exist . . . because they were first a picture—literally a vision—in the minds of those who built them." A recent article in *Advertising Age* reminds us that these visions matter in the marketplace: A survey of prospective automobile buyers showed that styling is still the major factor in choosing a car.

The need for training in visual thinking has begun to penetrate schools of engineering. A few teachers of engineering, like Stanford's Robert McKim, now emulate their colleagues in schools of architecture, who have always taught visual thinking. MIT professor of urban studies Donald Schön presents a rare glimpse of visual thinking and teaching in action in an architectural design studio, as a teacher and a student create a grade school that exploits a site with an unusual slope. Urban planners not only use the spatial skills of the engineer and the architect but are learning to take users' conceptions of built environments into account in order to design parks, plazas, and routes that make sense to those who use them as well as to those who design them.

Spatial intelligence works not only in the judgments that result in "hard" artifacts like cars, roads, and buildings but in clear, coherent, and powerful advertisements and logos that promote them. IBM's Chaplinesque tramp, Merrill Lynch's roaming bull, and Sinclair's dinosaur work because they are "right" in some way that words can't say. Similarly, trademarks and logos, like the three-pointed Mercedes star, often outweigh verbal messages. Rudolph Arnheim describes how the Chase Manhattan square-in-octagon conveys exactly what the emblem of a bank ought to convey. Arnheim is describing the Chase Manhattan trademark, but he could be describing the ideal of the bank itself:

> Closed like a fortress against interference and untouched by the changes and vicissitudes of time, the little monument is built of

sturdy blocks defined by straight parallel edges and simple angles. At the same time, it has the necessary vitality and goal directedness. The pointed units contribute dynamic forces which . . . compensate each other to an overall enlivened stillness or add up to the steady, contained rotation of a motor. Furthermore, the four components are tightly fitted to the whole, but at the same time preserve an integrity of their own, thus showing multiplicity of initiative. . . . The delicate balance between adjoining each other and interacting with each other by cooperative clasp further illustrates the nature of the internal organization.

In Business, Teaching, and Psychotherapy

Even in occupations where the raw materials are not spatial, a picture is worth much more than a thousand words. Graphic representations are incredibly efficient ways of storing, using, and communicating information. Successful managers, lawyers, doctors, and other practical-problem solvers routinely use flowcharts, bar graphs, critical paths, and other visual aids. Such spatial representations are absolutely essential to comprehension of complex situations where relations among many factors must be considered simultaneously. The commercial success of business software that uses graphic displays to control and communicate the output of word processors, spreadsheets, and data bases testifies to the practical importance of dealing deftly with spatial information. And when it comes to hardware, at least one successful personal computer owes its success to an iconic "user interface" that allows novices to use spatial as well as verbal and logical intelligences to communicate with their machines. A hint of the future of such devices is a product developed by the Garret AiResearch Company for NASA, which picks up the electrical signals that control eye movements and sketches the shapes they trace. When a man with a good visual imagination traced the outlines of an imagined car with his eyes, the machine produced a recognizable drawing.

Such a machine would be a valuable visual aid for teachers and other who use "chalk talk" to explain both spatial and more abstract concepts. It is ironic that although most primary and secondary school teachers receive training in the use of videotapes, overhead projectors, and other gizmos, no teacher training program includes instruction in the oldest and simplest visual aid of all: drawing.

Many practitioners of cognitive, psychoanalytic, and so-called humanistic psychotherapy use imagery in diagnosis and treatment of anxiety, depression, and other disorders of behavior, thought, and feeling. The "psychosynthesis" approach of Roberto Assagioli, for example, includes such exercises as the "dissolution of the body," in which one imagines one's body being consumed by flames, a fantasy that reportedly results in a sense of transcendence based on an awareness of the independence of the spirit from the body. Cognitive and behaviorally oriented therapists often use "systematic desensitization" to treat phobias: The therapist lists a series of scenes that progressively resemble the feared stimulus. If, for example, the client has a troublesome fear of snakes, the list might go: toy dinosaur, soft fuzzy plush snake, picture of dead baby snake, picture of live baby snake, etc. After conjuring up each image, one performs relaxation exercises until that image can be held without fear. Then one moves on to the next image. Eugene Gendlin of the University of Chicago encourages his clients (and readers of his book *Focusing*) to use "experiential focusing" to experience the full range and depth of their feelings about a person or situation. Gendlin says that such focusing in itself often leads to a "characteristic release" from previously unacknowledged emotional consequences.

In Everyday Life

Applications of spatial intelligence are ubiquitous in everyday life. To mention one banal but nontrivial problem of spatial memory, a recent study by Accountemps, a personnel firm, concluded that executives waste about four weeks a year, or about 7 percent of total work time, because they or their subordinates cannot find things. Almost everybody who works in a metropolitan area must solve the spatial problems posed by street crime, traffic jams, car pooling, rendezvous arranging, and errand running. This last task poses the problem of determining the shortest path through several points, which also concerns designers of transportation systems and sales routes. As soon as the number of points in such a route exceeds about ten, the problem of determining the optimal path taxes even the indefatigable intelligence of a medium-sized computer.

Besides such overt applications of SPI, covert applications abound. Many people solve problems that seem abstract by constructing spatial models. For example, in learning to operate devices like programmable microwaves or telephone answering machines, it is helpful to have in mind a "mental model" of how they work. (In Chapter 7, I describe how spatial intelligence in the form of such mental models plays a major role in everyday reasoning.)

Thus, even those of us who do not handle the spatial tasks of inventors, scientists, mechanics, engineers, architects, planners, designers, pilots, and psychotherapists use spatial intelligence to some degree.

Wayfinding in Natural Environments

Though spatial intelligence is important in the artificial environments of the office, classroom, and streets, it is at a premium in natural environments, which provide no verbal guides to wayfinding. To take an extreme case, the navigators of Puluwat Island in the South Pacific regularly sail to islands, some less than a mile across, over four hundred miles away in canoes twenty-five feet long and three feet wide, without motors, charts, or other aids to navigation (recently, some Puluwatans have begun to use magnetic compasses). Even those who carry a compass as a backup navigate by a "star course," a memorized list of points along the horizon marked by the rising and setting of certain stars. By sailing toward a star (or its position as inferred by the "shape of the sky") until it sets or gets too high, then toward another, and another, Puluwat navigators steer a series of courses that take them to their destination. Once the boat is within a few tens of miles of the objective, such clues as birds, cloud color, and "the loom of the land," a shimmering column of light reflected from sand and surf, allow them to approach to within ten miles, whence most islands are visible.

The Puluwatans rely heavily on spatial intelligence because of the relative featurelessness of the sea, but mineral and timber explorers; forest rangers; wildlife, botanical, and geological field researchers; and others who work in unmarked terrestrial environments depend on SPI too.

The Arctic equivalent of the Puluwatan navigators are the Avilik Eskimos described by Edmund Carpenter in his sensitive and moving portrayal of work and art in the far north, *Eskimo Realities.* Carpenter juxtaposes two maps drawn by Avilik men with a modern map constructed years later from aerial photographs. There are distortions in the Avilik maps, particularly in the exaggerated size of the peninsula that was their favorite hunting ground. Nevertheless, especially in the contours of the coast, the overwhelming impression is how accurate the Eskimo maps are. Carpenter echoes the student of visual memory who remarked on Eskimos' "extraordinary ability to find their ways through what appears to be a featureless terrain by remembering visual configuration." Carpenter identified these configurations as "relationships between, say, contour, type of snow, wind, salt air, ice crack. . . . two hunters casually followed a trail which I simply could not see, even when I bent close to scrutinize it; they did not kneel to examine it, but stood back, examining it at a distance." In the same vein, anthropologist Richard Nelson wrote: "I found that Eskimos in North Alaska, for example, would point out 'hills' in what looked like perfectly flat tundra."

The same spatial intelligence that makes Eskimos expert wayfinders makes them excellent mechanics. Carpenter writes:

> Avilik men . . . delight in stripping down and reassembling engines, watches, all machinery. I have watched them repair instruments which American mechanics, flown to the arctic for this purpose, have abandoned in despair. One day I was asked by a missionary to look at a complex machine of his that had stopped working. . . . I realized at a glance that it was too intricate for me to repair or even to understand. As I hesitated, an Avilik, who had been watching, slipped his hand under my arm, made a few quick adjustments, and it was fixed.

Carpenter claims that such mechanical aptitude is a product of dexterity and three spatial abilities.

The first spatial ability is perception and description of spatial relationships with the aid of a language with cases that treat space the way the tenses of English treat time.

The second is acute observation of details.

The third spatial ability is a dynamic conception of space as a process, direction, or operation. Eskimos can, for example, mentally rotate objects with great ease. Carpenter writes: "They carve a number of figures, each oriented . . . in a different direction, without moving the tusk. Similarly, when handed a photograph, they examine it as it is handed to them, no matter how it is oriented."

The spatial skills of the Avilik are rivaled by the professional fur trappers I studied in Minnesota and Colorado. These men regularly remembered the locations of hundreds of carefully concealed traps on lines many miles long and set over several months.

With Gun and Paintbrush

Because spatial intelligence is expressed so strongly in hunting and other work carried on in natural environments, as well as in art, I interviewed Barret Wynn, an extraordinarily successful hunting guide who is also gaining a reputation as a painter of wildlife. His two professions are both expressions of SPI.

Wynn has an uncanny ability to locate game. His clients pay handsomely for this ability: three thousand dollars and up for hunts that often last only a day. Working out of Santa Fe, New Mexico, Wynn shows his clients trophy deer, elk, and bighorn sheep in

Colorado and New Mexico, and Stone and Dall sheep in the Cassiar Mountains of northwest British Columbia. He has shown his paintings, for which he receives up to a thousand dollars, in Santa Fe, Jackson Hole, Scottsdale, and other habitats of connoisseurs of wildlife art. Unlike most painted animals, Wynn's look alive. I'm not sure why this animation is so rare, but it is. Perhaps artists who work from photographs and mounts tend to catch their subjects in random uncharacteristic poses, ones that animals only pass through, and never hold. In any case, I am tempted to attribute Wynn's lifelike creations to his experience with living creatures.

When I asked him to walk me through a successful search for big game, he began with his "homework" back in Santa Fe: reading about the animals and the country. Popular-magazine accounts are full of conflicting "facts" and "tips," but by "sortin' and siftin' " and talking to other guides and hunters, he built up a store of verbal information. Whenever he arrived in the field to set up his base camps and begin his own preliminary searches, he was able to draw on this fund of knowledge, to critically compare these articles and hunting stories to one another and to his own experiences. He opines that few other guides read so extensively. "They've been hunting all their lives," he said, "so they think they know more than any book. Well, I've been hunting all my life too, but I've got a lot to learn, and some of it'll be from books."

The first phase of a hunt is choosing a location to scan for game. Unlike most guides, who explore only just before (or during) a hunt, Wynn explores year-round in search of wildlife to paint. Because he actively scans terrain for feed, water, and sign as well as the game itself, he knows many more places to hunt than most other guides.

Being exposed to information is only the first phase of learning. The next phase is storing it in a way that will allow him to use it when he needs it. Painting provides the schemas that organize his spatial memories. It always takes several days of studio work to finish the paintings begun in the field, and these days reinforce his memories of the places he paints.

When it's time to plan a hunt, Wynn accesses this information with the aid of maps of large areas. Though their scale does not allow detailed planning, such maps do give the big picture: They show all the places he's been. Wynn pores over these maps, marking every possible place, including some that are far more attractive to painters than to hunters. The planning stage is where skill in getting the lay of the land and wayfinding come into play. One must learn not only where the game is likely to be but how to get there. Wynn plans his moves with the aid of highly schematic sketches of terrain. He illustrated one plan with a hastily scrawled map of the La Garita Mountains. When this oversimplified, rectilinear chart was done, it was hard to believe that it had been drawn by an artist. But it worked: I was able to understand how to get to where the sheep were.

The second stage of a hunt is scanning the chosen regions, attempting to find suitable prey. This is the most time-consuming and frustrating stage. "That's why they call it hunting," mutter frustrated hunters around the evening fire. People who don't hunt, and see game only at times and places when they cannot be hunted—in winter herds along roads or in national parks—do not realize how elusive game can be during hunting season. In most areas, the difficulty of finding game is compounded by regulations restricting hunting to mature males. And for Barret Wynn's hunters, a whole new dimension of difficulty is added: His clients want only the biggest, and hence oldest and smartest, males, the ones that will go into the record books.

Once the season opens, the decision to scan an area may involve substantial risk of a guide's most precious resource: time.

"Up in B.C., a dirt-bagger [geological surveyor who collects rock samples] told me about a band of old rams on top of a big mountain. The top was a big flat basin, like a skillet, and there was only one way up. I went up there with my dad and they were there all right, but it was so open and flat we couldn't get close enough for a shot. The next year, I set up a spike camp at the base of the mountain, which was around thirty-five hundred feet [in elevation]."

Barret and a client went up on a cloudy day and in the fog were able to approach close enough to get a "good-sized ram."

"What made you so sure the rams would be up there that you were willing to spend a whole day on sheep that might turn out to be inaccessible even if they were there?" I asked.

"I just knew they'd be there."

"But how? Something must have made you sure."

"O.K. Well, let me go back. I always hunt in places no one else goes. I prefer weird places, where no one would think to look for that kind of animal. So I know how animals are when they haven't been disturbed. And I could tell, when my dad and I were up there the year before, that no one had been screwing around with those sheep."

"How?"

"Well, for one thing, the high proportion of older rams—six out of eight were class four [eight years old or more, old for bighorn sheep]. And where they were . . . no one would hunt in that skillet because it's impossible to get a shot. And the way they acted . . . the ewes and lambs were more wary than the rams. I don't think they had ever heard a shot before."

Like many guides, Wynn is not reluctant to extend himself a liberal line of credit. He describes his success in scanning as "incredible." In his second year of guiding in the Cassiars, he claims, he showed his hunters more "big old rams than the guides who'd worked there all their lives." In response to a challenge to back up his braggadocio with some performance, Wynn took me into the mountains, where in a single day I saw more wildlife than I had in a month of daily fieldwork.

Wynn described several strategies he uses to perform such feats. "I always get as far away from where animals are as possible. That way, you can see more country, take your time, see where they go. With a good spotting scope, there's no need to be close enough for a shot. My clients are always saying, 'What'll you do if we do see something?' I just smile. The hard part is finding something in the first place. I worry about getting to them later. Sometimes I take the first day off and just ride around, looking for tracks. I can tell more about what the animals in an area are doing by sign than by watching the animals. This drives the hunters crazy, but it pays off. There was this lone ram over near Glenwood [New Mexico], on the Mogollon Rim—we called him 'Black Bart' because he was so dark. He lived in a deep dark canyon and the only way you'd ever see him was from the other side of the canyon, a four-hour drive from where you'd shoot. But we spotted him, saw where he bedded down, and went to where he was the next day. He was there all right, but my hunter missed him. He's still there."

Wynn separates scanning from later phases of the hunt. When he scans, he goes to places where scanning is best, and doesn't worry about stalking or getting a shot. Sometimes Wynn's separation of initial scanning from later phases of the hunt backfires, as when he and his father got to the skillet and saw sheep they could not shoot. In the long run, however, Wynn's strategy seems to be effective.

I asked Barret if he has any tricks for spotting game once he's in a place where animals are likely to be. He replied that game spotting is not so much seeing as imagination: visualizing what a deer would look like on that particular hill, hidden in that particular patch of oak brush with the light from that particular angle. He compared looking for animals to painting them. "It's like when there's an empty spot on the canvas and you know exactly what has to be there. I have it planned out. I know exactly how I want it to look."

Once suitable game has been spotted, the third phase of the hunt begins. The stalk may be a more or less direct approach using available cover, as in the skillet, or it may be circuitous, as in the four-hour drive to Black Bart. A stalk is seldom straightforward, and hunters often lose sight of their intended prey, and return to scanning. On such occasions, complex decisions are made under pressure. An example was a hunt in which Wynn's client was his wife, Pam.

"From camp we spotted three bull caribou on a steep slope four or five miles away. We saw 'em climbing, then they dropped out of sight into a basin. We went after 'em. It started to snow hard as hell, but this was Pam's first chance to get a really nice bull, so we kept going. We took a line that would intercept them, but when we got up to the basin, they had disappeared. . . . I knew which way they went, so we went after 'em."

"How did you know?"

"It's hard to say. I just know how to think like the animals I hunt."

"Tell me what you saw, what you were thinking, and what you decided to do."

"O.K. There was this steep cliff on the other side of the basin. They couldn't go that way. They couldn't have gone where we were coming from, so they either went left, climbing out of the basin, or right, dropping off the other side. I had a strong feeling that they went left."

"Why?"

"There wasn't any why. I just knew it."

"Well, what could it have been? More feed?"

"No. They eat lichen, and that was all over."

"Water?"

"That might have had something to do with it. It looked more like what they like. To the left there were a couple of little lakes—dwarf birch. [Long pause.] I've got it. It was that they had been climbing when we first saw them, and I figured they were getting up high to lie down where it's safe. Deer and elk do that. Caribou do that."

Thus, under cross-examination, Wynn's impulsive intuition about where the caribou went turns out to be an unconscious deduction based on verbal knowledge of animals' habits. Wynn's ability to put himself in the game animal's place is not simply the result of experience in hunting many different kinds of game. Many experienced hunters lack this ability. Rather, his spatial and verbal skills, when combined with a critical attitude, can create a kind of empathy for the animals he hunts.

WHAT SPATIAL INTELLIGENCE IS

Barret Wynn's intuitive grasp of how caribou move shows that spatial intelligences are, like social and body intelligences, intellectual abilities we share with nonhumans. Spatial problems are important in the ecology of wide-ranging species like caribou, and the human and other creatures, like wolves, who hunt them. Because our intelligence evolved to solve the sorts of spatial problems faced by wolves, my study of wolf spatial intelligence tells us a thing or two about our own spatial intelligence. For one thing, studies of nonhuman spatial thinking remind us that although we describe the operations of spatial intelligence in visual terms, spatial intelligence gets information through several other senses.

Wolves and other animals incorporate smell, sound, and touch into their spatial thinking, and so do we, when vision doesn't work. In fog or the dark, Eskimos find their way by using the smells and sounds of surf and the pressure of the wind. Urbanites, too, often solve spatial problems by touch, as when we feel our way down a dark corridor groping for a light switch, or tie knots without looking. Hearing also provides information about location and movement: foghorns, sirens, and train whistles. Recent experiments in Great Britain raise the intriguing possibility that humans navigate with the aid of yet another sense, magnetism, but the results are inconclusive. Thus, though much of our spatial intelligence is indeed visual, most psychologists use the general term "spatial" or "figural" to describe this form of intelligence.

Independence

We would not expect a form of intelligence that we share with other creatures to depend heavily on verbal or other abstract forms of thinking. Indeed, psychometricians have traditionally segregated spatial intelligence (and its cousin body intelligence) from verbal and mathematical intelligences. Any given person tends to do about the same on most of the abilities within one cluster, but may perform better or worse on tasks tapping the other. One investigator has even suggested that visual and verbal intelligences are opposed: People high in one may tend to be low in the other. Accordingly, British psychologist MacFarlane Smith, author of a standard text on spatial ability, suggests that candidates for programs in technical subjects be *penalized* if they get high verbal scores. Few others would go quite this far, but patterns of individual differences show that spatial abilities vary independently of other forms of intelligence.

Howard Gardner describes the extremes of this line of evidence in the form of spatial idiot savants, like a successful British painter with a subnormal IQ, or the autistic adolescent Nadia, who could draw scenes from memory with photographic detail but could not sort common objects into simple categories.

The hardest evidence about the independence of spatial intelligence comes from investigations of the aptitudes of patients who have suffered various forms of brain injury. The neurologist Kurt Goldstein described a patient who could throw balls into boxes at various distances but could not say which box was closest. Conversely, patients who have suffered damage to the right half of the brain show impaired visualization, rotation, and orientation without loss of verbal ability.

Psychometric, neurological, and other forms of evidence convince many (if not most) psychologists that there is something special about spatial thinking.

Varieties of Spatial Intelligence

Spatial information from several senses is processed in a variety of ways. Estimates of the number of more or less independent spatial abilities vary. Howard Gardner believes that spatial intelligence is a single "amalgam of abilities" that can be regarded as " 'of a piece.' " Lewis Thurstone divided spatial ability into three components. A recent review summarizing results of many previous studies also argues for three independent subabilities, roughly paralleling Thurstone's: visualization, relations, and orientation. Deferring to the mode among psychometricians, I discuss several different operations performed by spatial intelligence in terms of these three factors, without committing myself to a statement about how many fundamentally different subabilities are involved.

Visualization. Visualization is the ability to form and manipulate clear mental pictures. Pattern recognition is the simplest form of visualization. We are so good at recognizing patterns that psychologists are hard-pressed to find our limits. In one classic study, subjects were shown 2,560 slides of complex scenes. Recognition of repeats was 85 to 95 percent correct. Increasing the number of slides had so little effect that the investigator concluded, "The results would probably have been the same if we had used 25,000 pictures instead of 2500."

Even more amazing is our ability to respond to patterns that have been distorted. In the experiment just described, subjects' scores stayed high even when the slides were reversed, so that subjects saw mirror images. To take a real-world example, imagine yourself at your twentieth high school reunion. You could probably recognize many of your classmates even though most details of their faces had changed. What stays the same is the pattern, a family resemblance that's hard to specify in words or numbers. We take ability to recognize such variations on a theme for granted, but it is one of those tasks that are easy for people but extremely difficult for even the most powerful computer. The harder but more natural human task of detecting a distant and well-camouflaged animal, like a Stone sheep on a cliff, is all but impossible for computers. When we detect a concealed figure, our visualization is "seeing as" rather than simply seeing: The double-humped car roof in your rearview mirror can be seen as either a policeman's light bar or a ski rack.

Psychologists have developed paper-and-pencil versions of such natural visualization tasks. If the sheep is fully exposed, visualization consists of distinguishing its shape from the surrounding jumble of like-colored boulders. The Embedded Figure Test asks you to tell which of several complex figures contains a simpler target figure. If all that shows is part of a head and a rump, visualization is a matter of completing a pattern, as in the Gestalt Completion Test, in which you must identify fragmented images of dogs, violins, and other common items.

At a more sophisticated level, pattern recognition includes sensitivity to style, balance, and dynamics in graphic design—seeing the difference between an advertising layout that energizes the viewer and one that just "lies there."

Visualization includes pattern recall as well as pattern recognition. Francis Galton, a cousin of Charles Darwin, studied visual recall with a questionnaire about people's visual memory of their breakfast table: number, color, and position of cups, plates, napkins, etc. Galton himself was not particularly good at visual recall; he compared himself to a blind man who doubted the reality of vision.

Patterns of scores on various visualization tests convince some psychologists that the key operation in visualization is imagining movement among internal parts of complex figures. Mentally rearranging your living room is an everyday example of this factor at work. So are the judgments of volume described in the "conservation" experiments in the chapter on logical-mathematical intelligence.

The Minnesota Paper Form Board Test tests this factor by asking the subject to select the one of several figures that can be constructed by rearranging several simple geometric shapes. The widely used Differential Aptitudes Test (DAT) assesses the same subability by presenting flat, irregular forms and asking which of several complexly patterned boxes could be made by folding them. Other DAT items tapping dynamic visualization depict complex arrangements of pulleys, axles, and belts, and ask what movements would result from a twist in a given direction.

The highest-level operation of visualization is the creation of novel forms like Tesla's motors and generators. Students of creativity agree that what looks like a totally new construction is usually the rearrangement and combination of simpler, previously existing ones. Only God is able to create real things from void.

Spatial Relations. Oddly enough, people who are very good or very bad at visualizing objects tend to do no better or worse than average on other kinds of spatial tasks. This is good news for people like myself, whose visual images flicker dimly like a badly tuned TV in a fringe area. Even if you don't have vivid images, you may do much better than you would expect on other spatial tasks, as, for instance, when you mentally rotate a glove in order to compare it with your hands. Such judgments are applications of a second spatial subability, called "spatial relations." They are made by a mechanic sorting bolts, a mover figuring out whether a table will fit through a door, or a dentist deciding which is the rear end of a bridge.

We shouldn't be surprised that the ability to handle such spatial relations is independent of visualization. The key to visualization is changing the relationship among the parts of a figure to create a new one, as in the folding tasks. Spatial relations, on the other hand, is the opposite: the ability to preserve relationships among the parts of an object while transforming the object as a whole.

The best tests of this subability are the mental rotation tasks used by Stanford psychologist Roger Shepard and his colleagues. In a typical task, a subject is presented with two three-dimensional shapes and asked whether or not they are the same. A consistent result of tests of this type is the finding that the time it takes to give a correct "same" response is directly proportional to the degree of rotation. It is as though we solve such problems by mentally rotating an image at a constant average rate of about 53 degrees per second.

Humans are not the only animals who can perform mental rotations. At least, this is the inference drawn by Shepard and Lynn Cooper in an article in *Scientific American.* Returning with a stick that had been tossed over a fence, a German shepherd approached a hole in a fence that was not wide enough to allow the stick to pass. "Just as catastrophe seemed imminent, the dog stopped short, paused and rotated its head 90 degrees. With the stick held vertically it passed through the fence without mishap." Psychologists learned long ago to be skeptical about such anecdotes, but the inference that the dog solved the problem with some sort of mental imagery is supported by the results of my wolf research, which suggested that the German shepherd's wild cousins frequently take shortcuts and detours and solve spatial problems that would be extremely difficult without some sense of spatial relationships.

Orientation. Shortcuts, detours, and other "insightful" solutions to problems of finding one's way rely not only on spatial relations but on orientation, the most practical spatial subability for both wolves and human hunter-gatherers. Orientation is the ability to incorporate various points of view into thinking about a problem. For example, in imagining how a freeway exit, an airport, or a harbor would appear when approached from another direction, you use information not only about spatial relations but about where you are.

A classic test of orientation is Jean Piaget's "three-mountain" task, in which a subject is placed before a papier-mâché model and asked how a village or farm would appear if seen from various angles. Paper-and-pencil tests of orientation include items showing a figure from the side and asking the test taker to choose which of several top views depicts the same object. Other tests require imaginary journeys, as in the following (made-up) question: "If my house is on your left as you walk toward the setting sun, which direction does the street side of my house face?" If that one was too easy, try your hand at this orientation brainteaser: You walk south from camp for one mile, head west for a mile, then north for a mile, whereupon you find yourself back at camp, where you started. Unfortunately, a bear has destroyed your tent. What color is the bear? (This really does have an answer, given at the end of the chapter.)

As you worked on these problems, you had to combine visualized imagery and a knowledge of spatial relations with information about your own (imagined) location. Since orientation requires this third form of information, some people with an excellent "sense of direction," as orientation ability is often called, are very poor at visualization and rotation (and vice versa).

"Sense of direction" is a particularly misleading misnomer, because many people do believe in an "instinct" or a "sixth sense" of navigation. Though some people excel at orientation to an uncanny degree (and others are woefully deficient), there is no such instinct or sixth sense. There is a special ability to get and use the kinds of information that help you find your way, but as you will soon see, this ability is learned by better application of the senses we all share.

Cognitive Mapping. All three subabilities—visualization, spatial relations, and orientation—work together in a process called cognitive mapping. A cognitive map is a more or less vividly visualized mental image containing information about spatial relations among real places and your orientation to them. The amount of information in a cognitive map is prodigious. Think about how many words it would take to describe all the information in your mental map of your home town: the places you visit, the approximate distances between them and the enormous number of routes linking them, the landmarks you use to remember where to turn, and so on. Mental maps organize spatial information about where things are and verbal information about their names, uses, and attractiveness. The power of mental maps to organize large amounts of information is exploited in the "method of loci," a highly effective memory-improvement scheme described in the next chapter.

Harvard psychologist Stephen Kosslyn has studied mental maps by creating artificial ones. Kosslyn's subjects studied a map of a fictional island containing a beach, a rock, a tree, a patch of grass, a hut, a well, and a lake. After removing the map, Kosslyn asked his subjects to imagine a dot moving from, say, the rock to the tree, and press a button when the dot reached the tree. The time it took to press the button was directly proportional to the distance on the map. As in Shepard's mental rotation experiments, it was as though the subject were scanning a mental picture, and Kosslyn describes these representations as "quasi-pictorial."

Steve Kaplan, a cognitive scientist at the University of Michigan, has studied mental maps of cities, forests, and large buildings like hospitals. Arguing that mental maps were the earliest forms of complex memory to evolve, Kaplan views them as the fundamental structures underlying all thought. He writes: "The structure underlying the spatial map of the world that people carry around in their heads is not different from the structure that underlies *all* cognitive process."

Putting the Chart Before Discourse: The Relationship of Spatial Intelligences to Verbal Intelligence

Like Kaplan, Rudolph Arnheim, whose discussion of the Chase Manhattan trademark was quoted above, argues that all thinking is spatial. He quotes the anthropologist Benjamin Whorf: "I 'grasp' the 'thread' of another's arguments, but if its 'level' is 'over my head' my attention may 'wander' and 'lose touch' with the 'thread' of it, so that when he 'comes' to his 'point' we differ 'widely,' our 'views' being indeed so 'far apart' that the 'things' he says 'appear' 'much' too arbitrary, or even a 'lot' of nonsense." Arnheim comments, "Actually, Whorf is much too economical with his quotation marks, because the rest of his words, including the prepositions and the conjunctions, derive their meanings from perceptual origins also. . . . To put it more sharply: human thinking cannot go beyond the patterns supplied by the human senses."

Arnheim considers words mere currency that must be backed up by the solid bullion of real thought: "it is not possible to think in words," he writes, "unless one is satisfied with elementary statements such as: a sounds like b; or a comes before b. . . . The human mind needs better tools than that. . . . Purely verbal thinking is the prototype of thoughtless thinking."

Arnheim acknowledges the intimate cross-fertilizations between spatial and verbal modes of thought. He shows how language takes a mass of simultaneous sense impressions and organizes it into linear paths among the elements. Linguists have taken Arnheim's point of view seriously; one imaginative study has traced the translation of spatial knowledge of apartment layouts into verbal descriptions. As Arnheim would predict, the basic organization of such transcriptions is narrative: When people describe their apartment, they take an imaginary walk through it, beginning at the front door.

As a practical application of the fundamentally spatial character of even the most abstract thought, consider the utility of a concrete diagram in communicating even the most abstract of concepts. For example, most people find the verbal description of legal reasoning in Chapter 9 impossible to understand. Yet when I illustrate this process with a figure shaped like an upside-down tree, even my most verbally impacted colleagues get the point. A corollary to the old pedagogical saw that you don't understand it if you can't explain it might be: "You don't understand it if you can't draw it." Consequently, teachers of visual imagery prescribe exercises in which one draws pictures of such abstractions as "past, present, and future," "democracy," "good and bad marriage," and "youth."

In quoting Whorf on visual imagery in language, Arnheim was turning him on his head, for Whorf was the most famous spokesman for the opposite point of view: Language determines thought. Another anti-imagery position is that of the sophisticated, and outspoken Canadian psychologist–computer scientist Zenon Pylyshyn. Pylyshyn says that images are part of what the brain does, not part of the explanation of how it does it. The brain "does" imagery the same way it "does" language. According to Pylyshyn, Kosslyn's "fantasy island" scanning experiment shows only that subjects construe the experimenter's instructions as requiring them "to imagine various intermediate states . . . that they believe would be passed through . . . and that they spend more time visualizing those episodes that they believe (or infer) would take more time in the corresponding real task." In other words, Kosslyn is exploring, not images, but people's verbal "tacit knowledge" about them.

This theoretical controversy has practical consequences: If we are to enhance SPI, we need to know what it is we're enhancing. If spatial intelligence is really a child of language and logic, we can best foster its development by providing for its parents. If, on the other hand, it develops independently of other intelligences, we should concentrate on its special needs and provide it with its own educational trust fund.

One problem with the Whorfian theory that we process images verbally is that creatures like the stick-twisting German shepherd and shortcutting wolves solve spatial problems. Such creatures may be speechless, but they aren't "dumb." If they can think without words, why can't we? Another problem is the enormous amounts of information that can be stored in the form of images. Many of us feel that it's far easier to construct verbal descriptions of spatial information as needed than to construct a spatial image out of a mental gazetteer of verbal information.

An entire book could be written about the Kosslyn-Pylyshyn debate, but this one isn't it. The three spatial subabilities—visualizing, rotating, and orienting—work for hunters, psychotherapists, mechanics, and others who use spatial information and take their psychological reality of spatial images for granted. No one denies that some people *experience* images, and most psychologists who work with images are willing to take these experiences at face value, as consequences of a separate system that operates on spatial, picturelike, or "analogue" images. We might not use the same words, but we share the sentiment expressed by Rudolph Arnheim when he called the view that all thinking is verbal an "extraordinary perversion."

For practical purposes (and, I suspect, theoretical purposes as well), it makes sense to treat spatial intelligence as a separate intelligence, with its own best ways of being enhanced.

ENHANCING SPATIAL SKILLS: WAYFINDING USING MENTAL MAPS

Effective wayfinding prevents the stressful, wasteful consequences of being lost. Kevin Lynch, whose *Image of the City* is the classic study of urban mental mapping, describes these consequences: "To become completely lost is perhaps a rather rare experience for most people in the modern city. . . . But let the mishap of disorientation occur, and the sense of anxiety and even terror that accompanies it reveals to us how closely [orientation] is linked to our sense of balance and well-being. The very word 'lost' in our language means much more than simple geographic uncertainty: it carries a tone of utter disaster."

Lynch and others who claim that being lost is a rare experience in modern cities evidently don't frequent Denver's Stapleton Airport, where it seems that airlines are allowed to assign numbers to their competitors' gates, or Boston, where the locals, like Carpenter's Eskimos, orient to invisible hills long ago bulldozed into the Back Bay.

Nor do scholars who speak of the rarity of being lost work in wilderness, where "dead reckoning" sounds more ominous with every minute that an anticipated objective fails to appear. Experienced wilderness workers seldom get completely lost, but they are often irritated by uncertainty about where they are. Hundreds of wilderness novices do get lost every year, and some of them are found only as corpses. The National Park Service, the U.S. Forest Service, and local search-and-rescue organizations spend millions of dollars a year retrieving lost hunters, backpackers, and children.

Mental maps allow people not only to avoid getting lost but to imagine new routes connecting points never visited. The role of mental maps in wayfinding may be illustrated by contrasting my two favorite cities, Boston and Seattle, which is sometimes called the "Boston of the West." Boston is flat, compact, and shaped like a funnel, so you often get where you want to go without knowing how you got there. Seattle, on the other hand, is draped over seven hills separated by water. As a result, you can often see where you want to go, but you can't get there.

The consensus among experts is that everyone can learn to think visually. Over the last decade and a half, I've been testing this consensus. As a student and teacher of animal behavior in natural settings, I've sent scores of students into wilderness areas to record animal sign and behavior, and write and sketch descriptions of what they saw. Most were urbanites who had never traveled in an area without street signs. By adopting the sorts of strategies described below, they were all able to develop the sense of direction that most at the outset denied having. Therefore, I ask you to adopt, for the next few minutes, my working hypothesis that spatial skills can be developed.

We must first break the self-defeating positive feedback loop in which you tell yourself that SPI is a "talent" that you haven't got, thereby excusing yourself from further effort. An article published in the *Journal of Experimental Psychology* showed, as expected, that people who claim to have "good sense of direction" learned their way around a new environment better than those who judged themselves poor. However, this difference in learning occurred *only* when the subjects were informed in advance that they would be tested. When the test of spatial learning was a pop quiz, there was no difference in abilities between those who thought they had a good sense of direction and those who didn't. This result suggests that when confronted with a task requiring spatial ability, people psych themselves up or down, depending on their opinions of their own abilities, and handicap themselves when their opinion is low.

In the next few pages, I describe the mental maps of wayfinders, emphasizing the performance of experts, people who have acquired through experience highly organized masses of spatial information. All experts have had extensive experience with the areas they know, but not everyone who has lots of experience with an area is an expert wayfinder. We all know people who have lived in one city all their lives and still can't find their way around. As we go along, I'll prescribe some mental mapping techniques based on seeing key features of the environment, visualizing two-dimensional schematic maps, and drawing these maps in order to improve them.

Seeing

Expert teachers of spatial abilities agree that to visualize, remember, draw, or otherwise improve spatial skills, you must learn to see better. This does not mean getting better glasses. It means looking in new ways.

When Barret Wynn and I look at a cliff, and he sees sheep I don't, it's not because his eyes are better. It's because he knows how a sheep looks under different lighting conditions and in different contexts, and from different angles. Wayfinding experts usually have seen key landmarks and other orienting features in dim light, perhaps under snow. In unfamiliar country, they frequently look back to see how trail junctions or other features will appear on the return journey.

Another common characteristic of expert wildlife spotters is their willingness to risk false alarms. The cost of a false alarm in spotting an animal (or a landmark) is small: All you lose is the time and energy it takes to get a better look.

By paying lots of attention to subtle details, and making some mistakes, Richard Nelson, who studied Alaskan Eskimos' uncanny sensitivity to tracks, rises, and other signs, learned to recognize these features himself.

• Therefore, when in doubt, check it out.

Failure to notice subtleties of direction is a major obstacle to effective wayfinding. For example, like members of a psychological Corps of Engineers, we visually straighten the gradual curves of rivers and other edges and routes. Psychologist Stanley Milgram, who studied mental maps of Paris, wrote, "The Seine may course a great arc in Paris, almost forming a half circle, but Parisians imagine it a much gentler curve, and some think it a straight line." Kevin Lynch points out that "long slow curves, in almost all studies of orientation in cities, proved to be the most confusing and difficult to reconstruct." People wandering in natural environments who fail to notice the gentle curvature of their own routes may find themselves walking in circles.

A number of excellent books provide exercises designed to improve attention to such details. For example, Betty Edwards, in *Drawing on the Right Side of the Brain,* recommends exercise in seeing "negative spaces," the shapes enclosed by figures we attend to and ordinarily dismiss as ground. To heighten sensitivity to such shapes, she suggests contour sketching, drawing the silhouettes of complex objects. She believes that such exercises free one from the sorts of visual oversimplification that trick us into seeing curved routes as straight.

Robert McKim calls this process of overcoming visual stereotypes "recentering." He devotes a chapter of *Experiences in Visual Thinking* to exercises designed to "recenter vision away from stereotypes." For example, he suggests looking at objects upside down by peering between your legs, and observing distorted reflections. On city streets, such reflections are seen on automobile fenders and glass-sided office buildings. McKim claims that such tricks inhibit normal verbal labeling, with psychedelic consequences: "With habitual associations diminished, colors also seem more vivid and contrasts of light and dark more intense." Wayfinders might use recentering to heighten their ability to recognize landmarks from different points of view and in different lighting.

Such exercises in seeing promote creativity by freeing one's senses from the "cultural cocoons" of perceptual stereotyping. W. J. Gordon, author of *Synectics,* who describes this process as "making the familiar strange," also believes that it removes obstacles to creativity.

Though Edwards, McKim, and Gordon all warn about the ways in which verbal labels abet our tendency to stereotype, they would not deny that words provide useful "handles" for organizing and remembering what we see. Just as spatial memory improves verbal memory in the method of loci described in the following chapter, verbal memory can enhance spatial memory. For example, Ralph Norman Haber of the University of Rochester briefly showed subjects pictures of complex scenes and asked them to recall as much of the scenes as they could. When the subjects had related all they thought they could remember, they were prompted by nondirective questions until they ran completely dry. The experimenters then had some subjects free-associate (see Chapter 4) for about half an hour. Unlike control subjects, who played darts, the subjects who free-associated were able to recall details they had not mentioned before.

- Lawyers, detectives, and others who often need detailed descriptions of complex patterns ought therefore to encourage their informants to free-associate when they feel they can offer no further information.

General verbal categories for key environmental features can help you know what to look for as you learn a new place. In spite of the differences between artificial environments like Boston and natural ones like the northwest wilderness, the mental maps of cities and wildernesses contain the same five kinds of elements: paths and their junctions, regions and their edges, and landmarks. Let's take a quick tour of these five elements, one by one.

Paths or routes are the most basic elements of mental maps, because they represent the most direct transcription of spatial experiences: sequences of sensory impressions. In well-populated areas, paths are known by name or number. William Chase tested cabdrivers in Pittsburgh and found that experts (people with *real* street smarts) named more streets than novices and used their knowledge to plan shorter, faster routes.

- Knowing the basis on which routes are named can help you remember where they are.

In some cities, like Denver, the system is alphabetic, while in others, like Chicago's Loop, it is based on early U.S. Presidents. Actually, in the Loop there's just enough deviation from the true order to mess you up if you know your Presidents, so you may be better off *not* knowing the pattern, but this is the exception that proves the rule. A better example is the national numbering system for interstate highways: even numbers for east-west routes, odd for north-south, prefixes of 2 and 4 for routes going "to" or used "for" getting to a major one, such as Route 225, which goes to 25 in Denver, or Route 495, which you take out of New York City when you are headed for 95.

Paths are also fundamental elements in the mental maps of travelers in natural environments. Even wilderness is seldom "trackless": Anywhere animals have walked are systems of trails connecting the places most commonly visited. Such naturally occurring trails form the basis for human travel, and in turn become the elements of our mental maps.

Junctions of two or more major routes form a node, such as Columbus Circle in New York City, where Eighth Avenue, Broadway, and Fifty-ninth Street intersect. Nodes are useful because they are places where one can transfer from one route to another. When shown pictures of nodes, experienced cabdrivers recognized more of them than novices did.

Regions are more or less well-defined areas distinguished from their surroundings by form or function. New York's Central Park is a well-defined region, while Greenwich Village is a little fuzzier. Conceptions of neighborhoods are definite but idiosyncratic: You probably know where your neighborhood ends, but your mental neighborhood doesn't end exactly where your neighbor's does. Neighborhoods with especially fuzzy borders, like San Francisco's Tenderloin, provide opportunities for burglars, who, like lone wolves, tend to stay out of well-defined territories, where strangers are likely to be noticed. The expert cabbies studied by Chase also excelled in their knowledge of regions.

Edges divide regions, even when the regions are similar in form and function. Thus, Chicago's Loop has a well-defined edge, the elevated train tracks, but apart from the tracks overhead, you really can't tell when you've left the Loop proper. Edges can also be obstacles. Sometimes a street's status as an edge overrides its function as a route, as where Eighth Avenue becomes Central Park West in New York City. Edges often have a psychological reality far beyond their meager physical signs. Like edges of wolf territories, edges of gang territories are as real as a physical obstacle. I once tutored a young man on the south side of Chicago who would not cross Stony Island Avenue to walk on the shady side of the street.

Landmarks are salient and memorable places, like the World Trade Center, or the Transamerica Pyramid, often visible from a distance. As such, they are anchors for orientation and opportunities for rendezvous.

I have found these five elements in maps of open prairie, northern forest, southwestern desert, and Colorado mountains, drawn by housewives, inner-city children, West African high school teachers, college professors, wildlife scientists, guides, and accountants. Regardless of spatial expertise or degree of familiarity with a piece of terrain, people sketch and describe a mental map that contains these five kinds of elements. It is probably no coincidence that these elements are the features delineated by the scent marks of wolves. Since these elements appear in mental maps of such different environments, drawn (or squirted) by such different creatures, they may be viewed as the basic building blocks of cognitive maps.

These five kinds of elements fill the maps of expert guides who know an area well and untrained people who visit an area once. Expert wayfinders see and remember more examples of each kind of spatial elements than novices, but maps drawn by both experts and novices include some examples of all five kinds.

Two-Dimensional Schemas

The major difference between experts' and novices' mental maps is not in the kinds of elements but in how they are organized. Expert wayfinders use simple, two-dimensional, hierarchically organized mental maps. Novices, on the other hand, use literal, one-dimensional, list-like maps. The differences between the "survey" maps of experts and the "route" maps of novices suggest that learning to learn spatial structures means learning to integrate one-dimensional route maps into two-dimensional schemas.

Like Puluwat navigators, Avilik Eskimos, and their American peers, experienced London and Parisian cabdrivers have two-dimensional mental maps of their cities. However, there are some cities, including Boston and its suburbs, where even experienced cabbies are unable to form organized maps because routes are too complex and convoluted. In such places, as in unfamiliar ones, memories barely deserve the name "map." They are one-dimensional lists of locations strung along a single route, like the Triptiks provided by AAA. My "map" of London is like that: I can list lots of landmarks, and even put them in an order based on a sequence of underground stations, but I have no spatial schema to organize them, so I can't say whether Harrods is nearer to Westminster than to the Natural History Museum. Every trip away from the area around Grosvenor Square is a Magical Mystery Tour for me. Under stress, we sometimes revert to such route maps even when we know better. When you're late for a plane in heavy traffic, it's easier to remember "turn left at the Conoco station" than to visualize the best possible route.

When Barret Wynn sketched a map to show where he had found bighorns, his map, like those of most other expert wayfinders, was highly schematic: The irregular southern rim of the La Garita Mountains became a straight line, the complex configuration of the northwest corner of the San Luis Valley became a right angle, and his route became a straight line. Using a simple schematic form allowed him to remember and convey the general lay of the land, uncluttered by details that wouldn't matter until I got there. The designers of *Flash Maps* also used schematic distortions of geographic reality in order to help visitors find their way around New York City.

Similarly, expert taxi drivers in the U.S., Great Britain, and France all organize their knowledge of their cities in terms of a simplifying schema. A moment's consideration will show that they *must* use simplifying schemas because of the enormous amount of information they must generate. London cabbies, for example must pass a test on what they call "the knowledge": the four hundred fifty routes that connect the twenty-two or so points of interest separated by taxi rides.

Stephen Kosslyn says that we can improve our imagination of structures if we can find the right schema. He describes a technique used by students who must memorize the structures of large organic molecules: Memorize each of several pieces, then the structure as a whole. He further states that "almost anyone can improve his or her ability to maintain images." In support of this contention, he cites experiments in which subjects were asked to imagine sequences of up to ten line segments, each pointing in a specified direction: "South, west, southwest, east, northeast, northeast." At the end of the sequence, the subjects were asked whether the end point of the irregular line they had imagined was above or below the start. Although most people are terrible at this task, difficulty was not always determined by the length of the sequence: Longer sequences that formed regular patterns (schemas) were easier to visualize than irregular short ones. Moreover, people got better with practice. Since Kosslyn's task is exactly like constructing a two-dimensional survey map out of one-dimensional verbal instructions, we would expect the same conclusion to apply to learning real routes: Practice in integrating routes into mental maps helps.

Your mental map of any area you know well is organized hierarchically, or "top-down": You divide the U.S. into regions, regions into states, states into counties, etc. When we plan trips, we choose a major route that connects the two superordinate regions, then follow it until we find landmarks, which we use to choose minor routes through subordinate neighborhoods. Knowledge of minor routes through neighborhoods is accessible only when cued by actually being there. For example, expert cabdrivers, unlike nonexpert control subjects, always do better on the street than they do in the lab: They remember more when environmental cues are present. With spatial as with other kinds of information (see the following two chapters), hierarchical analysis is the best way to maximize the amount of information you retain.

A good way to get a two-dimensional, schematic, hierarchical sense of the lay of the land is to use vantage points: hills or tall buildings, like the Prudential Building in Boston. People who live in cities like San Francisco and Seattle, where hilltops provide a bird's-eye view, have more cohesive images of their cities than people who live in flatter cities like St. Louis or Chicago. Because vantage points incorporate the observer, they may be better integrators of spatial information than aerial photographs and conventional maps, which do not contain a point of view.

Movement seems to be even better exercise than elevation for developing integrated survey maps. Cognitive pioneer Ulrich Neisser argues that movement is an essential component of all schemas, and his point seems to be especially true of mental maps. Moreover, active exploration seems to be better than passive passengering. A number of independent studies have shown that people who walk develop more accurate, complete, and integrated maps than those who ride. But walking is too slow for most people, so the optimum method of learning a city would be that wonderful device that in cities combines the mobility and freedom of walking with the speed of a car: the bicycle. Indeed, prospective London cabbies spend a year on bicycles, integrating the four hundred fifty routes they need to know to pass the licensing exam.

- Therefore, play tourist: Go to the top of the Pru, the Mark, or whatever. Walk or bicycle around. You'll never generate a usable cognitive map just by poring over paper ones.

Spatial Therapy: Exercises, Crutches, and Relaxation

For readers reluctant to enhance their spatial skills by risking their lives on the street, exercises that can be performed in the safety of one's living room may be more appealing. Such exercises cannot provide direct experience with the city itself, but to the extent that they enhance visualization in general, they are useful for visualizing mental maps in particular.

It should be good news to sedentary readers that many writers, including Robert McKim, prescribe relaxation as a way of enhancing imagery. Freud used the couch to help his patients relax enough to associate freely, and in his early years used the images they reported as a basis for analysis. There is good experimental evidence showing that visual imagery improves with monotony and inactivity.

The most dramatic demonstration of this principle is the so-called sensory deprivation experiment, in which subjects spend days floating in a warm tub, blinded by half a Ping-Pong ball over each eye, deafened by the hiss of an air conditioner, and numbed by foam rubber cuffs. To the typical stressed-out urbanite, this may sound like nirvana, but after a few minutes of bliss, most people find that they are bored stiff, and after several hours many begin to halluci-nate. In some cases, the hallucinatory images are so vivid that sub-jects mistake them for reality. You don't need an isolation tank to enhance your imagery. Any comfortable, boring environment will do. Some of my most vivid dreams (of landscapes, of course) have occurred while I was nominally conscious, on long flights made longer by delays at Stapleton.

A variety of imagery crutches require only slightly more effort than relaxation. Francis Galton noted that chess players find it easier to visualize a game if they have a blank board to stare at. Even Bruce Jenner, the decathlon champion in the 1976 Olympics, was not above such armchair training: He kept a hurdle in his room and used it to help him visualize his progress through the steeplechase.

Finally, some real exercises.

Robert McKim offers exercises designed to enhance your spatial fluency. Here's one, just to give you an idea of what McKim is up to: Given a plank with three holes of equal size, one an equilateral triangle, one a circle, and the third a square, can you imagine a single solid that would just fit through each of the holes? In working on this spatial brainteaser, which has kept me awake more than once, I found it useful to think of a related problem. McKim's exer-cise reminded me of Richard Hofstadter's remarkable wooden block, which when illuminated from the top and two sides, projects the initials *G, E,* and *B* (for *Godel, Escher, Bach*). I solved McKim's problem by mentally projecting a light through each of the holes onto a block from each of three directions. My success suggests that simple problem-solving tricks (others are discussed in Chapter 8), like relating a problem to similar ones, may be as effective in solving spatial problems as in more abstract thinking. For what it's worth, I found that even I could mentally manipulate shapes with greater ease after working through McKim's book.

Unfortunately, there is little hard evidence about how effective such exercises are in the real world. What we have instead are mostly titillating hints, hypotheses, and conjectures. For example, Stephen Kosslyn suggests that the method of loci in Chapter 7 improves speed of forming images, and psychologist Lynn Cooper, another leading investigator of spatial intelligences, suspects that differences in spatial abilities depend on differences in the kinds of strategies people adopt, and that these strategies can be manipulated.

Nevertheless, we are not completely at a loss for demonstrably effective techniques for improving imagery in techniques. Kosslyn's line segment experiment is very close to the real-world task of visualizing verbal directions, and his practice effects are encouraging. Furthermore, my research on the training of map drawing in natural environments shows that people can learn to form more accurate mental and real maps by learning to eliminate common distortions.

Drawing Maps

My approach assumes that the best way to portray, manipulate, explore, communicate, and enhance the use of spatial information is via a spatial medium. It further assumes a direct relationship between maps in the mind and maps on paper. It attempts to establish a positive feedback loop in which drawing maps and receiving feedback about them leads to more accurate observation of key features in the field, and more insightful travel choices, whose validation in turn leads to more accurate drawings. My students were able to learn to find their way in wilderness and near-wilderness environments by daily map drawing, combined with training in basic "orienteering" skills: use of topographic maps, compass bearings, and triangulation.

You can, too. Let me anticipate your objection that you can't draw. First of all, the sketches I suggest are not supposed to be pretty or accurate, and you don't have to let anyone else see them. Second, computer graphics packages with "zooms" now make it easy for anyone to draw. Finally, in the many cases in everyday life where you have to tell someone how to get somewhere, you can save lots of time and energy by drawing a simple sketch rather than relying on words. Since you ought to be drawing maps anyway, you might as well get better at it.

Here are some hints for correcting your maps based on simplified generalizations from this research:

- Orient your map. Mark your position in the center of the map.
  Point north. Mark north on your paper. Point to the most

distant landmark you can see, and mark it on the map with the appropriate bearing in relationship to your position.

- Get into the habit of maintaining your orientation. Staying oriented is mainly a matter of paying attention. This sense of orientation not only will help you avoid getting lost but will help you with the next suggestions. (Later, look at your maps from different angles. Practice doing this mentally, without rotating the paper.)
- Don't put the chart before the source. All the information *you* need for *your* mental map is in the relations among places *you* need to go. These places are all in your head to start with, and the map you draw is a means to the end of improving the map you have in your head. You can worry about details later.
- Don't show more than you know. Make your first map highly schematic. Remember, you are striving not for topographical accuracy but for an accurate representation of what's in your head, in order to improve it. By drawing an intentionally oversimplified map, you will make it easier to correct your image. The objective is to make your images "debuggable."

Once you've got a sketch to work with, the next step is to correct your map by comparing your sketches with topographic or street maps. Look for the common kinds of distortions described below. These distortions are inevitable vicissitudes of verbal and spatial schemas, which oversimplify and stereotype reality even as they provide the categories and images that allow us to think. For example, in one experiment, graduate students misrecalled details of apartments they had lived in for years: They included details, like light switches near doors, common to apartments in general but not in their own.

- Therefore, check your map for common features that ought to be there, but aren't: roads that you think connect but don't quite, neighborhood borders that get fuzzy where you least expect it, phantom freeway exits.

Verbal labels distort not only what we remember but where we think it is. A recent article in the *Journal of Experimental Psychology* describes how our memories of locations are influenced by natural clusterings. We all have schemas for the kinds of places that ought to go together: playgrounds, beaches, and a golf course form a "recreational cluster," while courthouses, post offices, and police stations form a "government cluster," and so on. Subjects who saw maps in which, say, a point was labeled "courthouse" remembered its location as closer to "police station" than when the same point was labeled "golf course."

- Check your map for such natural clusters, and make sure they haven't distorted your memory for locations.

Other distortions are due to spatial schematization rather than verbal categorization. For example, most people rely on visual images when they answer questions like: "If you were to fly from Miami to Panama City, in what direction would you head?" Contrary to what most people say, the answer is "southeast." In our imaginations we tend to straighten out the Isthmus, so that it lies north and south instead of curving southeast. Similarly, in Paris, the underestimated curvature of the Seine leads to other distortions. Since a straightened Seine leaves no room for the Auteuil and Passy districts, they are mentally razed or relocated on the Left Bank.

Most spatial distortions are due to a combination of verbal and spatial simplifications. When asked which is farther west, Reno or San Diego, most people say San Diego, but Reno is farther west. We think of California as west of Nevada and think of San Diego as part of California and Reno as part of Nevada. Similarly, people incorrectly place Seattle southwest of Montreal, because they think of Canada as lying to the north of the United States. In both these cases, a kind of assimilation distorts our spatial reasoning.

- Therefore, check your map and if necessary redraw it to take such irregularities of regions and edges into account.

The most prevalent errors on sketches of both natural and artificial environments are distortions of distance.

- You will be least accurate in judging distances along seldom-used routes. In particular, since you probably make more trips toward town than away from town,
- You will tend to overestimate distances away from the center of town.

Terence Lee, a British psychologist whose doctoral dissertation was the first modern study of mental mapping of real-world (as opposed to laboratory) environments, attempted to understand why people in Dundee, Scotland, patronized a downtown shopping center rather than a similar and closer shopping center. This seemingly simple question opened what is now, thirty years later, one of the most complex and richly contradictory areas of spatial intelligence: recall of travel distance. Lee concluded that downtown was more familiar and attractive, and that satisfaction with the city center led people to imagine distances toward downtown as shorter than those away from town. A practical implication for retailers and providers of services:

- Locate your business downtown of your target market.
- You will overestimate distances along busy routes.

The more cognitive elements (nodes, landmarks) there are along a route, the greater your overestimation will be. As Francis Galton pointed out almost a hundred years ago, "It is difficult to estimate, by recollection only, the true distances between points in a road that has once been travelled over. There are many circumstances that may mislead, such as the accidental tedium of one part, or the pleasure of another. . . . recollection of an interval of time is, as we all know, mainly derived from the number of impressions that . . . memory has received." In an experiment in which subjects traveled from a shopping center to two equidistant locations, the route that passed more intersections, traffic, and businesses and took more time was judged longer. However, your distance estimates will be more accurate when the configuration of the cognitive elements of a city correspond closely to the schemas they suggest. For example, the central malls and radial avenues of a highly "legible" city like Washington, D.C., provide a simple cognitive structure that makes it relatively easy for even casual visitors to gauge distances correctly.

The converse of the overestimation of busy distances is:

- You will underestimate distances when travel is through relatively featureless terrain.

In some cases, this effect can override the effects of familiarity and attractiveness. A study in Columbus, Ohio, showed that people underestimated distances away from downtown and imagined trips into town as longer than out-of-town trips of equal length. This is the opposite of what Lee found in Dundee, where the surrounding countryside is far hillier and more varied than that around Columbus.

- You will underestimate distances to places with emotional valences.

An extreme example of this phenomenon is a *Newsweek* article that reported that a "Marxist has taken over on America's doorstep in Chile." As one acerbic reader pointed out, Santiago, the capital of Chile, is farther away from New York City than is Moscow.

Learning to learn your way in cities, forests, hospitals, airports, and other large-scale environments is not only a practical goal in itself but also an excellent model for enhancing other spatial skills. Because wayfinding with mental maps taps all three spatial subabilities, it is an example of what Howard Gardner calls "genetic primary examples," problems or lessons that can be handled by the novice but, at the same time, harbor within them the most relevant abstractions within that domain.

About that bear: The only place where two ninety-degree right turns would bring you back to your starting point is the North Pole, so the bear is white.

PART FOUR

ACADEMIC INTELLIGENCES AND SKILLS

8.
Verbal Intelligence

He gripped more closely the essential prose
As being, in a world so falsified,
The one integrity for him, the one
Discovery still possible to make . . .

—WALLACE STEVENS

Wallace Stevens, one of America's great modern poets, concealed his literary success from his colleagues in the insurance business until late in life, when his fame threatened to blow his cover. In the skyscrapers of Hartford, Connecticut, there are no suites for poets, but there should be. Business and poetry both require a way with words. In policies as in poems, loose language is a liability, so we pay a premium for precision. The secret success of Wallace Stevens is a lesson in how practical yet unappreciated verbal abilities are.

In this chapter, I want to convince you that even if you have a terrific secretary and a fifth-generation word processor with a built-in spelling checker, your own verbal skills are still crucial. I show you how valuable writing and speaking are when they are good, and how expensive they can be when they are bad. Then I describe the obstacles to enhancing verbal intelligence (VI), and explain how to overcome them by enhancing your own verbal abilities and those of your associates.

You use these abilities whenever you listen, read, speak, write, or think in English, French, COBOL, or any other language. Words are our major medium for both communication and thought. In the philosopher Ludwig Wittgenstein's words, "The limits of my language are the limits of my world." This is not to say that *all* communication and thinking is verbal. But verbal media always shape as well as express verbal messages.

Particular verbal abilities like comprehension, fluency, vocabulary, and other skills go together: People who are good at understanding verbal material tend to have large vocabularies, a good grammar sense, and lots of general knowledge. These verbal abilities go together whether the words used are written or spoken, so they seem to be incarnations of an underlying way with words. Words are important in so many different domains that psychologists who believe in general intelligence consider vocabulary size the best single measure of IQ or other manifestations of *g*.

IQ and *g*, as you will remember, are indices of "school smarts." Verbal abilities are one place where school smarts, street smarts, and office smarts overlap. This connection between academic and verbal intelligence does not, however, mean that schools do much to enhance verbal intelligence. In fact, most schools stifle such practical verbal skills as razor-lipped repartee, defusing humor, and natural style.

Let's look at how the same verbal abilities that let Wallace Stevens write masterpieces of lyric poetry allowed him to thrive in the profession that paid his bills—the law.

The legendary quantity and complexity of legal language weeds out lawyers and judges with mediocre verbal skills. A study in New York, for example, revealed that appellate court judges read an average of 309,750 pages per year. From the earliest days of the profession, when scriveners were paid by the word, lawyers have had to read prodigiously. In *Gulliver's Travels,* published in 1726, Jonathan Swift described the bar as "a Society that hath a peculiar cant and jargon of their own, that no other mortal can understand, and wherein all their laws are written, which they take special care to multiply; and whereby they have wholly confounded the very essence of Truth and Falsehood, of Right and Wrong."

In order to stabilize the chaos of human conflict, legal language has to be copious and complex. University of Chicago law professor Edward Levi describes case law as "classifying things as equal when they are somewhat different, justifying the classification by rules made up as the . . . classification proceeds." This is not a criticism; Levi argues that legal categories "must be left ambiguous to permit the infusion of new ideas. . . . The words . . . must come to have new meanings." In other words, judges must be able to "deem" virtually anything to be anything else.

Moreover an attorney's success often depends on the ability to create as well as to penetrate confusion. This is especially true in criminal law, where a successful defense attorney must merely raise "reasonable doubt" in the mind of the jury. Sometimes this can be done by creating confusion, sometimes by eliminating it. Both require VI. As Ed Gray, a lawyer with R. R. Donnelley in Chicago, put it: "Never underestimate the value of obfuscation."

The sheer mass and inherent complexity of the law, further muddled by lawyers' competitive obfuscation, make for a kind of "survival of the fittest" that selects for extremely high verbal abilities. It is no wonder that the law contains not only some of the worst writing in the world but some of the best.

Like lawyers, managers put verbal intelligence to work every day. In his classic *The Nature of Managerial Work,* Henry Mintzberg reported that 78 percent of managers' time and 67 percent of their activities involve verbal media: memos, phone calls, meetings, and reports. All ten of his key managerial roles require processing verbal information, and one of the four prime characteristics of successful managers' work is "attraction to verbal media."

Verbal intelligence comes up again and again in studies of factors promoting managerial success. The AT&T Management Progress Study listed competence in oral presentation, discussion, and writing as key factors in promotion within the Bell System. In *In Search of Excellence,* Peters and Waterman describe the value of verbal skills at Procter & Gamble: A new assistant brand manager's first memo traditionally requires at least fifteen drafts. And as I mentioned at the end of Chapter 5, verbal skills play a key role in Richard Boyatzis's cluster of leadership competences.

The recent trend toward decentralization ("intrapreneurialism") in several major corporations has increased the need for communication skills at all levels. Here's what chairman Roger Smith said about his priorities at GM: "Managers must be able to convey their vision in an inspiring and forceful way. . . . To do that you need communication skills. . . . We must import them. . . . And we must impart them."

Even Smith's rival at Chrysler, Lee Iacocca, agrees with him about the importance of verbal abilities: "The most important thing I learned in school was how to communicate."

No wonder many major law and business schools require courses in the communication skills that are the expression of VI. Harvard Business School prescribes a two-semester course (taught by nine writing specialists) that covers style, tone, oral presentation, editing, grammar, and logic. Similar courses are required at the University of Chicago, Stanford, Wharton, and Columbia business schools, to name but a few.

If you think verbal intelligence is for professionals only, consider this: A study conducted for the U.S. Army showed that verbal ability is related to the performance not only of supply clerks but of armored vehicle crews, mechanics, and cooks. In fact, soldiers' verbal ability predicted performance in these jobs about as well as it predicted their grades in college courses. The authors of the study are not surprised: They point out that nowadays all jobs require lots of verbal instructions. And people who perform well on jobs that don't require much verbal ability are in danger of being promoted into positions that do.

In the law, in business, the army, and everywhere else, we use language not only to inform but to persuade, to stay in touch, and to think. Verbal intelligence is human capital.

Nevertheless, a survey conducted by Robert Sternberg and his colleagues at Yale showed that most people believe verbal intelligence is for poets and professors, not for everyday problems, that it is different from practical intelligence. Though we pay lip service to communication skills, we don't value them enough to crack down on bad writing and speaking. "It's hard for me to believe that grown men write the kinds of things I see in some client organizations," says Jack Shaw, a partner at Touche Ross & Co., one of the Big Eight accounting firms. And Roger Smith writes: "All too few business people understand the importance of good, clear communication; all too few practice it in the daily performance of their job."

Poor communication sometimes wreaks havoc through misunderstanding. The most dramatic example of this is related in Stuart Chase's book *Power of Words.* When the Japanese cabinet replied to the Allies' Potsdam ultimatum in 1945, they used the word *mokusatsu,* which has two meanings: (1) to ignore, and (2) to refrain from comment. Their intended meaning was the second, but the Allies inferred the first. The result of this poorly chosen and interpreted word was the devastation at Hiroshima and Nagasaki.

The same thing happens repeatedly on a smaller scale. British cognitive psychologist P. C. Wason describes an investigation of a plane crash. The repair manual for the aircraft contained the following instruction: "Remove the pin, examine it, and if it is bent, replace it," which is exactly what the mechanic did. He was not instructed to replace it with a new pin, and he didn't.

Even when it is not a matter of life or death, crummy communication wastes time and money and erodes a company's image. E. A. Locke, president of the American Paper Institute, cites a contract lost because of the bad tone of a subordinate's memo.

Communication is the lifeblood of our information society. Healthy writing and speaking deliver meaning as hemoglobin delivers oxygen—on words bright red with iron. Healthy prose pulses powerfully but fluidly through well-organized channels. But the bloodstream of our businesses and governments is not healthy. Teachers, communication consultants, and managers agree in their diagnoses. The industrial diseases of the information age are:

- Anemia—weak, watery words that don't deliver a load of meaning: "utilize" instead of "use," "terminate" instead of "fire."

- Leukemia—too many verbal platelets, hypertrophied defensiveness about details that wins the battle against infection but kills the patient it's supposed to protect. A. Z. Carr, in *Business as a Game,* calls this "legalism." Early warning signs are the passive voice and the double negative. "It was not unexpected that it was received late."

- Hemorrhaging—disorganized paragraphs that bleed all over the place instead of flowing in clear channels.

- Infections of bad spelling and usage—"criteria" and "media" used as singulars, "infer" used for "imply," and "it's" ("it is") used as a possessive.

Our productivity suffers from these diseases even more than we do when we are exposed to them. And it's getting worse: Pepsi-Cola Co. president Victor A. Bonomo sees "an erosion of writing skills in a lot of the young people we bring in here who are very bright."

There are several reasons for our continuing failure to foster verbal intelligence. One is the sheer complexity of language itself. We take language for granted, but learning how to speak occupies most of our waking hours during our first four years of life. Learning how to read and write simple sentences takes another four years. And it takes at least another eight years for most people to master written and spoken language. There's not much we can do about the complexity of language. But we *can* do something about the remaining problems.

We can do something about how verbal skills are taught. Some of my fellow teachers can't sign a check in fewer than a hundred words—and we're the ones who teach the teachers who teach our students to write. Our logorrhea is contagious: In spite of what we academics profess, what our students end up learning is the academic style that drives readers (including us professors) crazy. The disease incubates in grammar school with essays with an arbitrary required minimum length—expressed in number of words, not quality of ideas. It goes into remission in high school, where writing is seldom required, but in college the symptoms are florid. "In today's society it may be seen as looked upon from different points of view . . ." begins a typical sophomore term paper. Consultant Albert Joseph, president of Industrial Writing Institute, said of business writers: "Those with PhDs may be the worst of all. The higher the education, the worse the writing they've been exposed to."

Obsolete status symbols are another removable obstacle to clear communication. It's no coincidence that autocrats are known as "dictators": One way you know you're in control is that you've got a secretary who handles a lot of your reading and writing. That makes reading and writing menial "girl stuff," and some (mainly male) executives refuse to use word processors. "That's what I've got a secretary for," one executive sniffed when I pointed out that when much depends on the precise wording of documents, who's really in control is the one who dots the *i*'s and crosses the *t*'s.

Another treatable problem is the attitude that to sound serious and businesslike, you've got to speak and write like a bureaucrat. According to William Zinsser, executive editor of the Book-of-the-Month Club and author of *On Writing Well,* businesspeople are infected with the idea that "a simple style reflects a simple mind." Consequently, subordinates emulate the poor speaking and writing of their leaders in order to sound "businesslike." Robert Shankland, who offers writing courses for businesspeople in San Francisco, gets resistance from students who claim that their bosses *like* a heavy-handed style. Joseph Williams, who teaches English at the University of Chicago Law School, quotes a student who complained, "I just spent three years learning how to write like a lawyer and now you're telling me to write just like everyone else."

There's curious inconsistency here: We embrace the age of information, elect a "great communicator" as President, and nod knowingly when Smith, Iacocca, and Forbes deplore bad writing, but we continue to emulate the worst writing and speaking in the world.

The fundamental problem with this view of communication is that it is egocentric: It ignores the abilities and needs of the audience. Egocentrism is wired deep in our brains, and it can't be easily eliminated. We can cope with it, though, by applying knowledge of the cognitive needs, biases, and abilities of our audience. To communicate well isn't to communicate "just like everyone else," and if I can convince you of that, I'll have taken the first step toward a cure of our epidemic of bad communication.

This brings us to the biggest enemy of enhanced verbal intelligence, the old bugaboo "talent": the peculiar idea that verbal abilities are gifts of the gods, the silver tongue, the platinum pen, and that there's nothing we can do to develop them. You *can* improve your verbal intelligence, your ability to acquire, use, and express verbal information. Verbal intelligence is crystallized intelligence, the kind that depends on knowledge and special skills (see Chapter 2). Since like all forms of crystallized intelligence, verbal intelligence depends on knowledge, building the vocabulary and other knowledge bases can increase verbal ability throughout adulthood. In other words, you can increase your own verbal intelligence and that of your workers because it depends on processes that improve with practice. It's like staying in shape. Some people are in better shape in their forties than they were in their twenties. They stay in shape all their lives by exercise.

That's not to say that you or I can become a Wallace Stevens just by practice. No amount of training will allow me to write a poem like "Peter Quince." But I can improve my basketball lay-ups 1000 percent and I can learn to imitate Stevens's style for a line or two. Studs Terkel's *Working* is full of powerful speech by interviewees who never considered themselves eloquent. The point is that verbal intelligence can be increased not only by hard work but also by play: not just reading and writing, but crossword puzzles, Scrabble, Botticelli, and other games verbal people play.

In the next sections, I show how an understanding of the needs and abilities of the audience can make you not only a better reader and listener but a better speaker and writer as well. I show you how to raise your verbal intelligence. The proof will be in the efficacy of the suggestions I present, but in order to get you to take my suggestions seriously, I'm going to have to show you why they work.

READING AND LISTENING

Bad writing and speaking not only waste time and create confusion; they create bad reading and listening habits. We've all learned to tune out much of what we hear, and to read the way we watch TV —passively. Expert readers and listeners are not passive. They actively seek out and transform what they read and hear through several stages.

The first stage of active processing is sensory: focusing our eyes on the words, which is really focusing the words on our eyes. Listening also begins with an active process of attention, called the "cocktail party phenomenon." The next time you are at a party, tune in on surrounding conversations one at a time. It's quite easy.

Once we have captured verbal information, we process it at several levels. The second stage is coding: translating the sound or image into auditory or visual symbols. The next stage for both spoken and written language is the lexical: converting these sounds or shapes into words: "I scream" or "ice cream." Then comes the syntactic level, where we "parse" or figure out relationships among words in terms of rules of grammar: word forms and word order. At the semantic level, we figure out what sentences and phrases mean. Finally, at the discourse level, we try to understand relationships among sentences: the point.

All of these processes work "bottom-up": Identifying letters or sounds allows you to identify words, which in turn allows you to understand their meanings, which in turn helps you to figure out what the point is.

These processes also work "top-down." Knowing what the writer or speaker is getting at allows you to deduce the meanings of words, which in turn tells you how these words are formed. Consider this sentence: "The millwright on my right thinks it right that some conventional rite should signify the right of every man to write as he pleases." Understanding or transcribing this sentence depends on both bottom-up ("data driven") and top-down ("conceptually driven") processes. The spellings depend on the meanings as much as the meanings depended on the spellings. A stenographer can infer top-down from the meaning of each phrase to how the word should be spelled, but these top-down processes are the major obstacle in the development of the "voice typewriter," a (so far) imaginary device that will take dictation.

Let's talk about these stages or levels of processing one by one, with an eye to ways to improve our performance at each of them.

Eye Movements and Coding

As you read these words at the adult average of about 250 per minute, your eyes jump like someone crossing a stream by leaping from rock to rock. The words are the rocks. Some, especially small ones, we skip, while on others we pause for a few seconds to gain our balance. These teetering pauses are called "fixations," during which we focus a word on the fovea, a small dishlike depression in the light-sensitive part of each eye. Your foveae allow you to look at one thing at a time, and to see it acutely and in color. Each fovea sees less than a degree of visual angle, or about four to eight letters of average-sized print. When we read, our fixations vary tremendously in duration: Some words (especially small function words, like "to") are often not fixated at all, while others (especially unfamiliar ones, like "fovea") are fixated for seconds at a time, sometimes more than once. We extract most information during fixations.

Speed-reading courses train you to increase your reading speed by fixating each line once, at a point near its center. Speed-reading teachers presume that it is possible to increase the amount of information extracted during a single fixation. Unfortunately, this does not seem to be possible. We simply don't get the information from the ends of the line. It's true that good readers (those who read faster and with greater comprehension) have shorter and fewer fixations than poor ones. However, good readers vary their fixation patterns according to the difficulty and structure of what they read. The amount of information we get from each fixation varies, but only as a function of the type of information being conveyed, not as a result of fixating the center of each line.

Furthermore, though good readers are both faster and comprehend more than poor ones, for any one person there is a nearly perfect trade-off between speed and comprehension. Speed-readers who fixate once per line show very poor comprehension. They know it too—when they expect to be tested for comprehension, they revert to normal fixation patterns. The American Speedreading Academy recently approached cognitive psychologist Don Homa at Arizona State University, asking him to investigate two of their star pupils, both of whom claimed to read at over 100,000 words per minute. Homa submitted the speed-readers to several tests, including a test of reading comprehension. He concluded that "the only extraordinary talent exhibited by the two speed readers was their extraordinary rate of page-turning."

Is the two hundred to four hundred dollars spent on a typical speed-reading course a waste of money? Not necessarily. Speed-reading may be useful for people who have trouble learning how to skim, a valuable skill if you must scan lots of written material, only a little of which is worth reading. For reading that requires high levels of comprehension and retention, the time and money spent on speed-reading courses would be better invested in slower, more careful reading.

Lexical Access

The second stage of processing is "coding": translating the visual or auditory input into symbols. We can code words visually, as a shape, or orthographically, as a sequence of letters. Children who learn to recognize words at extremely early ages are usually using purely visual codes, like a distinctive shape or color.

We can also code words phonologically, as sounds. When we talk about the millwright's right to a rite, we use several different orthographic codes for the same phonological code.

Here's an illustration of how top-down processes in coding influence fixation patterns, which in turn influence what we see. Count the number of *f*'s in the following sentence: THE FIRST FINE FISHING DAY OF THE YEAR WE FINALLY FLEW TO ALASKA FOR FIVE DAYS OF REAL FISHING. Did you get eight? Most people do, but there are ten. Try it again. Still got eight? That's because you either skipped the two "of"'s or coded the *f*'s phonologicaly, as *v* sounds.

The next stage of processing is called "lexical access." In this stage we use our visual or phonological codes to come up with the word we've just read or heard. The difference between coding and lexical access is illustrated by the "tip-of-the-tongue" phenomenon. In this peculiar state, which William James compared to the moment before a sneeze, you know that you know a word, but you can't quite spit it out. In their classic study of this phenomenon, Harvard psychologists Roger Brown and David McNeill found that you can often remember the approximate length and beginning sound of a word on the tip of your tongue. Evidently, in the tip-of-the-tongue state, phonological codes are accessible even when the word itself isn't. You can use this fact when you've got to come up with a word on the tip of your tongue. For example, if you need to introduce someone whose name you know but can't come up with, guess the first sound, then run through names beginning with that sound while you engage in small talk. Even if it feels like a shot in the dark, more often than not, your guess about the sound of the name will be correct. This trick has saved me embarrassment more than once.

Lexical access seems to be a key to differences between good and poor readers. For one thing, good readers take only about sixty-five milliseconds to recognize a word, while poor readers take almost twice as long. Good readers also code words more flexibly than poor readers. They switch smoothly from unconscious automatic (silent reading) visual codes to consciously controlled phonological codes whenever they encounter unfamiliar material. Poor readers are good at coding common words phonologically, but when they hit an unfamiliar word, they trip. They don't have the ability to "sound out" new words. They are at the mercy of their automated top-down codes—they respond to word shapes and often misread unfamiliar words without knowing it.

Just as you literally could not see the extra *f*'s in the sentence about fishing, you often ignore words you don't know. Have you ever learned a new word, only to see it in print the very next day? Probably you ignored it before you learned it.

A large *reading* (as opposed to speaking or writing) vocabulary is thus even more important than most people realize. There are three ways to build our reading vocabularies. The best way is to learn and use some tactics for deducing the meanings of words from context. If you can pretty much understand the passage or if you've got some notion of what a new word means, make an educated guess and keep your eyes open for other places the word is used to see if your guess makes sense. Otherwise, reread the passage to see if a synonym appears nearby.

These tactics don't always work, so expert readers have a backup strategy. They read with a dictionary at hand; they don't mind admitting they don't know a word, and regard new words the way wine tasters regard new wines. Make it a habit to use a dictionary, and to make it easy, use the smallest one that meets your needs.

A third strategy is brute force, using rote learning exercises like the ones described in the vocabulary-building books listed in the references for this chapter. These techniques seem to be most effective for people who have a hard time learning words from context.

Because using context or a dictionary engages you actively in finding the meaning of a word, you are more likely to remember it than if you learn it by rote. For most of us, time spent on vocabulary-building courses would be better spent in careful reading with a dictionary handy.

The bottom-up and top-down processes are integrated in a system called "working," or "short-term," memory. This is the system you use to remember the beginning of a sentence in order to make sense out of the end. It's what you use to remember a new phone number long enough to dial it. Working memory lasts only about twenty seconds. If anyone has ever asked you a simple question like "Where's the stapler?" or otherwise interrupts you for more than a few seconds while you're in the middle of dialing, you usually have to look up the number again. Without such interruptions, we are able to keep items in working memory indefinitely by reciting them to ourselves, aloud or silently. For most of us, working memory holds no more than about seven unrelated items, which is why phone numbers are seven digits long. People of high verbal ability can often hold nine or ten items in working memory. Thus it is another important determinant of verbal ability; such people can remember what the word "it" at the beginning of this sentence stands for.

The most powerful intelligence amplifier available to the human mind is not a drug or a machine but a mental process that goes by the unpretentious name "chunking." Chunking allows us to transcend the seven-item limit of working memory by treating groups of items as units. We can hold only about seven items in working memory, but the seven items can be chunks, each of which contains about seven items, each of which is itself a chunk. Try to memorize this number: 14092171376195069. Not easy, is it? But suppose I give you a chunking strategy. Instead of seventeen unrelated numbers, you've got three important dates in U.S. history, each with the number of states existing at that date in the middle. Now you've got seven chunks: three dates, three numbers, and a rule for combining them. You'll find that you will be able to come up with that number even after you've finished this chapter.

Even with chunking, working memory is still a bottleneck. This has several practical implications. In both reading and listening, most of us bite off more than we can chew. If you need to remember what you read, pause at least every fifteen seconds or seven items, whichever comes first. Use the pause to recite what you've just read.

In listening, the limitations of working memory mean we've got to take notes. However, research on notetaking shows that listeners who try to write points down as they are made are liable to overload their working memory. Educational psychologist D. L. Peters presented material either at the normal pace of lectures and business presentations, or at a much faster pace. At both rates of presentation, notetaking helped people with good working memories, but hindered those with poor ones. In other experiments, listeners, especially those with poor working memories, were better off using their working memories to understand the sense of a message and writing it down at natural breaks in the material, or even at the end.

Shorthand can help you take notes quickly in natural pauses. Develop your own, or have someone who knows the Gregg or other system show you a few tricks. Even a handful of the common abbreviations can help enormously. And if nothing else, learn to leave out all vowels. Y wll fnd tht y cn stll ndrstnd yr nts jst fn.

Getting the Point

The highest level I'll consider here is getting the point, seeing how the sentences or other parts of the discourse relate to the whole. (The higher level, evaluating, is the subject of Chapter 10.) Memory depends on comprehension: Memory for uncomprehended material is poor, as the following passage shows:

> If the balloons popped, the sound would not be able to carry since everything would be too far away from the correct floor. A closed window would also prevent the sound from carrying since most buildings tend to be well insulated. Since the whole operation depends on a steady supply of electricity, a break in the middle of the wire would also cause problems. Of course the

fellow could shout, but the human voice is not loud enough to carry that far. An additional problem is that a string could break on the instrument. Then there could be no accompaniment to the message. It is clear that the best situation would involve less distance. Then there would be fewer problems. With face-to-face contact, the fewest number of things could go wrong.

Even though every sentence is clear, this is gobbledygook. Yet everything in the passage makes sense if you know what's going on: A modern-day Romeo serenades his sweetheart by playing a guitar and singing into a microphone. His voice is carried by long wires to a loudspeaker suspended from a batch of helium-filled balloons outside his sweetheart's sixth-floor window.

When experimental subjects were provided with a cartoon depicting this scene, they had no trouble understanding and remembering the passage, but without the cartoon, they got very little. The point is that to understand and remember, you must relate the new material to some meaningful notion, or schema. (To refresh your memory, a schema is an organized system of knowledge that provides "slots" for a wide variety of relevant information.) Thus, if you have a good schema for a topic, it is easy for you to learn more about it. College students who knew a lot about baseball recalled much more of half an inning of a fictitious baseball game than students who knew little about the game. It wasn't that the knowledgeable students had better memories: They remembered *less* than the other students about details irrelevant to the game (like the attendance figures). In other words, knowledge provides the schemas you need to learn more.

This is the phenomenon of the "apperceptive mass" described in Chapter 2: The more you know, the easier it is to associate new material to what's already there. Note that this principle violates the "filing cabinet" schema most people have for memory. That schema applies pretty well to working memory, which is like a very small filing cabinet with only seven files. The more we put into a filing cabinet, the harder it is to get more in. On the other hand, long-term memory (which is any memory that lasts longer than the twenty seconds of working memory) is infinitely expandable. The more files you've got in long-term memory, the easier it is to handle new information—if you can get new information into the right file.

To do this, you must continually monitor yourself to make sure you are really getting the point. Keep the big picture in mind as you read or listen. Most of us have a tendency to ignore not only the forest but the trees, as we chew like caterpillars on leaves. Ask yourself where you are, where you've been, and try to guess what's coming next. If you can't, you're lost, and you'd better climb up the trunk (main point) for a look-see.

Looking at large units like forests and trees also allows you to take advantage of chunking. Chunking makes material easier to remember not only by organizing it but by adding information to it. This is called "elaboration." You can use the principles of chunking, organization, and elaboration to take notes that will help you remember and review. You can usually write things down (especially if you keep a notebook on you—mine is built into my wallet). Make your notes schematic: Keep them brief and organized, preferably in the form of an outline with fewer than seven items at each level of organization. This may sound like a lot to do while you're trying to keep up with a stream of (especially aural) information, but like many other skills, chunking and organization improve with practice and eventually become almost automatic.

Academicians love rote memory because it's easier to test and investigate than discourse-level memory, but memorizing is only occasionally a practical skill. Once in a while, though, you may need to remember, say, the names of ten regional managers and may be unable to consult notes, as in an "extemporaneous" pep talk you know you'll be asked to give. When Cicero and other Roman orators had to commit long speeches to memory, they used the method of loci. This effective memory-improvement scheme uses the enormous storage capacity of spatial memory (described in Chapter 7) to file verbal material. Start with an imaginary trip you know well, such as a tour of your home. Construct an image for each name, and place that image in a particular place. The image should have lots of associative "hooks." An easy way to get lots of hooks is to make the images bizarre, or at least as vivid as possible. Thus, Norman Linton, the first manager, is a Viking with lint on his tunic, standing in the foyer. Preston Sommers is a Mountie in a bathing suit under the chandelier; Gloria Manucia is a shining piece of fine print next to the light switch, and so on. If you take the time to construct such images and practice retrieving them, you will find that you can come up with the names even in the middle of your "impromptu" presentation.

You can make rote memory even more effective by using a phenomenon called "state dependent learning." The more closely the conditions of recall approximate conditions of learning, the better. If, for example, you will have to recall information in the morning, memorize it in the morning. If you know you'll be caffeinated and nervous when you are recalling the information, make yourself nervous when you learn: Drink coffee and set a time limit for memorizing each item. State dependent learning even extends to the physical surroundings—you're better off learning and recalling in the same room.

Like chunking, organization, and elaboration, formal memory improvement techniques become automatic with practice. Therefore, the last three practical suggestions for improving your reading and listening and memory are practice, practice, and practice. Practice in organizing and elaborating written and spoken information is probably the single most important function of law school and other professional programs that deluge students with far more information than they could ever hope to remember, even with the aid of memory-improvement schemes. Processes at sensory, lexical, syntactic, semantic, and discourse levels are not only learnable but automatable. With lots of practice, they become second nature: swift, smooth, and unconscious.

Choose the material you practice on according to the other abilities you want to foster. To enhance lexical abilities, read masters of words: poets like Wallace Stevens, or novelists like Henry James and Thomas Berger; for syntactic skills, read masters of grammatical construction: Edward Gibbon, William Faulkner, William Styron. Even if you aren't fond of these writers to start with, research shows that repeated exposure leads to increased enjoyment. In selecting the level of difficulty, it's a good idea to adopt a tactic from tennis: Play with someone only a little above your level.

WRITING

Playing with the masters has another practical payoff: It can help you criticize and organize your own writing. However, although reading great literature provides momentary relief from the symptoms of bad writing, it is no panacea. To treat the disease itself, we need some specific remedies. That's why major corporations pay writing consultants fees that blanch their academic counterparts: up to one thousand dollars a day for small groups. These courses are worth the expense. After one of them, executives at AT&T condensed the average three-hundred-word memo to about one hundred words, and pared writing time from an hour and a half to half an hour. At Pepsico, an executive's plan for reorganizing his unit was turned down. He took a writing course from Barbara Minto, who works out of London, and rewrote and resubmitted the plan two weeks later. It was approved. Attorney James Minor, who learned the art of legislative drafting from a master, Reed Dickerson, professor of law at Indiana University, was able to reduce Federal Aviation Administration regulations to one fifth their original length—and make them clearer in the process.

The remedies prescribed by professional writing consultants work. In this section, I describe *how* they work.

Effective writing remedies must take the limitations of working memory into account. Working memory is the aorta of language—most diseases of writing are the results of pumping too much information at once. When you try to think of what to say, how to say it, and how it reads, all at the same time, you risk a disease even more deadly than verbal anemia, hemorrhaging, or leukemia: thrombosis, the obstruction of the flow of words called writer's block. That's why Peter Elbow, author of *Writing with Power* and an expert writing teacher, calls trying for an acceptable first draft "the dangerous method."

Thus, the cure for bad writing begins with a kind of quarantine: separating the processes of writing in order to treat them. The basic processes of writing are planning, generating, organizing, rewriting, and editing. Let's treat them one by one.

A simple piece of practical advice: Use a word processor (a computer *program* that turns a microcomputer into the ultimate electronic typewriter). Using a state-of-the-art word processor is far easier than placing a long-distance credit card call and almost as inexpensive: Useful word processing programs are available for as little as fifteen dollars. Try one. Within half an hour, you'll have recouped your investment. Word processors drastically reduce the mechanical hassles of writing. More significantly, by making it easy to edit and reorganize, they reduce the pressure on your working memory. All the remedies described below are far easier on a word processor than on a tape recorder or a conventional or an electronic typewriter.

You may think that "real executives don't type," but dictation isn't much better than even old-fashioned typing. A study at IBM showed that experienced dictators could dictate a business letter in 10.2 minutes but that it took them only one minute longer to write it. Dictation does make one feel important, but successful executives are willing to try anything that promises to boost their productivity.

In most cases, a writer must begin by gathering information. Indexes like *Business Periodicals Index,* and on-line data bases like Dialogue, can reduce legwork.

The next step is to define your purpose. Ask yourself why you are writing. Do you mean to persuade, to attack, to explain, to inform, to move, or just to stay in touch? With your goals in mind, do a "front-end analysis": Consider the costs and benefits of writing in the first place. Might some other medium (telephone, skywriting) serve your purposes better, with less effort?

For short pieces of writing, like memos, Elbow recommends spending half your available time writing briskly, "helter-skelter," with no concern for spelling, wording, or grammar, but with your purpose in mind so you don't repeat or digress. Save the other half of your time for editing. When your writing time is up, ruthlessly cut the worst parts and the ones that don't belong and mark the best and most essential points. Then number them in the order that makes them clearest, add an introductory statement of purpose, and finally edit for spelling and usage.

For longer pieces of writing, like letters, proposals, or reports, you need a plan. Elbow suggests that writers begin by considering not only their goals but the audience. Linda Flower, a psychologist at Carnegie-Mellon and author of *Problem-Solving Strategies for Writing,* suggests that you sketch (not write) out a plan in the form of a tree. The tree I used for this chapter looks like this:

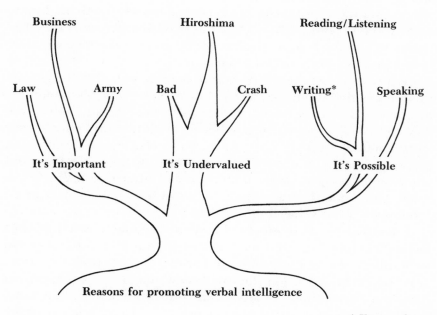

* You are here.

Once you've got a plan, describe it to your reader. The commonest complaint about business writing is failure to present a clear conclusion. Writer-editor-entrepreneur Malcolm Forbes advises:

"Plunge right in. Tell what your letter is about in the first paragraph."

Now for the first form of quarantine, separate what you want to say from how you plan to say it. Psychologists Allan Collins and Dedre Gentner at Bolt Beranek and Newman, a firm that conducts psychological research for businesses, studied the cognitive processes of writing. They concluded that "It is important to separate idea production from text production. The processes involved in producing text . . . must produce a linear sequence that satisfies certain grammatical rules. In contrast, the result of the process of idea production is a set of ideas with many internal connections, only a few of which may fit the linear model desirable for text." In other words, when you think about what you want to say, you see all kinds of connections, but when you plan how to say it, you've got to write one word at a time.

The next step is to generate lots of ideas, enough so you won't mind discarding the worst ones. This is a good time to practice brainstorming, synectics, lateral thinking, tagmemics, idea tracking, and the other approaches to creativity described in Chapter 12. Remember the quarantine: This is not the time to figure out how to express the ideas—get them down as sketches, phrases, or clichés. Never worry about poor spelling and grammar. Show connections between ideas with lines or circles.

When you separate the process of figuring out what to say from the process of writing, you can capitalize on the well-oiled cognitive machinery that allows us to speak fluidly and fluently. "Write the way you talk," advises Malcolm Forbes. This is even better advice than it sounds. Speech is five to six times faster than writing. We form a syntactic outline of what we mean to say, select content words, and decide on affixes unconsciously and automatically. At this stage, you want to bring these powerful automatic, unconscious processes to bear on writing.

Peter Elbow has a wonderful way of making your writing like talking and loosening up your creative writing. It's a kind of verbal yoga called freewriting: You write nonstop without pause, revision, or reflection for as long as you can. Freewriting is transcribing your stream of consciousness. Follow your thoughts wherever they lead, even if they seem to take you away from your topic. You can check later to see if these side trips really were digressions. Freewriting overcomes writer's block by preventing the censor from intruding on the creative process. Freewriting has the therapeutic effect of a high-fiber diet: It scrubs out your verbal arteries. It even feels good, like meditation or running.

If you have to write an important memo to your boss, and you can't get your freewriting started, imagine a different audience. If you're having a hard time getting words on paper, write a letter to a friend who makes you feel witty and articulate.

For practical writing tasks like reports, an especially effective use of freewriting is what Elbow calls "loop writing." Start out with a point you need to handle, and use it to trigger a burst of freewriting. If another major point emerges, use it as a launching pad for yet another. Then go back to your plan and select what you need from your freewriting. Repeat as needed.

Only after you've let your right hemisphere run wild is it time for left-brained systematic exploration. Go back over your research notes or other input, marking or listing all the relevant points, noting connections and items that are subtopics of others. What you've got at this point is a plan and an intentionally incoherent mess of notes, selections from your freewriting, comments, and connections.

The next step is the critical stage of the primary defense against hemorrhaging: combining the plan and the mess into a clear functional outline. Writing consultants agree that organization is the rarest ability to find and the hardest to teach.

To develop your outline, begin by revising your plan on the basis of any new connections that may have emerged at the end of the last stage. If necessary, sketch your new plan as another tree. Then climb through your tree, keeping a record of each fork and branch as you go. This record is your outline. Since working memory (yours and your reader's) holds only about seven items, prune mercilessly or chunk by adding more forks. Keep the outline lean but not scraggly. If you've got a lot of suckers around the base of the trunk, lop 'em off. If you've got a long, thin branch that takes you off into empty space, prune it.

The end of each branch will be a paragraph: one or more sentences that make a point. Paragraphs should be as short as possible, and often a single short sentence makes a punchy paragraph. A paragraph is a unit of thought, not a certain number of words, so if they have to run over the 320 words some writing consultants recommend, let them.

When you finish writing the paragraph at the end of each limb, jump down to the fork just below, write a transition sentence if necessary, and climb the next branch. Repeat this procedure until you have climbed through the whole tree. Then you can put all the notes, comments, and freewriting fragments into the order dictated by your outline. Now you have a (very) rough draft.

Revision: From Me to Meaning

Now take a break to let your draft cool down. The longer the interval between the caffeinated brilliance of that first draft and the sobering reading of what you actually wrote, the more your reaction will resemble the reader's. The only substitute for letting your first draft cool off is your own editor, and few of us can afford one. Write something else if you have to, go skiing, get out of town, do anything but stew over what you've written. This is not goofing off; it is an essential part of problem solving. Psychologists call it "incubation." The longer your writing incubates the better, right up to and beyond the point where you forget what you've written. This period of incubation will help you impose the second quarantine, between writing and editing, between vision and revision.

Healthy writing is a dynamic balance of these two separate, contradictory, and mutually exclusive processes—composing, which is primarily creative, and editing, which is primarily analytic. Creative and analytic processes are equally important, but separate even at an anatomic level: They take place in different parts of the brain. Trying to do both at the same time is like making love on a bicycle.

When you come back to your writing, try to put yourself in your reader's mind. Linda Flower describes the critical process of revision as a transformation of "writer-based" into "reader-based" prose. Writer-based prose is egocentric. It considers only the needs of the writer: to show what he knows, how hard he's worked, or how clever he is with words. Reader-based prose, on the other hand, is informed by a concern for the goals, abilities, and knowledge of the reader.

Your reader probably cares less about the topic than you do, so part of your job may be to make him or her care at least enough to read what you have to say. On the other hand, he or she may care more than you do, in which case your job is to avoid being flip.

Remember the reader's information-processing needs and limitations. At the sensory level, neatness counts. As my teacher Steve Kaplan used to say whenever he insisted that I clean my typewriter before rewriting a report: "To you it's ideas, but to me it's a visual stimulus." Don't overload the reader's working memory with sentences that are too long, that contain references to nouns mentioned far before, or that list more than about seven items in a row. Get feedback on your writing.

At the word level, it's fine to have a large vocabulary for reading, but don't practice your word power on others. Basic English, which is all you need for nontechnical communication, is eight hundred words—out of the fifty thousand words of the unabridged dictionary. You can get by in a foreign land with four hundred, and Dr. Seuss tells stories adults love to read using as few as two hundred words. When you use a bunch of words no one else knows, you alienate your reader. And you're liable to say something you don't mean, like using "negative reinforcement" when you mean its opposite, the everyday word "punishment."

Rather than pumping up your prose with fancy words, play with everyday words to increase your verbal dexterity.

- Do crossword puzzles, write poems.
- Make up and solve verbal analogies like the ones in Robert Sternberg's *Intelligence Applied:* ITT is to Geneen as GMC is to _____.
- Make up "daffynitions": Tirade—a summer drink made from automobile tires. Demonstration—devil's food cake. Manslaughter—a male expression of delight.
- Create tendentious triplets: I am firm; you are obstinate; he is pig-headed. I am thrifty; you are parsimonious; she is a tightwad.
- Pun. (But only in private.)

Don't hesitate to use technical terminology, as long as it's not lost on your reader. There is a big difference between jargon and gobbledygook: Jargon is the technical terminology that specialists need to communicate fine but important distinctions. Gobbledygook is what you get when you try to *sound* like a specialist.

A quick and dirty way to evaluate the demands your writing places on the reader is Robert Gunning's Fog Index, which measures writing in terms of the grade level of the brightest reader who could be expected to understand it. *Business Week* and the Gettysburg Address have a Fog Index of about 10. Most news magazines, like *Time,* run a little higher, around 11 or 12. This paragraph is about 8 or 9. To calculate your own Fog Index, take a short paragraph of about a hundred words. Count the number of words, rating dates and other numbers as single words. Then count the number of sentences. Divide the number of words by the number of sentences to get the average number of words per sentence. Now get a polysyllable tally. Count the number of words of three or more syllables in your sample. (Don't count proper names; you don't have control over those.) Now add your polysyllable count to your words per sentence. Multiply the sum by .4. If the product is higher than 16, you're writing over the heads of average college graduates.

Don't take the Fog Index too seriously; occasionally, especially in technical fields, you have to write foggy prose, and sometimes you can write a paragraph with a high Fog Index that is nevertheless perfectly clear. This paragraph, for example, has a Fog Index of approximately 19.

Remember that the reader doesn't know what you know, especially about your plan. Typically, your reader knows less about the topic than you do. Peter Elbow describes the writer's privilege and the reader's plight with a delightful metaphor: "The writer steers sitting in the stern, facing forward; the reader does all the work, rowing and also facing backwards without even knowing where she is going until she gets there." This makes it essential that you provide a structure that makes sense from the reader's point of view. Such a structure may not do justice to the intricacies of a technical field but is better than a structure that is incomprehensible or unread.

Give your reader plenty of cues to structure. Readers climb trees like cats—going up is a lot easier than going down. Make sure those transition sentences help you down from each branch of your plan and point the way into the next one. In each major section, follow the old adage: Tell 'em what you're going to tell 'em; then tell 'em; then tell 'em what you told 'em.

By now, your draft looks even worse than it did when you started. Take advantage of the copious flow you produced while freewriting, and be ruthless: cut, cut, and cut some more. Eliminate whole paragraphs where possible, sentences where necessary, then get in there with a scalpel and excise spare words. William Strunk and E. B. White, whose book *The Elements of Style* is the industry standard for clarity and brevity, warn about the words "rather," "little," "very," and "pretty," which they call "leeches that infest the pond of prose, sucking the blood of words."

Once you've cut to the bone, get a clear copy so you can read what's really there. It's time for the final phases of editing. Sit back and try to read what you've written through your reader's eyes.

"Write so he'll enjoy it," advises Forbes. Enjoyment may be too much to strive for in a letter about investment credit deductions, but you can at least spare your reader unnecessary suffering. Avoid fancy metaphors: If they don't work perfectly, they make you and your reader look stupid. Here's a metaphor by a famous CEO that almost makes it but ends up derailing itself: "The mechanics of management enable you to stay on the rails so that your emotional firepower does not drive you over the cliffs of bankruptcy." If the guy who wrote that can unintentionally end up with a candidate for *The New Yorker*'s "Block That Metaphor" feature, so can you. Don't get cute. Writing so your reader will enjoy does not mean adding fancy rhetoric or gratuitous humor.

Write in your own voice. Above all, using your own voice means being natural. Read your writing aloud. You should be able to do it naturally and easily, without feeling twinges of phoniness. It should ring with your voice, the way William Buckley's columns drawl and Andy Rooney's columns whine.

Adapt your tone to your audience. In a proposal to a prospective client, you might project yourself as a serious, no-nonsense trouble-shooter, but in a memo to your associates about an office party, strive for a lighter touch. In either case, adopt the attitude described by Peter Elbow: Say "I'm *me*, I'm saying *this*, and I'm saying it to *you*."

Writing naturally means using the active voice, avoiding words ending in "-tion," like "implementation." The two comments I most frequently add to the grant proposals I review are "KISS" (Keep It Super Simple) and "SWYM" (Say What You Mean). George Orwell, an expert on practical uses of language, contrasts two versions of a famous piece of prose. Here's the original, from Ecclesiastes: "I returned, and saw under the sun, that the race is not to the swift, nor the battle to the strong, neither yet bread to the wise, nor yet riches to men of understanding, nor yet favour to men of skill; but time and chance happeneth to them all."

Contrast this punchy, precise prose with Orwell's translation into institutionalese: "Objective consideration of contemporary phenomena compels the conclusion that success or failure in competitive activities exhibits no tendency to be commensurate with innate capacity, but that a considerable element of the unpredictable must invariably be taken into account."

If you're writing this sort of gobbledygook, don't sink, SWYM. Talk out loud to your dog, your computer, or the invisible rabbit in the corner of your office. Say, "What I'm really trying to say is . . ." You may get some weird looks, but talking instead of writing works.

Once you've edited for style and voice, have someone else edit for spelling and usage, which may require typing another draft. This may seem like a lot of drafts to you—but remember the fifteen drafts it's supposed to take managers at Proctor & Gamble.

If you can't get someone else to edit, read it aloud. Reading aloud will force you to look at each word, and avoid the "proof-reader's error," the the powerful tendency to see what you think is there, not what's really there. Did you notice that "the" appears twice in a row in the sentence above? Word processors with built-in spelling checkers don't catch the most lethal spelling errors, which are not typos but homophones—"there" instead of "their" or "they're." Remember the rite of the right to write.

Reading aloud for spelling and usage also gives you one last chance to hear how it sounds. If you've done your job, you will have written something you'd be proud to read aloud to an audience.

SPEAKING

You may indeed be proud to read your writing aloud, but unless you are an Orson Welles, don't read your speech. Reading aloud is a good way to check your writing for tone, but it's a terrible way to deliver a speech. There is a good reason why we read aloud to put our children to sleep. Most of us read in a monotonous drone.

Most of us are even less effervescent when we recite material we've memorized, so don't try to memorize your presentation—you will end up sounding as bored as you're bound to be. Monotony is the disease that most often kills oral presentations. Richard Boyatzis singled out "spontaneity" in speaking as one of his major managerial competencies.

Howard Edson, a Denver management consultant, bears out Boyatzis's point. Edson runs workshops for his clients, so effective speaking is his bread and butter. "People made some comments to me about my monotone, and I began to realize I wasn't using the full range of my voice," Edson said. He sought professional treatment from a "voice doctor" named Kerry McGuirk, who runs SoundVoice, a voice-coaching business. Most people never use their full ranges of pitch and loudness, especially their lower register, so McGuirk prescribes vocal exercises. Edson is pleased with the results: "I feel much more capable of driving home points dramatically in my workshops."

It's fear of appearing foolish or of forgetting an important point that tightens the speaker's throat and tempts most speakers to read or memorize (and forget what they've memorized) in the first place. To some extent, this anxiety is justified. Writing is like painting: you can paint over what you've done as many times as time allows; but speaking is like sculpture: when a piece has been chipped away, it's gone. On the other hand, if you know how to use your own anxiety, it can be a powerful prophylactic for monotony. Peter Elbow notes that experienced speakers "let themselves feel excitement and even anxiety because they know what to do with those emotions . . . if you are . . . tired . . . or bored . . . an audience can get you up so you can concentrate again." Therefore, stay in touch with your audience. Get a critique when you're done. You may be good or bad in ways you don't suspect.

But what if you're so anxious about speaking in public that the mere thought of it sends a flash of fear through your guts? The cure is "desensitization." Start with a completely nonthreatening situation and gradually move toward the real, scary one. Begin by delivering some real material exactly as you would to a real group—but do it under nonthreatening circumstances: in your basement, with no one else at home. The oddity of the situation is part of the treatment—you *want* to feel awkward, but not uptight. Practice until you're at ease talking alone in your basement.

Then move by the *tiniest* step to a slightly tenser situation: with your cat as an audience, present your talk again. Then add a full-length mirror to make you more self-conscious. Then record your talk. Knowing you're being recorded will boost your anxiety until you get used to it. Moreover, the recording will let you hear what your voice sounds like to others. If at any stage you feel the slightest twinge of anxiety, back up to the previous step and repeat it until you feel at ease. Otherwise, you'll be conditioning yourself to be tense. At the end of this stage, you've got a nonthreatening audience of three: your mirror image, a tape recorder, and a cat.

Sooner or later, you will be tempted to rush the cure, but don't. This is a radical procedure, intended for the many people with real speaking phobias.

Eventually you'll feel ready for the critical step: Exchange your audience for one nonthreatening human being: a child, the plumber —anyone who won't make you feel nervous. Repeat until you feel completely at ease, then add one more nonthreatening person. At this point you may be able to exchange your nonthreatening audience of two for one person whose opinion matters—a colleague or your wife.

One day you'll be ready for your first public appearance, which should be under the friendliest possible circumstances. Prepare a short joke or other very brief bit for your poker cronies, your sewing circle, or friends you meet for lunch. Deliver longer and longer pieces at larger and larger gatherings. Toastmasters' or other warm, supportive groups can help you make the final transition to true public speaking.

Most nervous speakers can be cured by a much less radical procedure. They can use a microphone, a pointer, or another prop as an emotional crutch, like Linus's blanket in the *Peanuts* comic strip. You can practice with such a crutch, which psychologists call a "transitional object," by talking to it. Then, when you've got to give a real talk, talk to the transitional object instead of the audience. Eventually you'll be able to wean yourself away from your crutch by gradually tuning in to the audience.

Desensitization and transitional objects are defensive tactics, designed to cure anxiety and thereby eliminate the temptations to read or memorize. A far more positive approach is to organize information in the form of a story. Harvard psychologist Jerome Bruner calls the ability to spin events into a story "narrative intelligence," and he regards it as independent of IQ. Words are the usual medium for storytelling, so narrative intelligence is a form of verbal intelligence. We don't ordinarily think of storytelling as practical, but in their book *Corporate Cultures*, Terence Deal and Allan Kennedy argue persuasively that "90% of real business goes on in the cultural network" of organizations. The bearers of a corporation's "oral tradition" are in a powerful position because they can "change reality." They are probably people who have high levels of narrative intelligence.

If you are a gifted storyteller, don't keep your light under a wastebasket. Organize your talk as a story or a cycle of stories that make your point for you.

For those of us who are not storytellers, and for technical information that doesn't fit the narrative form, an outline is the best way to ensure you don't leave anything out and that you form fresh sentences. An outline reduces anxiety by keeping your attention focused on how to say what you mean, not on how you're doing. Most important of all, if you're careful to describe your outline's structure, it will adapt your presentation to the cognitive capacities of your audience. Ruth Day, a professor of psychology at Duke University, points out that an outline in the form of a tree allows you to see relationships among sections and points at a glance, which is valuable when you have to answer questions. And if you run short of time, you can easily prune the ends of branches of major points, while leaving the point itself intact, or eliminate whole branches if necessary.

In preparing the outline for a speech, follow the suggestions for preparing a written report. Above all, keep the number of points and subpoints to fewer than seven. Recapitulation is a good way to protect a talk at its most vulnerable moment: the end. Many good talks are killed by weak, abrupt endings ("I guess that's all").

A talk without a clear conclusion is liable to be maintained by heroic measures long after it is brain-dead. This risk is especially high when you're nervous. The best piece of advice on speaking I got came when I needed it most. I was in the Oval Office to address President John F. Kennedy on behalf of a group of young scientists. As I rose, ready to orate, someone slipped me a note. It said: "Stand up. Speak up. Shut up."

9.
Logical-Mathematical Intelligence

Think 'til it hurts.
—LORD THOMSON

For twenty years, *Star Trek*'s Mr. Spock has rescued the crew of the starship *Enterprise* from comets, Klingons, and critics. He is logical-mathematical intelligence in the flesh. Logical-mathematical intelligence (LMI) is the ability to think systematically and abstractly, using the concepts of logic and mathematics. We need Spock's skills in everyday life just as much as Captain Kirk does in outer space.

LMI incorporates verbal and spatial abilities, and like them (and unlike some other forms of practical intelligence), LMI shines in school and IQ tests. It also provides the ground rules for the complex and critical cognitive styles described later on.

Though LMI incorporates and mediates other ways of being smart, according to Howard Gardner LMI develops independently of them. LMI has its own system of symbols, the language of symbolic logic and mathematics. It also seems to have its own sequence of stages, as described by developmental psychologist Jean Piaget. It has its own pathologies, in the forms of retardation and delusion, and its prodigies, like the mathematician Carl Gauss, who discovered an error in his father's accounting at age three, derived the formula for the sum of an arithmetic progression at ten, began work on the first non-Euclidean geometry at twelve, and discovered the prime number theorem at sixteen. Because logical-mathematical intelligence develops independently of other intellectual abilities, political leaders and other convincing communicators are not always logical thinkers, while engineers and other people high in LMI are not necessarily good at communicating their ideas.

We depend on people who are high in LMI, but we distrust them. Mr. Spock's flat voice and pointy ears are symbols of our ambivalence: Like the abstract ratiocination he embodies, Spock is indispensable, yet alien. By making Spock an unemotional alien, the creators of *Star Trek* capture our uneasiness about LMI but misrepresent intelligence itself. Within and across species, high intelligence and high emotion go hand in hand. If we ever encounter extraterrestrials with IQs of 600, they will probably be highly emotional, more like E.T. than Mr. Spock. Though we link LMI with Vulcans, whiz kids, and mad scientists, this way of being smart is as warm and human as any other.

Our alienation from LMI would be an amusing anomaly were it confined to science fiction. Unfortunately, shelves of how-to-succeed books sell the seductive message that success is based on impulsive action, not reflective thought. They have provided a whole generation with yet another welcome excuse to shun science and mathematics.

As a result of our distrust of LMI, mathematical decision theory and other intelligence amplifiers rarely influence the day-to-day practice of physicians, lawyers, and managers. Most real-world decisionmakers prefer "clinical" approaches, in which the ways of combining data vary from case to case, to "actuarial" ones, in which the same rule is applied to all cases.

This is a pity. There are many ways in which rational, systematic approaches surpass intuitive, clinical ones. In *The Proactive Manager,* Lorne Plunkett and Guy Hale point out that actuarial techniques are teachable, persuasive, efficient, reliable, repeatable, and delegatable. The superiority of actuarial approaches in diagnosis and planning has been well documented by decades of research in real-world situations. Decision theorist R. M. Dawes summarizes such research: "The statistical analysis was thought to provide a floor to which the judgment of the experienced clinician could be compared. The floor turned out to be a ceiling."

People who distrust statistical models are unlikely to be convinced of their superiority by statistical arguments. Fortunately, the strongest argument requires no statistics, but only the realization that the clinician's intuition can be built into an actuarial model. This process is called "bootstrapping." One form of bootstrapping has been used to simulate the on-the-job decisions of radiologists, stockbrokers, admissions committees, and judges of corn quality and human beauty. In each of these fields, the statistical models not only matched the judgments of the decisionmakers but exceeded the accuracy of many of the individuals from whom the models were derived.

Actuarial judgments surpass clinical ones because they include the intuitions of the expert and because they are consistently comprehensive. Though clinical judgments may use many different variables over several different cases, in any particular case most clinical judgments use only one or two. By consistently weighting variables according to their diagnostic value, actuarial judgments include all the factors used by clinicians, and avoid the distractions and biases that we all too often bring to individual cases.

The commonest argument against actuarial judgments is that they are "inhuman," but what is really inhuman is not to make the best possible judgment as often as possible. There is nothing inhuman about being rational.

Advocates of clinical as opposed to actuarial judgments often argue that the real world is too complicated, changeable, and unpredictable for LMI. This is often true. In many cases, we simply haven't enough experience or time to use actuarial models, and impulsive, intuitive action is often essential. In other situations, however, to be impulsive is to invite disaster. An actuarial model can include "escapes" whereby under specified conditions one rationally decides to be impulsive.

Another argument against actuarial methods is that some variables cannot be quantified. However, subjective qualitative judgments ("I know it when I see it") can be scaled even if the scale is "present" or "absent," as in the "balance" of dog breeders and wine tasters. Moreover, actuarial models can weight these variables flexibly, according to their reliability and relative contribution to good decisions in different categories of decision. The policies of wine tasters whose confidence and concern about judgments of "earthiness" and "dryness" depend on whether the wine under consideration is a Bordeaux or a Rhine can be captured by a model that weights earthiness or dryness accordingly. Finally, real-world decisions, regardless of how subtle or subjective their inputs are, typically result in categorical outputs: to buy or not, hire or not, prescribe or not. At some point, ineffable "judgment" must become objective choice. Actuarial models place this point at the beginning, where it is most easily examined, and revised.

Although it is true that many successful people attribute their success to impulsive, intuitive judgments, studies of what these people actually do reveal lots of rational, Spock-like thought. In their in-depth study of industrial leaders Reg Jones of GE, Walter Wriston of Citicorp, Thomas Watson, Jr., of IBM, and Arthur Sulzberger of the *New York Times,* management consultant Harry Levinson and psychiatrist Stuart Rosenthal concluded that "what we see among these leaders is a great deal of thinking."

Consider, for example, how LMI is used by trial lawyer F. Lee Bailey, who has successfully pleaded the cases of a dockload of defendants, including accused murderer Dr. Sam Sheppard, whose story inspired the TV series *The Fugitive.* In his book *The Defense Never Rests,* Bailey describes his defenses of Dr. Carl Coppolino, a physician accused of a double murder. The first victim was William Farber, a neighbor and the husband of Coppolino's lover. New York medical examiner Dr. Milton Helpern showed Mr. Farber's larynx (in a jar) to the jury, pointing to fractures in the outer cartilage as prima facie evidence of strangulation. Bailey, however, argued that if Mr. Farber had been strangled, there would be signs of internal bleeding. There was no such bleeding, so Farber could not have been strangled. The verdict was not guilty.

Coppolino was also accused of murdering his wife, Carmela, by injection. The prosecution's case rested on traces of succinylcholine (a powerful sedative) in her body. These traces were the sole basis for the prosecution's claim that death was caused by injection. Bailey described other possible causes for the chemical traces, including the possibility that they were due to the chemical action of embalming fluid. Given the strength of other evidence against Coppolino, the verdict of Second-degree murder was a minor victory for Bailey.

Any good lawyer must become what Martin Mayer, author of *The Lawyers,* calls "one of the world's experts in any technical subject that is crucial to the issue." Acquiring such expertise requires attorneys to think like doctors, engineers, or detectives; the planning that precedes trials, hearings, and negotiations makes them think like generals; and civil cases involving money make them think like accountants. Finally, the mathematical symbols that are beginning to crawl across the pages of legal journals are signs that some lawyers are already thinking like mathematicians. It is no wonder that the undergraduate major preferred by several of our most prestigious law schools is mathematics.

Lawyers must also be able to think like lawyers. According to University of Chicago law professor Edward Levi, legal reasoning goes like this:

A [a case] falls more appropriately in B than in C [legal concepts]. It does so because A is more like D [another case] which is of B than it is like E [another case] which is of C. Since A is in B and B is in G [another legal concept], then A is in G. But perhaps C is in G also. If so, then B is in a decisively different segment of G, because B is like H which is in G and has a different result from C.

If you had a hard time with Levi's explanation, not to worry. That's exactly the point: Legal reasoning requires high levels of LMI.

Managing, too, requires substantial logical-mathematical intelligence. The languages of business are no longer only English, German, French, and Japanese. They now include the only universal language: mathematics, including its dialects COBOL, FORTRAN, and C. In his autobiography, *Managing*, Harold Geneen, former CEO of ITT, wrote, "The drudgery of the numbers will make you free." Managers, he says, must have the "ability to act upon the early warning system provided by the numbers. . . . The professional's grasp of the numbers is a measure of the control he has over the events that the figures represent." Geneen ought to know. One of his associates at ITT described him as a "genius" and a "master of professional business management." With his background in accounting, Geneen had the rational component of business down, as we say, to a science. He is the embodiment of logical-mathematical thought applied to managing a large organization.

Textbooks of business administration have long been full of the sigmas, integrals, and other mathematical creatures that have begun to slither across the pages of legal journals. The ability to use these tools is essential to what Beck's Management Progress Study of Bell System management called "administrative skills, especially planning, organizing and decisionmaking." These skills were among the main factors promoting advancement in AT&T management.

Anyone who deals with complex realities needs high levels of logical-mathematical intelligence, and no one deals with realities more complex than those faced by physicians. To a greater extent every day, the day-to-day tasks of doctors require spreadsheets, critical paths, and other mathematical planning models. This is especially clear at the frontiers of medicine, in the no-man's-land between basic research and experimental treatment. In the next section, I take you into this no-man's-land to show you how a doctor uses LMI. Then I analyze his performance step by step to convince you that you, too, can learn to think like Spock.

James Fuller treats patients other doctors don't. A graduate of Northwestern University Medical School, he specializes in chronic pain, a problem all too often dismissed as neurosis or malingering. With neurosurgeon Benjamin Crue, formerly of the University of Southern California, Fuller operates one of the most comprehensive and advanced neurological facilities in the Southwest. Some of his patients travel a thousand miles to see him because he's the only doctor who takes their problems seriously. He takes the time to explain his treatments, and patients often wait well into the evening. They don't seem to mind. All the ones I talked to appreciated his explanations; several described him as their only hope.

Fuller's diffidence belies his patients' admiration. A faint and slightly one-sided smile comments ironically as he speaks, and his turtleneck, beard, and glasses are reassuringly academic.

As a young physician at Cook County Hospital in Chicago, he saw patients who didn't fit the pigeonholes of conventional medicine: impulsively violent, often indigent men, usually brought to the hospital in handcuffs. Conventional wisdom had it that these patients were feigning brain injury to avoid prosecution. When their symptoms failed to match conventional diagnostic categories, the mismatch was regarded as evidence of malingering. There was a discrepancy here that nagged at Fuller: The patients acted as though they had "no control over their actions—they'd get mad and stick scissors through somebody's chest. They'd do heinous things but be remorseful. To me they seemed to be sincere people who hated their impulsivity—they would plead to be locked up." Try as he would, Fuller could find no way to relate known patterns of brain injury to the kinds of behavior that got these men in trouble. Nevertheless, he took their complaints seriously.

Needless to say, Fuller's views seemed naive to his case-hardened colleagues. Few other doctors took the trouble to investigate a problem that seemed mainly a matter for the police, but Fuller couldn't get the inconsistency out of his mind. He let it be known that he was interested in cases of impulsive violence and soon had plenty of referrals, many from psychiatrists. The psychiatric workups provided some clues: an occasional query about the possibility of seizures; the puzzling ineffectiveness of Valium, the drug of choice for controlling excessive emotion.

Fuller's next step was to do what any scientist does with a puzzling group of phenomena: He searched the literature and classified his cases. He soon realized that physicians throughout the world had arrived at the same classifications he had. He began to interview people close to the patients, some of them several times, often at personal risk.

"I always sat down, so I wouldn't be threatening—and I always left a clear way to the door," he said, smiling one-sidedly.

"For you or for the patient?" I asked.

He smiled again, this time bilaterally. "For whoever could get there first, I guess."

The next phase of his thinking was the crucial one, but in his attempts to gloss over technical details, Fuller was deliberately vague. After asking my third follow-up question, I began to wonder if I was blocking the door. Then he leaned back in his chair, stared at the ceiling, and quietly uttered the clearest reflection on practical thinking I have ever heard: "I'm not sure I know what I know, but I know what I should do."

What he did was try certain treatments. These treatments were not hunches, they were backed by logic. Fuller saw each type of violence as somehow similar to the neurological disorder it most resembled, even though the match was far from perfect. He experimentally treated each problem as though it were the corresponding neurological disorder. He used drugs no one had ever prescribed for impulsively violent behavior: antidepressants, anticonvulsants, adrenaline antagonists. The result was one of the high points of Fuller's career: "I had this guy on lithium [an antidepressant]. One day he told me that he had started to get mad at someone in the waiting room and that he was going to hit her, but then for the first time in his life he had time to think and he controlled his impulse." Eventually Dr. Fuller "got a large number to where they had some choice."

As a result of this and similar experiences with patients whom other doctors considered "crocks," years later, as chief clinical resident at the University of New Mexico Medical School, Dr. Fuller had a "turning point" in his career. "I saw a patient who fit the [malingering] pigeonhole perfectly. He had been in an automobile accident, he was in litigation, and he had arm and shoulder pain on one side. The pattern of his pain was incompatible with traditional neurological theory. . . . I knew in my heart that the guy was for real. . . . My fund of knowledge was inadequate. I had to go outside mainstream neurology. I did a literature search—I covered more than five thousand articles and copied four hundred in one year. I found articles describing these patients in highly acceptable journals, but outside neurology." Another interview and more tests confirmed the diagnosis Fuller had formed as a result of his literature search—the one-sided pain was a clue that the patient had a form of migraine. Fuller tested this hypothesis by prescribing drugs used for migraine. The arm pain disappeared.

As a result of this turning point, Dr. Fuller now specializes in patients who suffer from migraine and other forms of chronic pain. Today, he is in the vanguard of neurological research, pursuing an effective treatment for migraine based on his own theory and practice. Fuller's painstaking explanations, and his patience with my questions, were reminders that *doctor* is Latin for "teacher."

We can dissect six phases of LMI from Fuller's story of his neuro-logical successes:

1. Detecting an opportunity to bring LMI to bear: Fuller began by detecting discrepancies between a model of an illness and the symptoms the patient presents. He seems to have an unusual sensitivity to such dissonance. As he says, "Others aren't bothered by what bothers me."

2. Gathering information: the literature search and in-depth interviews.

3. Defining the situation in a productive manner by relating it to a familiar pattern: Seeing similarities among cases allowed him to see impulsive violence as several types. Fuller has an unusual ability to recognize subtle and complex patterns.

4. Choosing tentative diagnoses based on the similarities between these types of disorders he'd seen, the ones in the literature, and his knowledge of conventional neurological disorders.

5. Planning a course of diagnosis through treatment: This is where he knew what to do even when he wasn't sure what he knew. His plan of action was also a plan of investigation. He planned his treatment to help him learn what he didn't know.

6. Checking to see how the plan works and feeding back information into diagnoses: Like all good doctors, Fuller continued to monitor his patients to verify the effects of his treatment. The understanding gained by acting and thereby gathering additional data sometimes led him back to phase 2 and a new definition of the problem.

This description of LMI in action parallels classic descriptions of the psychology of problem solving, based on artificial puzzles solved under laboratory conditions. There is, however, an important difference. The classic descriptions present problem solving as a linear, one-way process. This may be true for the artificial one-right-answer puzzles of psychology laboratories, but students of clinical and other real-world thinking see it as cyclic and dialectical. Though I have dissected his thinking into a series of phases, Fuller did not deduce diagnosis from symptoms or treatment from diagnosis in a straight-forward, linear manner. Any of the last three phases may result in returning to phase 2 to gather more data or to phase 3 to redefine the problem.

Fuller's alternation between reflection, data gathering, and action is typical of experienced diagnosticians. Not only is the process cyclic and tangled, but the boundaries between one phase and another are seldom clear. Like good mechanics, programmers, and managers, Fuller swings smoothly from reflection through data collection into action and back. LMI acts in phases, but they are not the phases of a linear journey from problem to solution; they are more like a waltz, in which action and investigation embrace each other, creating yet fighting the centrifugal forces that threaten to spin them apart.

Fuller used intuition, but he did not rely on it. Experience and unconscious judgment were, in his words, "backed by logic." Fuller's abilities, though unusual and complex, are amenable to rational analysis and therefore learnable. The thesis of this chapter is that actuarial and other rational approaches to life can boost your LMI. In the following pages, I waltz you through the epicycles of real-world LMI one phase at a time. At each phase, I show how people often trip, and describe some simple tricks to help you become more surefooted.

PHASE 1: DETECTING OPPORTUNITIES

In the real world, opportunities to use LMI don't come neatly numbered, with a space for the right answer. That's why the first item on management consultant George Klemp's list of essential abilities is "identifies the most important issues in complex situations." For example, a personnel officer must be able to tell the difference between absenteeism due to a seasonal change in weather patterns on the one hand, and a morale problem on the other. Realizing that an opportunity exists is often decisive.

Sometimes these opportunities are problems, as when Dr. Fuller focused on discrepancies instead of ignoring them, as others had. Often, however, the solution comes first. Hardly anybody needed a microcomputer in 1980, and nobody needed a pet rock. To this day, Joe Weizenbaum, a computer wizard at MIT, calls microcomputers "a solution in search of a problem." The explosion of the microcomputer industry in the early 1980s recapitulates a pattern seen several times before: Better ways of doing things emerge before problems in the old ways are felt. In the dawn of the electronic computer, when Tom Watson decided to market IBM's punch-card calculator, he expected to sell two or three. He called it "the first electronic multiplier." It grew into the 604, IBM's first commercially successful electronic product. When electronic computers were new, experts' estimates of the total market for them had two digits.

People vary in their attention to problems or opportunities.

People with high LMI spend lots of time looking for opportunities to use it. Like Dr. Fuller, they are nagged or challenged, not daunted, by abstraction and complexity. Students of management call this tendency "proactivity," and describe it as the opposite of "reactivity." Proactive physicians counsel their patients about diet, tobacco, and alcohol. They are more interested in health than in disease. Proactive marketing managers don't wait for R&D to develop a product. They anticipate opportunities as well as problems.

How can you cultivate sensitivity to opportunities to use your LMI? First of all, by developing mental models so you can tell when something doesn't fit or where there's room for a new idea. Mental models are conceptual prototypes. They are more concrete than the schematic outlines discussed in the previous chapter, but they are not as concrete as the mental pictures we call "images." Your mental model of a car is not a pure abstraction like a dictionary definition; nor is it as concrete as your image of the battered 1981 Plymouth parked down the street. Creating and manipulating mental models combine LMI with spatial intelligence, and psychologists find that people high in spatial ability often excel at abstract problems.

A good model allows you to see a situation in a productive way. Like a schematic diagram of an electrical circuit, a good mental model is concrete enough to help you visualize and abstract enough to help you think. Experts have a rich vocabulary of mental models. Sometimes, for example, it's useful to regard electricity as a fluid under pressure (voltage) moving through constrictions (resistance). The fluid model can't handle the phenomenon of capacitance, however, so it's also useful to be able to think of electricity as, say, a crowd of people who gather under certain conditions. Experts' multiple models are organized so that they can move smoothly from one level to another (as when you move from your car model to your model of a dashboard). Experts have lots of cross-references connecting the elements of different models (as when you remember different locations of shift levers).

Just as your mental model of an automobile may be highly concrete if you've been in only one car, so are the models of novice physicians who know only the classic case. As a result, when they see symptoms that don't match the textbook example, they are liable to ignore real problems. In the absence of adequate cross-referencing, a novice may be able to reject diagnoses but unable to come up with a plausible new one. Alternatively, overestimation of the variability of the symptoms of a given disease may result in detecting a problem when there isn't one.

The experts' mental model is an abstract, global schema that includes relevant details as special cases of general principles. Doctors' mental models of diseases are more concrete and complete than a textbook description, but less concrete than images of particular patients. For example, a study conducted at MIT focused on physicians' models of kidney disease. The investigators found that their mental models consisted of a small set of "objects" (albumin, blood vessels, osmotic pressures, etc.) and relations among them. The model handled relationships among these objects in purely qualitative terms: directions of flow, increased and decreased albumin, low albumin.

Mental models allow the "chunking" described earlier. When expert electronic technicians were asked to sketch circuits from memory, they drew functional units: filters and amplifiers. Novices' sketches, on the other hand, looked more like pictures of circuits than like schematic diagrams. A similar pattern emerged in a study of architects' sketches of buildings. In both studies, the experts' memories were organized in terms of models that encapsulated enormous amounts of information in efficient, readily accessible chunks.

If you've got a bunch of good models, you'll trust your sensitivity to discrepancy. Too often, we deny our confusion and sweep opportunities under the rug. According to one White House adviser, those in a position to head off the impending gasoline shortage of 1973 by programs promoting conservation and independent production displayed "a general lack of interest." Their denial was responsible for a crisis that called for far more extreme measures than would have been required had they acted proactively.

When we recognize an opportunity to use LMI, we often whine to ourselves in a self-defeating mental monologue: "This doesn't make sense, so I must be dumb." Experts at LMI are often confused, and they admit it. But they interpret confusion and inconsistency as opportunities. The best way to develop the courage of your confusions is by developing multiple mental models. So let's get on with it.

Once you have detected a problem or another opportunity to use LMI, you must decide how much time to allocate. In most cases, LMI depends more on choosing the appropriate pace than on simply being fast. As Thurstone pointed out in the 1920s, intelligent action more often requires inhibiting than performing snap judgments. He who hesitates is lost, but so is he who leaps without looking. Practical LMI requires deciding which adage to obey.

Though IQ tests' time limits place a premium on speed, rarely do major real-world decisions have to be made in a minute or less. One exceptional situation is the medical emergency, as when a patient's heart has stopped. In such cases, physicians must make impulsive, intuitive snap decisions.

In cases other than emergencies, your decision about how much time and other resources to put into your deliberations depends on an appraisal of the benefits and costs of thinking about the situation. Thinking can cost a lot more than time; an often unanticipated cost is the confusion that thinking is liable to create. Before thinking through a problem, you need to decide if you can afford the risk of greater uncertainty, which may make your actions less decisive. Once you are morally, legally, or economically committed to, say, using CAT scans in all cases where tumors might be present, it is rational not to agonize over the trade-offs implicit in your commitment.

If you decide that the situation is worth thinking about, the next phase is gathering information.

PHASE 2: GATHERING INFORMATION

Information gathering appears in Mintzberg's competencies, Klemp's competence model, and Boyatzis's concept of proactivity. Such skills are mainly a matter of knowing the ropes: abstracts, indexes, on-line data bases, people. What makes Dr. Fuller different from many of his colleagues is a willingness to reach for a journal before making a judgment. Though rare among physicians and engineers, such integration of research into a plan of action is often required.

This realization has penetrated medical school curricula and assessment. Paul Cutler, in his book on clinical decisionmaking, describes the new Problem Based Learning approach to teaching medicine as "a major breakthrough in medical education . . . a process whereby students learn by using a problem as a stimulus to discover what added information they must acquire in order to move toward a solution." The "tab item" technique assesses diagnostic skills in medicine, electronic troubleshooting, and elsewhere by presenting tests the problem solver might perform in order to obtain information. By lifting covering tabs, testees leave a permanent record of their information gathering.

There is evidently nothing like Problem Based Learning or tab item assessment in the schools of architecture whose graduates continue to transplant San Diego designs to Colorado ski towns, where ski bums support themselves by shoveling snow off the roofs of condominiums that are on the verge of physical and fiscal collapse.

PHASE 3: FORMULATION

The next phase is the crucial one: defining the situation in ways that will help you work. So important is this phase that it is one of the few places where highly intelligent people take *more* time than less intelligent ones. We will emulate them by spending lots of time on formulation, where, as in detection, success depends less on native ability than on diagnostic skills that you can learn.

This ability to diagnose problems in productive ways comes up again and again in accounts of real-world problem solving. Both Richard Boyatzis and George Klemp describe diagnosis by competent executives as recognizing patterns in new problems and relating them to other problems with known solutions.

Opportunities to use LMI often become clear as soon as a situation is diagnosed properly. Rolex watches are so expensive that many are bought on an installment plan, giving new meaning to the phrase "time payments." They are so expensive to repair that many buyers also purchase maintenance contracts. In order to get such prices, André Heiniger, chairman of Rolex Corporation, needed only to diagnose his market. As he pointed out to marketing consultant Mark McCormack, "Rolex is not in the watch business. We are in the *luxury* business." McCormack says that the essence of marketing is "knowing what business you're really in."

Practical diagnosis has been most thoroughly investigated in medicine, but wherever it has been studied, it seems to follow similar rules. Above all, successful diagnosis depends on knowledge that is not just masses of facts, but facts organized into intricately cross-referenced mental models. A study at the University of Minnesota found that expert cardiologists' "disease models were sufficiently rich in detail to allow combinations of weak clues to serve in the place of fewer strong clues." This is exactly what we saw in Dr. Fuller's diagnoses of the disorders responsible for impulsive violence, where mentally cross-referenced constellations of symptoms allowed him to form plausible tentative diagnoses. Expert diagnosticians use their vocabulary of models to move quickly beyond the patient's complaint to educated guesses about the disease.

Micheline Chi and Robert Glaser are cognitive psychologists at the University of Pittsburgh, a world center for the study of LMI. They describe the critical difference between experts and novices in a variety of fields as an ability to see the situation in a way that restricts the number of possible "moves" toward success. Experts' models give them an "ability to choose the best path to solution without considering the others." Arthur Elstein, a pioneer in the study of clinical problem solving, found that experienced physicians integrate a small number of cues obtained early in a workup into tentative diagnoses. They begin to test these models right away. Though they ask fewer questions than novices, they ask the right ones. Novices, on the other hand, tend to stay close to the patient's description of the problem, and gather more information than they really need. Similarly, experienced radiologists see each X-ray as an example of diagnostic categories, while novices interpret X-rays by focusing on details.

The same pattern emerged in studies of other technical fields. When expert and novice computer programmers were asked to complete programs with missing lines, the experts used abstract, high-level goals and plans, while the novices used low-level, concrete, syntax-based approaches similar to those taught in programming classes. Working with Nobel laureate Herbert Simon, cognitive psychologist Jill Larkin and her colleagues found that expert physicists formulate problems in terms of what she calls "large functional units." Like the radiologists and the programmers, their initial descriptions of problems were abstract and general, not the literal ones of novices.

Even in chess, a purely abstract game where pure intellectual power (if there is such a thing) has a home-field advantage, it is knowledge organized into models, not superior cognitive skills, that creates mastery. The chess masters studied by Herbert Simon, Micheline Chi, and others "looked ahead" the same number of moves as novices, but their vocabulary of models allowed them to diagnose situations quickly and efficiently. Chess masters can remember board configurations better than novices only when the boards match their models. They surpass novices in their memory for real board configurations arising from real games, but are no better than novices at memorizing random configurations. Experts' models allow them to organize lots of information into meaningful chunks, while novices define problems concretely, in terms similar to those in which they are posed. They can't see the forest for the trees.

When it comes to the strategies that follow from the initial formulation, the experts aren't thinking faster or more cleverly, but they're working on the right problem. The management adage applies equally to other fields: "It's more important for a manager to do the right thing than to do things right."

How do the experts develop the models that create their superior diagnostic ability? Not by mental power or other underlying abilities. In none of these studies did the experts create global problem descriptions out of void by sheer intellectual power. In fields as different as cardiology, radiology, chess, physics, baseball, agricultural planning, and computer programming, experts perform better not because of who they are but because of what they know. That's why expert systems for medical diagnosis, oil exploration, and other technical fields depend no longer on larger, faster computers but on well-organized technical knowledge.

The crucial roles of diagnosis in LMI and of knowledge in diagnosis are good news—knowledge, unlike "talent" and other godlike "gifts," is learnable. If microchips can be taught to diagnose problems like experts, so can you. Let's look at how experts do it.

Edwin Land, inventor of the Polaroid photographic process, once said, "Insight is the sudden cessation of stupidity." What appears to be stupidity is usually only an unsuccessful attempt to apply a faulty model. Our minds are not blank slates—we've all got lots of mental models, and many are very good on their own turf. The problem is that we use them where they don't work. This implies that if we want to increase our LMI, we need first of all to avoid faulty diagnosis through the wrong models.

Using the wrong model gets us into trouble in mathematical problems based on real-world situations. Even people who are good at algebra and arithmetic typically have a hard time with story problems, not because they can't solve simple equations but because they solve the wrong equations. More than half the college students asked to write equations for statements like "For every six bottles of beer, we sell eleven cans of cola" wrote incorrect equations. When a comparable group translated the statement into a simple program in BASIC, the error rate was almost halved. Evidently, it is easier for people to apply concrete procedural models (like "multiply the number of bottles by six, multiply the number of cans by eleven, and set them equal") than more abstract algebraic models.

Even with questions like "Which is heavier—a pound of lead or a pound of feathers?" not having the right mental model can cause adults to err. Consider the following experiment by psychologists Vernon Hall and Richard Kingsley. They flattened one of two identical balls of clay into the shape of a feather, surreptitiously removing some clay. When they weighed the two pieces of clay on a laboratory balance, fewer than half the graduate students they tested diagnosed the problem correctly. Most accepted the demonstration at face value, and fabricated ingenious (but wrong) diagnoses: the scale was defective, the clay was off center. This "failure to conserve" is no mere laboratory curiosity: The art of packaging is to a considerable extent the art of fooling consumers into similar failures of conservation. It is unlikely that anyone would fall for such a ruse with unpackaged pâté on a conventional scale at the delicatessen. Other psychologists have reached similar conclusions: People who think logically on familiar ground are rubes when the context, whether it is a laboratory gadget or an artfully designed cereal box, prevents use of good models. The moral is: Translate problems into ones for which you have models that are tried and true.

Let's see how good your models are. The Fourteenth Psalm tells us: "The fool hath said in his heart, There is no God." If we make the reasonable assumption that "the fool" refers to fools in general, we can translate this statement into "All fools are atheists." Suppose we add to this questionable premise a true one: "Prime Minister Gorbachev is an atheist." *If* we accepted both premises, what, if anything, could we conclude?

The answer is "nothing." If you answered "Gorbachev is a fool," you're in good company. Majorities of audiences of faculty and students at the universities of Chicago, Michigan, and other institutions of higher education fell for it too. The point of this example is not to show, as its victims often complain, that they are stupid. On the contrary, it is to show that even intelligent people fall for simple fallacies when unfamiliar materials trick them into using the wrong model. Where we go wrong is in using a model that puts the first premise backward. To say that all fools are atheists is not to say that all atheists are fools. The psalm leaves room for people who, like Gorbachev, are atheists but nobody's fool. If you are an atheist, you will of course gain absolutely no comfort whatsoever from this demonstration that the psalmist is not calling you a fool.

Syllogistic slips like the foolish atheist occur in real-world diagnosis every day. Robin Hogarth of the University of Chicago Graduate School of Business illustrates the same error with a scenario in which an executive must evaluate the credibility of one of his salesmen, who has just reported information that strongly suggests the opening campaign of a price war. In this case,

> the estimation of the salesman's credibility was done by considering instances where you already knew the truth of something he reported to you . . . "given that I know the competitor has booked advertising space, how likely is my salesman to report this . . ." However, the appropriate question is: "Given that my salesman reported that a competitor has booked advertising

space, what is the probability that the competitor has indeed booked advertising space?" . . . To assume that both statements represent the same estimate of the salesman's credibility is to commit a logical error of the form "All women are human; therefore all humans are women."

Note how easy it is to see the problem with women and humans, where you have a good model.

As remedies for slippery syllogisms, logicians prescribe Venn diagrams, models using overlapping circles. The problem with Venn diagrams is that many logical relationships can be diagrammed ambiguously or in misleading ways. Philip Johnson-Laird's solution is to build a model of the first premise by constructing lists of every possible type of individual instantiating it. Thus, "All fools are atheists" would be instantiated:

> foolish atheist
> clever atheist
> clever believer

Only one combination is ruled out by the first premise: foolish believer.

The next step is to add similar instantiations of the second premise to the model of the first. "Gorbachev is an atheist" eliminates the last term and we are left with:

> Gorbachev foolish atheist
> Gorbachev clever atheist

Finally, one formulates a conclusion that describes all the remaining combinations. Gorbachev might be foolish, but he might be clever, are the two possible conclusions following from the premises.

The value of this procedure is that it guarantees validity. This was a simple case, but since all possible combinations must be taken into account, some superficially simple syllogisms require combining several mental models, and this step, though mechanical, can be laborious. A more practical implication is the general rule that when you must engage in abstract reasoning, translate the statements into ones for which you have accurate models.

In the real world, we typically must handle unpredictable uncertain events, and we don't have good models for them. We tend to overdiagnose, to see patterns in what are really random occurrences. Conversely, our models of how to create randomness are often too broad. People are incapable of recognizing or producing random strings of numbers. A notorious example was the 1970 draft lottery, in which capsules containing the numbers 1 to 365 were mixed in an urn for several hours. Most of us have a model that tells us that this should be plenty of mixing. The mixing did not, however, randomize the order in which the numbers were drawn from the urn. In fact, birthdays tended to be drawn in a nonrandom, reverse-chronological order: the first ones drawn tended to be from December, the last ones from January.

An example of our tendency to impose patterns on chaotic events is the "gambler's fallacy," the incorrect belief that lightning never strikes twice. If you toss a coin and it comes up heads five times in a row, you'll be tempted to think that it's "due" to come up tails. But successive tosses of a fair coin are independent events. If anything, five heads should lead you to suspect that the coin isn't fair, so you should bet on heads. A real-world analogy occurs in stock markets, where short-term fluctuations are random. Yet even some sophisticated buyers use "systems" based on short-term patterns, like predicting a drop after three successive days of gain.

In his *Judgment and Choice,* Robin Hogarth presents the "unfolding test," a simple test for trends or randomness in data that vary with time, like the performance of a stock. Accordion-pleat a graph plotting price against time, making each vertical pleat just wide enough to hold one point. Now examine each pleat one at a time, using each point to predict where the next will be. If you can predict most points, the variation in stock prices is indeed nonrandom. For more complex data—in which, for example, you suspect a secular trend with cyclic variation—Hogarth recommends technical aids, like computer packages for analysis of time series. For simple series, however, "quick and dirty" tests like unfolding are excellent prophylaxes against overdiagnosis.

Another common cause of overdiagnosis is seeing spurious or illusory correlations—seeing a pattern of association when in fact the associations are random. As a result of our susceptibility to spurious correlations, we often create models relating events that are really unrelated. For example, at a flight school in Israel, psychologists had advised instructors to reward every successful maneuver with praise. However, there was considerable day-to-day variation in performance. Because the maneuvers were difficult, after a good flight pilots were liable to do worse the next time. As a result, the instructors came to believe that praise was *reducing* performance, and balked at continuing to deliver praise. Similarly, when psychologists presented nurses with cases in which a symptom (say, fever) was associated with an illness (say, chicken pox) exactly half the time, the nurses detected a correlation. The association was of course illusory, since a patient with that symptom was equally likely to have or not have the disease.

The tendency to see spurious correlations is universal. They are responsible for the longevity of racial and sexual stereotypes, of quack cures and other superstitions. The ritualistic behavior around slow elevators resembles the "superstitious behaviors" of pigeons placed in a device that delivers a food reward at random intervals. The pigeons soon adopt ritualistic bowlings, cooings, and hops. They act as though they are being rewarded for those behaviors, which of course they are if they keep them up long enough. A chance association between a random reward and a random behavior is enough to stamp a simple causal model into the pigeon's brain.

People are reluctant to test their syllogistic slips and spurious correlations by looking for negative instances: clever atheists and professors who never forget. This reluctance is greatest on unfamiliar terrain. Suppose you've got four cards, each bearing an abstract symbol like a letter or a number on each side. Suppose the sides you can see have E, K, 4, 7. Test the rule "Vowel on one side means even number on other" by turning over two cards. Which cards would you turn over?

Almost everyone correctly chooses the "E" first. However, Philip Johnson-Laird finds that almost everyone, including philosophers and others trained in formal logic, go on to pick the "4." But the crucial card is the "7." What if "7" has a vowel on other side?

However, if the task is made concrete, with cards bearing names of cities, like "Chicago" and "New York," and vehicles, like "car" and "airplane," and you are asked to test the rule "Every time I go to Chicago I travel by air," you will probably turn over the correct cards. Eighty percent of Johnson-Laird's subjects did.

Many bad models come from the tendency to take one's intuitions based on a small number of experiences too seriously. We have all had lots of experience with small groups of people, and we have learned that on your birthday, you can invite up to, say, ten of your friends without having to worry about someone else also having a birthday that day. In fact, in groups of fewer than ten people, the chance of two people having the same birthday is less than twelve out of a hundred. Your experience, however, does not prepare you to deal with larger parties. What's the chance of having two people with the same birthday at a party with twenty-five people? Most people guess way too low. In fact, the chances are better than even for any group of more than twenty-three people.

We all tend to base our models on a single familiar case instead of on the average or typical outcome. Yale University psychologist Richard Nisbett and his colleagues describe the discriminating buyer who on the basis of extensive surveys conducted by *Consumer Reports* decides to buy a Volvo. Just before concluding the sale, however, he is at a party where an acquaintance cites problems his brother-in-law had with his Volvo: fuel injection computer, rear end, transmission, clutch. As Nisbett put it, "The logical status of this information is that the N [number] of several hundred Volvo-owning *Consumer Reports* readers had been increased by one and the mean frequency of repair record shifted up by an iota on three or four dimensions. However, anyone who maintains that he would reduce the encounter to such a net informational effect is either disingenuous or lacking in the most elemental self-knowledge." In fact, a single vivid example is far more persuasive than "hard" statistics, as is demonstrated by the dramatic increase in appointments for breast exams following the publicity surrounding the mastectomies performed on two first ladies. The Yale psychologists cite numerous similar cases in which the models we use to diagnose a situation are built entirely of personal experience, and incorporate little reliable statistical data.

When they don't use the correct model, experts are just as liable as novices to succumb to fallacies based on trusting their unaided numerical intuitions. Surgeons who specialize in risky operations, where the mortality rate is 2.42 percent, were asked to judge the average risk of surgery. Their estimates were twice as high as the estimates made by surgeons who specialize in safer operations. Judgments by both groups were skewed by their professional experience. Physicians are just as liable as the rest of us to disregard the results of surveys showing that a treatment is ineffective if they have used the treatment successfully. A recent study found that physicians were equally likely to overestimate or underestimate the risks of various procedures. The investigator concluded that "the doctors were guessing."

Nowhere is this tendency to ignore the facts more strongly embedded than in diagnostic reasoning that requires inferring from the symptoms the odds that a patient has a disease. Suppose your new employer requires you to get a chest X-ray. You feel fine, but you comply. The physician tells you that X-rays are 95 percent reliable: If you don't have TB, 95 times out of 100, the X-rays will be negative; and if you do have TB, 95 times out of 100, the X-rays will catch it —will be positive. Assuming that your X-rays come out positive, what are the chances that you have TB? A simple calculation shows that the odds that you have TB are about nine out of ten, but most people don't buy it. Similar indifference to mathematical logic was found in a study of horse-race handicappers who refused to revise their predictions about a horse's performance on the basis of its long-term track record.

Failures of conservation, slippery syllogisms, the gambler's fallacy, spurious correlations, ignoring negative evidence, and trusting small numbers demonstrate that novices' LMI is low not because of limited intellectual power but because they use the wrong models. When experts use the wrong models, they do just as badly. As psychologist Amos Tversky points out, "Whenever there is a simple error that most laymen fall for there is always a slightly more sophisticated version of the same problem that experts fall for." Knowing the kinds of mistakes you are liable to make will help you prevent them. That's why I spent so much time on the most common bad models.

The practical thrust of all this is to develop a vocabulary of models suited to your occupation, so you can apply several different models to every case. Donald Schön refers to this as the "ability to use a Rashomon of problem settings," and psychologists call it the "generate and test" strategy.

Some of these models can be quite simple—as simple as the pâté on your grocer's scale or a list of logical possibilities like foolish and clever atheists. A map is useless if it is as detailed as the territory. It's far better to have a simple model you understand than a complicated one you don't. Legend has it that Andrew Carnegie's model of production at his steel mills was based on the number of chimneys belching smoke. Russell Ackoff, one of the founders of operations research, describes a case in which market researchers at a major oil company built a complex mathematical model of service station sales. They pared seventy variables down to thirty-five, which they built into a much simpler model. Another team built a simple model based on one variable: customers' perception of how long they would have to wait. This model not only made better predictions than the thirty-five-variable equation; it showed *why* the big equation worked: The important variables all had something to do with anticipated delays in getting gas.

There's no room in this book for all the models readers need, but that's O.K. Mental models work best if you build them yourself, so you can see how and why they work. In their *Harvard Business Review* article on management models, Robert Hayes and Richard Nolan point out that "Managers are beginning to realize that the real value of a model comes not just from *using* it but from *creating* it."

James R. Manion creates complex mathematical models for a living, but he uses simple mental models to manage them. He is Range Visibility Officer at the China Lake Naval Weapons Center. China Lake is in the northern Mojave Desert and has been dry for thousands of years—a strange place for a navy base. The Naval Weapons Center is located there because the clear air of the Mojave allows long-range observation of rockets and other ordnance. The clarity of the air is what Manion's models are about. As we talked, I could see sharp gray crags just over his shoulder. I had passed those crags on my drive to China Lake, so I knew that they were more than an hour away.

"Could you walk me through a project where you were at your best?"

"Sure. Right now we're studying the ways particles in the air degrade optical images. The navy would have to spend three million dollars on this study, so I had to decide whether this thing was worth tackling at all. I started with existing data. Air quality goes up and down year to year, season to season, but it looked to me like we have a problem. The old-timers are right—the air isn't as clear as it used to be. And if we can't run our tests here, we're out of luck.

"Turns out the EPA has a sophisticated mathematical model for air pollution. In this business, you've got to be careful not to reinvent the wheel, so I started with the EPA model. I tried to match their parameters to data we've been collecting. I wasn't getting a very good fit, so I diddled with the model, adding parameters, and pretty soon it was a real mess. Eventually I realized I was spinning my wheels."

"What led you to use the EPA model in the first place?"

"I always leave a trail of bread crumbs back to the big picture. One of the reasons I'm out here is because of the air—used to live in Riverside, where half the time I couldn't see across the street. My work for the navy is really about environmental issues."

"What did you do when you realized you were spinning your wheels?" Manion's reply. was lost as an A-6 jet fighter blasted past low enough to raise whirlwinds on the dusty valley floor. He raised his finger for silence, and a few seconds later there was a muffled crump as a rocket exploded on a far-off hill. Manion smiled, and started again.

"I went back to the big picture again. I mean, remembering it's our navy in the free world really helps—suppose we find that all the crap in the air comes from the San Joachin Valley? So what? This isn't Russia: *We* can't tell farmers to stop plowing. The EPA model ignores local sources, so I'm working on a new model, based on local sources, the ones we can do something about."

"How do you do that?"

"One step at a time. We grade these target rings, some almost a mile across. That raises dust. Once I get the effects of grading nailed down, I'll work on things like what they're burning at the county dump. The trick is to try to vary these things one at a time so we can see which ones are the worst problems. The worst sources may be the easiest to handle. You know, 'Please don't burn tires on Tuesdays, we've got some rounds scheduled.' "

"Then what do you do?"

"Then I test the model when we've got all these things working together. There are always unexpected effects of combinations of variables: Maybe dust polarizes the light one way, smoke another. You just hope the model doesn't blow up."

"How do you come up with the right models for your problems?"

"I've been involved in electromagnetic opacity research off and on for twenty years, but my background has been eclectic. I'm no wizard, but I'm good at what I do because I know where to look for what I need to know. I stay dabblingly current in a broad range of fields: atmospheric physics and chemistry, mathematical modeling. I'm not a specialist in physics, math, or chemistry, but I'm good at combining them."

"Would you say, then, that your ability is based on redefining problems in terms of the big picture, your experience in building models, and feeding back the results of what you do?"

"No. *You'd* say that. But I'd agree."

Phases 4 and 5: Choosing a Diagnosis and Planning Action

After gathering information and formulating multiple diagnoses, ideally the next phase is to choose one diagnosis as a basis for your action plan. However, neither Manion nor Fuller could afford this luxury. Real-world decisionmakers must often swing into action before they have reduced the number of diagnoses to one. In such cases, they need a plan of action that allows them to choose among multiple diagnoses. Whether or not such a plan works, it leads to better understanding of the situation.

As we move from diagnoses to plans of diagnosis through action, we can apply four general principles demonstrated in the earlier phases.

First, allocate plenty of time to high-level planning. Manion's recourse to the "big picture" is typical of the thinking of expert problem solvers. Consider several plans of action, not just the first plan that comes along.

Second, optimize when you can. Optimizing is an exhaustive search for the best possible plan. The epitome of optimizing decisionmaking approaches is the ideal decision procedure developed by Irving Janis and Leon Mann. According to them, there are seven steps. The perfect decisionmaker:

1. thoroughly canvasses a wide range of alternative courses of action;

2. surveys the full range of objectives;

3. carefully weighs whatever he knows about the costs and risks of negative consequences, as well as the positive consequences, that could flow from each alternative;

4. intensely searches for new information relevant to further evaluation of the alternatives;

5. correctly assimilates . . . any new information . . . to which he is exposed;

6. reexamines the positive and negative consequences of all known alternatives, including those regarded as unacceptable, before making a final choice;

7. makes detailed provisions for implementing . . . the chosen course of action, with special attention to contingency plans that might be required if various known risks were to materialize.

In their book *Decision Making,* Janis and Mann examine each of these steps in detail, describe cases in which decisions went wrong because of failure to adhere to them, and show how to follow them.

One of the most effective optimizing techniques is also the simplest and oldest. In a 1772 letter to his friend the British physical scientist Joseph Priestley, Benjamin Franklin described what he called his "prudential algebra." It is still prescribed in modern texts of decisionmaking. Here's how Franklin described it:

When these difficult cases occur, they are difficult, chiefly because while we have them under consideration, all the reasons pro and con are not present in the mind at the same time. . . . To get over this, my way is to divide half a sheet of paper by a line into two columns; writing over the one Pro and over the other Con. Then during three or four days consideration, I put down under the different heads short hints of the different motives, that at different times occur to me, for or against the measure. When I have thus got them all together in one view, I endeavor to estimate their respective weights; and where I find two, one on each side, that seem equal, I strike them both out. If I find a reason pro equal to two reasons con, I strike out the three. If I judge some two reasons con, equal to some three reasons pro, I strike out the five; and thus proceeding I find at length where the balance lies; and if, after a day or two of further consideration, nothing new that is of importance occurs on either side, I come to a determination accordingly. And though the weight of reasons cannot be taken with the precision of algebraic quantities, yet when each is thus considered, separately and comparatively, and the whole lies before me, I think I can judge better.

Janis and Mann evaluated the effectiveness of the balance sheet in real choices of college and career, and found that it was effective in several respects: Those who used it considered many more factors than those who simply talked about their situations for the same amount of time; those who used the balance sheet were more open to negative information about consequences of their choices and they were less likely to express regret about their decision. Janis's colleague Mary Ellen Colten found that women at a diet clinic who used a balance sheet to weigh the advantages and disadvantages of the clinic's program were significantly more likely to follow the diet than a control group who got the same information but didn't construct balance sheets. As a result, they lost more weight.

Because the balance sheet is a paradigm of Spock-like actuarial techniques, it should be noted that people do not find it at all cold and calculating. Janis and Mann describe the intense emotions typically associated with the discovery of the relative costs and benefits of real-life decisions.

Balance sheets are typically used to choose among action plans, but they also assist in diagnosis. Arthur Elstein, the student of medical problem-solving describes a weighting procedure similar to Benjamin Franklin's balance sheet. Elstein's rule states that the diagnosis should be the one with the highest sum of positive or negative weights of one, two, or three points to various symptoms. This rule allows anyone with the right information to choose among alternative diagnoses at least as well as experienced physicians.

The third step for moving from diagnosis to plan is to satisfice when you must. To "satisfice," according to Herbert Simon, is to choose a course of action that's good enough. Sometimes satisficing is all there's time for, as in triage, where physicians must handle large numbers of acute cases and deal first with the ones they can help, postponing action on the patients who will live or die no matter what they do. Manion engaged in a form of triage when he ignored distant sources of pollution because he couldn't do anything about them. Satisficing is often a rational alternative to the "vigilant scanning" model of Janis and Mann.

"Heuristics," or rules of thumb, are satisficing plans for diagnosis and action. Heuristics are powerful aids for choosing among diagnoses as you act, but they don't guarantee the best solution. For example, means-ends analysis is a search for a move that will bring you closer to your goal. Means-ends analysis doesn't guarantee a solution, because real-world problems often require detours. Working with Herbert Simon and others, Jill Larkin found that physics novices adopt a sort of means-ends heuristic: They work backward from the unknowns in a problem to its givens. Experts, on the other hand, typically begin by encoding the givens in ways that allow them to work forward.

Sociologist Amitai Etzioni advocates a mixed strategy, optimizing in major decisions and satisficing in minor ones. Robert Townsend, former chairman of Avis, agrees. He says, "There are two kinds of decisions, those that are expensive to change, and those that are not. A decision to build the Edsel or Mustang (or locate your new factory in Orlando or Yakima) shouldn't be made hastily. . . . But the common or garden variety decision—like . . . what brand of pencil to buy—should be made fast."

Fourth, whenever possible, plan your action to eliminate diagnoses. The most powerful model for choosing a diagnosis is not a search for confirming evidence, but turning over the right card, seeking information that eliminates alternative diagnoses. This method is what Nobel Prize winner Konrad Lorenz had in mind when he said, "It is a good morning exercise for a research scientist to discard a pet hypothesis before breakfast." Just as scientists work not by proving but by disproving, and doctors diagnose by eliminating possible diseases, effective diagnosis in other realms depends on a process of elimination by data gathering.

Like other practical experimenters, Fuller and Manion eliminated diagnoses by action. Fuller prescribed drugs suggested by his tentative diagnoses and Manion got the "grader people" to keep records. If he detected no difference in air quality when target rings were being scraped, he would have eliminated the grader dust diagnosis.

One of the most powerful ways to eliminate diagnoses through action is control. Control eliminates causes by isolating them or holding them constant. You can get control by comparison. A lawyer friend described a trial in Miami in which the prosecution presented traces of cocaine on several hundred-dollar bills in the defendant's possession as proof of illegal activities. The defense ordered a similar analysis of hundred-dollar bills taken at random from a bank vault. Many of these bills were contaminated with cocaine. The defense cast the prosecution's diagnosis into doubt by eliminating the defendant as a factor and holding the size of the bills constant; there was no way he could have been responsible for the cocaine on the bills in the Fed. The defendant walked.

Another way to achieve control is by doing one thing at a time so you know which treatment worked. In some scientific experiments, controls are provided by using two groups of subjects, experimental and control. The experimental group gets the treatment; the control group is treated exactly like the experimental group in every way except the treatment. Manion checked one thing at a time: first grader dust, then dump smoke. If your car won't start, trying to start it after replacing or restoring one component at a time will help you understand what went wrong.

As means of choosing among diagnoses and action plans, optimizing, satisficing, and elimination require you to gather more information.

The final stage of planning is choosing the sequence of steps you will go through. A powerful planning tool is the "top-down" approach, sometimes called "subgoaling." This is a divide-and-conquer strategy, in which a big problem is divided into bite-sized pieces, as in the issue trees and writing outlines of Chapter 8. Dr. Fuller used this approach when he divided the problem of impulsive violence into several different and smaller problems that he could attack one at a time.

Similarly, good computer programmers begin with a description of what the program is to do, break it down into large functional units, then divide each of the units into routines, and the routines into subroutines. This highly structured form of thinking is the only way to handle the mind-boggling complexities of programming. Top-down planning allows reuse of the same modules (subroutines) as parts of different functional units. Most important of all, top-down design allows debugging. When something goes wrong in a top-down plan, it is relatively easy to isolate.

All these advantages apply to human planning as well, as you can see in the simplified chart diagrammed below. Suppose the goal is to increase profits. This goal breaks down into decreasing overhead, speeding up accounts receivable, reducing inventory, and boosting sales. Speeding up accounts receivable breaks down into accelerating deliveries and collections. Boosting sales depends on satisfying customers and providing incentives to the sales force. Satisfying customers depends on several things, but one of these is a module we've seen before: accelerating deliveries. Since you can kill two birds by accelerating deliveries, begin by dividing this module up into doable chunks: finding ways to prepare invoices faster, allowing dispatchers to use the best carriers, etc. With this sort of system in operation, debugging a delayed order is a simple matter of walking through the chart.

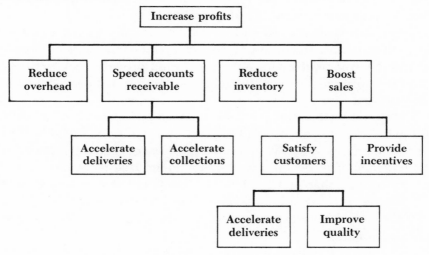

MONITORING AND FEEDBACK

In the next phase of LMI, you are finally committed to a course of action. Arizona governor Bruce Babbitt has a poignant way of explaining what "committed" means to most real-world actors. Over a breakfast of ham and eggs, he described the difference between "involvement" and "commitment" like this: "The chicken is involved in our breakfast—the pig is committed." To workers in the trenches, commitment is a drastic don't-look-back plunge. Real-world action requires sticking to a decision long enough to reap the consequences, but no real-world thinker should be willing to emulate the pig's commitment. Commitment is not the end of the line, but a way to do better next time around.

The link that completes the cycle of LMI is feedback of action outcomes into future diagnoses. It is not feedback per se that matters, though. Simply knowing the results of your decisions does not automatically lead to better decisions. In order to forge a strong link and make better decisions, you must build feedback from your decision into your diagnostic and planning models. Such "process" feedback, as psychologists call it, can have dramatic effects on thinking.

For example, Dr. Fuller fed his experience with impulsive violence back into his models of patients other doctors considered "crocks." He was willing to take the accident victim with arm pain seriously enough to embark on the cycle of information gathering, tentative diagnosis, and experimental treatment that led to his successful chronic-pain practice.

That it is the effect of the feedback on our models that matters and not the feedback itself is demonstrated by the effectiveness of role playing. Janis and Mann found that role playing was effective in getting people to come to terms with the consequences of continuing to smoke, drink, etc. Psychodrama provides not feedback but "feedforward," information about outcomes that precedes decisionmaking.

Most of us get all the feedback we need to develop good models, but we are reluctant to incorporate it into our models of situations and of planning. When Wagner and Sternberg studied the practical intelligence of successful people, they found that it wasn't amount of experience that mattered. They concluded that practical tacit knowledge is "not automatically acquired with experience. It is what we learn from experience rather than experience per se that seems to matter."

The RAND corporation has developed a model for building feedback into the problem-solving process. In order to evaluate various methods of training crews of soldiers to handle the complex decisions involved in air defense, RAND's System Research Laboratory ran a series of two-hundred-hour simulations in which "hostile" and "friendly" aircraft appeared on simulated radar scopes at rates of up to three hundred a minute. Though the soldiers were provided with feedback about the outcomes of their actions, none of the training methods produced much improvement, and it appeared that the problem was too complicated for humans to handle. Then the RAND scientists tried a radical approach called the Cogwheel Experiment, in which teams were provided with a special form of feedback: a public display of the whole team's pattern of response. They soon learned to ignore half of the incoming information, and by the end of the experiment they were effectively handling unprecedented traffic loads—up to three times higher than any real levels.

In his *Reflective Practitioner*, Donald Schön describes how the

Cogwheel model, with its emphasis on process feedback to participants in a decisionmaking process, has dramatically improved thinking in action on problems as different from air defense as Third World nutrition. By monitoring our solutions, we can build better and better models and avoid what Janis and Mann call "justification of effort," the reluctance to reassess old decisions that keeps us throwing good money after bad.

This final phase, the restructuring of diagnostic and planning models, is the hallmark of real-world LMI. In his book on clinical problem solving, Paul Cutler uses what he calls a "data-logic-data-logic approach." He describes patient management as a reflective cycle of data gathering, diagnoses, choice, treatment plan, and modification of diagnoses and treatment plans by feedback. Effective users of LMI are what Donald Schön calls "reflective practitioners." They regard action not only as a way of getting things done but as a way of testing new models. They plan not only for action but for understanding.

In this chapter, I have walked you through the cycle of LMI: detection, information gathering, formulation of multiple diagnoses, formulation of multiple plans that eliminate diagnoses, and feedback into diagnostic models. As I took you through each of these phases, I argued that in medicine and other professions, logical-mathematical intelligence is practical. I tried to show that what appears to be stupidity is usually only use of the wrong model, and therefore you can boost your LMI by learning to use the right ones.

No one ever said that this is easy. There are, however, several things you can do:

- Draw pictures of every problem you work on. Sometimes it'll slow you down, but the time you save in the ones it does work with will make up for the rest. And your diagrams will get better with practice.
- Invest time in the early stages of thinking: detecting opportunities to practice your LMI, gathering information, formulating and reformulating diagnoses and plans.
- Learn to use abstracts, on-line data bases, and other tools for finding information.
- Learn the conceptual tools needed in any trade: probability, algebra, elementary set theory, etc. These tools are like various kinds of pliers: If you've got the right tool, it's easy to get a grip on your problem. The references for this chapter include several books designed to provide the general reader with a working knowledge of these basic tools.

- Learn where your models fit and where they don't. Turn over the cards that could falsify your diagnosis.
- Optimize when you can, but satisfice when you must.
- Reevaluate all important decisions, incorporating what you've learned by making them. Commitment to a course of action on one occasion shouldn't mean being locked into it on later occasions.
- Think till it hurts.

10.
Critical Thinking

One horse-laugh is worth ten thousand syllogisms.
—H. L. MENCKEN

At a time when the stock market was booming and the President
was sure the economy was "absolutely sound," one financier was
bailing out. He was called a negativist and an iconoclast. The time
was 1928 and the financier was Bernard Baruch.

Four years later, after the total quoted value of stocks on the
New York Stock Exchange had crashed from almost ninety billion
to just over fifteen billion dollars, Baruch attributed his prescience
to Charles Mackay's *Extraordinary Popular Delusions,* a book on
critical thinking.

Today, critical thinking is itself a growth industry, with no crash
in sight. In 1980, all the recent articles on critical thinking fit in one
fat folder. By the middle of the decade, that folder would contain
2,500 articles.

A recent front-page story in the *Wall Street Journal* covered the
Committee to Scientifically Investigate Claims of the Paranormal or
Other Phenomena, or "csicopps." Founded by astronomer Carl
Sagan and other critical thinkers, the csicopps debunk astrology,
clairvoyance, and other popular cults. Why front-page coverage?
Because, the article explains, "a lot of money is wasted" on "pseu-
doscientific mumbo-jumbo," and because bad ideas must be de-
bunked to make room for better ones. Now that employers can buy
an expert system on a floppy disk, they hire humans with expecta-
tions they will think in ways that computers can't: creatively, intuitively, and above all critically.

There is little relationship between measures of academic aptitude like IQ and measures of critical thinking ability. Thus, like
other practical skills, ways of working smarter, critical thinking com-

bines multiple intelligences. Critical thinking is a skill that combines rhetorical and technical knowledge, verbal and logical-mathematical intelligences, the skeptical "Show me" attitude of the Missouri state motto, and the analytic, reflective, and complex cognitive styles described in Chapter 11. Practical critics must also be able to act when the time for reflection is over.

Pragmatic philosopher John Dewey called critical thinking "reflective thought," which he defined as "active, persistent, and careful consideration" of an argument "in the light of the grounds that support it and the further conclusions to which it tends." The word "reflective" snaps softly, like pages turning, and accentuates the positive. Criticism, whether practical or literary, appreciates; policies and books that survive critical scrutiny are taken more seriously than those that are never reviewed. I use the phrases "critical thinking" and "reflective thinking" interchangeably.

THIS GUN'S FOR HIRE: A MODERN WESTERN

Although critical thinking has been in the news, none of the news stories is exactly a scoop. Critical or reflective thinking has, in one form or another, been around at least since the time of Socrates. The founding fathers regarded it as the foundation of democracy. So did journalists Walter Lippmann and H. L. Mencken. The founding fathers' intellectual heirs are Senator William Proxmire, with his "golden fleece" awards, and columnist William Buckley, with his "jeweler's eye" for liberal cant. Critical thinking is what teachers have in mind when they say they try to teach students to think. Only recently, however, have business and political leaders begun to ask for critical thinking as a form of psychological capital. As was once said of psychology in general, critical thinking "has had a long past but a short history."

Business leaders, with their impulsive, action-oriented cognitive styles, are understandably impatient with academics' reflective skepticism about reflective skepticism. Executives are, however, themselves divided about critical thinking. They want critical thinkers, but only in their place. The perfect sheriff was Harold Geneen, whose six-gun was a spreadsheet. It was accounting, he said, that "taught me analytical approaches to business problems, objective reasoning, and the highest order of discipline in making factual presentations." A better description of critical thinking applied to business would be hard to find.

The problem is that, like gunfighters hired to clean up a cow town in the old West, hired guns who are good at shooting holes in weak arguments are liable to turn their weapons on the arguments of their employers. Board members know they need critical thinkers, but they also fear them.

A. Z. Carr describes this attitude perfectly in his book *Business as a Game,* a manual for corporate gunslingers. Carr argues for critical thinking, but only within narrow limits. Although the critical thinker "is at a disadvantage in business, every now and then circumstances arise in which dissent, confined to a single issue, can prove sound strategy." Such circumstances include situations in which the issues at hand don't affect major policies, are obsolete on purely monetary grounds, or are supported only by "habit and fear"; or those in which the chief advocate of the proposal to be criticized is certain to back down because the critic is invulnerable. In other words, most corporate leaders want criticism directed only at the "bad guys," whether the bad guys are a competing nation, corporation, or division. Critical thinking is O.K. at the corral, but keep it out of the boardroom.

The significance of this wariness was not lost on prospective Wyatt Earps. At about the time Carr was writing *Business as a Game,* a 1964 article in the *Wall Street Journal* warned that the brightest college graduates were rejecting careers in business because they were repelled by demands for conformity. They saw Kennedy's problem with the Bay of Pigs invasion, GM's problems with the Corvair's handling, Ford's with the Pinto's gas tank, to say nothing of the Edsel's styling, as consequences of corporate conformity and failures to listen to criticism.

Meanwhile, back at the boardroom, a modern Wild Bill Hickok was showing his timid constituents why businesses need straight shooters. As chairman of the board at Avis, Robert Townsend offered aid and comfort to the critical outlaws, the "subversives" who conduct "nonviolent guerrilla warfare, dismantling our organizations when we're serving them, leaving only the parts where they're serving us." Townsend's *Up the Organization* books extol "disobedience and its necessity." They are case studies of the rewards to be collected when we give critical thinking a badge, a gun, and a blank arrest warrant.

Still, no one was ready when Bob Woodward and Carl Bernstein drew down on the Nixon gang. The Watergate showdown, more than any other single victory, showed all of us why we can't do without gunfighters, even if some of their shots go wild.

Today, as a result of the efforts of gunfighters like Townsend and Bernstein and Woodward, our fear of reflective thinkers is giving way to respect. Workers and managers alike define success not only in terms of dollars but in terms of increased personal, social, and ecological responsibility. The theme that emerges in Studs Terkel's interviews with workers in *Working* is the triumph of meaning over money. Successful corporations, especially high-tech firms like Hewlett-Packard and Apple Computer, have adapted to the new values. These firms are hiring young potential Billy the Kids and encouraging them to bring their equalizers with them. As a result of this new openness to criticism, many bright young gunfighters are working for banks, not blowing them up. Their values, combined with the independence provided by two-income households, encourage them to exercise their critical faculties and to challenge the assumptions of their employers in ways unthinkable a generation ago.

The new interest in putting critical thinking to work, led to educational regulations requiring courses in critical thinking as graduation requirements throughout the California State University system. As usual, other states quickly followed California's lead. Public and private colleges and universities all over the country sent faculty members to a recent international conference on critical thinking at Sonoma State University (SSU). I went too. I go to a lot of conferences on critical thinking, and I amuse myself by checking out the parking lots to see what kinds of cars critical thinkers drive. At SSU, I was surprised to find the usual mob of Plymouths, Toyotas, and VWs dignified by a delegation of Mark VIIs and Mercedes 300s. I walked into the opening session wondering what else was going on there that would attract such upscale vehicles, and got a bigger surprise when I saw the audience. The usual denim patchwork had a border of designer dresses and pinstripe suits. This conference was attended not only by academics but by executives, who like good students had taken the front row.

One of the front-row suits was SSU president David Benson, who expressed the theme of the conference in his welcome: "The biggest problem is how to get people who know how to critically think to do something." This theme was echoed by conference organizer Richard Paul in his opening address. Paul said, "Practice without theory is blind; theory without practice is empty." Later the same day, Albert Shanker, president of the American Federation of Teachers, reported on a meeting of the Business Round Table. He said that business leaders are asking educators for critical thinking and creativity, which they see as essential weapons in international competition. Leaders of industry, because they know we need to rebuild the "human infrastructure," are asking educators to send them critical, creative thinkers, not just "empty suits."

Many business leaders see how critical thinking can promote corporate productivity and personal success. At the 1985 national meeting of the American Association of Colleges (AAC), as at SSU, business leaders begged their academic colleagues to stop arguing about what critical thinking is and start doing something about it.

We *are* doing something about it, but we need the business leaders' help as much as they need ours. The best way they can help us to help them is by sending unequivocal messages. As it stands, CEOs are asking for gunfighters, but their recruiters, perhaps responding to ambivalence in the CEOs themselves, are perceived by students as still looking for accounting skills first and thinking skills second (if at all).

What are academics doing? First, we have (of course) studied the problem, and written books. Critical thinking has been in the education journals all along, but academics now know that it is the heart of education that prepares people for citizenship and work, not just for more education. Like the conference itself, the journals bring some bad news and some good news.

The bad news is that even the hardest-nosed scientists, executives, and other critical thinkers are remarkably fallible, gullible, and credulous when operating on unfamiliar terrain. How typical is this gullibility? Very. At SSU, David Perkins reported on his studies of the ability of high school, college, law, and medical students and graduates to reason about real-world proposals. The proposals used had many different arguments for and against them. They included buying a house, resurrecting the draft, and requiring deposits on bottles. The subjects were encouraged to consider both sides of each issue. Their critical-thinking performance was measured by the number of different lines of argument for and against each proposal. By this standard, performance was poor: The overall average was fewer than three arguments for the subject's position and one against it. What's worse, education seems to have no effect. Each year of education added an average of one tenth of a line of argument.

More bad news: The experts are as divided about what to do about this deplorable situation as they are about other issues having to do with intelligence. Some experts think that we can teach critical thinking by teaching logic. One such expert is Edward Glaser, president of the Human Interaction Research Institute, and one of the world's leading critical thinking consultants. Glaser is coauthor of the Watson-Glaser Critical Thinking Appraisal, the most widely used measure of critical thinking ability. Like other measures of critical thinking that view it as logic, the Watson-Glaser tests one's abilities to draw inferences, recognize assumptions, make deductions, and interpret and evaluate arguments. Unlike IQ and other tests of academic skills, the Watson-Glaser is based on real-world situations. As you might expect, people with high IQs often do poorly on this test.

Other experts believe that critical thinking is many different skills, and that how you think critically depends on what you want to think about. For practical purposes, this pluralistic point of view makes more sense: Real-world problems are seldom reducible to mere logic. Thus, although critical thinking includes the logical skills measured by the Watson-Glaser, there is more to real-world critical thinking than logic.

The good news is that programs designed to promote critical skills in academic domains lead to limited but significant increases in real-life reasoning performance. Programs designed specifically to enhance critical thinking in practical realms work even better. Glaser trains executives, pilots, and other workers interested in enhancing their critical skills, and usually succeeds in raising their scores on his test.

Glaser's approach is based on the view that critical thinking is simply a matter of logic. A broader approach, based on a view of practical critical thinking as several different skills, ought to work even better.

How to Think like Spock

A decade ago, I developed a course in clinical decisionmaking for medical students. It was designed to teach multiple critical skills, not just logic. I called the course "How to Think like Spock." The title referred both to Mr. Spock of *Star Trek* and to Dr. Benjamin Spock, an outspoken critic of several controversial national policies. I wanted to teach critical thinking not only to medical students but to law and business students as well, so I needed a scheme that was flexible enough to be used in real-world situations and yet simple enough to teach in a one-semester course.

I began by collecting cases of practical critical thinking by the Spocks and other masters, including executives, lawyers, scientists, police officers, detectives, investigative reporters, and political columnists. Perhaps because I used such a variety of cases, I was impressed above all by how different these modes of thought were. Yet they were all in some sense critical. I sifted and sorted the cases until I found a way to describe, compare, and contrast them.

What I came up with after an analysis of these cases was a

description of the tacit procedural knowledge constituting critical thinking in a variety of fields. My analysis was flexible enough to fit all the cases I considered and simple enough to fit a simple mnemonic: Give 'em SOME LIP.

GIVE 'EM SOME LIP

Scientists, lawyers, doctors, managers, and other professional skeptics perform seven critical tasks: considering *S*ources, maintaining *O*pen minds, defining *M*eanings, evaluating *E*vidence, analyzing *L*ogic, examining *I*mplications, and unearthing *P*resumptions. These methods are easy to remember: The next time someone tries to sell you a product or an idea, give it SOME LIP. Some arguments stand up to SOME LIP, but many do not.

Consider the Source

"Consider the Source" is step one for all critical thinkers. It's good advice, but it's easier said than done. All sources are liable to be biased in one way or another.

Even people who should know better have a lot to learn about sources. The unwarranted credibility of authoritative sources is so well documented that it has received a name: the "Dr. Fox effect." "Dr. Fox" was not a doctor at all, but an actor who presented a lecture to students and faculty at a major medical school. The lecture was amusing, and it was carefully written to include contradictions and nonsense, and to avoid conveying any real information. The audience rated the lecture on an eight-item questionnaire, and Dr. Fox's evaluations were favorable. When sources seem authoritative, even experts grant them more credibility than they deserve.

The Dr. Fox effect occurs every day in courtrooms, when a doctor testifies as an expert witness. The problem with competing experts, according to the great jurist Learned Hand, is that they impose a "practical closing of the doors of justice upon the use of specialized and scientific knowledge," leaving the jury "as badly off as if they had none to help." The trial of John Hinckley, who shot President Reagan in 1981, was a horrible example of competing experts on mental illness. As a result, the American Bar and Psychiatric associations submitted to Congress proposals to restrict the role of the expert witness in Not Guilty by Reason of Insanity (NGBRI) defenses.

Though controversies about legal standards for expert witnesses have yet to be resolved, courts have procedures to help jurors and judges evaluate sources. The law requires two witnesses in serious cases such as trials for treason and can declare sources incompetent on the basis of age, reputation, pecuniary interest, prejudice, or prior conviction. Because the law is a reflection of a changing society, its standards for appraising sources change too. For example, restrictions on testimony from spouses, children, and perpetrators of criminal acts are being relaxed.

Even when protected by legal and other safeguards, most of us are susceptible to the Dr. Fox effect. But not Harold Geneen. He is notorious for his cross-examinations of his executives. There is a reason for the intense probing: Geneen considers the source of facts as important as the facts themselves. The "good guys want you to ask the right question," he writes. "Only . . . phonies squirm when confronted." In a section of his autobiography on how to think like a manager, Geneen advises ambitious "good guys" to rely only on firsthand information from several sources.

Geneen's advice applies to politics as well as business. Much of the time and effort that *Washington Post* reporters Carl Bernstein and Robert Woodward invested in the Watergate investigation went into considering sources. The reporters preferred firsthand accounts, and went to considerable lengths to obtain them, such as Woodward's series of secret rendezvous with "Deep Throat." Like Geneen, they considered a source's emotional state an important part of the story. Deep Throat's "dispassionate" sincerity and the uncharacteristic outrage expressed by a Justice Department attorney during a discussion of "dirty tricks" made these sources more credible. On one occasion, Woodward made twelve telephone calls to check the reliability of one source. Bernstein and Woodward always checked one source against another—anything they published had to have two independent sources. In following these procedures, Bernstein and Woodward operated much like rational-model managers and lawyers.

On the other hand, when appropriate, Bernstein and Woodward employed a personal style more like a clinical psychologist's than a scientist's. They established rapport with sources (like Hugh Sloan, assistant to presidential counsel Maurice Stans) in order to win their confidence, or angered them to get them to spill more than they wanted to. Woodward deliberately provoked Deep Throat by accusing him of playing a "chicken shit" game, and purposely angered a college student by accusing him of spying.

All critical thinkers prefer multiple, firsthand, objective sources whenever possible, but it is not always possible. Thus, although "consider the source" is good advice, how to go about considering sources can't be reduced to a simple formula. The best we can do is learn tricks from experts like Harold Geneen, Carl Bernstein, and Robert Woodward.

Here are some of those tricks:

- Remember Dr. Fox. The "expert" may not be what he or she seems. Find out who's who. Ask others in the field. Check credentials, publications, experience. Every field has its quacks.

- Remember the Edsel. Even real experts are sometimes wrong.

- Use firsthand information whenever possible. When you can't, get as close to the primary sources of information as you can. Remember the game of "telephone," in which a story passes from one person to the next, each retelling multiplying old distortions by new ones until the product is almost unrecognizable. Secondhand information degrades rapidly.

- Trace it down. Usually you depend on information that is at least secondhand, and usually third or fourth hand. Like secondhand cars, secondhand information is often damaged by previous owners in ways that do not meet the eye. You can learn a lot by finding out about that original owner. "Pyramid power" started as a joke in Martin Gardner's column in *Scientific American.* Now people in Mill Valley run their garden hoses through tetrahedrons made of coat hangers.

- If you can't find the original source—look out! Someone may be setting you up.

- Use multiple sources. Even when people see the same event, accounts disagree. In order to make this point to my experimental-psych class, I stage a mock assassination and ask the class to jot down a brief account. On a typical occasion, the class correctly reported the weapon (a cream pie), but most omitted one or more details, such as the assassin's dress (a Union Jack cape, ski goggles, and a wet suit) or his getaway vehicle (a skateboard). By putting several accounts together, however, you can often get a pretty good picture. A combination of the assassination reports, while far from complete, was better than any one of them.

- Use reputable sources: *Harvard Business Review, New England Journal of Medicine,* or the handful of newspapers and magazines that have similar editorial standards—*Science, Scientific American,* and *Byte,* or the equivalent in your field. These sources have biases, but they are generally up-front about saying what their biases are. Magazines make money by selling space to advertisers, and selling space means having a big circulation. For a magazine editor deciding if or how to run a story, the bottom line is not accuracy but circulation. Journals, on the other hand, have few ads, soft paper, and no pictures. Professional journals' revenues come mainly from subscribers, not advertisers. They get subscribers by supplying the confusing details that interest only specialists. They reveal all their sources. Articles are never anonymous, and authors' credentials and professional affiliations are always provided. Reference lists at the end of each article allow the interested or skeptical reader to check the authors' sources.

- Get it in writing. When a document passes from hand to hand, the words stay the same, no matter who looks at them.

- Watch out for "I've read somewhere that . . ." as an attempt to cite a source. Not even Will Rogers believed *everything* he read in the papers.

- Beware of sources who get defensive when probed. Remember: "The good guys want you to ask the right question."

Open Your Mind

Once you've considered a source's biases, the next step is to confront them with your own. And we all have biases, whether we know it or not. As we saw in Chapter 3, overconfidence in our own judgments is imposed by the totalitarian ego. "The only impartiality possible to the human mind," wrote English jurist Lord Hewart, "is that which arises from an understanding of neither side of the case." That's why the *O* in SOME LIP stands for "Open Your Mind."

When people are asked to estimate upper and lower limits for figures on unemployment, foreign automobile imports, and other indices so that they are 98 percent certain that the real figure is between their limits, they make their range too narrow about a third of the time. Managers congratulate themselves on their judgment when they review their personnel decisions, but like subjects in the card-flipping experiment described in the preceding chapter, they never consider crucial evidence about the successful people they *didn't* hire.

Open-mindedness is a principle of U.S. law. Judges are sworn to be impartial and their decisions are subject to reversal on appeal, but the real protection against partiality is the adversary method. In his essay *Legal Reasoning,* Edward Levi wrote, "The ideas have had their day in court. . . . that is what makes the hearing fair, rather than any idea that the judge is completely impartial, for of course he cannot be completely so."

Similarly, the Sixth Amendment guarantee of the right to an "impartial" jury is implemented not by attempting to open jurors' minds but by excluding those with closed ones. Some protection against partiality based on race, class, sex, or employment is supposed to lie in the representation of all major groups on lists of prospective jurors. However, partiality is so difficult to avoid that the constitutional guarantee is effected by the right to disqualify prospective jurors by "challenges for cause"—i.e., on account of partiality. In federal courts, the number of such challenges for cause is unlimited.

Good physicians, like other practical scientists, make an art of open-mindedness. They are eager to learn new theories that can lead to better treatments. Doctors used to view schizophrenics like John Hinckley as victims of mental conflicts created by parents. This view may be correct, but it is impractical because it doesn't tell us how to treat schizophrenia. New medical technology like Positron Emission and Computerized Axial Tomography (PET and CAT) scans has led many physicians to adopt a more practical view based on brain physiology, which we can treat.

One man who learned the value of open-mindedness the hard way was Richard Nixon, who ended the Vietnam war, opened China, and would have been remembered as one of our most successful Presidents if it had not been for his lack of open-mindedness. Watergate is a cautionary tale about the dangers of unrecognized bias. From John Dean on down, the convicted principals in the Watergate cover-up apparently believed that they were performing their duty. The political biases that blinded them to the questionable legality and morality of their actions were as invisible to them as they were obvious to those who did not share the biases.

In contrast, although Bernstein and Woodward were also biased, they were aware of their bias against the administration and guarded against it. For instance, they overcame their conviction that H. R. Haldeman was in charge of the secret fund. They were assisted in overcoming their biases by their editor, Benjamin Bradlee, who "served as prosecutor, demanding to know what each source had said." Personal involvement also helped them to remain open-minded, as in Bernstein's empathy for "the excruciating depths of [Attorney General] John Mitchell's hurt."

You can't escape biases, but you can confront them. Here's how:

- Get feedback on your judgments. Weather forecasters, bookmakers, and others who receive frequent feedback are quite accurate at assessing their accuracy.
- Go back to the suggestions at the end of Chapter 4 on self-understanding. The best guide to your biases are your values.

- What are your vested interests? Do the stocks or real estate you own bias you toward the status quo? Do you owe a lot of money at fixed interest? Pay social security? Work for a multinational? Your answers point to interests that bias you for or against a wide range of attitudes and policies. You're better off knowing what your biases are than denying that they exist.

- How did you vote? If you didn't, do it next time, if only to learn about yourself.

- Expose yourself. If you're a liberal, liberate yourself with a subscription to *National Review*. If you're a conservative, invest in a subscription to *New Republic*. If you're middle-of-the-road, try *Mother Jones*. These sources will open your mind by forcing you to confront new meanings, evidence, logic, implications, and presumptions. The adversary method has been around for a long time. It works. Remember Alfred Sloan's advice about developing disagreement, quoted in the chapter on social intelligence.

Meanings

M stands for "Meanings" of words and phrases. "When *I* use a word," said Humpty Dumpty, "it means just what I choose it to mean." Humpty Dumpty's arrogance didn't work even in Wonderland. In the real world, those who insist on choosing what words mean are liable to share his fate. The Watergate conspirators left us a legacy of ironic new meanings for old terms, including "national interest" and "executive privilege." Not even the President's men can put these words together again without echoes of "dirty tricks," "deep sixing," and "twisting slowly in the wind."

Like all critical thinkers, the Watergate investigators were scrupulous in their attention to meanings. Woodward, for example, paid particular attention to Henry Kissinger's use of phrases like "almost never" to describe wiretaps, and inferred that wiretaps had been authorized. By paying attention to the meaning of Nixon's denial that anyone "presently employed" at the White House was involved, the investigators focused on former employees.

The problem with careful use of meaning is that people in the same field often emulate Humpty Dumpty, and choose meanings that suit their purposes. Remember the definitions of "intelligence." Think about the differences in the way the word "energy" is used in physics, economics, and pop psychology. The same word has different meanings in different fields. Worse, different fields have different standards for what constitutes a good definition. Doctors, who by and large apply the methods of science, continually confront lawyers, whose standards are far different. In a discussion of differences between scientific and legal meanings, the great legal scholar and jurist Edward Cleary wrote: "scientific language insists that concepts be defined in terms of the operations producing them. Evidence operates on the reverse basis that the concept produces the result. Legal water runs uphill."

We encountered one example of scientific definition in terms of operations in Chapter 2. Boring used the operation of giving an intelligence test to define the concept of intelligence. Cleary's point is illustrated by the Hinckley jurors' confusion, in which the "mental disorders" of psychiatrists clashed with the "mental diseases" of law. The legal term "insanity" is itself having a breakdown. It is no wonder that during their deliberations, the jurors asked (in vain) for a dictionary.

As a manager, teacher, counselor, or citizen, you will often deal with terms whose meanings determine a decision. There are several things you can do to clarify meanings:.

- Make it a habit to ask "What does that mean?" Overcome the natural tendency to regard requests for clarification as confessions of ignorance. You'll be amazed at the answers you get (and don't get).

- Check definitions. Many words have more than one meaning. Find out which one is intended.

- Try definitions on for size. Like a leather belt, a good definition is long enough and has enough adjustment to fit all the good examples. A good definition is also tight enough to exclude cases that don't fit. "One size fits all" is a sign of an elastic definition. It may look good, but like an elastic belt, it may not hold up.

- Read the headlines in *National Enquirer.* Then read the stories.

- Practice spotting incomplete statements: comparisons like "makes your clothes whiter" (than what?) or "saves you money" (relative to what?).

- Listen to George Carlin, the comedian, and read the columnist William Safire. They have a knack for spotting howlers such as "fresh frozen" or "guest host."

Evidence

E stands for "Evidence." Evidence is not just common sense. Common sense tells us that sharp knives are more dangerous than dull ones. The evidence tells us the opposite: Accidents are more likely with dull knives. For most practical purposes, the best kind of evidence is facts, true statements about observable events. When Harold Geneen cross-examined his executives at ITT, the answers he wanted were "facts and opinions backed by facts." In one of his terse memos, he asked for not just ordinary facts but "unshakeable facts."

The difference between mere facts and unshakeable ones is shown by the (literal) exposure of Uri Geller. Uri Geller is a famous Israeli stage magician who claimed that his supernormal powers came from a computer in a UFO. For years, Geller convinced skeptics, including some highly trained physicists, that he employed some as yet unknown method of transferring images to photographic film. Then *Psychology Today* published a picture of Geller caught in the act by a wide-angle lens with unusual depth of field. He had by simple sleight of hand shown something far more interesting than supernormal powers—that outside their laboratories, scientists are as gullible as anyone else. He never would have fooled a *real* expert on sleight of hand. That's why he refuses to perform in front of other stage magicians and why he has yet to collect the ten thousand dollars offered by the Amazing Randi, another stage magician, who claims only that his hands are quicker than your eye. Geller can collect if he can do a trick that Randi can't. "Seeing is believing," but the evidence of the untrained eye is often not good enough to catch a Uri Geller.

A more practical illustration of the importance of good evidence comes from studies of the effects of biorhythms on accident rates. Biorythms are real, but biorythm theory goes beyond biorythms. Biorythm theory says that there are three kinds of rhythm: physical, emotional, and intellectual well-being each with positive and negative phases. Since each cycle has its own period, there are times ("bad days") when all three cycles are negative. According to the biorhythm theory, on these bad days we are especially liable to accidents, depression, and even suicide. When workers are warned about their "bad days," the accident rates on those days often drop. That's evidence. But accident rates drop on *any* day when workers are warned to be especially careful. That's better evidence.

Unfortunately, industrial accidents and other tragedies are influenced by many factors unrelated to biorhythms, and most early studies did not control these other factors. One way to do this is to compare crashes involving pilot error (presumably subject to the effect of biorhythms) with those caused by major equipment failure, wind shear, and other factors not subject to the influence of the pilots' biorhythms. Thirteen such controlled studies showed no association between pilots' biorhythms and the likelihood of a crash.

Nevertheless, like other simple explanations for complex events, biorhythm theory is appealing; people who want to believe don't want to be confused by the facts. Several large corporations continue to spend time and money applying biorhythm theory. Biorhythm theory would be only a harmless marketing scheme if it didn't blind those responsible for our safety to the real significance of the evidence: Workers can reduce accidents by being more careful not just on "bad days" but all the time. Good evidence can save lives.

What constitutes good evidence depends on what you want to do with it. Judge Cleary contrasts legal methods with those used by physicians and other scientists. "In the realm of honest searching after the truth, nothing could be further removed from scientific method than the rules governing procedures used in courts."

Cleary's point is highlighted in trials involving the NGBRI defense, where differences between legal and medical standards for judging evidence are brought into focus. In making judgments about mental disorder, CAT scans are the sorts of hard evidence doctors prefer. They can give the physician who knows how to interpret them a layer-by-layer look at the inside of a brain. They are used routinely in the diagnosis of various neurological disorders, like brain injuries and tumors. In the Hinckley trial, however, Judge Barrington Moore twice refused defense motions to admit CAT scans of Hinckley's brain. He eventually allowed them to be shown but insisted that they be projected on a small screen on the side of the courtroom away from the jury, and without dimming the lights. There was a reason for Moore's waffling: He feared that the CAT scans, which showed abnormalities in Hinckley's brain, would, for a jury of laypersons, carry more weight than they should. The judge's indecisiveness is testimony to his awareness of the different ways doctors and juries deal with evidence like CAT scans. The jury's verdict of NGBRI testifies to the persuasive power of facts that can be seen firsthand.

In spite of major differences in medical and legal standards for evidence, the law does share a few principles of evidence with other systems of critical thinking. For one thing, the law of evidence distinguishes facts from inferences, "conclusions on the part of the witness." For another, the law excludes hearsay testimony and all information other than a document itself as evidence of its content.

Bernstein and Woodward applied these principles for evaluating evidence to their Watergate investigation. They separated the facts from what they thought those facts meant. "Hard" evidence was preferred. Their editor "always felt better when he knew that somewhere . . . there was a piece of paper that could support a story." Such hard documentary evidence included address books, library checkout slips, canceled checks, a telephone list, and office rosters.

So . . .

- Check it out yourself. Get something *you* can see, hear, or touch.
- Remember Uri Geller. Believing is seeing, so don't trust your eyes too much—or your ears. My wet-suited cream pie marksman shouted, "I should have done this next year, when I had the chance!" as he hurled the pie. Everyone recorded "next" as "last," because that is what they expected to hear.
- Write it down right away. Take a tip from detectives, reporters, field scientists, and other experts in real-world evidence. Don't trust your memory. You don't have to carry a notebook —a small pad will fit in your wallet with no bulge.
- Get it in numbers. Numbers can't always be precise, but they can be precise about how imprecise they are. Ask your mechanic if he can have it done in a week, plus or minus six days.
- Learn some elementary descriptive statistics: Know your way around the bell-shaped curve. Huff's *How to Lie with Statistics* is a good source.
- Beware of anecdotes. We are unduly persuaded by a single vivid story: one miracle cure, one airplane crash, instant success.

Logic

Even the hardest evidence is useless without *L*ogic, the rules about how evidence can be used. The problem is that the rules of logic are often disobeyed. Here's a real-world example of the same backward logic we saw in the case of the foolish atheist in the preceding chapter. Consider the argument made by Wilson Brian Key on subliminal advertising. Key argues that many advertisements are successful, not because they are striking and attractive, but because they contain hidden figures that stimulate unconscious fears and desires. One reason so many people find Key's argument convincing is that firsthand evidence in the form of advertisements is all around. Look for hidden faces or other figures in the sky or in the surf. You are sure to find some.

The problem is not in Key's evidence; it's in his logic. The logical problem was described by Shakespeare, in *Hamlet.*

HAMLET: Do you see yonder cloud that's almost in shape of a camel?

POLONIUS: By the mass, and 'tis like a camel indeed.

HAMLET: Me thinks it is like a weasel.

POLONIUS: It is backed like a weasel.

HAMLET: Or like a whale?

POLONIUS: Very like a whale.

Subliminal advertisers on Madison Avenue are clever indeed; they have been putting shapes into clouds for over three hundred years. I asked Key about this in a public question period after one of his lectures. He dismissed my question, saying that it came from a "sexually repressed" college professor. Key is an example of someone who *doesn't* want to be asked the right question. He got a good laugh from the audience but didn't answer the question I asked. Fortunately, most advertisers are skeptical enough to save their money for ads that work not subliminally but superliminally, that are striking and appealing in ways we can see.

Backward logic misleads those who conclude that running is bad for you because some people die while running and that marijuana smoking leads to heroin addiction because most heroin addicts smoked dope first. (As George Carlin points out, they *all* drank milk first, so milk "leads to *everything.*") This form of backward logic is so common that it received a name back when the language of logic was Latin: *post hoc propter hoc*—after this, therefore because of this.

Psychologists David Perkins, Amos Tversky, Irving Janis, and others have developed a virtual encyclopedia of logical fallacies. How can we protect ourselves against such fallacies? The best way is to become familiar with valid forms of argument and their common misuses.

Scientists use several powerful and versatile logical techniques. One of them is "strong inference," the logical method described by Sherlock Holmes in "The Sign of the Four": "When you have eliminated the impossible, whatever remains, however improbable, must be the truth." Holmes's method is the essence of scientific logic. Scientists work not by proving but by disproving. For example, doctors diagnose by eliminating possible causes of the symptoms they observe.

One of the most powerful scientific techniques for eliminating alternatives is control. Controls eliminate causes by isolating them or holding them constant. In some scientific experiments, controls are provided by using two groups of subjects. The experimental group gets the treatment. The control group is treated exactly like the experimental group in every way except the treatment. For example, if we want to find out if subliminal advertising affects sales, we would use two groups of subjects: an experimental group that gets the subliminal ad, and a control group with the same average age, income, and background that gets exactly the same advertisement but without the subliminal content. If the only difference between the two groups is the treatment, the treatment must be responsible for any difference in test scores. Such controlled experiments have been performed and the results show no difference. Because controls are such simple and powerful ways of eliminating rival hypotheses, it is ironic that so many studies, especially in non- and semiscientific publications, do not use them.

In the law, the adversary method forces alternative versions of the truth to compete, so there is something like strong inference in legal logic. However, the law does not use either controls or other forms of strong inference in any systematic way. Adversaries present not only different pieces of evidence but different versions of the logic to be used by the jury in arriving at a verdict. In criminal trials, prosecutors typically attempt to hang the defendant with a rope made of separate strands of evidence; strands may give way without significantly weakening a rope. Defense attorneys, on the other hand, attempt to raise reasonable doubts by comparing the prosecution's logic to a chain whose links are pieces of evidence. Unlike a rope, a chain is broken if any one link is cut.

Because there is no single system of rules jurors may use to decide between such logics, the adversary method, in Edward Cleary's opinion, is only "a dog fight between two conflicting versions out of which the trier is expected to emerge triumphantly carrying in his teeth the bone of 'truth.' As Edward Levi wrote, "The law has a logic of its own." Actually, the law has two main systems of logic: In criminal trials, guilt must be proven beyond a reasonable doubt, while in civil cases, a preponderance of evidence suffices. In either case, the law's practical aims are different from the theoretical goals of formal logic and pure science. Levi also wrote, "The contrast between logic and the actual legal method is a disservice to both."

Watergate investigators Bernstein and Woodward opportunistically used both scientific and legal logics. They eliminated impossibilities one by one: the "crazy Cubans" theory that the burglars acted on their own, the "Chotiner" theory about the involvement of Nixon's staff, the "set up" theory that the two of them were being deliberately misled, and the "Haldeman" theory that Nixon's top aide controlled the secret espionage fund. Soon only the improbable remained: that knowledge of the cover-up went all the way to the Oval Office.

On the other hand, Bernstein had formulated the conspiracy theory long before evidence could support it. Like prosecutors, the investigators cross-examined sources in a search for data that supported their theory. Although they were themselves cross-examined by their editors, their search for supporting rather than falsifying evidence was a form of advocacy closer to the methods of the law than to those of science. They were aware of this when they called their initial story "interpretive—risky."

No one ever said using logic is easy. In fact, as we saw in Chapter 9, logical reasoning requires a special form of intelligence. There are, however, several things you can do to analyze logic:

- Look out for common sense. The "sense" in the fallacy of the foolish atheist is all too common. It tells us to look before we leap. However, it also tells us that he who hesitates is lost. Common sense does *not* tell which applies to a given decision.

- People who want you to buy a procedure, policy, or product offer explanations of why it works, so always ask, "Are there other explanations?" Then ask if there were controls to eliminate these other explanations.

- Learn the valid logical forms of argument: induction, deduction, and example. There's a whole genre of books with the words "straight" and "thinking" in the title.

- Learn to recognize the weak forms of argument: analogy, authority, straw man, and so on. The straight-thinking books will help here too.

- Look for logical fallacies like the backward logic of the foolish atheist and subliminal advertising.

- Learn some elementary probability. In a risky world, you've got to play the percentages, so you'd better know how they work.

- Remember that logic is not enough. You gotta know the territory.

Implications

*I*mplications are, in John Dewey's definition of reflective thought, "the further conclusions to which an argument tends." In other words, if the argument is true, then what? Sometimes an otherwise sound argument has unacceptable practical consequences; implications often reveal inconsistencies not apparent in arguments themselves.

For example, consider the controversies about abortion and capital punishment. People who favor one tend to oppose the other, and both sides base their arguments on the sanctity of human life. Yet use of this sanctity implies that both are wrong.

In *Shooting Ourselves in the Foot,* Bernard O'Keefe elaborates the implications of a belief in the inherent superiority of capitalism to other forms of economic organization. O'Keefe is a laissez-faire capitalist who believes that nuclear power is "inherently safe," and fondly recalls the days when "a smokestack meant jobs, not pollution." If we really believe in capitalism, he argues, we should let it work; we shouldn't undermine it (hence the title) by spending money on wasteful military defenses against Communism. Capitalism is itself the best defense. He cites the "recognition by China of the superiority of the democratic capitalistic system" as evidence that capitalism unfettered by military spending can convert the Communist bloc by example.

When an implication of an argument benefits the source, we are justifiably skeptical. Implications do not affect an argument's internal validity, but critical thinkers are often less likely to accept an argument when they realize where it leads or who stands to gain. Public officials attempt to avoid this skepticism by putting their investments into blind trusts.

Medical arguments are often judged by their practical implications. For example, many psychiatrists prefer theories about mental disorder based on brain chemistry to those based on repression simply because an understanding of brain chemistry has more direct therapeutic implications. We can do more about chemistry than we can about repression.

Implications are the whole point of legal argument. The implications for John Hinckley and for society of a NGBRI verdict were as much a part of his trial as were the facts of the case. The attorneys who argued and the psychiatrists who worked on John Hinckley's behalf tried to get him the best possible treatment. Across the courtroom, the prosecution argued in terms of the verdict's implications for society.

The Watergate investigators let the implications fall where they might. However, for many politicians and political columnists, the major criteria for judging the validity of Bernstein and Woodward's case were its political implications. You could predict most people's attitude about the validity of the accusations by knowing how they had voted.

Here's how you can use implications to test an argument:

- Use the Golden Rule: Would you like the argument applied to you? to your friends? to your competitors?

- Take the premises one step farther. If an argument depends on a belief, explore the other consequences of that belief.
- Ask who stands to gain from your acceptance. The source? The source's organization or allies? Knowing that there are vested interests doesn't make an argument wrong, but knowing who they are often tells you where to look for unacceptable implications. Someone always stands to gain, otherwise you wouldn't be exposed to the argument in the first place.
- Sometimes implications are not to your liking, but they are nonetheless true. Be open-minded enough to accept the argument and its implications even if it's your ox that gets gored.

Presumptions

The final step is to go back and examine the *P*resumptions on which the argument rests. This is the last step because presumptions are often unstated. You can't see what they are until you've got the rest of the argument laid out. Here's an example of how unacknowledged presumptions interfere with solving a simple problem.

A man and his son had a car crash. The father was killed. The son was rushed to a nearby hospital. Upon seeing the boy, the surgeon said, "I can't operate—he's my son." Who was the surgeon? People who have a hard time answering this question are victims of the hidden presumption that the surgeon must be male.

David Perkins finds that most flaws in practical thinking are caused by presumptions like that one. He calls the presumptions in terms of which situations are initially conceptualized "situation models." For example, Bernstein and Woodward used the Teapot Dome and other scandals as situation models for Watergate. They explicitly presumed that something was going on. They tacitly presumed that they could discover that something, using general principles of how humans act. Similar tacit presumptions are made by doctors, lawyers, engineers, and anyone else who hopes to get and use scientific understanding. These principles must be presumed because there is no way to test them. As critical thinkers, the best we can do is recognize them for what they are: acts of faith. Acts of faith they may be, but they are highly practical. Without these working presumptions, no scientific or other practical enterprises could proceed. If they are not true, we'll find out soon enough.

Other practical presumptions include the explicit presumptions of innocence under English law and of guilt under the Napoleonic code. Other legal presumptions, like the doctrine of the "reasonable man," are tacit; everyone is supposed to know what "reasonable" means. Cleary satirized this presumption with his doctrine of the "reasonable chicken," which everyone knows comes home to roost. The continuing controversies about the NGBRI defense show that we do not know how to decide to whom the presumption of the "reasonable man" applies.

All critical thinkers evaluate Sources, try to remain Open-minded, define Meanings of key terms, appraise Evidence, apply Logic, deal with Implications, and examine Presumptions. These tasks are more easily described than accomplished, because every field has its own ways of accomplishing them. The **SOME LIP** scheme is like training wheels. If you've been picking away at it all along, finding the tasks arbitrary or out of order, you probably don't need it. If it sounds pretty good, you ought to try it. But remember, training wheels are meant to help people learn a new skill, not to slow those who have mastered it.

Failures of critical thinking can be serious obstacles to productivity, excellence, health, and life itself. If we are willing to die for a theory and to risk taking the world along with us, we had better be critical about that theory.

PART FIVE

PRACTICAL STYLES AND CREATIVE SKILLS

11.
Cognitive Styles

Much I owe . . . to the Lives that fed—
But most to Allah Who gave me two
Separate sides to my head.

          —RUDYARD KIPLING

The preceding chapters show how skilled workers employ various combinations of six intelligences in a wide variety of occupations, and how verbal and logical intelligences work together in critical thinking. Each intelligence tells a different story, and together these stories are far richer than the one told by IQ alone. But there is more to the working mind than combinations of abilities. What is missing is what psychologists call "cognitive style."

People with similar patterns of intelligence (high verbal and spatial, low mathematical, etc.) often differ in the ways in which they apply their abilities to a given task. For instance, when you use spatial intelligence to decide how to move a table through a doorway, you may act impulsively and intuitively, immediately "seeing" that two legs will hit the inside wall unless the table goes in on its side. I, on the other hand, would plod methodically through, imagining every possible orientation, and would eventually arrive at the same answer you did. Multiple intelligences measure *how well* you think. Cognitive styles describe *how* you think.

Psychologists distinguish cognitive styles from intellectual abilities. But there's a complication. Most investigators define "intelligence" as IQ. Therefore, some of the differences they describe as stylistic I consider differences in patterns of MIs. As you will see, some styles seem to bear a very direct relationship to some MIs. In many cases, as psychologist Nathan Kogan puts it, "a particular type of intelligence is actually assimilated within the cognitive style at issue."

YIN AND YANG

Kogan's point is illustrated by the table below. Cognitive styles are organized along dimensions, or scales, running from analytic to holistic, from methodical to intuitive, and from reflective to impulsive. Most practicing psychologists find it useful to summarize the first end of each of these continua as more or less left-brained and the other end as more or less right-brained.

LEFT BRAIN SYSTEM	RIGHT BRAIN SYSTEM
Multiple Intelligences	
verbal	spatial
logical	body
Cognitive Styles	
analytic	holistic
methodical	intuitive
reflective	active

MULTIPLE INTELLIGENCES AND COGNITIVE STYLES

Like all polar dimensions, the table's left-right continuum is an oversimplification. Nevertheless, individuals tend toward one pole or the other: Analytic people tend to be methodical and reflective, while holistic people tend to be intuitive and active. Consequently, industrial psychologists and management consultants find the left–right distinction useful. For example, Henry Mintzberg's *Harvard Business Review* article "Planning on the Left Side and Managing on the Right" contrasts the two modes of thought. As with all Mintzberg's work, his conclusions in this article are based on a detailed, minute-by-minute analysis of managerial behavior. The article's title, implies Mintzberg's main point: that each style has its place not only in the brain but in the decisionmaking process. In a 1981 article in *Organizational Dynamics,* management consultant Patrick Nugent contrasts these two modes and discusses several practical implications, including the value of intentionally and explicitly alternating between them during problem-solving sessions.

Even left-brained experimental psychologists sound a little mystical when it comes to cognitive styles. Textbook definitions of cognitive style are full of allusions to "preferred modes" of thinking, "the unconscious," "insight," "intuition," and other slippery characters that you can never pin down long enough to get a story from. In this chapter, I describe how left- and right-brained styles work and help you learn where you are on each of the style dimensions. I also discuss how to use your style in choosing occupations and career strategies. Finally, I mention some (arduous) ways to develop and adjust your own cognitive style.

My main point is that what Dolph Kuss claimed for style in skiing is true of style in thinking: Style is largely the product of training and experience. As you will see, the highest stages of stylistic development are flexibly integrated combinations of left- and right-brained modes of thinking. Developing expertise is in part an increase in the range of styles you can use.

For example, in spatial intelligence, we move from linear route maps to holistic survey maps. In body intelligence, we move from conscious verbal analysis toward automatic, holistic motor programs, as when we go from letter-level to word-level typing. We move from methodical to intuitive as we automate our responses; and we move from reflective to impulsive as we wean ourselves from verbal rules. In each of these examples, we may seem to be replacing left-brained modes with right-brained ones. For this reason, a small industry has arisen around techniques for training right-brained thinking.

Indeed, experts *are* capable of more right-brained thinking than novices. However, they are often more left-brained as well. Experts have fully developed left- *and* right-brained styles and can shift flexibly from one mode to the other as the situation requires. For example, I discussed how expert cabdrivers "downshift" from survey maps to route maps when they enter less familiar areas. As you will see, the culmination of stylistic development is not simply a matter of left or right, but a master style called "cognitive complexity," which cuts across the others, flexibly combining analysis with holism, method with intuition, and reflection with action.

FOXES AND HEDGEHOGS

The distinction between analytic and holistic styles is at least as old as an epigram attributed to the Greek poet Archilochus: "The fox knows many things, but the hedgehog knows one great thing."

Foxes are analytic—they are good at making fine, "legalistic" distinctions. Thomas Reed Powell of Harvard Law School expressed the analytic quality of legal thinking when he described the legal mind as one that "can think about a thing inextricably attached to something else without thinking about the thing which it is attached to." Such analytic habits are what professors mean when they describe the real lessons of law school as learning to "think like a lawyer."

Holistic hedgehogs, on the other hand, are good at seeing similarities, at constructing the "big picture." Like the senior managers studied by Daniel Isenberg of Harvard's Graduate School of Business Administration, hedgehogs "synthesize isolated bits of data and experience into an integrated picture, often an 'aha!' experience."

How deep the analytic-holistic distinction runs is shown by a study conducted in the 1940s by psychologist Herman Witkin, a pioneer in the study of cognitive style. Witkin investigated claims that at night and in clouds, some pilots become so disoriented that they emerge from cloud banks upside down. These pilots, whom Witkin called "field dependent" because they depend heavily on their surroundings, process information holistically: They rely on context. When clouds or darkness deprives them of other contexts, so that the only context they have is the cockpit, "up" becomes "toward the canopy." "Field independent" pilots, on the other hand, rely not on context but on the vestibular sense I mentioned in Chapter 6. They tend to handle information analytically: They can separate vestibular or other information about up and down from the conflicting information provided by their immediate surroundings.

Witkin soon discovered that the degree to which someone relies on internal versus external cues generalizes to a wide range of situations other than perception of up and down. One such situation is the basis of a common test of the analytic-holistic dimension, the Embedded Figures Test, an adult version of the children's puzzles that ask how many bunnies you can find in a picture. Others, like the Rod and Frame Test and the Tilting Chair Test, which require judgments of vertical, are more like the real-world tasks that originally captured Witkin's interest.

Because of the association between analysis and field independence, on the one hand, and between field dependence and holism, on the other, in the psychological and management-science literature "high analytic" and "field independent" are used interchangeably, as are "low analytic," "field dependent," and "heuristic." In any case, foxes and hedgehogs do more than think differently; they see differently, and can disagree about even so basic a "fact" as which way is up.

David Halberstam's *The Best and the Brightest* shows the fox and hedgehog styles in action during the deliberations that led to Lyndon Johnson's escalation of the Vietnam war. Robert McNamara's style was foxy: analytic and field independent. He saw the situation in Vietnam in strictly military and economic terms. His analysis was structured, deductive, meticulous, and precise as far as it went. Indeed, from military and economic points of view, there seemed to be no way we could lose. Chester Bowles, however, was more holistic and field dependent: He saw the problem in a historical and geographical context, and argued that there was no way the U.S. could win.

Given the advantage of hindsight, we might conclude that the holistic hedgehog style may be well adapted to problems where social context matters. Indeed, people who maintain a consistently field-dependent style are good at remembering social interactions and conversations, and prefer "people work": teaching, sales, and other services. Such a generalization suggests an intimate and profitable relationship between the hedgehog style and the social intelligences described in Chapter 5. Researchers in social intelligence and cognitive styles may be working on the same case and might well compare notes.

Conversely, in many tasks, such as flying a plane, the field-independent style has a real advantage. In fact, most professional schools consider inculcating an analytic style a major part of the curriculum. As you might expect, people who use a consistently analytic style prefer legal, technical, and other occupations where they can work with information divorced from social context. This style smacks of the distinction between visualizers and verbalizers discussed in Chapter 7, and suggests another potentially profitable collaboration between investigators in different precincts.

One researcher on management information systems has recommended that foxy executives get reports that emphasize quantitative data, and use information systems that allow them plenty of time to break these data down as they see fit. Hedgehogs, on the other hand, should get mainly qualitative information and systems that let them handle data quickly.

To get an idea of where you are on the hedgehog-fox dimension, compare your pattern discrimination performance with that of your colleagues. Use the materials you work with to create a real-world version of the Embedded Figures Test: For example, are you good at finding misplaced objects that are in full view but camouflaged by clutter? Or do you suffer from "desk blindness"? How do you do on the real-world Rod and Frame Test? When it comes to straightening pictures, are you usually the one who asks or the one who helps? Do you like to argue by making distinctions, or are you likely to exclaim, "What's the difference?" Do you tend to believe the last argument you've heard, or do you tend to stick to your guns? None of these informal tests has the precision of a psychological assessment, but they all have one big advantage: They test your style in the real situations where your style works (or doesn't work).

The distinction between foxes and hedgehogs is useful because most of us use a consistent intellectual approach to solving all problems—verbal, spatial, mathematical, etc. This does not mean, however, that you are stuck in either the analytic or the holistic mode. We do not know the extent to which fox and hedgehog styles depend on experience, but it may be considerable. To return to the example above, it is to be expected that Robert McNamara, whose analytic approach to finance worked so well at Ford Motor Company, would apply the same approach to the new realm of politics. The old hand Chester Bowles had been used to context-rich situations for years: It was he who five years before had advised against the Bay of Pigs invasion.

In fact, whether they consider style a matter mainly of nature or of nurture, most psychologists think of cognitive development as moving generally from field dependence to field independence. We have seen this progression in several domains. In self-intelligence, for example, we saw how field-dependent looking glass selves develop into a field-independent totalitarian ego. Similarly, in the motor domain, as motor programs become more autonomous, they move from field dependence to field independence. By the same token, in spatial intelligence, mental survey maps render expert wayfinders independent of their immediate surroundings.

This picture of development from dependence (associated with holism) to independence (associated with analysis) is complicated by developmental trends in the opposite direction: Progress toward empathy in the social domain is in part a matter of becoming more field dependent, as is learning to generate reader-based prose in the verbal domain. In many areas, acquiring expertise means moving from analysis to holism. In the domain of the self, multiple looking glass selves become a whole ego. In body intelligence, motor acts initially handled analytically become smooth wholes with appropriate practice. In verbal domains, propositions unite to form systems of belief. Finally, in spatial and logical-mathematical domains, with experience we form unifying mental maps and models. In fact, some psychologists regard fostering holistic processing as a major goal of education.

One way to solve these developmental complications would be to separate the field dependent–independent dimension from analysis–holism. Another way to handle these slippery styles is to say that progress along the analytic–holistic, field-dependent dimension (if indeed it is a single dimension) is, like other forms of cognitive development, a matter of increasing differentiation and flexibility. As we master the rules of a new enterprise, we become more flexible: We can move freely between analytic and holistic, field-independent and -dependent processing. Nor does such progress proceed independently of abilities, skills, and other styles.

HUNCHES IN BUNCHES

In particular, development of flexibility along the fox-hedgehog dimension is intimately involved with the most mysterious and influential figure in our gang of cognitive styles—intuition. Intuition teeters at one end of a beam on whose opposite extreme sits the systematic, methodical, vigilant style described in the chapter on logical intelligence. Intuition is a willingness to use those vague, ineffable inklings we call "hunches," what Lee Iacocca calls "street smarts, the things you just *know*."

The opposite of intuition is systematic planning, the formulation of a strategy. Systematic thinkers prefer the left-brained, hierarchically organized forms of thinking described in the chapters on verbal and logical intelligence and critical thinking.

Our old friends Richard Wagner and Robert Sternberg found that systematic strategies allow successful executives to defer decisions until the time is ripe. An example of one such strategy is what the psychologists described as "managing career": "knowing what activities lead to the enhancement of one's reputation and success in one's field of endeavor." Successful managers "knew the ropes," were clever at choosing tasks and positions that led to the top. In the Yale study, managing career was the strongest predictor of executive success. As an industrial chemist once told me, "You can get a lot farther by being clever than you can by being smart."

Studies of why executives fail support the importance of long-range strategic planning for individual success. According to Morgan McCall and Michael Lombard, project managers at the Center for Creative Learning in Greensboro, North Carolina, among the major reasons executives are fired or demoted is "inability to think strategically" or "to take a broad, long-term view."

In earlier chapters, I have filed my brief for the practical importance of systematic thinking, so in the next few pages I argue that intuition has its place alongside more methodical, top-down forms of thinking.

In order to experience your own style on the methodical–intuitive scale, try your hand at the problems on the next few pages. You'll get a rough idea of where you stand on the continuum.

Here's the first one: Imagine that you've been hired by Gonzo Motors to style a new family sports car—the Mustang of the 1990s. The CEO insists that you study other manufacturers' styling trends and tailor your design to the niches they create. You can think all you want, but the sooner you can come up with a design, the better. What's your first step?

In case you couldn't care less about cars, here's another one: Rate on a scale from 0 to 1, with 0 meaning "definitely will not happen" and 1 meaning "definitely will happen," the chances of a major (millions of deaths) thermonuclear war by the year 2000. What do you do first?

Too heavy? Here's one in between: Name the next Democratic presidential candidate. Step one?

In confronting real-world problems like these, systematic people begin by formulating a plan. The first part of the plan might be to gather more information: they would study competitors' designs for five years. Or the plan might begin with a mathematical model of the situation: a list of all the factors that could lead to a war and the probabilities of each. Or they might proceed by elimination: begin by listing all the possible candidates and their liabilities. Other people, however, don't bother to plan; they already have all the data they need: They "sense" a design that will sell, something that looks like a Porsche 944 but costs less; they "just know" that no world leader will press the button, and that the time is right for Gary Hart. Which pattern is yours? The systematic? Or the intuitive?

Even if you answered the questions intuitively by taking a shot at an answer, your shot was not in total darkness, but was illuminated by your experience. In designing the Gonzo 472, you might realize without further inquiry that the market is defined by competitors and buyers, and take those factors into account (albeit in a seat-of-the-pants sort of way), or you might unconsciously but reasonably assume that competitors' designs will change according to gradual and somewhat predictable progressions because each year's body panels are usually produced by retooling the dies of previous years. Your hunch would then be based on your grasp of the whole structure of the market. This year, for example, no one is making a high-performance four-seater with lots of compound curves; and you have seen world leaders and presidential candidates on television often enough to have some idea about how likely they are to press buttons and appeal to voters.

Psychologist Malcolm Westcott, author of a classic book on intuition, devised simple paper-and-pencil tests of cognitive style. As in each of the real-world problems above, the simpler problems below present you with a progression. Cover each progression in turn and uncover one item at a time. As soon as you've seen enough items to be pretty sure you know the answer, write it down.

Here they are:

1	2	3	5	8	13	?
MN	NO	OP	PQ	QR	RS	?
247–5956	624–7595	562–4759	956–2475	595–6247		?

Westcott devised his test in the belief that intuition is the ability to reach a sound conclusion on the basis of limited information. You operate intuitively when you get a correct answer after only two or three items. Westcott found no clear relationship between the number of items uncovered and the percentage correct: There were some (highly intuitive) people who got good scores based on a few clues, and there were others who did poorly, even though they used all the clues. To those who claimed that Westcott was testing IQ rather than intuition, he was quick to point out that intuition as measured by his test was a poor predictor of grades and other measures of academic achievement.

Note that in each case, what is called for is spotting a pattern, either by systematic search (simple computer programs do well at number sequence problems) or by holistic perception: seeing each number in the first series as the sum of the two preceding ones, seeing the second series as a double alphabet, seeing the third as rotation. Holistic perception is what creates the hunch. How did you work the problems? Systematically, by developing a plan? Or by intuitively reaching for answers?

In a *Harvard Business Review* article, James McKenney and Peter Keen describe intuition as a mode of evaluating information that can be measured by standard tests, including the Myers-Briggs Type Indicator. Their subjects were rated as "intuitive" or "systematic," and then given the following cipher to decode:

VEY CO XTS XCMS BEF IDD . . .

Once again, what is required is detecting a pattern, and once again, the pattern can be detected either by following a systematic plan, as by substituting common letters in the order of their frequency, or, intuitively, by grasping the message as a whole: It looks like "Now is the time for all . . ."

Both systematic and intuitive thinkers adopted a consistent style as they approached a variety of problems, instead of matching their style to the demands of the task at hand. Intuition went along with the Jungian "feeling" mode, a tendency to evaluate in terms of emotional reactions (likes and dislikes, good and bad, pleasant and unpleasant) rather than logical abstractions. The intuitive subjects broke the code, some of them in a "dazzling" manner. Because intuitive thinkers frequently redefine problems in a trial-and-error fashion as they go along, they often reinvent the wheel, and waste time and effort. Systematic thinkers, by contrast, allocate considerable time to high-level planning, and once they have formulated a plan, they stick to it.

None of the systematic subjects broke the cipher, but they did better than intuitive thinkers on well-structured problems, and there was no overall difference in performance between the two groups.

Real-world hunches require a sensitivity to subtler or more complex patterns than the ones in Westcott's test. Intuitive designers see such subtle patterns in the trend to curvier automobile shapes. Daniel Isenberg has discovered another subtle pattern: trouble ahead. Isenberg emulated Harry Mintzberg's observational approach to managerial behavior, which I described in Chapter 2. In a recent *Harvard Business Review* article, Isenberg reports on the results of interviews and observations of twelve executives for periods of up to twenty-five days. Senior managers "intuitively sense when a problem exists." The chief financial officer of a leading technical products company, for example, "based on a vague gut feeling that something was wrong, decided to analyze one business group. 'The data on the group were inconsistent and unfocused,' he said after doing the analysis. 'I had the sense that they were talking about a future that just was not going to happen, and I turned out to be right.' "

Notice the phrase "after doing the analysis." This executive used rational, systematic thinking to fuel his intuition. Yet ever since Freud's prodigal disciple Carl Jung relegated it to the unconscious, intuition has had an uneasy relationship with rationality. As the first psychologist to discuss the psychology of entrepreneurs, whom he regarded as "intuitive extroverts," Jung has continued to influence students of intuition in practical contexts. His theory of personality is the foundation of the Myers-Briggs Type Indicator, one of the major measures of cognitive style.

The Jungian notion that we must often act nonrationally gained respectability in management circles with the publication in 1945 of Herbert Simon's *Administrative Behavior*. Simon argued persuasively that the limitations of human information processing make nonrational, intuitive techniques essential in complex decisionmaking. Though Simon never regarded satisficing and other heuristics (see Chapter 9) as substitutes for rationality when rationality could be applied, advocates of intuitive decisionmaking during the reaction to the hyperrational "operations research" movement of the 1940s and '50s found it useful to cite a Nobel laureate; the result was a kind of academic "Simon says." Another Nobel laureate, economist Paul Samuelson, wrote: "For most problems there is usually only time for quick and dirty solutions." Nowadays, after the heyday of left-brain versus right-brain pop psychology, most responsible management scientists agree that real-world decisionmakers need both intuition and more systematic approaches.

My discussion thus far has relied on examples from business, but the complexity of medical decisionmaking requires intuition too. Paul Cutler's influential *Problem Solving in Clinical Medicine,* a monument to the benefit of formal, logical mathematical skills, contains the following passage: "When a physician sees a patient, how does he decide what is wrong? Ask him how and he cannot really explain. He may use terms such as 'hunch,' 'intuition,' 'judgment,' 'experience,' 'deduction,' and so forth."

"Intuition" is not a nice word for lawyers, who like everything spelled out in bulletproof boilerplate. Jurists spurn the word "intuition" in favor of phrases like "lawyer's judgment," but whatever you call it, it is essential to the decisions made by lawyers and judges alike. Judge Joseph Hutcheson, in "The Judgment Intuitive: The Function of the Hunch in Judicial Decision," wrote that the judge "does and should decide difficult and complicated cases only when he has the feeling of the decision."

The more we learn about intuition, the more rational it seems. Weston Agor, author of *Intuitive Management* and *The Logic of Intuitive Decision-Making,* sees "intuition as a very logical skill . . . a product of real life experience, of working with one's self, of good training and education." Most of the two hundred highly intuitive managers Agor investigated viewed intuition as a way to integrate past experiences. As Daniel Isenberg puts it, intuition is "not the opposite of rationality, nor is it a random process of guessing. Rather, it is based on extensive experience both in analysis and problem solving and in implementation, and to the extent that the lessons of experience are logical and well-founded, then so is the intuition." Isenberg's Harvard Business School colleague James McKenney says: "The intuitive mode is not sloppy or loose. It seems to have an underlying discipline at least as coherent as the systematic mode." This point of view puts a different slant on the common finding that top managers use intuition more than their subordinates: It's not that they are less rational, but that they have the experience that makes intuition work.

Experience drives the holistic pattern recognition that allows experts to perform fluidly, unconsciously, and intuitively, according to Hubert and Stuart Dreyfus, twin brothers at the University of California at Berkeley who studied the development of expertise. As cognitive pioneer Jerome Bruner put it: "Individuals who have extensive familiarity with a subject appear more often to leap intuitively into a decision or a solution."

If intuition is based on experience, we would expect people to perform intuitively in domains they know well, and less intuitively on foreign turf. Westcott found that people who did well on the sorts of problems presented above did not do particularly well on visual versions, in which each succeeding clue consisted of a more complete sketch of an object to be identified. Thus, there is at least a suggestion that intuition is indeed domain specific.

One practical implication of domain specificity is that it may be possible to learn to operate intuitively. The Dreyfuses describe one case in which this appears to have happened. The case has to do with the critical but undervalued skill of chicken sexing. Poultry breeders need to be able to separate commercially valuable female chicks from the nearly worthless males as early in the life cycle as possible. In the 1930s, U.S. breeders hired Hikosoboro Yogo, an expert chicken sexer whose gender judgments were 98 percent accurate. Yogo worked intuitively—he couldn't describe how he did it. However, by watching him work, apprentices were able to acquire similar skill within a few months.

Is intuition learnable in tasks other than chicken sexing? To the extent that each of the multiple intelligences is learnable, and that development moves toward intuitive performance as an end point, it is. Self-knowledge is often intuitive. As described in the chapter on social intelligence, empathy seems similarly unconscious. One "just knows" how someone will react; there is no conscious chain of abstract reasoning. The development of automation in body, verbal, and logical intelligence certainly parallels the growth of unconscious hunches. Thus, we should expect that it is possible to become more intuitive and that the way to do so is by cultivating the various multiple intelligences, not by artificially fertilizing intuition itself.

Books like Robert McKim's *Experiences in Visual Thinking*, which promotes unconscious-level automation in the spatial domain, or Robert Sternberg's *Intelligence Applied* and Suzette Elgin's *The Gentle Art of Verbal Self-Defense*, which provide experiences in verbal and logical modes (already recommended as enhancements of multiple intelligences), are the best route to the development of this cognitive style.

Since there are certain to be practical limits on how intuitive each of us can become, we ought also to match our levels of intuition to our jobs. You remember that McKenney and Keen found that the intuitive cognitive style is well suited to jobs where problems are poorly structured or open-ended: marketing manager, psychologist, historian, architect, and bond salesperson. Conversely, more methodical styles are well adapted to jobs like auditor or financial analyst.

Intuition is generally considered the most mysterious and influential of intellectual styles. By now, it should be clear why. When it comes to a positive identification, we have no eyewitnesses; all we have are glimpses of black sedans disappearing in the fog, and rumors.

I have followed Westcott, who used intuition specifically to refer to the use of hunches, even though most of the investigators mentioned here use the term more broadly, to tag styles that look to me more like holism, and that others call flexibility. Intuition is the Kingpin of the right-brain gang, but there are so many aliases, false beards, and costumes that it's hard to tell how many styles there are. At times, they seem to be different disguises for the same character, intuition. Holism whispers in intuition's ear, and intuition is the muscle behind the active style.

THINKING VERSUS DOING

The active style is a tendency to act effectively, but quickly, without much research. "He who hesitates is lost," says the active decision-maker. The opposite of active is reflective, the tendency to look before you leap.

My favorite image for the distinction between these two styles is the faculty meeting, where the only relief from unrelenting tedium is watching administrators (who tend to be relatively action oriented) as they go quietly nuts while their reflective faculties agonize over semicolons. Dean watching is best at the climax of the meeting, when the issue that required convening is, by a narrow margin of votes, tabled.

Reflective thinkers do as much (or more) thinking as is necessary to get a good decision. They weigh alternatives, carefully examining all imaginable consequences. Clearly, the reflective style resembles the systematic, but there is a difference in emphasis. Reflective thinking is thoroughly researched, while systematic thinking is meticulously planned.

The active style is similar to the style psychologists call "impulsive," a tendency to "go for it" without considering all the consequences or gathering all the information. Impulsive decisionmakers sacrifice accuracy for speed, and high error rates are hallmarks of impulsiveness. In the real world, this trade-off is often effective. "Close enough for government work" is sometimes all there's time for. Because "impulsive" smacks of going off half-cocked, I use "active" to refer to practical impulsiveness that is matched to the demands of a job.

Most of us tend to equate speed of thinking with intelligence; we describe highly intelligent people as "quick-witted," less intelligent ones as "slow." The active-reflective scale does not, however, seem to have much to do with IQ. If anything, as Robert Sternberg likes to point out, in academic domains the reflective style is associated with problem-solving ability. Nevertheless, of two people who get the same score on an intelligence test, one may err by impulsively choosing the first answer that "looks right," and the other by reflectively running out of time.

The active style depends on whatever MIs are appropriate to deal with the decision at hand. The active style also depends on other cognitive styles, especially intuition. Malcolm Westcott's definition of intuition in terms of the amount of information needed to reach a correct decision is very close to the standard psychological definition of "impulsive."

Further collusion between intuition and action is documented by McKenney and Keen, the Harvard investigators who studied systematic and intuitive problem solvers. McKenney and Keen found that intuitive problem solvers not only spent less time on planning than systematic ones but explored and abandoned alternatives very quickly: They jumped right into a solution. And Daniel Isenberg found that intuitive senior managers not only performed "well-learned behavior patterns rapidly" but tended to "bypass in-depth analysis and move rapidly to come up with a plausible solution." People who have hunches are inclined to act on them.

In business, the active style is expressed by what Henry Mintzberg calls a preference for "live action." Richard Boyatzis calls "efficiency orientation" a skill and describes it as a concern for measurable results: production, sales, peer ratings, or the bottom line.

No one exhibits the active style better than H. Ross Perot. Perot is a crew-cut self-made billionaire who, as a computer salesman for IBM, found the corporate style a little too reflective. (In those days, IBM's slogan was "Think.") When IBM rejected his proposal to offer computer consultants along with their computers, Perot left the company to found Electronic Data Systems (EDS), which he built into the nation's second-largest provider of computer services. Impatient with State Department attempts to help American POWs, he personally flew to North Vietnam in a 707 loaded with Christmas supplies. He managed the rescue of two EDS employees from an Iranian prison. Perot and EDS reorganized GM's corporate communications. He worked with GM's computer engineers to integrate data flow into one quickly reacting nervous system: the revolutionary Saturn marketing/sales/manufacturing system, which will allow customers to sit at a terminal and design their own car from "menus" of options. Ultimately, the system should deliver the desired robin's-egg-blue Saturn two-door with vinyl seats, tinted windows, no carpets, four speeds, and cruise control in one week. Perot has learned to harness his impulsiveness, and to act by leading.

A similar "bias for action" pervades the culture of excellent organizations. Peters and Waterman quote a young engineer at Hewlett-Packard who describes the importance of making working prototypes of new devices "for people to play with. . . . the fellow walking around playing with your gadget is likely to be a corporate executive, maybe even Hewlett or Packard." Peters and Waterman relate a piece of corporate culture. One Saturday, Bill Hewlett found a lab stockroom locked. He personally cut off the lock and replaced it with a note forbidding anyone to relock the door. From our point of view, these organizational characteristics work because they provide scope for corresponding personal characteristics. Hewlett-Packard succeeds because it allows everyone, even senior managers, to express their "hands-on" orientation.

Platoon leaders, air traffic controllers, Emergency Medical Technicians, and other decisionmakers are often forced to follow FDR's advice "But above all try something." Action delayed is often no action at all. Thus, the active style is even more essential in these arenas than in the offices where most students have watched it work.

The active style sometimes seems like sleight of hand. How can some people be both faster *and* more effective than others?

Daniel Isenberg's research may provide the answer. He describes the intellectual component of the action style as "integrating action into the process of thinking." On the basis of his interviews and observations of senior executives, Isenberg concluded that their

> Thinking is inextricably tied to action in what I call thinking/ acting cycles, in which managers develop thoughts about their companies and organizations not by analyzing a problematic situation and then acting, but by thinking and acting in close concert. . . . What may appear to be action for action's sake is really the result of an intuitive understanding that analysis is only possible in the light of experience gained while attempting to solve the problem. . . . Senior managers often instigate a course of action simply to learn more about an issue. "We bought that company because we wanted to learn more about that business."

Isenberg's notion resembles George Gilder's concept of the "epistemological function" of enterprise. In his recent book, *The Spirit of Enterprise,* Gilder argues that enterprises are experiments. Like all experiments, whether or not they succeed in financial terms, they always pay off in knowledge. They tell us, for example, whether certain production and marketing systems will sustain a new service or product. As the microcomputer explosion has shown, the only way to find out what will fly is to try it out, to "put it on the train and see if it gets off at Westport," as advertising executives used to say.

Like Gilder's earlier *Wealth and Poverty, The Spirit of Enterprise* is a tribute to "the act of faith" that distinguishes the entrepreneur. Emphasis should be placed on the word "act," for it is the doing that makes the difference. Gilder writes eloquently about the successful acts of entrepreneurship, but he does not write about impulsive acts that fail, like Harding Lawrence's dramatic expansion of Braniff's routes or his successor's untimely 11 percent boost in management salaries. Those who leap without looking are as liable to lose as those who hesitate, but neither is the stuff of Horatio Alger stories. Without intellectual abilities and the other styles, acts of faith are only examples of Twain's oversimplified formula for success: "ignorance plus confidence."

Though educators have traditionally concerned themselves much more with training impulsive children to be reflective than with teaching reflective adults to be impulsive, by now it should be clear that in some cases, training for action is desirable. It should be equally clear that impulsiveness should not be taught as an end in itself (we've plenty of reckless decisionmaking as it is) but be allowed to emerge as the natural consequence of complex, holistic, intuitive expertise.

CAN YOU HOLD? COGNITIVE COMPLEXITY

Fully developed cognitive styles, when combined with fully developed verbal and logical intelligence, culminate in a pattern of decisionmaking that psychologists call "cognitive complexity." Cognitive complexity is ability plus style: It is the ability to juggle large amounts of information by alternating and integrating left- and right-brained modes of thinking. Through the realistic international business simulations described in Chapter 2 and other methods, Siegfried Streufert, a leading investigator of cognitive complexity, has found that people with approximately equal IQs often differ widely in cognitive complexity, so he, like most psychologists, calls it a cognitive style. He further finds that this style is a major factor in executive success.

Though Streufert and others refer to complexity as a single style, it is really a syndicate of conflicting styles, as I learned during my interview with John Peters of Zoetrope Studios.

Diversification from films into wines was a long-term strategy for Coppola and Peters; the cabernet about to go on the market had been put up six years before. Peters and I were interrupted several times by phone calls, and at one point Peters was on two different phones at the same time. On one phone, he patiently explained the varieties of California wines to a new customer. During long pauses in which his interlocutor was presumably occupied (perhaps in calculation, perhaps in another conversation of his own), on the other phone Peters conducted a no-nonsense, rapid-fire discussion of the fine print of the film distribution contracts spread out before him. At the end of this conversation, he got in a quick plug for the cabernet.

The episode exposed the distinguishing feature of cognitive complexity: a flexible resolution of psychological paradoxes. These paradoxes combine the opposite poles of the three previously mentioned dimensions of cognitive style: analytic–holistic, systematic–intuitive, and reflective–active.

Multidimensional Thinking

The first paradox is what Streufert and his colleagues call multidimensionality, a flexible combination of analytic and holistic styles. Peters was handling this information multidimensionally: He differentiated among the minutiae of several different contracts, and integrated these discriminations into decisions about what to change and what to let be. And though he had master plans for producing and marketing wines and negotiating contracts, he was flexible: The new customer was not one of the Bay Area restaurateurs for whom the wine was intended. Furthermore, as he switched from one conversation to the other, he adapted his tone to the goals of each.

When you operate at the simplest level of differentiation in domains you don't know well, you analyze in black-and-white terms (or red-and-white, using wines as an example). To someone unfamiliar with wine, these categories are rigid, so rosé is forced into the red-wine category, or considered "no wine at all." With experience, you add not only shades of difference along this dimension (white, rosé, red, robust) but more dimensions: dry–sweet, foreign–domestic, more or less expensive. Similarly, inexperienced teachers monitor their classes along one dimension: attentiveness. More experienced teaches distinguish boredom at the back, frustration at the front, and confusion in the corner.

As you might expect, when you make richer differentiations, you can make better predictions: A student who is frustrated will respond to mild teasing quite differently from one who is bored. Moreover, the multidimensional teacher is aware of several ways of handling frustration or boredom. Streufert describes this awareness as seeing the "multiple implications even in single items of information."

Differentiation's cohort is integration: combining information from different dimensions. The degree of integration is the number of different dimensions and values along each of them that are taken into account in making a decision. For instance, our hypothetical cognitively simple wine novice probably does not integrate the price dimension with the color dimension, and will be unable to say whether cheap white wines are preferable to cheap red wines. Moreover, our novice has extremely simple rules for integrating the small number of dimensions into decisions about what to serve: white with fish, red with beef, the wine the boss likes whenever he or she comes to dinner. These rules are strained by new information (the boss's spouse likes rosé with lamb) and they don't give an inch until they break under an overload. When they do snap, there are no new rules to replace them. If God is dead, anything goes, even Riesling with burritos.

When you operate at higher levels of integration, you can combine dimensions, and note that dry champagnes cost more than sweet ones. You can act according to more highly articulated standards—you know *why* expensive wines are generally better than the cheaper ones. You can act independently, and buy a cheap red to wash down the boss's pasta. Rules accommodate inconsistencies by becoming more complicated and specific.

Streufert and his colleagues describe the highest levels of multidimensionality as characterized by a "theoretical outlook." This term may seem odd as a feature of an intensely practical working mind, but it is well chosen: The extremely complex executive, like a good theory, handles a diversity of situations. A great number of interactions among dimensions generates new patterns of interaction among schemes (hypotheses), and the complex executive copes with all this with the aid of highly abstract formulations. Once again, there seems to be nothing quite as practical as a good theory.

At the highest levels of differentiation and integration, you can distinguish and combine whole systems of rules into coherent points of view, others' as well as your own. Rules defer to taste. For instance, you might be able to imagine that the boss and his or her spouse would disagree about what wine to have with canapés, and come up with several ways to please them both. This empathic ability to imagine, transcend, and use two or more points of view, which we discussed in Chapter 5, is considered the hallmark of integrative complexity.

Physicians, nurses, and other health care providers are often forced to juggle multiple points of view. Decisions to treat, to refer, or to dismiss typically involve integrating physiological, ethical, psychological, and legal constraints, so it's likely that multidimensionality is a prerequisite to even moderate levels of competence in health professions. Such juggling also seems to be essential to high-level managerial success. Richard Boyatzis, whose *The Competent Manager* has been cited throughout this book, describes a competence he calls "perceptual objectivity," the ability to take multiple perspectives simultaneously.

Reflective Action

The cognitively complex decisionmaker is, paradoxically, both reflective and active. Peters was acting on lots of information quickly and without getting overwhelmed by details. According to Streufert, maintaining adequate information flow without being overwhelmed is one of the identifying features of cognitive complexity.

Reflectiveness, you will remember, is the tendency to ponder as much information as possible before making a decision. Successful executives have what Mintzberg calls a "thirst for current information."

Such executives may envy what they perceive as the more leisurely pace enjoyed by their attorneys, but their envy is misdirected. Plato's description of the paper chase is more valid today than when he wrote it over 2300 years ago in the *Theaetetus:* "the lawyer is always in a hurry; there is the water of the clepsydra [water clock] driving him on . . . he has become keen and shrewd."

Nor should the attorneys envy their physicians. The availability of automated and therefore relatively inexpensive tests makes it extremely easy for physicians to overload themselves with information about each patient's problems. Accordingly, a recent article describing the intellectual competence of the successful physician lists "control of flow of information."

Managing a high information flow is learnable. Experts like Peters use chunking (see Chapter 8) to organize information into a number of pieces small enough to "get a handle on."

The reflective thirst for information is slaked at considerable cost. Streufert points out that cognitively complex decisionmakers arrive at decisions slowly and thus appear less decisive than their more "reactive" peers.

At the same time that they reflectively take in information, complex decisionmakers cope with rapidly changing, fragmented demands for quick decisions: They act quickly and flexibly.

In *The Nature of Managerial Work,* Henry Mintzberg says that the primary characteristic of the manager's job is "much work at an unrelenting pace." His or her work is characterized by "brevity, variety, and fragmentation." The typical manager studied by Mintzberg handled thirty-six pieces of mail, five calls, and eight meetings every day. The average executive had thirty-six written and sixteen oral contacts per day, and the average interval of uninterrupted desk work was fifteen minutes. In large organizations, half, and in small ones 90 percent, of managers' activities lasted less than nine minutes. Successful organizations take this into account, designing into their systems what Peters and Waterman describe as "fluidity." Fluidity is the organization's ability to alter agendas to fit new priorities. For example, at United Airlines and at Hewlett-Packard, this flexible openness is called "MBWA—Management by Walking [or Wandering] Around."

Janet Gale's study of how physicians interview patients contains a nice illustration of flexibility. In a quality she calls "patient-determined interview structure," "the course of the interview as directed by the doctor is determined, or follows on from, the flow of information as presented by the patient." By the same token, when Carol Schneider and Susan Kastendiek studied effective teachers of adults, they found that the behavior used "to shape and adapt teaching process" includes the ability to use student "feedback *at the time,*" to bear "in mind a reserve of alternative approaches," and to try them out.

McCall and Lombardo's study of factors in executive failure uncovered "Inflexibility: inability to adapt to new boss or new problems." Such failures of either flexibility or strategy are common. An example of how difficult it is to reconcile the opposing imperatives of strategy and flexibility is provided by no less a manager than Harold Geneen, who as CEO of ITT topped Procter & Gamble's one-page limit on memos with his one-sentence memo: "There will be no more long-range planning." By opting for flexibility over strategy, Geneen deferred to the difficulty of having both. In fact, managing such contradictions is so stressful that cognitively complex executives face a greater than average risk of heart attacks.

Geneen's memo is a reminder that even the highest-ranking executives find it difficult to tolerate ambiguity. Yet tolerance for ambiguity appears to be one of the most important features of flexibility. Daniel Isenberg found that "In making their day-by-day and minute-by-minute tactical maneuvers, senior executives tend to rely on several general thought processes such as . . . dealing with ambiguity, inconsistency, novelty, and surprise."

Systematic Intuition

The third paradox of cognitive complexity is combining systematic long-range planning with an intuitive grasp of relationships among problems. Resolving this paradox allows decisionmakers to plan strategically and act opportunistically.

According to Streufert, complex managers are strategists who "plan long into the future, taking into account all possible events that can be anticipated." How long is "long into the future"? Two hundred fifty years, if you are Konosuke Matsushita, the entrepreneur who founded one of Japan's largest home appliance companies. On the other hand, most Western CEOs plan less than ten or twenty years ahead, and most senior managers operate within time frames of five years or less.

Elliott Jacques, director of the Institute of Organisation and Social Studies at Brunel University in England, believes that the time frames used in planning are the major factor in determining cognitive power. Time frames of a year or so allow what Jacques calls "reflective articulation," a kind of abstract, objective tactical planning. Ten-year frames permit a qualitatively different form of thinking—he calls it "shaping whole systems"—in which one imagines changing the internal configuration of an organization as well as its exterior boundaries by, say, moving into new markets, and the long-term reverberations such moves will have. Jacques notes the direct relationship between rank in an organization and the size of the time frame in which people are expected to function: production workers day by day, foremen quarter by quarter, managers from year to year. Since people differ in the time frames they prefer to deal with, in setting your goals for promotion you might well contemplate your own willingness to extend your time frame.

Daniel Isenberg describes how a systematic analysis paves the way for an intuitive grasp of similarities and relationships.

> Approximately two-thirds of the senior managers I studied were preoccupied with a very limited number of quite general issues, each of which subsumed a large number of specific issues. . . . For instance, a bank CEO had a "network" of at least 19 related problems that he was concerned about . . .: establishing credibility in international banking, strengthening the bank's role in corporate banking, increasing the range of financial services and products, being prepared to introduce new products to respond to competitors' innovations, developing systems to give product cost information, reducing operational costs, standardizing branch architecture, and using space efficiently.

The CEO integrated these highly differentiated problems into two long-term strategies: expanding competences and standardizing systems. He and the other senior managers studied by Isenberg had an "organized mental map of all the problems and issues facing them."

Matching People to Enterprises

Like other cognitive styles, complexity has been regarded as a more or less permanent personality trait. Consequently, most practical applications have more to do with matching people to environments than with enhancing complexity. In selecting people or environments, it is important to bear in mind Harold Schroder, Michael Driver, and Siegfried Streufert's (inverted) "U-curve hypothesis." After examining results of simulations of island assaults, stock market decisionmaking, and other real-world problems, they concluded that as environmental complexity increases, so does the amount of information processed, up to some optimal point. Beyond this point, as environmental complexity increases, the amount of information processed begins to drop.

Environmental complexity is measured by the number, range, rate of change, or uncertainty of the events the decisionmaker must respond to. Information processing is measured in terms of the amount of differentiation (number and fineness of dimensions used to categorize inputs) and integration (number and complexity of rules combining different dimensions).

More complex people not only process more information at all levels of environmental complexity but reach their peaks at higher levels of environmental complexity. Thus, in environments of low to moderate complexity, highly complex people process all information their jobs provide. They will raise their level of processing to match increased environmental complexity, right up to their peak. This means that you are better off saving your most complex people for your most complex jobs. Specifically, Streufert suggests that people of high cognitive complexity should be in charge of planning.

Enhancing Complexity

Matching people and environments is one way to take advantage of differences in complexity. Fortunately, there is good reason to believe that you don't have to take your level of complexity as a given —complexity, like the MIs, can be enhanced. Streufert and his colleagues describe multidimensionality as specific to domains in which decisionmakers have acquired expertise. People probably choose to work in domains for which they are somehow prepared in advance to be complex, but it nevertheless seems likely that, given the right environment, experience in an area can promote cognitive complexity.

Complexity can be developed by providing appropriate combinations of challenge and support. The lowest level of complexity is a rigid, authoritarian, black-and-white style like that of the wine novice above. Contradictions like the rosé create tensions. Given enough challenges of this sort, and enough support to avoid a complete conceptual breakdown, most people move into what is known as the "relativist" position: All rules are relative, it all depends "on where you live." There are lots of different rules but no way to relate them, so all decisions are purely matters of taste or opinion. It's liberty hall, as long as you buy the wine.

Again given appropriate challenge and support, a small fraction of us attain the highest level of cognitive development, "commitment." This is the abstract, independent, theoretical style described above.

Schroder, Driver, and Streufert describe the optimal environment for training a multidimensional, "flexibly integrated" style as providing "information interdependence." Such an environment "does not overwhelm . . . [but] encourages explorations and allows . . . [one to] experience the consequences of trying out self-generated rules." It "provide[s] sufficient supporting structure for relating and comparing these rules and schemata." People trained in such environments learn to "explore and delineate alternate rules."

Robert McKim devotes much of his *Experiences in Visual Thinking* to exercises designed to promote flexibility in the levels, operations, and media of problem solving. For instance, he suggests using the "abstraction ladder" of semanticist S. I. Hayakawa to free thinking from the concrete anchors that prevent perception of the essential issue.

Perhaps without knowing about the optimal environments described by Streufert, McKim, and others, several successful organizations have created environments that promote flexibility at all levels. In *In Search of Excellence*, Peters and Waterman argue that such environments are clues to the success of Hewlett-Packard and 3-M, for example. Systematic application of psychological research on optimal environments might lead to even greater gains for these corporations and those that would emulate them.

A LINEUP OF STYLES

Recently, designers of computerized information systems, who tend to be left-brained thinkers themselves, have begun to incorporate our growing knowledge of intuition and other right-brained cognitive styles into their user interfaces. As a result, users may now match systems to their styles. Such matches make it easier for more people to use data bases, spreadsheets, and other information systems. More important, they should increase the quality of decisions; several studies in *Management Science* reported that people tend to discard recommendations when the supporting data don't match their cognitive style.

Another direct application of differences in styles has to do with group decisionmaking. A researcher who studied groups that were either homogeneous or mixed with respect to cognitive styles concluded that mixed groups were more effective because their members tended to see flaws in one another's approaches. Therefore, you should include people of different cognitive styles on committees and other decisionmaking teams.

In his influential article "Management and Modes of Thought," Patrick Nugent recommends that discussion leaders let styles alternate, so that right-brained thinking dominates the discussion during goal-setting phases, and left-brained thinking dominates during planning and evaluation phases.

Cognitive styles provide a convenient way to summarize development within each of the multiple intelligences: In all cognitive domains, development is an increase in the range of styles available. Novices tend to operate in a left-brained manner, systematically following verbal, specified rules one at a time. Experts typically operate unconsciously, holistically, intuitively, and actively, but they "downshift" to more analytic, systematic, linear processes when they encounter unexpected difficulties. Thus, differences between experts and novices are most pronounced at the right end of continua of styles, but it would be incorrect to characterize expert performance as uniformly right-brained.

The practical implication of this developmental denouement is that although cognitive styles are considered entrenched and trait-like, they can be learned. Viewing them developmentally suggests a new way to learn them: not by training in complexity, holism, intuition, impulsiveness, and creativity as such, but by cultivating the multiple intelligences on which they depend. Since intelligences in turn depend on knowledge and connections gained through experience, the best way to enhance the development of styles seems not to be exercises in right- (or left-) brained thinking, but the basic approach I've advocated all along: mastery of a domain of knowledge.

Throughout this chapter, the conventional dichotomy of left- and right-brained styles has served us well. There is a family resemblance among analytic, systematic, and reflective forms of thought, on the one hand, and holistic, intuitive, active modes, on the other. Moreover, members of each family seem to stick together: Systematic thought requires analysis and reflection. Similarly, intuition provides the connections for holistic comprehension, which in turn urges us to act.

Like all dichotomies, the left–right distinction works best if we don't take it too seriously. One of the largest structures in the brain, the corpus callosum, is devoted to the integration of right and left brains, so that in any real-world task they work as a team. Although cognitive complexity relies heavily on logical and verbal intelligences, and produces rational choices among listable alternatives, it draws on and integrates styles and intelligences from both sides of the brain. Complexity might be regarded as a "software" corpus callosum, integrating left- and right-brained intelligences and styles into fluid, flexible performance. In the next chapter, you will see that creativity, commonly considered a denizen of the right brain, like its partner complexity moves freely across the corpus callosum.

12.
Practical Creation

Imagination rules the world.
—NAPOLEON BONAPARTE

The creation, as opposed to the choice, of alternatives requires a combination of abilities and styles that is different from complexity but just as practical. Cognitive psychologist Jerome Bruner once described creation as "effective surprise." To get a description of practical creativity, we need only qualify Bruner's felicitous phrase with the requirement that "effective" means useful in attaining some biological, economic, or political end. Bruner's colleague David Perkins defines creation in similar terms, as work of high quality and originality.

The Apple II is a practical example of effective surprise. This personal computer and its later stages the II+, IIe, and IIc launched a three-person enterprise into a billion-dollar orbit; Apple Computer rocketed into the *Fortune* 500 faster than any other business. It did so because it provided people with a simple yet powerful tool for handling information. The Apple II was not only commercially and technically effective; it was also original. Although the first Apple was only an enhanced version of existing "home brew" microcomputers, the Apple II was the first multipurpose computer designed for a mass market. It was an implementation of Steven Jobs's highly original vision of the ultimate personal computer, a portable, powerful, "friendly" information genie.

Many people think of creativity as a rare gift useful only in advertising, inventing, and a few other peculiar occupations. But as the growth of the personal computer industry and other new markets shows, opportunities for practical creativity abound in work and everyday life. Richard Boyatzis includes a kind of verbal creativity, "spontaneity in self-expression," in his list of managerial competencies. A. Z. Carr, in *Business as a Game,* lists "creative imagination" as an essential quality for high-level executive positions. Indeed, psychologists find that scores on tests of creativity predicted leadership abilities of air force captains, "customer service" of retail saleswomen, peer ratings of U.S. government administrators, and success in "creative" occupations like advertising and public relations.

The growth of industries (and regulations governing them) based on information storage and exchange and other goods and services unheard of a decade ago shows that business provides plenty of opportunity for the exercise of creativity and imagination. Sticky notepads, autofocus cameras, personal computers, laser discs, and data bases required imagination at their conception, and still need a steady diet of new ideas for marketing and development.

Nevertheless, many managers are suspicious of creative solutions. Their subordinates feel, quite rightly, that their organizations value consistency and adherence to corporate conventions more than innovation. In such organizations, a kind of Peter Principle allows creative people to rise only until they threaten a superior. What advertising executive David Ogilvy said about his trade applies to business in general: "The business community wants remarkable advertising, but turns a cold shoulder to the kinds of people who can produce it."

Managers' unwonted suspicion of creative work is easy to understand if not to condone. In popular imagination and psychological theory alike, creativity has always been seen as somehow allied with madness. Creativity is threatening in the same way madness is, because it is by nature unpredictable. This view was immortalized by John Dryden: "Great wits are sure to madness near allied, And thin partitions do their bounds divide." Albert Einstein's line of doggerel shows that not even he was immune to this prejudice: "A thought that sometimes makes me hazy: Am I—or are the others crazy?" Einstein notwithstanding, you need not risk madness to become more creative. As you will see, creativity can be far more mundane than is commonly believed.

Recipes for practical creation are similar to those for creation in the arts and sciences, where Jerome Bruner, David Perkins, and most other psychologists have analyzed it. Most psychologists regard creation as a combination of ingredients, including intelligences, styles, strategies, knowledge, and beliefs. Since all these ingredients can be learned, so too can creativity. According to Robin Hogarth of the University of Chicago's Graduate School of Business and Centre of Decision Research, "given even a minimal level of intelligence, most people are both imaginative and creative." He goes on to argue that all most of us need to realize our creative potential are appropriate kinds and amounts of mental effort.

Therefore, as in earlier chapters, my approach is practical. I see creativity not as a separate ability to be cultivated in isolation, but as the ultimate stage of development of multiple intelligences and cognitive styles. After briefly discussing creativity in terms of originality, effectiveness, IQ, and multiple intelligences, I explain the major strategies for enhancing creative work. I argue that these strategies can in fact help you be more creative *if* you know a lot about the problems and materials you work with. As we go along, I present practical applications of creativity in order to get you to believe that creativity is worth cultivating.

EFFECTIVE SURPRISE

Originality is ordinarily defined in terms of rarity or novelty. For example, consider the inventions that allow us to drink our morning coffee as we drive to work: spouts, valves, and narrow necks. None of these solutions is original—all have been used for preventing spills of other liquids, in baby bottles, water pumps, and chemical flasks. Gimbals attached to the dash are a more original solution, in the sense of novel: Gimbals have been used to keep compasses and other navigational instruments level for centuries but only recently to prevent spilling. We could apply the same criterion to the various ways of preventing these commuters, who are too busy drinking coffee to buckle their seat belts, from bashing into their dashboards. Current solutions include buzzers, air bags, automatic belts like the ones in Rabbits, seat belt legislation and enforcement, and ignition locks that prevent the car from starting until the seat belt is buckled. By our criterion, the most original of these solutions is the air bag, because it introduces a new element, unlike any other part of any car. Note that the most original solution in each case was not the most complicated, or necessarily the best. It was the one that depended least on other solutions to the problem and other, similar problems.

Psychometricians regard originality as the central component of a cluster of abilities they call "divergent production"—that is, producing unusual responses. They measure divergent production by asking questions like "How many uses can you think of for a brick?" Try it yourself—write down as many uses as you can in five minutes. When you run dry or out of time, score your answers for total number, originality, detail, and variety. For example, using a brick as a paperweight, doorstop, and bookend would get low scores on all four scales, while bedwarmer in an igloo in Minneapolis, weapon for defending against soft-skulled extraterrestrials, and grinder for finishing a dugout canoe made from teak would yield higher scores. Factor-analytic investigations of divergent production suggest that people vary independently along the four divergent-production scales. Thus, even this component of creation is itself a clique of several distinct characters.

Divergent production is measured in terms of how many and how well. The originality component, especially the highly individualized originality we associate with creative geniuses, is also partly a matter of style, of process rather than product, of "how" rather than "how well." We consider the telephone an original invention not because of what it is but because the two men who invented it did so independently, without relying on each other's work.

There is no necessary connection between divergent production and the other component of creation, effectiveness. Rube Goldberg's inventions are original without being effective, and some extremely effective devices (like sonar) are more copies of natural phenomena. Indeed, tests of divergent production virtually ignore effectiveness, and scores are not strongly related to real-world creativity, at least not in science and invention, the fields where most data are available. There is as yet no test or group of tests that can predict who will be judged to be creative in real-world or academic pursuits.

All too often, judgments of effectiveness seem to be matters of opinion. For instance, experts still disagree about the relative effectiveness of automatic seat belts, air bags, and other restraints. Really creative innovations are inherently hard to evaluate because they violate the rules we customarily apply in judging quality. Thus, we should not be too hard on psychometricians and other students of creativity who have not done as well with "effectiveness" as they have with "surprise."

CREATIVITY AND INTELLIGENCES

Most psychologists who have studied the relationship between creativity and intellectual ability have relied on IQ as a unitary measure of intellectual ability. Divergent production is not strongly related to grade point average, IQ, or other measures of "school smarts." Correlations between IQ and measures of creativity suggest that a minimal ("threshold") IQ is a prerequisite for creative work in most fields. Below this threshold, one rarely sees much creative work at all, and above it, IQ and creativity are unrelated. Thus, two people with IQs of 85 (below average) and 100 (the average) are likely to be equally uncreative, and two people with IQs of 120 (about average for professionals) and 150 ("genius" level) are likely to be equally creative. The "creativity threshold" for any occupation depends on the extent to which it requires the verbal and logical skills measured by IQ. For most occupations the threshold seems to be around 115, which is about average for college graduates, but for occupations like physics, where even minimal performance requires mathematical skill, the creativity threshold is somewhat higher. On the other hand, in occupations like sales, where social intelligence matters more than mathematical, the threshold IQ may be much lower.

As the sales example suggests, creative work in practical realms depends less on IQ than on a high level of development of one or more of the intellectual abilities discussed in earlier chapters. Creative self-understanding means knowing yourself by becoming the self you choose. Social intelligence becomes creative when you empathically imagine others' points of view, inventively negotiate agreements, or persuasively construct an argument. Mastery of body and spatial intelligences allows skilled making, manipulating, drawing, designing, and dancing, and well-developed mental maps foster insightful new solutions to problems of finding your way. Written and spoken products of verbal intelligence are almost always creative in the sense of being novel, and at high levels of expertise, expository writing and extemporaneous speech can be highly creative. Original hypotheses, powerful theories, and elegant experiments are creative products of logical-mathematical intelligence.

Such a Gardnerian description of creation in terms of multiple intelligences, when combined with threshold theory, would suggest that there are multiple intelligence thresholds. Thus, even people with below-average IQs may be capable of creative work, if they have well-developed personal, social, body, or other intelligences untapped by IQ. As David Perkins puts it, "any normal person can be creative in terms of whatever abilities he or she has or can acquire."

DARE TO CREATE

In order to get you to try some strategies for enhancing your practical creativity and to get you to share psychologists' belief that you can learn to be more creative, I'll give you two problems to work on. The first asks for a real-world invention: a new way of marketing any familiar product. Spend a minute or two on this one now. Don't be discouraged if you're not successful right away, and don't stop with the first idea you get.

When you get tired of working on that one, switch to an impractical but easier problem, of the sort used in tests of creativity: the classic nine-dots problem that asks you to draw only four straight lines that go through all nine dots, without lifting your pencil.

```
o     o     o

o     o     o

o     o     o
```

Beat your head against this one for a few minutes, then read on.

However creative your solution to the nine-dots problem (soon I'll describe some highly creative ones), it will not be an example of *practical* creativity: The world won't be any better when you're done. Nevertheless, give it a shot—precisely because it is so simple, this problem is a good way to illustrate strategies for increasing creativity. We'll come back to the practical problem soon enough. Another reason for providing you with the nine-dots problem is that creative solutions to this artificial problem often come within a few minutes. If you do solve it, you'll experience one of the most powerful and pleasurable incentives to do creative work: the "creative flash" or "Aha!" As with sneezes and other releases from tension, the longer it takes to do, the better it will feel, so keep trying.

Unlike the "Aha!" people get when they solve simple problems, insight in real-world situations is more commonly the product of long, thorough steeping in all the relevant knowledge. The projects of Darwin, Tesla, Fuller, Einstein, and other creative thinkers usually took years, sometimes decades. They did not, however, achieve their insights by unrelenting concentration, but rather by what Howard Gruber of the University of Geneva calls "networks of enterprise": The creative scientists Gruber studied worked on several projects simultaneously to avoid being stymied or discouraged when they hit a snag.

Work on one project that helps another, unrelated one is what psychologists call "incubation," an extremely effective strategy for creative work. Incubation is not just forgetting about the project. It requires the kind of flexibility and integration I discussed in the preceding chapter as parts of cognitive complexity: shifting gears, combining different kinds of information, and coming back to your project.

Most psychologists believe that incubation works in several ways. First, by getting away from a situation, you overcome "functional fixedness," a tendency to see things only in terms of their usual roles. A classic demonstration of the power of functional fixedness is the finding that in response to a typical divergent-production question, employees of the AC Spark Plug Company listed fewer uses for spark plugs than were listed by comparable employees of a heavy-equipment company. Second, incubation allows new, seemingly unrelated information to be processed, and some of it may eventually be associated with information about the creative project. Third, incubation provides opportunities for brief, calm returns to your creative project from another point of view.

All three of these processes operate both consciously and unconsciously; often their conscious operations are so fleeting that they are soon forgotten, and we are left with the anecdotes of the insight literature, like the classic case described by the great French mathematician Henri Poincaré, who distracted himself from his mathematical work by embarking on a geological excursion. "Having reached Coutances," Poincaré wrote,

> we entered an omnibus to go some place or other. At the moment when I put my foot on the step the idea came to me, without anything in my former thoughts seeming to have paved the way for it, that the transformations I had used to define the Fuchsian functions were identical with those of non-Euclidian geometry. I did not verify the idea; I should not have had time, as upon taking my seat in the omnibus, I went on with a conversation already commenced.

Poincaré's anecdote and many others like it are frequently cited as arguments that creative insight is instantaneous and therefore uncontrollable. However, as David Perkins points out in his analysis of Poincaré's account, the same conversation that prevented verification of the insight, when combined with Poincaré's surprise at his discovery, would have prevented accurate memory of the processes preceding it. Poincaré notwithstanding, practical creation is a long-term process that takes advantage of incubation and networks of enterprise. Thus, by giving you two problems to work on, and by distracting you with this discourse on incubation, I'm increasing your chances of finding solutions to both problems. If you think you've incubated long enough, try both problems again.

TRY EVERYTHING ONCE

The most popular strategies for enhancing creativity emphasize divergent production. These approaches stress quantity, originality, and variety of ideas, and leave the problem of evaluating effectiveness and selection for later. For example, in applying Peter Elbow's freewriting technique described in Chapter 8, one writes down everything that comes to mind; the only rule is to keep writing.

Freewriting is a lot like "brainstorming," a widely used technique for enhancing the creativity of groups, and probably the best-known quantity-based technique. Brainstormers are encouraged to produce and record as many ideas as possible, using each other's ideas as foils, while withholding all judgment and criticism. There is no evidence that brainstorming by groups is more effective than brainstorming by individuals. In fact, it appears that the effects of group brainstorming are pernicious. One study, using advertising personnel as subjects, revealed that people produced 30 percent more ideas (with no drop in quality) when working alone than when brainstorming in teams. This is especially true of the most creative people, who, in spite of the rule against criticism, are often unwilling to be really wild and crazy when surrounded by peers and superiors.

You might try a little brainstorming on your marketing project and the nine-dots problem. If nothing else, brainstorming legitimates ideas you might otherwise consider too weird to consider.

Even more influential than brainstorming in recent years has been Edward DeBono's "lateral thinking," the exploration of "least likely" directions by relaxing logic and using chance. Although not emphasizing sheer quantity to the extent that brainstorming does, lateral thinking is equally nonevaluative. "With vertical thinking [conventional problem solving] one is trying to find the best approach, but with lateral thinking one is generating different approaches for the sake of generating them. Vertical thinking moves only when there is a direction to move, lateral thinking moves in order to generate a direction." The main technique recommended by DeBono is using the word "PO," which is the positive, inclusive, intuitive, impulsive, lateral counterpart to the vertical thinker's "no." PO can be used in many ways, including as a kind of intellectual emetic, as when you try to invent a new form of marketing by constructing sentences like "PO salespeople play canasta" or "PO sales pay no commission." You might also try some lateral thinking on the nine-dots problem: Nobody said the lines have to stay within the square defined by the dots. So try a literally lateral move. If this hint didn't help, read on. The answer will come soon enough.

Himself a lateral thinker par excellence, Edward DeBono has been more interested in promoting his ideas than in evaluating them. Consequently, the task of evaluation has fallen to academicians, most of whom are impressed primarily by the absence of evidence that PO or other lateral-thinking techniques have benefited anyone other than Edward DeBono. However, the absence of evidence should never be used as an argument; as experimental psychologists like to say, you can't prove there is no Santa Claus, so we should laterally reserve judgment about lateral thinking and give DeBono the last word: When it comes to comparing lateral thinking to other ways of promoting creativity, the best evidence is PO.

Brainstorming and lateral thinking may be regarded as mainly right-brained: they are impulsive, intuitive, and flexible rather than reflective, systematic, and regulated. Brainstorming and lateral thinking attempt to promote divergent production by teaching you how to move in random and unusual directions. Other, somewhat more left-brained approaches to divergent production provide more or less systematic ways to combine unrelated or even contradictory ideas.

Many original inventions have been based on such combinations. The air bag, for example, combines the contradictory ideas of safety and explosion. It is difficult today to remember how improbable the combination of the words "personal" and "computer" was in the mid-1970s. Then computers were the ultimate symbol of the impersonal. When Jobs combined computing power with easy operation, he illustrated what Arthur Koestler called "bisociation," simultaneously seeing an object or idea in terms of two different sets of rules. F. Scott Fitzgerald described this quality when he wrote, "The test of a first-rate intelligence is the ability to hold two opposed ideas in the mind at the same time, and still retain the ability to function."

A quote from Poincaré testifies to the power of combination: "one evening, contrary to my custom, I drank black coffee and could not sleep. Ideas rose in clouds. I felt them collide until pairs interlocked, so to speak, making a stable combination." Like Poincaré's coffee, combinatorial strategies are artificial aids to integration, but they attempt to be more controllable. Unlike brainstorming and lateral thinking, they leave as little to chance as possible. These methods might well be called Lullian, after Raymond Lull, a thirteenth-century Spanish theologian who developed techniques for systematically listing all possible combinations of ideas in a particular realm. For instance, Lull derived all the important truths about God by listing all His attributes, then examining all possible combinations: His goodness we determine is great and powerful, just as His greatness is good and eternal, etc.

Let's apply Lull's technique to our problem of inventing a new form of marketing. We construct a table with forms of marketing across the side and bottom, and fill it in with all possible pairs. Among these pairs we are sure to find some odd or even contradictory combinations, but some of them might be interesting: for instance, marketing mobile homes like conventional homes, by selling both a mobile home and a lot. Certainly there's a contradiction here: Who would buy a mobile home and an immobile lot? But contradictions in logic are not always contradictions in psychology. People buy mobile homes not because they are mobile but because they are cheap. In fact, although many people like the feeling of mobility "mobile" homes give them, they almost never move them. Moreover, what prospective buyers dislike most about trailers is their tacky impermanence. So you display trailers in a lot, on wheels, ready to roll. That appeals to the desire for mobility. Next you take the customer to a nicely landscaped development where trailers are elegantly and permanently planted on firm foundations. So much for tacky impermanence. The Lullian method generated a new and not entirely implausible marketing solution. Call my 800 number to place your order.

Modern Lullian methods based on systematic and exhaustive search of combinations include "morphological analysis," developed by the Swiss aeronautical engineer Fritz Zwicky, the K-J method of Japanese anthropologist Kawakita Jiro, and "morphological forced analysis," described by Don Koberg and Jim Bagnall in *The Universal Traveler* as a "fool-proof invention-finding scheme."

These techniques all begin with exhaustive lists of "attributes," "dimensions," or "observations." For example, to invent a new kind of manufacture, we might list its important dimensions: materials, operations, and products. We would then list as many alternatives as we could under each dimension. Under materials we might have aluminum, wood, paper, words, numbers, etc. Under operations we might have glue, weld, staple, rivet, peg, etc. Under products we would put cars, trailers, houses, real estate, etc. Finally, we would construct lists or "morphological tables" in order to examine all possible combinations.

These neo-Lullian strategies do have some limitations. They work only when dimensions and alternatives are listable. Moreover, because they combine alternatives only in different dimensions, they would never produce the immobile-home marketing scheme, which was a combination of two alternative methods on the same dimension.

In spite of these limitations, some engineers do find these methods effective. And at least one psychologist has found them useful aids to invention. If our dimensions of manufacture sounded vaguely familiar, it is because they are also the terms of Guilford's structure of intellect model (described in Chapter 2). Guilford gives Zwicky credit for Guilford's own discovery of new intellectual abilities arising from systematic morphological combinations of, for example, figural and behavioral contents operations like divergent production and evaluation, to produce products like classes and transformations. David Perkins must have had these combinatorial methods in mind when he claimed that some genuinely creative enterprises are "products of the kind of searching we do when we systematically pick lint off a sweater."

BEYOND QUANTITY

In contrast to the divergent "quantity versus quality" approaches to creativity, other strategies emphasize quality rather than quantity. Such approaches are heuristics (see Chapter 9). They are shortcuts, not foolproof exhaustive searches like Lullian methods. Advocates of these techniques agree with Poincaré that "Anyone could make new combinations. . . . to create consists precisely in not making useless combinations, and in making those which are useful, and which are only a small minority: invention is discernment, choice."

Proponents of lateral thinking and other hit-or-miss methods are fond of pointing out that creative acts break rules. Creators break rules, however, only in service of other, more abstract, higher-order rules. My Lullian marketing scheme, for instance, broke a rule by making mobile homes immobile, but only to obey a more fundamental rule that says people like to eat their cake and have it.

The invention of the first Apple computer exhibits a similar sacrifice of concrete rules for more abstract ones. At a time when the rule for commercial success in computer design was to make a more powerful and complicated machine, Steven Jobs and Stephen Wozniak made one that was small and simple, in order to obey a more fundamental rule: To sell, give people what they want.

My favorite example of creative rule-breaking is the physics student whose answer to the question "How would you measure the height of a building with a barometer?" was "Drop the barometer off the roof, time it, and substitute time into the formula $s = 1/2gt^2$." This student broke the rule that says you should answer questions about barometers with statements about atmospheric pressure, in order to obey a more abstract rule that says the purpose of a physics exam is to show you've learned some physics.

And here's one solution to the nine-dots problem, which violates the (self-imposed) rule that keeps most people within the boundaries of the figure in order to satisfy the more general rules of the puzzle:

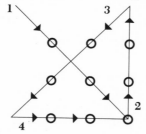

Truly creative solutions to the nine-dots puzzle, like the ones reported by James Adams in *Conceptual Blockbusting*, violate other tacit low-order rules in order to satisfy the stated higher-order rules. You can make three diagonal lines fat enough to go through the edges of the dots; you can fold the paper in several ways, so that one straight line will pass through all the dots; or you can crumple the page into a ball, stab a pencil through it, and repeat until by chance you happen to poke the pencil through all nine dots.

Teachers of creativity recommend defining problems at the highest possible level of abstraction as a way to determine which rules to break, thereby restricting one's search to fruitful alternatives. David Perkins recommends that when you're stuck on a problem, redefine it in terms of the "real problem," which is often more abstract. As an example, he describes how, in the early years of the space program, NASA engineers spent a lot of time and money looking for the right stuff to shield the nose of the space shuttle. Protecting the capsule, they eventually realized, was only a concrete means to the more general goal of protecting the astronauts inside. The engineers solved the problem by working on this "real problem." By redefining the problem at a higher level of abstraction, they arrived at a creative solution: The ablatable shield burned away, sacrificing the integrity of the craft to obey a higher-level rule.

William Gordon, in his book *Synectics*, also prescribes abstraction as a way of finding higher-order rules. For example, he suggests that urban designers attempting to invent new ways of parking in cities think about storage in general. Designers adopting his advice proposed several new schemes based on hanging, stacking, and other storage systems never before applied to cars.

To apply abstraction to our marketing project, we might, define "marketing" in the broadest possible terms: anything that promotes exchange. This abstract definition includes war, natural disasters, general prosperity, and other impractical "solutions." We might think of ways to obtain the marketing benefits of, say, a heat wave, without the destructive consequences. We could, for example, concentrate our pitches for air conditioners or soft drinks in places like subways, where people are likely to be overheated. Abstraction also frees us from incidental barriers: Marketing doesn't require advertising, a product, or even sales. Thus, we might think of ways to promote barter or other forms of cooperation, as by opening an outdoor market to which people could bring broken appliances, and trade their own skills or goods for repairs.

Although abstraction's style is left-brained, other techniques are more right-brained: They depend heavily on creativity's mysterious accomplice, intuition, and its sidekick, metaphor, which Aristotle called the sign of genius. Skill at constructing metaphors, which Howard Gardner attributes variously to spatial and to logical-mathematical ability, is based on seeing delineated similarity between two previously unrelated items, as when Steven Jobs imagined the personal computer as like an older friend who would answer questions, offer advice, and play games. Metaphor also guided the paintbrush developers described in the preceding chapter.

Metaphor is at the heart of Gordon's synectics, a technique for creative problem solving. "Synectics" means "combining what has been separate"; Gordon describes it as making "the strange familiar" and "the familiar strange." Synectics is used by groups. After discussing different perspectives on a problem, group members combine them or select one problem definition as the basis for future work.

The next stage is a kind of structured incubation, in which group members discuss other matters in search of productive metaphors. Nature is a rich source of solutions to practical problems, so synectics sessions often begin with a search for natural metaphors. Natural solutions to the problems of marketing include the attractive scents of dogs, moths, and other animals, so we might consider ways of enhancing the allure of a product with subtle sexual scents. "Personal" analogies are another synectic tactic: We might discuss what it would be like to be a can or another container. Or we might act out the response of someone shopping to a waft of sexual attractant while passing a shelf of canned fruit. Such playacting might help us detect a problem with our method: Odors diffuse, and might not single out our product; perhaps we could solve this problem with large or isolated displays. A third tactic for finding metaphors is "symbolic" condensations of our problem into a single word or image. We might, for example, describe marketing as like skywriting or finding a mate, or imagine a moth fluttering upwind, in the hope that these condensations will generate further ideas. Finally, we might engage in "what if" fantasies: What if we could cast spells, and could get people to buy things without their knowing that they were in our power?

Finally, we would return to the problem as initially defined, evaluating ideas suggested by each analogy. We might end up with a new form of marketing that uses subtly scented containers backed up by magazine ads that emit the same subliminal olfactory messages.

You Got to Know the Territory

Finally, we get to a strategy you never find in creativity training books because it can't fit between two covers. By now, you ought to be able to guess what it is: acquiring well-organized knowledge in all the domains relevant to the ones you work in. This view of creative work as requiring expertise and knowledge runs counter to conventional views that regard creativity as a talent or a gift of muse, chance, or DNA. It is also challenged by psychologists who argue that there is nothing new under the sun, that creative work consists only of new combinations, and that combinatorial techniques are the royal road to creativity.

On the other hand, the "work ethic" approach to creation is widely shared among psychologists. Howard Gardner, whose theory of multiple intelligences is the spine of this book, writes: "genuinely original or novel activities can come about only when an individual has achieved mastery in the field where he has been working." Thus, we find that "originality or novelty does in fact occur principally, if not exclusively, within single domains: one rarely if ever encounters individuals who are original across the intellectual board." Anne Roe found that extensive knowledge was a prerequisite for creative work in science, and David Perkins argues effectively that there is "no substitute for knowledge."

Jobs and Wozniak could not have created the Apple without expertise gained through years of experience with small computers and other electronic devices. My somewhat less significant immobile-home marketing scheme, though mediated by Lull's technique, depended on knowledge of what people like and hate about trailers. Even abstract problems like the nine dots are solved more creatively by people who have worked on other, similar problems, and who apply this knowledge by looking at similarities and differences between the problems at hand and other problems they know how to solve.

Robert Sternberg points out that it is not just the amount of knowledge that promotes creativity, but the richness of interconnections among knowledge units. Jobs and Wozniak, for example, knew not only about computers but about the appeal of electronic games, and were, because of their experiences tinkering with games, able to make connections between what they liked and what they could build.

The practical implication here is the same as it was for developing cognitive styles: We become creative not by working on creativity as such but by mastering a domain. Once again, we have moved ahead to basics.

DOING IT

Powered by well-developed multiple intellectual abilities and guided by flexibly integrated cognitive styles, creation is the payload of practical intelligences. All the techniques for boosting creativity described in this chapter fuel multiple intelligences or refine cognitive styles. These strategies can be summarized in a few direct suggestions:

- Pick your shots. Creativity depends on multiple intelligences and cognitive styles, so if you don't have the luxury of picking your problems, pick approaches that use the kinds of intelligence you have or can develop. Solutions based on creating new products will most likely require logical, analytical abilities and styles; inventing new services, on the other hand, will require more right-brained, people-oriented skills and styles.

- Relax! There's plenty of good evidence that creation needs a calm, receptive attitude to get off the ground.

- Brainstorm! Freewrite and freethink. Be impulsive: Turn off your critical monitor and leave it off until you run dry.

- Analyze and combine. Take a bottom-up approach to the problem, using Lullian and neo-Lullian combinatorial schemes on the smallest units you can handle. Real-world problems have lots of attributes, so use newsprint or other large formats for your tables of combinations.

- Abstract! Switch to a top-down approach. If necessary, write out your problem, and replace every term with the most generic one you can come up with. Then abstract some more, by dropping qualifying phrases. Once you've defined the problem in the most general terms possible . . .

- Saturate! Soak yourself in the material you will work with. Eat, sleep, drink, and dream it. Creation depends on expertise. After you saturate . . .

- Incubate! When you hit a snag, work on it for a little while. Then work on something else: your design for the perfect desk, or a new arrangement for your office. You want your project out of sight but orbiting nearby, so you can . . .

- Look for metaphors as you incubate. When you get an analogy or other idea . . .

- Try it! As the inventive electrical engineer Charles Kettering once said, "I have never heard of anyone tumbling on something sitting down."

Kettering's comment echoes a statement made by Aristotle in his *Nicomachean Ethics:* "In practical matters the end is not mere speculative knowledge of what is to be done, but rather the doing of it." You've read enough. As you get back to work, I hope you'll use the suggestions in this book. They have worked for me, and if they work as well for you, you too will be able to say, "I'm practically intelligent."

Notes

PAGE   *1. Empires of the Mind*

3   **There is nothing as practical:** Kurt Lewin, in *Field Theory in Social Science,* ed. D. Cartwright (New York: Harper & Row, 1951).

3   **many ways for people to be smart:** Ulrich Neisser, DCL in Daniel Goleman, "Successful Executives Rely on Own Kind of Intelligence," *The New York Times,* July 31, 1984, p. C11.

5   **are not aggressive:** George Klemp, personal communication, Nov. 17, 1985. Quote from Goleman, "Successful Executives."

6   **Coppola nearly dueled:** *New York Magazine,* May 7, 1984, p. 59.

7   **empires of the mind:** Winston Churchill quote: in Anne Keatley, "Knowledge as Real Estate," *Science,* 222, Number 4625, Nov. 18, 1983, p. 1.

7   **historic transition:** *Business Week,* June 30, 1980. Quoted by Morton Meltzer, *Information: The Ultimate Management Resource* (New York: AMACOM, 1981), p. 3.

7   **working smarter:** "People and Productivity: A Challenge to Corporate America," *New York Stock Exchange Office of Economic Research,* Nov. 1982.

7   **80 percent of their time:** H. D. Toong and A. Gupta, "Personal Computers," *Scientific American,* 247(6), 1982, p. 107.

7   **the manager's capital:** Peter Drucker, "Managing the Information Explosion," *The Wall Street Journal,* April 10, 1980, p. 24.

8   **the mental strategies:** Silvia Scribner, "Studying Working Intelligence," in *Everyday Cognition,* ed. Barbara Rogoff and Jean Lave (Cambridge, Mass.: Harvard University Press, 1984).

9   **The middle class handles:** Rudolph Arnheim, *Visual Thinking* (Los Angeles: University of California Press, 1969), pp. 2, 203.

9   **bureaucratic competencies:** John Raven, *Competence in Modern Society* (London: H. K. Lewis, 1984).

9   **theory G:** Harold Geneen, *Managing* (New York: Doubleday, 1984), p. 17.

10   **Practical men:** John Maynard Keynes, *The General Theory of Employment, Interest, and Money* (New York: Harcourt Brace Jovanovich, 1936).

10 **axial principle:** Daniel Bell, *The Coming of Post-Industrial Society* (New York: Basic Books, 1973).

11 **differences between school and the real world:** Ulrich Neisser, "General, Academic, and Artificial Intelligence," in *The Nature of Intelligence,* ed. Lauren Resnick (Hillsdale, N.J., 1976), p. 137; Robert Sternberg, "Teaching Critical Thinking, Part 1: Are We Making Critical Mistakes?" *Phi Delta Kappa,* Dec. 1986, pp. 277–80.

12 **range of alternative solutions:** Frederick Bartlett, *Thinking* (New York: Basic Books, 1958).

2. The Politics of Intelligence

14 **A good theory:** Donald Hebb, *Psychology Today,* 3, Nov. 1969, p. 21.

14 **new look:** Daniel Keating, "The Emperor's New Clothes: The 'New Look' in Intelligence Research," in *Advances in the Study of Human Intelligence,* ed. Robert Sternberg (Hillsdale, N.J.: Lawrence Erlbaum, 1984).

15 **independent and unequal:** Alfred Binet, *Les Idées Modernes sur les Enfants* (Paris: Flammarion, 1909). Quoted in Stephen Jay Gould, *The Mismeasure of Man* (New York: Norton, 1981) p. 149.

15 **to different ends:** Ibid., pp. 174–76, 251–55.

16 **different definitions of intelligence:** "Intelligence and Its Measurement: A Symposium," *Journal of Educational Psychology,* 12, 1921, pp. 123–275.

17 **Intelligence is what the tests test:** Edwin G. Boring, "Intelligence As the Tests Test It," *New Republic,* 34, 1923, pp. 35–37.

17 **without saying what it was:** Richard Hernnstein, *IQ in the Meritocracy* (Boston: Little, Brown, 1971), chap. 2.

17 **Intelligence, like electricity:** Arthur Jensen, *Genetics and Education* (New York: Harper & Row, 1972), p. 72.

17 **electricity is easy to define:** Hilary Putnam, "A Philosopher Looks at Quantum Mechanics," in *Beyond the Edge of Certainty,* ed. R. G. Cooley (Englewood Cliffs, N.J.: Prentice-Hall, 1965), p. 76.

18 **Adler's CR Test:** F. Adler, "Operational Definitions in Sociology," *American Journal of Sociology,* 52, 1947, pp. 438–44.

18 **the last thing:** George Miller, *Psychology: The Science of Mental Life* (New York: Harper & Row, 1962), p. 79.

18 **The first step:** Daniel Yankelovitch, quoted by "Adam Smith," *Supermoney* (New York: Popular Library, 1972).

18 **a mere vocal sound:** Charles Spearman, *The Abilities of Man* (New York: Macmillan, 1927).

19 **King *g*:** Hans Eysenck, *Know Your Own I.Q.* (London: Penguin, 1962).

20 **material energy:** Spearman: Gould, *Mismeasure of Man,* p. 267.

20 **extent that they do:** Hernnstein, *IQ in Meritocracy,* p. 71.

20 **whatever has received a name:** John Stuart Mill: Gould, *Mismeasure of Man,* p. 320.

21 **thermometer readings:** Eysenck, *Know Your Own IQ,* p. 9.

22 **an ordinal scale:** Joy Paul Guilford, *Psychometric Methods* (New York: McGraw-Hill, 1954), p. 17.

PAGE

22   **No one has seriously tried:** Robert Plutchik, *Foundations of Experimental Psychology* (New York: Harper & Row, 1968), pp. 229–36.

23   **make-believe operation:** Eysenck, *Know Your Own IQ,* p. 19.

23   **pure illusion:** Raymond Cattell, "Are IQ Tests Intelligent?" in *Readings in Psychology Today,* ed. James Maas (Del Mar, Calif.: CRM, 1974).

23   **Not much:** N. J. Block and Gerald Dworkin, "IQ, Hereditability, and Inequality," in *The IQ Controversy,* ed. N. J. Block and Gerald Dworkin (New York: Pantheon, 1976); E. E. Ghiselli, *The Validity of Occupational Aptitude Tests* (New York: Wiley, 1966); Hernnstein, *IQ in Meritocracy,* pp. 125–27. Christopher Jencks et al., *Inequality* (New York: Basic Books, 1972), pp. 144–45, 186–87, appendix B; Arthur Jensen, *Genetics;* Arthur Jensen, "Another Look at Culture Fair Testing," in *The Disadvantaged Child,* ed. J. Hellmuth (New York: Brunner Mazel, 1970), p. 63; Richard Wagner and Robert Sternberg, "Practical Intelligence in Real-World Pursuits: The Role of Tacit Knowledge," *Journal of Personality and Social Psychology,* 49, 1985, pp. 436–58; David McClelland, "Testing for Competence Rather than for 'Intelligence,'" *American Psychologist,* 28, Jan. 1973, pp. 1–14.

24   **correlation of .7:** Hernnstein, *IQ in Meritocracy,* p. 114.

24   **the Pygmalion effect:** Robert Rosenthal and L. Jacobson, *Pygmalion in the Classroom* (New York: Holt, Rinehart & Winston, 1968).

25   **vice-president of General Motors:** Nicholas Von Hoffman, "The View from the Top," *San Francisco Examiner and Chronicle,* Sept. 23, 1973.

25   **groupthink:** Irving Janis, *Groupthink* (Boston: Houghton Mifflin, 1983).

27   **fluid and crystallized:** Raymond B. Cattell, "I.Q. Tests."

28   **intellectual abilities:** Cyril Burt Guilford, *Nature of Human Intelligence,* pp. 2, 11.

29   **verbal-educational ability:** Phillip Vernon, *The Structure of Human Abilities* (New York: Wiley, 1950).

30   **Primary Mental Abilities (PMAs):** Guilford, *Human Intelligence,* pp. 174–76, 251–55.

30   **Multiple Intelligences (MIs):** Howard Gardner, *Frames of Mind* (New York: Basic Books, 1983). Guilford, *Human Intelligence,* pp. 60–66.

31   **Cognitive psychologists began:** For an early history of cognitive science see Howard Gardner, *The Mind's New Science* (New York: Basic Books, 1985).

32   **Steven Jobs:** Michael Moritz, *The Little Kingdom* (New York: Morrow, 1984).

32   **rational model:** G. Allison, *Essence of Decision: Explaining the Cuban Missile Crisis* (Boston: Little, Brown, 1971).
    Departure from the rational model in real-world decisions: Hugh Mehan, "Intellectual Tasks of Warehouse Workers and Truck Drivers," in *Everyday Cognition,* ed. Barbara Rogoff and Jean Lave, (Cambridge, Mass.: Harvard University Press, 1984).

33   **design of an expert system:** Douglas Lenat, "Computer Software for Intelligent Systems." *Scientific American,* 251(3), 1984, pp. 204–13.
    Expert Systems as "designer jeans": Alan Kay, "Computer Software,"

Scientific American, 251(3), 1984, pp. 204–13. Sternberg's triarchic theory: Robert J. Sternberg, *Beyond IQ* (Cambridge: Cambridge University Press, 1985).

34   **new look:** Keating, "Emperor's Clothes," Wilbert McKeachie, "The New Look in Instructional Psychology: Teaching Strategies for Learning and Thinking." Invited address delivered at the First European Conference for Research on Learning and Instruction, Catholic University of Leuven, Belgium, June 12, 1985. Richard E. Snow, "The Training of Intellectual Aptitude," in *How and How Much Can Intelligence Be Increased?,* ed. Douglas Detterman and Robert Sternberg (Norwood, N.J.: ABLEX, 1982).

34   **IQs of identical twins:** P. Watson, "Uncanny Twins," *London Sunday Times Weekly Review,* May 25, 1980, pp. 1–6; R. S. Woodworth, *Heredity and Environment: A Cultural Study of Recently Published Materials on Twins and Foster Children* (New York: Social Science Research Council Bulletin, 1941). Cited in Howard Gardner, *Developmental Psychology* (Boston: Little, Brown, 1982), p. 309.

35   **learning to learn:** Harry F. Harlow, "The Formation of Learning Sets," in *The Transfer of Learning,* ed. Henry Ellis (New York: Macmillan, 1965). Wallace Stevens, "Reality Is an Activity of the Most August Imagination," in *The Palm at the End of the Mind: Selected Poems and a Play,* ed. Holly Stevens (New York: Vintage, 1972) p. 396.

36   **darkling plain:** Matthew Arnold, "Dover Beach," in *Seven Centuries of Verse,* ed. A. J. M. Smith (New York: Scribner's, 1957), p. 476.

36   **subnormal IQs to superior ones:** Changes in IQ: M. C. Jones, N. Bayely, J. MacFarlane, and M. Honzik, *The Course of Human Development* (Ann Arbor: Xerox College Publishing, 1971).

36   **What any person:** *Developing Talent in Young People.* ed. Benjamin Bloom (New York: Ballantine, 1985).

36   **recent book:** Sternberg, *Beyond IQ.*

37   **Psychometrician E. E. Ghiselli:** E. E. Ghiselli, *The Validity of Occupational Aptitude Tests* (New York: Wiley, 1966).

37   **ethological approach:** William R. Charlesworth, "Human Intelligence as Adaptation: An Ethological Approach," in *The Nature of Intelligence,* ed. Lauren B. Resnick (Hillsdale, N.J.: Lawrence Erlbaum, 1976).

37   **classic ethological study:** Henry Mintzberg, *The Nature of Managerial Work* (New York: Harper & Row, 1973).

37   **really psychological:** David McClelland, *The Achieving Society* (New York: Van Nostrand, 1961).

38   **Norman Fredericksen of ETS:** Norman Fredericksen, "Toward a Broader Conception of Human Intelligence," *American Psychologist* 41, 1986, pp. 445–52.

38   **realistic simulations:** Siegfried Streufert, "The Stress of Excellence," *Across the Board,* 20(9), 1983, pp. 8–16; Harold M. Schroder, Michael J. Driver, and Siegfried Steufert, *Human Information Processing* (New York: Holt, Rinehart & Winston, 1967) pp. 57–58; Siegfried Streufert, *Behavior in the Complex Environment* (New York: John Wiley and Victor Winston, 1978).

39   **a sense that is not clear:** Robert Sternberg and Richard Wagner, "Practical Intelligence," in *Practical Intelligence: Nature and Origins of Competence in the Everyday World,* ed. Robert Sternberg and Richard Wagner (Cambridge: Cambridge University Press, 1986).

39   **questionnaires:** ibid.

3. A Practical Approach to Practical Intelligence

41   **Behavioral Event Interviews:** *Critical Behavior Interviewing* (Boston: Charles River Consulting, 1985).

42   **multiple intelligences:** Howard Gardner, *Frames of Mind* (New York: Basic Books, 1983), p. 239.

43   **depend heavily on spacial intelligence:** Robert Sternberg, "Human Intelligence: The Model Is the Message," *Science,* 230, Dec. 6, 1985, pp. 1111–18.

44   **crap detector:** Ernest Hemingway, quoted in Neil Postman and Charles Weingartner, *Teaching As a Subversive Activity* (New York: Delacorte, 1969).

44   **impulsive to reflective:** Jerome Kagan, *Developmental Studies of Reflection and Analysis* (Cambridge, Mass.: Harvard University Press, 1964).

44   **Cognitive complexity:** Harold M. Schroder, Michael J. Driver, and Siegfried Steufert, *Human Information Processing* (New York: Holt, Rinehart & Winston, 1967), pp. 57–58. Siegfried Streufert, "The Stress of Excellence," *Across the Board,* 20(9), 1983, pp. 8–16.

46   **ignorance plus confidence:** Mark Twain, quoted in A. A. Carr, *Business As a Game* (New York: New American Library), p. 212.

4. Self-Understanding

51   **What am I doing:** Arthur Miller, *Death of a Salesman* (New York: Penguin, 1985), p. 132.

51   **Who in the world:** Lewis Carroll, *Alice in Wonderland* (New York: Grosset and Dunlap), p. 15.

51   **Lido:** Lee Iacocca, *Iacocca* (New York: Bantam, 1984).

53   **intrapersonal intelligence:** Howard Gardner, *Frames of Mind* (New York: Basic Books, 1983), pp. 242–73.

53   **best-sellers:** *Chronicle of Higher Education,* Apr. 6, 1986, p. 2.

53   **self-actualization:** Daniel Yankelovitch, *New Rules* (New York: Random House, 1982), pp. 76–85.

53   **recent study:** Robert Beck, *The Liberal Arts Major in Bell System Management* (Washington D.C.: Association of American Colleges, 1981). Richard Wagner and Robert Sternberg, "Practical Intelligence in Real-World Pursuits: The Role of Tacit Knowledge," *Journal of Personality and Social Psychology,* 49, 1985, 436–58.

54   **people who excel:** Charles Garfield, *Peak Performers: The New Heroes* (New York: Morrow, 1986).

55   **race is for his life:** Plato, *Theaetetus,* in *The Dialogues of Plato, Volume II,* trans. Benjamin Jowett (London: Oxford University Press, 1871), p. 177.

55   **lawyers were psychoanalyzed:** Benjamin Davis, quoted by Martin Mayer, *The Lawyers* (New York: Dell, 1967), p. 50.

55   **large ego:** Iacocca, *Iacocca,* pp. 37–8.

55   **John Z. DeLorean:** John DeLorean and Ted Schwartz, *DeLorean* (Grand Rapids, Michigan: Zondervan, 1985).

56   **dark side:** Daniel Goleman, "The Psyche of the Entrepreneur," *The New York Times Magazine,* Feb. 2, 1986, pp. 63, 68.

56   **Willy Loman:** Miller, *Salesman,* Requiem.

56   **worse than alchoholism:** Harold Geneen, *Managing* (New York: Doubleday, 1984), p. 177.

56   **Braniff:** John Nance, *Splash of Colors* (New York: Morrow, 1984), pp. 140–41.

56   **self-perception:** David G. Meyers, in "How Do I Love Me? Let Me Count the Ways," *Psychology Today,* May 1980, p. 16.

56   **self-assessment:** Richard Boyatzis, *The Competent Manager* (New York: Wiley, 1982), p. 29.

56   **Mark McCormack:** Mark McCormack, *What They Don't Teach You at Harvard Business School* (New York: Bantam, 1984), p. 161. Lyle Spencer, quoted in Goleman, "Psyche."

57   **Psychologist Bill McKeachie:** Wilbert McKeachie, *Teaching Tips* (Lexington, Mass.: Heath, 1969), p. 2.

57   **adult education programs:** Carol Schneider, George Klemp, and Susan Kastendiek, *The Balancing Act: Competencies of Effective Teachers and Mentors in Degree Programs for Adults* (Center for Continuing Education, University of Chicago, 1981).

57   **your values:** Howard Gardner, *Frames of Mind,* pp. 238–39.

61   **common cold of psychopathy:** J. Coleman, J. Butcher, and R. Carson, *Abnormal Psychology and Modern Life* (Glenview Ill.: Scott, Foresman, 1984), p. 325.

61   **Wall Street psychiatrist:** Jay Rohrlick, in A. Brown and E. Weiner, *Supermanaging* (New York: McGraw-Hill, 1984), p. 157.

61   **thoughts of the pistol:** William James, in Robert Watson, *The Great Psychologists* (New York: Lippincott, 1978), p. 372.

61   **Type A:** Meyer Friedman and Ray Rosenman, *Type A Behavior and Your Heart* (New York: Fawcett, 1974), pp. 69–96, 143.

61   **The Gamesmen:** in Alice G. Sargent, *The Androgynous Manager* (New York: AMACOM, 1983) p. ii.

62   **The Crab Nebula:** Walker Percy, *Lost in the Cosmos* (New York: Farrar, Straus & Giroux, 1983), pp. 2–5.

63   **psychodynamic theory:** Sigmund Freud, *An Outline of Psychoanalysis* (New York: Norton, 1963), pp. 13–17.

64   **Transactional Analysis:** Eric Berne, *Transactional Analysis in Psychotherapy* (New York: Grove Press, 1961), pp. 3, 11, 24, 32; Eric Berne, *Games People Play* (New York, Grove Press, 1964), pp. 26–7.

64   **cognitive perspective:** Anthony Greenwald, "The Totalitarian Ego," *American Psychologist,* 35, Number 7, July 1980, pp. 603–18.

65   **management consultant:** Harry Levinson, *The Exceptional Executive* (New York: Mentor, 1971), pp. 34–41.

65   **Rational Emotive Therapy:** Albert Ellis, *A New Guide to Rational Living* (Hollywood, Calif.: Wilshire, 1975), pp. 2–4.

65   **schema repair:** Daniel Goleman, *Vital Lies, Simple Truths* (New York: Simon & Schuster, 1985), p. 238.

67   **P. T. Barnum effect:** Bertram Forer, "The Fallacy of Personal Validation: A Classroom Demonstration of Gullibility," in *Readings in Social Psychology,* ed. Dennis Krebs (New York: Harper & Row, 1982).

67   **Chauncey:** Jerzy Kosinski, *Being There* (New York: Harcourt Brace Jovanovich, 1971).

68   **looking glass self:** Charles Horton Cooley, in Mark Snyder, "The Many Me's of the Self-Monitor," in *Social Psychology in the Eighties,* ed. Lawrence S. Wrightsman and Kay Deaux (Monterey, Calif.: Brooks/ Cole, 1981).

68   **development of the sense of self:** Erik Erikson, *Childhood and Society* (New York: Norton, 1950).

68   **boundaries of the physical self:** William James, *Psychology* (New York: Fawcett, 1963), p. 168.

68   **labeling theory:** Stanley Schachter and J. E. Singer, "Cognitive, Social and Physiological Determinants of Emotional State," *Psychological Review,* 69, 1962, pp. 95–106.

71   **social selves:** William James, *Psychology,* pp. 170–2.

72   **different person in each one:** Kenneth Gergen, *The Concept of Self* (New York: Holt Rinehart & Winston, 1971); Kenneth Gergen, "The Healthy Happy Human Being Wears Many Masks," in *Readings in Psychology Today,* ed. James Maas (Del Mar, Calif.: CRM, 1974).

72   **Parent of TA:** Berne, *Transactional Analysis,* pp. 17–19.

72   **self as theory:** Seymour Epstein, "The Self-Concept: A Review and Proposal for Integrated Theory of Personality," in *Personality: Basic Assumptions and Current Research,* ed. E. Staub (Englewood Cliffs, N.J.: Prentice-Hall, 1980).

73   **spiritual me:** James, *Psychology,* p. 167.

73   **ego states:** Berne, *Transactional Analysis,* pp. 4–20.

73   **vertical organization of the brain:** Paul MacLean, in Charles Hampden-Turner, *Maps of the Mind* (New York: Collier, 1981), p. 80.

74   **The trinity of selves:** Norman Geschwind, in Jonathan Miller, *States of Mind* (New York: Pantheon, 1983), pp. 118–34.

74   **a curious case:** Goldstein, in ibid., pp. 120, 123.

75   **well dressed and a great athlete:** James, *Psychology,* pp. 174, 175, 177.

75   **totalitarian ego:** Greenwald, "Totalitarian Ego."

76   **code of coherence:** Gergen, "Healthy Happy Human Being."

77   **transcend personal polarities:** Sargent, *Androgynous Manager.*

77   **article in the *New York Times:*** Marilyn Loden, "A Machismo That Drives Women Out," the *New York Times,* Feb. 9, 1986, p. 2 (Business).

77   **large corporations:** Eli Ginzberg and George Vojta, *Beyond Human Scale* (New York: Basic Books, 1986).

77   **Social critic:** Philip Slater, *The Pursuit of Loneliness* (Boston: Beacon, 1970), p. 3.

77   **consistent patterns:** Gergen, "Healthy Happy Human Being."

78   **goal of psychoanalysis:** Sigmund Freud and Joseph Breuer, *Studies in*

Hysteria, in Janet Malcolm, "The Impossible Profession," *The New Yorker*, Nov. 24 and Dec. 1, 1980.

78 **Cognitive scientist:** Donald Norman, in Goleman, *Vital Lies*, p. 72.

78 **show down:** Lee Iacocca, *Iacocca*, pp. 121–22.

79 **defenses:** Matthew Erdelyi and Benjamin Goldberg, "Let's Not Sweep Repression Under the Rug: Toward a Cognitive Psychology of Repression," in John Kihlstrom and Frederick Evans, *Functional Disorders of Memory* (Hillsdale, N.J.: Lawrence Erlbaum, 1979).

79 **recent study:** "Clod May Find Room at the Top," *Rocky Mountain News*, July 13, 1985, p. 48.

80 **character armor:** Wilhelm Reich, *Character Analysis* (New York: Farrar, Straus and Giroux, 1972).

80 **forgets that one has forgotten:** R. D. Laing, *The Politics of the Family* (New York: Pantheon, 1969), pp. 28–42.

80 **blind spots:** Goleman, *Vital Lies*, pp. 15–16.

80 **knows nothing of it:** Anna Freud, in *The Ego and the Mechanisms of Defense*, in Goleman, *ibid.*, p. 125.

80 **A study by:** R. Lynn, "Anxiety and Economic Growth," *Nature*, 219, 1968, pp. 765–66.

81 **cognitive biases:** Greenwald, "Totalitarian Ego."

82 **reflected glory:** Robert Cialdini, *Influence* (Glenview, Ill.: Scott, Foresman, 1985).

83 **As one:** psychoanalyst: in Malcolm, "Impossible Profession."

84 **have faith:** Jerome Bruner, *In Search of Mind* (New York: Harper & Row, 1983).

5. Social Intelligence

85 **the Johnson treatment:** Arthur M. Schlesinger, Jr., *A Thousand Days* (New York: Fawcett, 1965), pp. 18–19.

86 **studies of managers:** Henry Mintzberg, *The Nature of Managerial Work* (New York: Harper & Row, 1973), pp. 36–38, 58–60, 127.

87 **"people sense":** Thomas Peters and Robert Waterman, *In Search of Excellence*, (New York: Harper & Row, 1982).

87 **empathic skills:** Thomas Peters and Nancy Austin, *A Passion for Excellence* (New York: Random House, 1985).

87 **managing others:** Richard Wagner and Robert Sternberg, "Practical Intelligence in Real-World Pursuits: The Role of Tacit Knowledge," *Journal of Personality and Social Psychology*, 49, 1985, pp. 436–58.

87 **Fatal flaws:** Morgan McCall and Michael Lombardo, "What Makes a Top Executive?," *Psychology Today*, Feb. 1983, pp. 26–31.

87 **No one familiar:** "Showdown in Silicon Valley," *Newsweek*, Sept. 30, 1985, pp. 46–57.

87 **Interpersonal skills:** Carol Schneider, George Klemp, and Susan Kastendiek, *The Balancing Act: Competencies of Effective Teachers and Mentors in Degree Programs for Adults* (Center for Continuing Education, University of Chicago, 1981).

88 **flattery and deception:** Plato, *Theaetetus*, in *The Dialogues of Plato, Volume II*, trans. Benjamin Jowett (London: Oxford University Press, 1871), p. 177.

88   **Interpersonal skills:** Martin Mayer, *The Lawyers* (New York: Dell, 1967), pp. 2, 18, 21, 61, 62.

88   **Nizer's sympathy:** Louis Nizer, *My Life in Court* (New York: Doubleday, 1961), pp. 139–50.

88   **dark side:** Medina, in Mayer, *Lawyers,* pp. 43–44.

89   **an outstanding officer:** Lyle Spencer quote, in Daniel Goleman, "Influencing Others: Skills Are Identified," *The New York Times Magazine,* Feb. 18, 1986, p. C15.

90   **social intelligence:** Edward Thorndike, "Intelligence and Its Uses," *Harper's,* 140, pp. 227–35.

90   **elaborated this definition:** Phillip Vernon, "Some Characteristics of the Good Judge of Personality," *Journal of Social Psychology,* 4, pp. 42–51; Howard Gardner, *Frames of Mind* (New York: Basic Books, 1983), p. 239.

91   **sensitivity to these signals:** Roger Peters, *Mammalian Communication* (Monterey, Calif.: Brooks/Cole, 1980).

91   **Several standardized tests:** Robert J. Sternberg, *Beyond IQ* (Cambridge: Cambridge University Press, 1985), pp. 260–61.

92   **Three tests:** Joy Paul Guilford, *The Nature of Human Intelligence* (New York: McGraw-Hill, 1967), pp. 106–7, 236–38; Gardner, *IQ,* p. 263.

92   **system of abilities:** Norman Fredericksen, Sybil Carlson, and William Ward, "The Place of Social Intelligence in a Taxonomy of Cognitive Abilities," *Intelligence,* 8, 1984, pp. 315–37.

92   **women generally out perform:** David G. Myers, *Social Psychology* (New York: McGraw-Hill, 1983), p. 194.

93   **managing others:** Wagner and Sternberg, "Practical Intelligence."

94   **a daring firefighter:** Craig Anderson, Mark Lepper, and Lee Ross, in Myers, *Social Psychology,* p. 112.

94   **fundamental attribution error:** Lee Ross, "The Intuitive Psychologist and His Shortcomings: Distortions in the Attribution Process," in *Advances in Experimental Social Psychology,* 10, ed. Leonard Berkowitz (New York: Academic Press, 1977), pp. 173–220.

94   **data entry clerk:** Richard Boyatzis, *The Competent Manager* (New York: Wiley, 1982), pp. 166–67.

95   **Peter Principle:** Lawrence Peter and Raymond Hull, *The Peter Principle* (New York: Morrow, 1969).

95   **conceptions of empathy:** Charles F. Manucia, "Some Aspects of Empathy Operationally Defined," Unpublished Ph.D. Dissertation (Ann Arbor: University Microfilms, 1967), pp. 16, 69–70.

95   **Boyatzis includes a trait:** Boyatzis, *Competent Manager,* pp. 179–81.

96   **see clearly:** Lyle Spencer, in Goleman, "Influencing Others."

96   **caring more important:** G. G. Reader, L. Pratt, and M. C. Mudd, "What Patients Expect from Their Doctors," *Modern Hospital,* 89, 1957, p. 88.

96   **researchers at University of North Carolina:** William Stiles, Samuel Putnam, Matthew Wolf, and Sherman James, "Interaction Exchange and Patient Satisfaction with Medical Interviews," *Medical Care,* 17, June 1979, pp. 667–79.

97   **"buying off"**: Harry Levinson, *The Exceptional Executive* (New York: Mentor, 1971), pp. 84–87.

98   **Reg Jones:** Harry Levinson and Stuart Rosenthal, *CEO: Corporate Leadership in Action* (New York: Basic Books, 1984), pp. 23, 70.

98   **teachers who were perceived:** Schneider, Klemp, and Kastendiek, *Balancing Act.*

98   **150 nonverbal signals:** E. O. Wilson, *Sociobiology* (Cambridge, Mass.: Harvard University Press, 1975), p. 556.

99   **fly in the face of decades of research:** Albert Scheflen, *Body Language and the Social Order* (Englewood Cliffs, N.J.: Prentice-Hall, 1971).

99   **70 to 90 percent:** Ray Birdwhistell, in *Introduction to Kinesics* (Louisville: University of Kentucky Press, 1952); Albert Mehrabian, in "Communication Without Words," in *Readings in Social Psychology,* ed. Dennis Krebs (New York: Harper & Row, 1982), p. 95.

99   **sensitivity to nonverbal communication:** Robert Sternberg, *Intelligence Applied* (San Diego: Harcourt Brace Jovanovich, 1986), pp. 303–16.

99   **Ralph Exline tricked:** Michael Argyle, "The Laws of Looking," *Human Nature,* Jan. 1978.

100   **Freud was guilty:** Sigmund Freud, *Psychopathology of Everyday Life* (New York: New American Library, 1959).

100   **an informal network:** John P. Kotter, *The General Manager* (New York: Free Press, 1982).

100   **withs:** Scheflen, *Body Language,* p. 32.

100   **frames:** ibid., p. 28.

101   **Gaze time:** Mehrabian, "Communication without words."

101   **congruence:** Albert Scheflen, "Significance of Posture in Communications Systems," *Psychiatry,* 27, Nov. 1964.

101   **enhance her emotional empathy:** Mehrabian, "Communication without words."

101   **pupils dilate measurably:** Eckhard H. Hess, "The Role of Pupil Size in Communication," *Scientific American,* Nov. 1975.

102   **Anthropologist Ray Birdwhistell:** Julia Davis, "The Way We Speak 'Body Language,'" in Krebs, *Readings in Social Psychology,* p. 87.

102   **similar to those:** ibid., pp. 92–3.; Peters, *Mammalian Communication,* chap. 9.

102   **Touching:** N. M. Henley, *Body Politics* (Englewood Cliffs, N.J.: Prentice-Hall, 1977).

103   **Dominant members of a group:** Mehrabian, "Communication Without Words."

103   **Recent articles:** John E. Lochman and Robert N. Dain, "Behavioral Context of Perceived Physician Empathy," *Family Practice Journal,* 2, fall 1982, pp. 28–36; Stephen Feldman and Kent Wilson, "The Value of Interpersonal Skills in Lawyering," *Law and Human Behavior,* 5, number 4, pp. 311–22.

104   **terminal markers:** Scheflen, *Body Language,* p. 31.

104   **social networks and shared schemas:** Terence E. Deal and Allan A. Kennedy, *Corporate Cultures* (Reading, Mass.: Addison-Wesley, 1982), p. 86.

104 **managing group process:** Boyatzis, *Competent Manager,* pp. 80, 129.

105 **other groups:** Levinson, *Exceptional Executive,* pp. 69–70.

105 **how to resolve conflicts:** Roger Brown, *Social Psychology: The Second Edition* (New York: Free Press, 1986), p. 620.

106 **a collective hunch:** Lily Tomlin, in Jane Wagner, *The Search for Signs of Intelligent Life in the Universe* (New York: Harper & Row, 1987).

106 **Social constructionists:** Peter Berger and Thomas Luckman, *The Social Construction of Reality* (New York: Doubleday, 1966).

107 **games:** Eric Berne, *Games People Play* (New York: Grove Press, 1964).

107 **Dealing with social processes:** Abe Wagner, *The Transactional Manager* (Englewood Cliffs, N.J.: Prentice-Hall, 1981).

107 **game theory:** John McDonald, *The Game of Business* (New York: Anchor, 1977).

107 **15 percent:** Daniel Yankelovitch, *New Rules* (New York: Random House, 1982), p. xii.

107 **risky shift:** H. Lamm and D. G. Myers, "Group-Induced Polarization of Attitudes and Behavior," in Berkowitz, *Advances.*

108 **How could I have been so stupid:** Kennedy quote, in Theodore Sorensen, *Kennedy* (New York: Bantam, 1966), p. 346.

108 **jurors:** David G. Myers and Morton F. Kaplan, "Group-Induced Polarization in Simulated Juries," *Personality and Social Psychology Bulletin,* 2, 1976, pp. 63–6.

108 **one observer:** Sorensen, *Kennedy,* p. 343.

108 **Social facilitation:** Robert B. Zajonc, "Social Facilitation," *Science,* 149, 269–74.

108 **Social loafing:** Bibb Latané, K. Williams, and S. Harkins, "Many Hands Make Light the Work: The Causes and Consequences of Social Loafing," *The Journal of Personality and Social Psychology,* 37, 1979, pp. 822–32.

109 **groupthink:** Irving Janis, *Groupthink* (Boston: Houghton Mifflin, 1983), pp. 13, 36.

110 **Gentlemen, I take it:** Sloan quote, in Peter F. Drucker, *The Effective Executive* (New York: Harper & Row, 1966), p. 148.

110 **verbal judo:** Suzette Elgin, *The Gentle Art of Verbal Self-Defense* (New York: Dorset, 1980).

111 **real champions of persuasion:** Robert Cialdini, *Influence: Science and Practice* (Glenview, Ill.: Scott, Foresman, 1985), pp. 36–7, 82.

111 **Instructions:** R. A. Whitney, T. Hubin, and J. D. Murphy, *The New Psychology of Persuasion and Motivation in Selling* (Englewood Cliffs, N.J.: Prentice-Hall, 1965), p. 13.

112 **any reason whatsoever:** Ellen Langer, A. Blank, and B. Chanowitz, "The Mindlessness of Ostensibly Thoughtful Action: The Role of 'Placebic' Information in Interpersonal Interaction," *Journal of Personality and Social Psychology,* 36, 1978, pp. 635–42.

113 **Joe Girard:** *Guinness Book of World Records,* in Cialdini, *Influence,* p. 142.

114 **LBJ flew in:** Theodore White, *The Making of the President, 1960* (New York: Pocket Books, 1961), p. 53.

115 **effective defenses:** Cialdini, *Influence,* pp. 88–92, 171.

115   **advancement at AT&T:** Robert E. Beck, "The Liberal Arts Major in Bell System Management" (Washington, D.C.: Association of American Colleges, 1981).

115   **leadership cluster:** Boyatzis, *Competent Manager,* pp. 99–120.

116   **"transforming leadership":** James MacGregor Burns, *Leadership* (New York: Harper & Row, 1978).

116   **charismatic leaders:** David McClelland, *Power: The Inner Experience* (New York: Irvington, 1975), pp. 59–60.

116   **parallelisms:** Elgin, *The Gentle Art,* pp. 212–33.

116   **images of achievement:** Charles Garfield, *Peak Performers: The New Heroes* (New York: Morrow, 1986).

116   **"mobilizing meaning":** Trudy Heller and Jon Van Til, "Leadership: The Management of Meaning," *Journal of Applied Behavioral Science,* 18, 1982, pp. 257–73.

6. Body Intelligence

121   **A moving part:** Wallace Stevens, "Looking Across Fields and Watching the Birds Fly," *The Palm at the End of the Mind: Selected Poems and a Play,* ed. Holly Stevens (New York: Vintage, 1972), p. 380.

121   **body intelligence:** Howard Gardner, *Frames of Mind* (New York: Basic Books, 1983), pp. 205–8.

122   **Reaction times are faster:** Ernest R. Hilgard, *Introduction to Psychology* (New York: Harcourt Brace Jovanovich, 1962), p. 14.

122   **I work with:** Studs Terkel, *Working* (New York: Pantheon, 1974), p. 397.

123   **Those who knew:** Peter Hewitt quote, in Eugene S. Ferguson, "The Mind's Eye: Nonverbal Thought in Technology," *Science,* 197, Aug. 26, 1977, pp. 827–39.

124   **To know what a wave is:** Eleanor Metheny, *Moving and Knowing* (Los Angeles: Peek Publications, 1975), p. 53.

124   **sensorimotor schemes:** Jean Piaget, *The Origins of Intelligence in Children* (New York: International Universities Press, 1952).

125   **brilliant young engineers:** Tracy Kidder, *The Soul of a New Machine* (New York: Avon, 1981), pp. 93, 216.

125   **Steven Jobs and Stephen Wozniak:** Michael Moritz, *The Little Kingdom* (New York: Morrow, 1984).

125   **LOGO:** Seymour Papert, *Mindstorms* (New York: Basic Books, 1980).

125   **relationship between thought and action:** Charles Solley and Gardner Murphy, *Development of the Perceptual World* (New York: Basic Books, 1960), p. 306.

125   **There are languages:** Norman Mailer, in Gardner, *Frames,* p. 207.

125   **The hand designs:** Martin Heidegger, in David Sudnow, *Ways of the Hand* (Cambridge, Mass.: Harvard University Press, 1978), p. ix.

126   **couldn't name common tools:** Gardner, *Frames,* p. 213.

126   **Joey:** Bruno Bettelheim, *The Empty Fortress: Infantile Autism and the Birth of the Self* (New York: Free Press, 1967), pp. 233–39.

127   **H.M.:** Brenda Milner, "Memory and the Medial Temporal Regions of the Brain," in *Biology and Memory,* ed. Karl Pribram and Donald Broadbent (New York: Academic Press, 1970).

127   **two separate factors:** D. K. Brace, "Studies in Motor Learning of Gross Bodily Motor Skills," *Research Quarterly,* 17, 1946, pp. 242–53.

127   **psychomotor skills of pilots:** E. A. Fleishman, *The Structure and Measurement of Physical Fitness* (Englewood Cliffs, N.J.: Prentice-Hall, 1964).

128   **refind analysis:** Joy Paul Guilford, "A System of Psychomotor Abilities," *American Journal of Psychology,* 71, 1958, pp. 164–74.

128   **general sensorimotor ability:** F. M. Henry, "Coordination and Motor Learning," *Annual Proceedings of the College Physical Education Association,* 59, 1956, 68–75.

128   **portraits:** Betty Edwards, *Drawing on the Right Side of the Brain* (Los Angeles: Tarcher, 1979), pp. 11–13.

131   **information-processing approaches:** Paul Fitts, "Perceptual Motor Skill Learning" in *Categories of Human Learning,* ed. Arthur Melton (New York: Academic Press, 1964).

132   **Alex Williams:** Paul Fitts and Michael Posner, *Human Performance* (Monterey, Calif.: Brooks/Cole, 1967), pp. 11–13.

134   **defined feedback as:** Norbert Wiener, *Cybernetics* (New York: Wiley, 1948).

134   **most critical element:** John N. Drowatsky, *Motor Learning* (Minneapolis: Burgess, 1981), pp. 99–101.

135   **knowledge of results (KR):** Matthew Kleinman, *The Acquisition of Motor Skill* (Princeton: Princeton Book Company, 1983), pp. 208–10.

136   **As performance becomes:** Paul Fitts, "Engineering Psychology and Equipment Design," in *Handbook of Experimental Psychology,* ed. S. S. Stevens (New York: Wiley, 1951), pp. 1287–1340.

136   **Proprioceptive feedback can be processed faster:** J. A. Scott Kelso and George E. Stelmach, "Central and Peripheral Mechanisms in Motor Control," in *Motor Control,* ed. George E. Stelmach (New York: Academic Press, 1976), p. 5.

136   **Speed enhances the shift:** ibid., p. 13.

137   **linear control to automatic:** Timothy Gallwey, *Inner Skiing* (New York: Random House, 1977); Timothy Gallwey, *The Inner Game of Tennis* (New York: Random House, 1974).

137   **the shift from visual:** Sudnow, *Ways of the Hand,* p. 12.

137   **Autonomous performance:** Fitts and Posner, *Human Performance,* p. 14.

138   **advanced typists:** Donald Gentner and Donald Norman, "The Typist's Touch," *Psychology Today,* Mar. 1984, pp. 66–72.

139   **a video game:** David Sudnow, *Pilgrim in the Microworld* (New York: Warner, 1983), p. 41.

139   **Chaining:** Robert Gagné, *The Conditions of Learning* (New York: Holt, Rinehart & Winston, 1965), pp. 92–94, 128–31.

140   **As my hands began:** Sudnow, *Ways of the Hand,* p. 9.

140   **TOTE:** George Miller, Eugene Galanter, and Karl Pribram, *Plans and the Structure of Behavior* (New York: Holt, Rinehart & Winston, 1960).

141   **handwired:** Walter Schneider and R. Shiffrin, "Controlled and Automated Human Information Processing I: Detection, Search, and Attention," *Psychological Review,* 84, 1977, pp. 1–66.

142   **half the errors went undetected:** Leonard J. West, *Acquisition of Typing Skills* (New York: Plenum, 1969), pp. 77–85.

142   **debugging philosophy:** Papert, *Mindstorms,* p 114.

142   **almost all losses:** Ralph Norman Habor, "Flight Simulation," *Scientific American,* July 1986, pp. 96–103.

143   **second visual system:** H. Knoche, *"Die Retino-Hypothalamische Bahn von Mensch, Hund, und Kaninchen," Jahrbuch Morphologische Mikroskopische Anatomie,* 63, pp. 461–486.

144   **sensory extension:** Charles Sherrington, *The Integrative Action of the Nervous System* (New York: Scribner, 1906).

144   **seventh sense:** Guy Goodwin, D. I. McCloskey, and P. B. C. Matthews, "Feedback . . ." *Brain,* 95, 1972, pp. 705–48.

145   **Now the computer:** Sudnow, *Pilgrim,* pp. 24–6.

7. Spatial Intelligences

146   **We should talk:** J. O'Neil, *Prodigal Genius: The Life of Nikola Tesla* (Hollywood: Angriff, 1981).

146   **Nikola Tesla:** ibid.

147   **Michael Faraday:** Arthur Koestler, *The Act of Creation* (New York: Dell, 1964).

147   **James Clerk Maxwell:** W. I. Beveridge, *The Art of Scientific Investigation* (New York: Vintage, 1957), p. 76.

147   **one commentator:** Eugene S. Ferguson, "The Mind's Eye: Nonverbal Thought in Technology," *Science,* 197, August 26, 1977, pp. 827– 39.

147   **Einstein's famous thought experiment:** Jacques Hadamard, *The Psychology of Invention in the Mathematical Field* (Princeton: Princeton University Press, 1945).

147   **Kekule's image:** Koestler, *Act of Creation.*

147   **We find that it was imagery:** J. C. Gowan, "Incubation, Imagery, and Creativity," *Journal of Mental Imagery,* 2, spring 1978, p. 26.

147   **scientists:** Anne Roe, "A Psychologist Looks at Sixty-Four Eminent Scientists," in *Creativity,* ed. Phillip Vernon (New York: Penguin, 1975), p. 133; Anne Roe, "A Study of Imagery in Research Scientists, *Journal of Personality,* 19, 1951, pp. 459–70.

148   **In his Visual Thinking:** Rudolf Arnheim, *Visual Thinking* (Berkeley: University of California Press, 1969).

148   **metaphorical thinking:** David Perkins, *The Mind's Best Work* (Cambridge, Mass.: Harvard University Press, 1981); Howard Gardner, *Frames of Mind* (New York: Basic Books, 1983), pp. 190ff.

148   **The pumpoid metaphor:** Donald Schön, *The Reflective Practitioner* (New York: Basic Books, 1983), pp. 184–85.

148   **The spacial problems pilots solve:** E. A. Fleishman and W. E. Hempel, "Factorial Analysis of Complex Psychomotor Performance and Related Skills," *Journal of Applied Psychology,* 40, 1956, pp. 96–104.

150   **Pyramids, cathedrals, and rockets exist:** Ferguson, "Mind's Eye."

150   **styling is still the major factor:** Roger Rowand, "Design Still Powers Buying Decisions," *Advertising Age,* June 16, 1986, pp. S26–27.

150   **schools of engineering:** Robert H. McKim, *Experiences in Visual Thinking* (Monterey, Calif.: Brooks/Cole, 1972); Robert H. McKim,

"Visual Thinking and the Design Process," *Engineering Education,* March 1968, pp. 795–799.

150   **schools of architecture:** Schon, *Reflective Practitioner,* pp. 93ff.

150   **Closed like a fortress:** Arnheim, *Visual Thinking,* pp. 144–46.

151   **eye movements and sketches:** Richard Coss, "Drawing with the Eye," *Leonardo,* 2, 1969, pp. 399–401.

152   **the psychosynthesis approach:** Roberto Assagioli, *Psychosynthesis: A Manual of Principles and Techniques* (New York: Hobbs, Dorman, 1965).

152   **experiential focusing:** Eugene Gendlin, *Focusing* (New York: Everest House, 1978).

152   **cannot find things:** "Executive Waste," *Rocky Mountain News,* July 13, 1986, p. 72.

152   **a mental model:** David E. Kieras and Susan Bovair, "The Role of a Mental Model in Learning to Operate a Device," *Cognitive Science,* 8, 1984, pp. 255–73.

153   **navigators of Puluwat Island:** Thomas Gladwin, *East Is a Big Bird* (Cambridge, Mass.: Harvard University Press, 1970).

153   **Avilik Eskimos:** Edmund Carpenter, *Eskimo Realities* (New York: Holt, Rinehart & Winston, 1973), pp. 10, 31, 40, 134.

154   **hills:** Richard Nelson, *Hunters of the Northern Forest* (Chicago: University of Chicago Press, 1973), pp. 90–91, 156–57.

159   **my study of wolf spacial intelligence:** Roger Peters, *Dance of the Wolves* (New York: McGraw-Hill, 1985).

159   **yet another sense, magnetism:** R. Robin Baker, "Goal Orientation by Blindfolded Humans After Long-Distance Displacement: Possible Involvement of a Magnetic Sense," *Science,* 210, 1980, pp. 555–57.

159   **visual and verbal intelligences are opposed:** Phillip Vernon, *The Structure of Human Abilities* (London: Methuen, 1950).

159   **subjects be penalized:** I. Macfarlane Smith, *Spatial Ability* (San Diego: Knapp, 1964).

160   **idiot savants:** Gardner, *Frames of Mind,* p. 188.

160   **a patient:** Arnheim, *Visual Thinking,* p. 191.

160   **three components:** Lewis Thurstone, "Primary Mental Abilities," *Psychometric Monographs,* 1, 1938.

160   **recent review:** D. F. Lohman, "Spatial Ability: A Review and Reanalysis of the Correlational Literature," Stanford School of Education Technical Report Number 8, 1979.

160   **classic study:** Ralph Norman Haber, "How We Remember What We See," *Scientific American,* May 1970, p. 104.

161   **pattern recall:** Francis Galton, *Inquiries into Human Faculty and Its Development* (London: Dent, 1907).

161   **imagining movement:** Steven E. Poltrock and Polly Brown, "Individual Differences in Visual Imagery and Spatial Ability," *Intelligence,* 8, 1984, 93–138.

162   **spatial tasks:** Smith, *Spatial Ability,* appendixes 11 and 12.

162   **ability to handle such spatial relations:** C. H. Ernest, "Mental Imagery and Cognition," *Journal of Mental Imagery,* 1, 181–216.

162   **spatial relations:** Roger N. Shepard and Lynn A. Cooper, *Mental Im-*

ages and Their Transformations (Cambridge, Mass.: The MIT Press, 1986).

162   **mental rotation tasks:** Roger N. Shepard and Lynn Cooper, "Turning Something Over in the Mind," *Scientific American,* 251, Dec. 1984, pp. 106–14.

163   **Orientation:** Stephen Kosslyn, *Ghosts in the Mind's Machine* (New York: Norton, 1983).

164   **mental maps:** Stephen Kosslyn, T. M. Ball, and B. J. Reiser, "Visual Images Preserve Metric Spatial Information: Evidence from Image Scanning," *Journal of Experimental Psychology: Human Perception and Performance,* 4, 1978, pp. 47–60.

164   **mental maps of cities:** Stephen Kaplan, "Cognitive Maps in Perception and Thought," in *Image and Environment,* ed. Roger M. Downs and David Stea (Chicago: Aldine, 1973), pp. 51–62.

164   **Benjamin Whorf:** quoted in Arnheim, *Visual Thinking,* p. 232.

165   **Words mere currency:** ibid., pp. 233–44.

165   **it is not possible:** ibid., pp. 120–34.

165   **images are part of what the brain does:** Zenon Pylyshyn, "The Imagery Debate: Analogue Media Versus Tacit Knowledge," *Psychological Review,* 87, 1981, pp. 16–45.

167   **urban mental mapping:** Kevin Lynch, *The Image of the City* (Cambridge, Mass.: MIT Press, 1960), p. 4.

167   **everyone can learn to think visually:** Robert Sommer, *The Mind's Eye* (New York: Delacorte, 1978), p. 138.

168   **psych themselves up or down:** L. T. Kozlowski and K. J. Bryant, "Sense of Direction, Spatial Orientation, and Cognitive Maps," *Journal of Experimental Psychology: Human Perception and Performance,* 3, 1977, pp. 590–98.

168   **learn to see better:** Sommer, *Mind's Eye,* p. 8.

169   **Eskimos' uncanny sensitivity:** Nelson, *Hunters,* p. 91.

169   **mental maps of Paris:** Stanley Milgram, "Psychological Maps of Paris," in *Environmental Psychology,* ed. Harold M. Proshansky, William H. Ittleson, and Leanne G. Rivlin (New York: Holt, Rinehart & Winston, 1976).

169   **seeing negative spaces:** Betty Edwards, *Drawing on the Right Side of the Brain* (Los Angeles: Tarcher, 1979).

169   **recentering:** McKim, *Experiences,* chap. 8.

169   **describes this process:** W. J. J. Gordon, *Synectics* (New York: Harper & Row, 1961).

170   **as much of the scenes:** Haber, "How We Remember."

170   **these five elements:** Lynch, *Image,* pp. 49–78.

170   **cabdrivers in Pittsburgh:** William G. Chase, "Spatial Representations of Taxi Drivers," Learning Research and Development Center Technical Report Number 6, (Pittsburgh: University of Pittsburgh Press, 1982), in Linda Flower and John R. Hayes, "Images, Plans, and Prose," *Written Communication,* 1, Jan. 1984, 120–60.

171   **Conceptions of neighborhoods:** Terence Lee, "Psychology and Living Space," in *Image and Environment,* ed. Roger Downs and David Stea (Chicago: Aldine, 1973), pp. 87–108.

171   **opportunities for burglars:** Sommer, *Mind's Eye,* p. 176.

172   **learning to integrate:** Roger M. Downs and David Stea, *Maps in Minds* (New York: Harper & Row, 1977), pp. 225–27.

172   **London and Parisian taxi drivers:** ibid., p. 230.

173   **Flash Maps:** T. Lasker, *New York in Maps* (New York: New York Magazine and Flashmaps, 1972).

173   **the right schema:** Kosslyn, *Ghosts,* pp. 184–86.

173   **organized hierarchically:** Kevin R. Cox and Georgia Zannaras, "Designative Perceptions of Macro-Spaces: Concepts, Methodology, and Applications," in Downs and Stea, *Image and Environment,* pp. 162–78.

174   **expert cabdrivers:** Chase, "Spatial Representations."

174   **cities like San Francisco and Seattle:** J. Porteus, *Environment and Behavior* (Reading: Mass.: Addison–Wesley, 1977).

174   **movement is an essential:** Ulrich Neisser, *Cognition and Reality* (San Francisco: W. H. Freeman, 1976), p. 110.

174   **people who Walk:** T. G. Bower, in Downs and Stea, *Maps in Minds,* p. 236.

175   **relaxation:** McKim, *Experiences,* Chap. 6.

175   **sensory deprivation:** Woodburn Heron, "The Pathology of Boredom," *Scientific American,* Jan. 1957.

175   **chess players:** Francis Galton, *Faculties.*

175   **Bruce Jenner:** Sommer, *Mind's Eye,* pp. 25–26.

175   **Robert McKim:** McKim, *Experiences,* p. 7.

175   **remarkable wooden block:** Richard Hofstadter, *Godel, Escher, Bach* (New York: Basic Books, 1978).

176   **the method of loci:** Kosslyn, *Ghosts,* p. 175.

176   **differences in the kinds of strategies:** Lynn Cooper, "Strategies for Visual Comparison and Representation: Individual Differences," in *Recent Advances in the Psychology of Human Intelligence,* ed. Robert J. Sternberg (Hillsdale, N.J.: Lawrence Erlbaum, 1982), p. 78.

177   **details of apartments:** Kovarsky and Eisenstadt, in John R. Anderson and G. H. Bower, *Human Associative Memory* (Washington, D.C.: Winston and Sons, 1973).

177   **natural clusterings:** Stephen C. Hirtle and Michael Mascolo, "Effect of Semantic Clustering on the Memory of Spatial Locations," *Journal of Experimental Psychology: Human Perception and Performance,* 12, 1986, pp. 182–89.

178   **Paris:** Milgram, "Paris."

178   **Reno or San Diego:** Hirtle and Mascolo, "Semantic Clustering."

178   **downtown shopping center:** Terence Lee, "Brennan's Law of Shopping Behavior," *Psychological Reports,* 11, 1962, p. 662.

179   **It is difficult:** Galton, *Faculties.*

179   **In an experiment:** Edward Sadalla and L. J. Staplin, "The Perception of Traversed Distance," *Environment and Behavior,* 12, 1980, pp. 167–82.

179   **highly legible city:** D. Canter and S. Tagg, "Distance Estimation in Cities," *Environment and Behavior* 7, 1975, pp. 59–80.

179   **Columbus, Ohio:** Reginald Golledge and Georgia Zannaras, "Cognitive Approaches to the Analysis of Human Spatial Behavior," in *Envi-*

ronment and Cognition, ed. W. Ittelson (New York: Seminar Press, 1973), pp. 59–94.

179 **Marxist has taken over:** *Newsweek,* Dec. 14, 1970, in Downs and Stea, *Maps,* p. 142.

180 **genetic primary examples:** Gardner, *Frames,* p. 389.

8. Verbal Intelligence

183 **He gripped more closely:** Wallace Stevens, "The Comedian as the Letter C," *The Palm at the End of the Mind: Selected Poems and a Play,* ed. Holly Stevens (New York: Vintage, 1972), p. 66.

183 **Wallace Stevens:** Milton J. Bates, *Wallace Stevens* (Berkeley: University of California Press, 1985).

183 **The limits of my:** Ludwig Wittgenstein, *Philosophical Investigations* (Oxford: Blackwell, 1954).

183 **Particular verbal abilities:** Earl Hunt, "Verbal Abilities," in *Human Abilities,* ed. Robert J. Sternberg (New York: Freeman, 1985), pp. 31–58.

184 **an average of 309, 750 pages:** Martin Mayer, *The Lawyers* (New York: Dell, 1967), p. 480.

184 **classifying things:** Edward Levi, *Introduction to Legal Reasoning* (Chicago: University of Chicago Press, 1948).

185 **In his classic:** Henry Mintzberg, *The Nature of Mangerial Work* (New York: Harper & Row, 1973), pp. 36–40.

185 **The AT&T Management Progress Study:** Robert E. Beck, "The Liberal Arts Major in Bell System Management" (Washington, D.C.: Association of American Colleges, 1981).

185 **value of verbal skills:** Thomas Peters and Robert Waterman, *In Search of Excellence* (New York: Harper & Row, 1982), pp. 150–52.

185 **Managers must:** Roger Smith, "Business and the Liberal Arts," *Michigan Today,* Dec. 1985, p. 4.

185 **The most important thing:** Lee Iacocca, *Iacocca* (New York: Bantam, 1984), p. 16. Soldiers: Hunt, "Verbal Abilities."

186 **a survey conducted:** Robert J. Sternberg, B. E. Conway, J. L. Ketron, and M. Bernstein, "People's Conceptions of Intelligence," *Journal of Personality and Social Psychology,* 41, 1981, pp. 37–45.

186 **It's hard for me:** Jack Shaw, in "Teaching the Boss to Write," *Management,* July 13, 1981.

186 **All too few:** Roger Smith, "Business and the Liberal Arts."

186 **mokusatsu:** Stuart Chase, *The Power of Words,* in Jagjit Singh, *Great Ideas in Information Theory, Language, and Cybernetics* (New York: Dover, 1966), p. 4.

186 **Remove the pin:** P. C. Wason, in *Cognitive Processes in Writing,* ed. Lee W. Gregg and Erwin R. Steinberg (Hillsdale, N.J.: Lawrence Erlbaum, 1980).

186 **E. A. Locke:** Advertisement (Elmsford, N.Y.: International Paper Company, 1979).

187 **legalism:** A. Z. Carr, *Business As a Game* (New York: New American Library, 1968), p. 167.

187 **an erosion:** Victor A. Bonomo, in Shaw, "Teaching the Boss."

PAGE
188   **Those with PhDs:** Albert Joseph, ibid.
188   **a simple style:** William Zinsser, in Nicholas Ronalds, "Employers Prioritize Utilization of Words to Impact Quality," *Wall Street Journal,* Nov. 6, 1979, p. 28.
188   **Robert Shankland:** ibid.
188   **I just spent:** Joseph Williams, "What Can We Glean from Cognitive Research About Understanding and Teaching Young Writers? A Pragmatic Interpretation," Lecture for Cognitive Strategies and Writing: A Dialogue Across Disciplines, University of Chicago, May 8, 1986.
189   **powerful speech:** Studs Terkel, *Working* (New York: Pantheon, 1974).
190   **millwright:** in D. I. Slobin, *Psycholinguistics* (Glenview, Ill.: Scott, Foresman, 1979), p. 8.
190   **your eyes jump:** Charles A. Perfetti, "Reading Ability," in Sternberg, *Human Abilities,* pp. 31–58.
191   **two of their star pupils:** Don Homa, "An Assessment of Two Extraordinary Speed Readers," *Bulletin of the Psychonomic Society,* 21, 1983, pp. 123–26.
192   **THE FIRST FINE:** P. Dunn-Rankin, "The Visual Characteristics of Words," *Scientific American,* 238, 1978, pp. 122–30.
192   **tip-of-the-tongue:** Roger Brown and David McNeill, "The 'Tip of the Tongue' Phenomenon," *Journal of Verbal Learning and Verbal Behavior,* 5, 1966, pp. 325–37.
192   **good and poor readers:** Perfetti, "Reading Ability."
193   **three ways to build:** Robert J. Sternberg, J. L. Ketron, and J. S. Powell, "Componential Approaches to the Training of Intelligent Performance," in *How and How Much Can Intelligence Be Increased?,* ed. Douglas Detterman and Robert J. Sternberg (Norwood, N.J.: ABLEX, 1982), pp. 155–72.
194   **research on notetaking:** D. L. Peters: in R. E. Snow and P. L. Peterson, "Recognizing Differences in Student Aptitudes," in *New Directions for Teaching and Learning,* No. 2, ed. Wilbert McKeachie (San Francisco: Jossey-Bass, 1980), pp. 12–13, 27–28.
194   **if the balloons:** J. D. Bransford and M. K. Johnson, "Contextual Prerequisites for Understanding: Some Investigations of Comprehension and Recall," *Journal of Verbal Learning and Verbal Behavior,* 61, 1972, pp. 717–26.
195   **a lot about baseball:** H. L. Chiesi, G. J. Spilich, and J. F. Voss, "Acquisition of Domain-Related Information in Relation to High and Low Domain Knowledge," *Journal of Verbal Learning and Verbal Behavior,* 18, 1979, pp. 257–74.
197   **executives at AT&T:** Shaw, "Teaching the Boss."
197   **Pepsico:** Ibid.
197   **James Minor and Reed Dickerson:** Martin Mayer, *The Lawyers* (New York: Dell, 1967), pp. 57–58.
198   **the dangerous method:** Peter Elbow, *Writing with Power* (New York: Oxford University Press, 1981).
198   **A study at IBM:** J. D. Gould, "Experiments on Composing Letters: Some Facts, Some Myths, and Some Observations," in Gregg and Steinberg, *Cognitive Processes;* J. D. Gould, "Writing and Speaking

Letters and Messages," *IBM Research Report,* RC-7528, in Michael Eysenck, *A Handbook of Cognitive Psychology* (Hillsdale, N.J.: Lawrence Erlbaum, 1984), p. 226.

199   **the form of a tree:** Linda Flower, *Problem-Solving Strategies for Writing* (New York: Harcourt Brace Jovanovich, 1981).

200   **Plunge right in:** Malcom Forbes, "How to Write a Business Letter," advertisement (Elmsford, N.Y.: International Paper Company, 1983).

200   **It is important:** Allan Collins and Diedre Gentner, "A Framework for a Cognitive Theory of Writing," in Gregg and Steinberg, *Cognitive Processes.*

200   **Write the way:** Forbes, "Business Letter."

200   **Speech is five to six times faster:** M. F. Garrett, "Syntactic Processes in Sentence Production," in *New Approaches to Language Mechanisms,* ed. R. J. Wales and E. Walker (Amsterdam: Elsevier, 1976); Michael Motley, "Slips of the Tongue," *Scientific American,* 253, Sept. 1985, pp. 116–27.

200   **freewriting:** Elbow, *Writing with Power,* pp. 50–75.

201   **the 320 words:** "How to Polish Your Writing," *Business Week,* July 6, 1981, pp. 106–10.

202   **reader-based prose:** Flower, *Problem-Solving Strategies,* pp. 144–64.

203   **Fog Index:** Robert Gunning, *The Technique of Clear Writing,* in "How to Polish Your Writing."

204   **clarity and brevity:** William Strunk, Jr. and E. B. White, *The Elements of Style* (New York: Macmillan, 1972), pp. 17–18.

204   **Write so he'll:** Forbes, "Business Letter."

204   **CEO:** Harold Geneen, *Managing* (New York: Doubleday, 1984), p. 272.

205   **I'm me:** Elbow, *Writing with Power,* p. 344.

205   **contrasts two versions:** George Orwell, "Politics and the English Language," in *Shooting an Elephant and Other Essays* (New York: Harcourt, 1950).

206   **People made some:** Verna Noel Jones, "The Voice of Success," *Rocky Mountain News,* Sept. 20, 1985, p. 90.

206   **Let themselves feel:** Elbow, *Writing with Power,* p. 182.

208   **the cultural network:** Terence Deal and Allan Kennedy, *Corporate Cultures* (Reading, Mass.: Addison-Wesley, 1982), p. 86.

208   **in the form of a tree:** Ruth Day, "Teaching from Notes: Some Cognitive Consequences," in McKeachie, *New Directions.*

9. Logical-Mathematical Intelligence

210   **Think 'til it hurts:** Lord Thomson, in Robin Hogarth, *Judgment and Choice* (New York: Wiley, 1980), p. 62.

210   **(LMI):** Howard Gardner, *Frames of Mind* (New York: Basic Books, 1983), pp. 128–62.

210   **Carl Gauss:** Eric Temple Bell, "Gauss, the Prince of Mathematicians," in *The World of Mathematics,* ed. James R. Newman (New York: Simon & Schuster, 1956).

211   **actuarial techniques:** Lorne C. Plunkett and Guy A. Hale, *The Proactive Manager* (New York: Wiley, 1982).

PAGE
211   The statistical analysis: R. M. Dawes, "Shallow Psychology," in *Cognition and Social Behavior,* ed. J. S. Carroll and J. W. Payne (Hillsdale, N.J.: Lawrence Erlbaum, 1976).

211   bootstrapping: L. R. Goldberg, "Man Versus Model of Man: A Rationale, Plus Some Evidence, For a Method of Improving on Clinical Inferences" *Psychological Bulletin,* 73, 1970, pp. 422–32.

211   exceeded the accuracy: Lee S. Shulman and Arthur S. Elstein, "Studies of Problem-Solving, Judgment, and Decision Making," *Review of Research in Education,* 1975.

212   what we see: Harry Levinson and Stuart Rosenthal, *CEO: Corporate Leadership in Action* (New York: Basic Books, 1984), pp. 23, 70.

213   Dr. Carl Coppolino: F. Lee Bailey, *The Defense Never Rests* (New York: Stein and Day, 1971), pp. 201–22.

213   one of the world's experts: Martin Mayer, *The Lawyers* (New York: Dell, 1967), p. 42.

213   A [a case] falls: Edward Levi, *Introduction to Legal Reasoning* (Chicago: University of Chicago Press, 1948).

214   The drudgery of the numbers: Harold Geneen, *Managing* (New York: Doubleday, 1984), p. 181.

214   advancement in AT&T: Robert E. Beck, "The Liberal Arts Major in Bell System Management" (Washington, D.C.: Association of American Colleges, 1981).

218   identifies the most: George Klemp, "Cognitive Abilities and Performance in the World of Work: Field Research and Implications for the Academy," Lecture presented at Cognitive Frameworks and Higher-Order Reasoning, University of Chicago, Nov. 17, 1985.

218   Tom Watson: Levinson and Rosenthal, *CEO,* pp. 180–83.
219   proactivity: Boyatzis, *Manager,* pp. 71, 77–78.
219   Mental models: P. N. Johnson-Laird, *Mental Models* (Cambridge: Cambridge University Press, 1983).

220   Doctors' mental models: Paul E. Johnson, Alicia S. Duran, Frank Hassebrock, James Moller, Michael Prietula, Paul Feltovich, and David Swanson, "Expertise and Error in Diagnostic Reasoning," *Cognitive Science,* 5, 1981, pp. 235–83.

220   models of kidney disease: Benjamin Kuipers and Jerome Kassirer, "Causal Reasoning in Medicine: Analysis of a Protocol," *Cognitive Science,* 8, 1984, pp. 363–85.

220   In both studies: Dennis Egan and B. J. Schwartz, "Chunking in Recall of Symbolic Drawings," *Memory and Cognition,* 7, pp. 149–58; O. Akin, *Models of Architectural Knowledge* (London: Pion, 1980).

220   gasoline shortage: *Time,* Dec. 10, 1973, pp. 49–50, in Irving L. Janis and Leon Mann, *Decision Making* (New York: Free Press, 1977), p. 108.

220   often requires inhibiting: L. L. Thurstone in "Intelligence and Its Measurement: A Symposium," *Journal of Educational Psychology,* 12, 1921, pp. 123–275.

221   competence model: Klemp, "Cognitive Abilities."
221   proactivity: Boyatzis, *Competent Manager,* pp. 71–73.

221 **a major breakthrough:** Paul Cutler, *Problem Solving in Clinical Medicine* (Baltimore: Williams and Wilkins, 1985), p. xxvi.

221 **tab item:** Shulman and Elstein, "Problem Solving," p. 13.

222 **recognizing patterns:** Boyatzis, *Competent Manager*, pp. 80–81; Klemp, "Cognitive Abilities."

222 **Rolex is not:** Mark McCormack, *What They Don't Teach You at Harvard Business School* (New York: Bantam, 1984), p. 113.

222 **expert cardiologists':** Johnson, "Expertise and Error."

223 **ability to choose:** Micheline T. H. Chi and Robert Glaser, "Problem-Solving Ability," in *Human Abilities*, ed. Robert J. Sternberg (New York: Freeman, 1985), pp. 227–49.

223 **tentative diagnoses:** Arthur Elstein, in Shulman and Elstein, "Problem Solving," pp. 5, 9; Arthur Elstein, L. S. Shulman, and S. A. Sprafka, *Medical Problem Solving* (Cambridge, Mass.: Harvard University Press).

223 **each X-ray:** Kuipers and Kassirer, "Causal Reasoning."

223 **computer programmers:** E. Soloway, K. Ehrlich, J. Bonar, and J. Greenspan, "What Do Novices Know About Programming?," in *Directions in Human-Computer Interactions*, ed. A. Badre and B. Shneiderman (Norwood, N.J.: Ablex, 1982), pp. 27–54.

223 **large functional units:** Jill Larkin, J. McDermott, D. P. Simon, and H. A. Simon, "Models of Competence in Solving Physics Problems," *Cognitive Science*, 4, 1980, pp. 317–45.

223 **chess:** William Chase and Herbert A. Simon, "Perception in Chess," *Cognitive Psychology*, 4, 1973, pp. 55–81.

224 **technical knowledge:** Robert Glaser, "The Role of Knowledge," *American Psychologist*, 39, 1984, pp. 93–104.

224 **Edwin Land:** in G. I. Nierenberg, *The Art of Creative Thinking* (New York: Simon & Schuster, 1982).

224 **Using the wrong model:** Johnson-Laird: *Mental Models.*

224 **concrete procedural models:** E. Soloway, J. Lockhead, and J. Clement, "Does Computer Programming Enhance Problem Solving Ability?," in *Computer Literacy*, ed. R. J. Seidel, R. E. Anderson, and B. Hunter (New York: Academic Press, 1982).

224 **the following experiment:** Vernon Hall and Richard Kingsley, "Conservation and Equilibration Theory," *Journal of Genetic Psychology*, 113, 1968, pp. 195–213.

225 **similar conclusions:** R. De Lisi and J. Staudt, "Individual Differences in College Students' Performance on Formal Operations Tasks," *Journal of Applied Developmental Psychology*, 1, 1980, pp. 201–8.

225 **the estimation:** Hogarth, *Judgment and Choice*, pp. 80–81.

226 **instantiating it:** Johnson-Laird, *Mental Models.*

227 **draft lottery:** Persi Diaconis, in Gina Kolata, "What Does It Mean to Be Random?," *Science*, 231, Mar. 7, 1986, pp. 1068–69.

227 **unfolding test:** Hogarth, *Judgment and Choice*, pp. 23–24.

227 **at a flight school:** Daniel Kahneman and Amos Tversky, "On the Psychology of Prediction," *Psychological Review*, 80, 1973, pp. 237–51.

228 **spurious correlations:** J. Smedslund, "The Concept of Correlation in Adults," *Scandinavian Journal of Psychology*, 4, 1963, pp. 165–73.

228   **superstitious behaviors:** B. F. Skinner, " 'Superstition' in the Pigeon," *Journal of Experimental Psychology,* 38, 1948, pp. 168–72.

228   **you've got four cards:** P. C. Wason and P. N. Johnson-Laird, *Psychology of Reasoning: Structure and Content* (Cambridge, Mass.: Harvard University Press, 1972).

229   **buy a Volvo:** Richard Nisbett, E. Borgida, R. Crandall, and H. Reed, "Popular Induction: Information Is Not Necessarily Informative," in *Cognition and Social Behavior,* ed. J. S. Carroll and J. W. Payne (Hillsdale, N. J.: Lawrence Erlbaum, 1976).

229   **risky operations:** D. E. Detmer, D. G. Fryback, and K. Gassner, "Heuristics and Biases in Medical Decision-Making," *Journal of Medical Education,* 53, 1978, pp. 682–83.

229   **The "Doctors were guessing":** Scott Crowley, *Zodiac News,* Mar. 31, 1986 (radio broadcast).

229   **Bayes' theorem:** Hogarth, *Judgment and Choice,* p. 38; Amos Tversky, in Howard Gardner, *The Mind's New Science* (New York: Basic Books, 1985), p. 360.

230   **Rashomon of problem settings:** Donald Schön, *The Reflective Practitioner* (New York: Basic Books, 1983), pp. 191–95.

230   **Andrew Carnegie's model:** Edward F. Konczal, "Models Are for Managers, Not Mathematicians," *Journal of Systems Management,* Jan. 1975, pp. 12–15.

230   **mathematical model:** Russell Ackoff, "Management Misinformation Systems," *Management Science,* Dec. 1967, pp. B147–56.

230   **Managers are beginning:** Robert Hayes and Richard Nolan, "What Kind of Corporate Modeling Functions Best?," *Harvard Business Review,* May–June 1974, pp. 102–112.

233   **Optimizing:** Janis and Mann, *Decision Making,* p. 11.

233   **Benjamin Franklin:** *The Complete Works of Benjamin Franklin,* vol. 4, ed. J. Bigelow (New York: Putnam, 1887), p. 522.

234   **diet clinic:** Mary Ellen Colten and Irving L. Janis, "Effects of Self-Disclosure and the Decisional Balance Sheet Procedure in a Weight Reduction Clinic," in *Counseling on Personal Decisions: Theory and Field Research on Helping Relationships* (New Haven: Yale University Press, 1978).

234   **Elstein's rule:** Elstein, Shulman, and Sprafka, *Medical Problem Solving;* Larkin, McDermott, Sion, and Simon, "Models of Competence."

235   **mixed strategy:** Amitai Etzioni, *The Active Society* (New York: Free Press, 1968), pp. 282–309.

235   **There are two kinds:** Robert Townsend, *Up the Organization* (New York: Knopf, 1970), p. 45.

236   **top-down approach:** Kenichi Ohmae, *The Mind of the Strategist* (New York: Penguin, 1983), pp. 28–31.

237   **The chicken is involved:** Bruce Babbit quote, Keynote address, Conference on Microcomputers in Education, Arizona State University, Tempe, Mar. 1984.

238   **Psychodrama:** Janis and Mann, *Decision Making,* pp. 379–88.

238   **not automatically acquired:** Richard Wagner and Robert Sternberg, "Practical Intelligence in Real-World Pursuits: The Role of Tacit

Knowledge," *Journal of Personality and Social Psychology*, 49, 1985, pp. 436–58.

238   **Cogwheel Experiment:** Schön, *Reflective Practitioner*, pp. 191–95.

239   **data-logic-data-logic approach:** Cutler, *Problem Solving*, p. xxii.

10. Critical Thinking

241   **One horse-laugh:** H. L. Mencken, in Martin Gardner, *Science, Good, Bad and Bogus* (New York: Avon, 1981), p. vii.

241   **Bernard Baruch:** Charles Mackay, *Extraordinary Popular Delusions* (New York: L. C. Page, 1932), pp. xiii–xv.

241   **Csicopps:** "People Will Believe Anything, Which Is Why Csicopps Exist," *Wall Street Journal*, July 19, 1985, p. 1.

242   **reflective thought:** John Dewey, *How We Think* (Washington, D.C.: Heath, 1933), p. 9.

242   **taught me analytical approaches:** Harold Geneen, *Managing* (New York: Doubleday, 1984), p. 63.

243   **is at a disadvantage:** A. Z. Carr, *Business As a Game* (New York: New American Library, 1968), p. 161.

243   **demands for conformity:** J. E. Harrison, in *Wall Street Journal*, Nov. 9, 1964, in Carr, ibid., p. 155.

243   **subversives:** Robert Townsend, *Up the Organization* (New York: Knopf, 1970).

243   **Watergate:** Carl Bernstein and Robert Woodward, *All the President's Men* (New York: Simon & Schuster, 1973).

244   **meaning over money:** Studs Terkel, *Working* (New York: Pantheon, 1974).

244   **Their values:** A. Brown and E. Weiner, *Supermanaging* (New York: McGraw-Hill, 1984), pp. 68–72.

244   **critical thinking as graduation requirements:** G. S. Dumke, "Executive Order No. 338," The California State University and Colleges, Nov. 1, 1980.

244   **The biggest problem:** David Benson, "Welcome," (Lecture) The Third International Conference on Critical Thinking and Educational Reform, Sonoma State University, July 20, 1985.

244   **Practice without theory:** Richard Paul, "Critical Thinking: The State of the Field," (Lecture), Ibid.

244   **human infrastructure:** Albert Shanker, "Critical Thinking and Educational Reform," (Lecture), Ibid.

245   **to reason about real-world proposal:** David Perkins, "Real World Reasoning and How It Grows" (Lecture), Ibid.

245   **by teaching logic:** Edward Glaser, "The Watson-Glaser Critical Thinking Appraisal," (Lecture), Ibid.

245   **measure of critical thinking ability:** Watson-Glaser Critical Thinking Appraisal (New York: The Psychological Corporation).

247   **Dr. Fox effect:** D. H. Naftulin, J. E. Ware, and F. A. Donnelly, "The Doctor Fox Lecture: A Paradigm of Educational Seduction," *Journal of Medical Education*, 48, 1973, pp. 630–35.

247   **as if they had none to help:** Learned Hand, "Historical and Practical Considerations Regarding Expert Testimony," in *Selected Writings on*

the Law of Evidence and Trial, ed. W. Fryer (St. Paul, Minn.: West
Publishing Co., 1957).

247   (NGBRI): Lincoln Caplan, "The Insanity Defense," *The New Yorker*,
July 2, 1984, pp. 45–78.

248   good guys: Geneen, *Managing*, p. 274.

248   Deep Throat: Bernstein and Woodward, *All the President's Men*, p.
137.

248   outrage: ibid., p. 134.

248   sources: ibid., p. 81.

248   Hugh Sloan: ibid., p. 99.

248   provoked Deep Throat: ibid., p. 141.

248   angered a college student: ibid., pp. 290–92.

250   The only impartiality possible: Lord Hewart, in Martin Mayer, *The
Lawyers* (New York: Dell, 1967), p. 464.

250   The ideas: Edward Levi, *Introduction to Legal Reasoning* (Chicago:
University of Chicago Press, 1948).

251   they were aware of: Bernstein and Woodward, *All the President's Men*,
pp. 203, 217–18.

252   Kissinger's use: ibid., pp. 345–46.

252   Nixon's denial: ibid., p. 59.

253   scientific language insists: Edward Cleary, "Evidence As a Problem in
Communicating," in Fryer, *Selected Writings*.

253   Hinckley jurors' confusion: Caplan, "Insanity Defense."

254   Harold Geneen: *Managing*, p. 9.

254   Uri Geller: Andrew Weil, in James Randi, *The Magic of Uri Geller*
(New York: Ballantine, 1975).

254   biorhythm theory: J. H. Wolcott, R. R. McMeekin, R. E. Burgin, and R.
E. Yanowitch, "Correlation of General Aviation Accidents with the
Biorhythm Theory," *Human Factors*, 19, 1977, pp. 283–93.

255   In the realm: Cleary, "Evidence."

255   Hinckley trial: Caplan, "Insanity Defense."

255   Hard evidence: Bernstein and Woodward," *All the President's Men*, p.
90.

256   the bell-shaped curve: Darrell Huff, *How to Lie with Statistics* (New
York: Norton, 1954).

256   subliminal advertising: Wilson Brian Key, *Subliminal Seduction* (New
York: New American Library, 1974).

257   Backward logic: George Carlin, *Toledo Window Box* (phonograph record) (New York: Little David, 1974).

257   Logical fallacies: Perkins, "Real World Reasoning." Daniel Kahneman,
P. Slovic, and Amos Tversky, *Judgment Under Uncertainty: Heuristics
and Biases* (New York: Cambridge University Press, 1982); Janis and
Mann, *Decision Making*.

257   Sherlock Holmes: Arthur Conan Doyle, *The Complete Sherlock
Holmes* (New York: Doubleday, 1927).

258   a dog fight: "Evidence."

258   The law: Levi, *Legal Reasoning*.

258   scientific and legal logics: Bernstein and Woodward, *All the President's
Men*, pp. 16, 90, 150.

PAGE
259   **the further conclusions:** Dewey, *How We Think,* p. 23.
260   **inherent superiority of capitalism:** Bernard O'Keefe, *Shooting Ourselves in the Foot* (Boston: Houghton Mifflin, 1985).
260   **The implications for John Hinckley:** Caplan, "Insanity Defense."
261   **situation models:** Perkins, "Real World Reasoning."
261   **Watergate:** Bernstein and Woodward, *All the President's Men.*
262   **reasonable chicken:** Cleary, "Evidence."

11. Cognitive Styles

265   **Much I owe:** Rudyard Kipling, "The Two-Sided Man," *Rudyard Kipling's Verse* (London: Hodder and Stoughton, 1927).
265   **a particular type:** Nathan Kogan, in *Moderators of Competence,* ed. Edith D. Neimark, Richard De Lisi, and Judith L. Newman (Hillsdale, N.J.: Lawrence Erlbaum, 1985).
266   **Cognitive styles are organized:** Anita Woolfolk and Lorraine McCune-Nicolich, *Educational Psychology for Teachers* (Englewood Cliffs, N.J.: Prentice-Hall, 1984), pp. 148–50.
266   **left–right distinction useful:** Henry Mintzberg, "Planning on the Left Side and Managing on the Right," *Harvard Business Review,* July–Aug. 1986, pp. 49–50.
266   **contrasts these two modes:** Patrick Nugent, "Management and Modes of Thought," *Organizational Dynamics,* spring 1981, pp. 45–59.
267   **Archilocus:** Isaiah Berlin, *The Hedgehog and the Fox: An Essay on Tolstoy's Theory of History* (New York: Mentor, 1957).
267   **can think about a thing:** Thomas Reed Powell, in A. Yarmolinsky, "The Core of Professional Education," in *What Is an Educated Person?,* ed. M. Kaplan (New York: Praeger, 1980).
268   **synthesize isolated bits:** Daniel Isenberg, "How Senior Managers Think," *Harvard Business Review,* 84, Nov.–Dec. 1984, pp. 81–90.
268   **field dependent:** Hermann Witkin, C. A. Moore, D. R. Goodenough, and R. W. Cox, "Field Dependent and Field Independent Cognitive Styles," *Review of Educational Research,* 47, 1977, pp. 1–64.
268   **the Vietnam war:** David Halberstam, *The Best and the Brightest* (New York: Random House, 1972).
269   **where social context matters:** T. J. Shuell, "Dimensions of Individual Differences," in *Psychology and Education: The State of the Union,* ed. F. H. Farley and N. J. Gordon (Berkeley: McCutchan, 1981).
269   **analytic style prefer:** P. R. Clar, "The Relationship of Psychological Differentiation to Client Behavior in Vocational Choice Counseling," Doctoral dissertation, University of Michigan, *Dissertation Abstracts International,* 32, 1971.
269   **management information systems:** M. A. Vasarhelyi, "Man-Machine Planning Systems: a Cognitive Style Examination of Interactive Decision Making," *Journal of Accounting Research,* 15, 1977, pp. 138–53.
271   **intuition:** L. Edson, "Intuition," *Across the Board,* June 1982.
271   **you just know:** Lee Iacocca, *Iacocca* (New York: Bantam, 1984).
271   **managing career:** Richard Wagner and Robert Sternberg, "Practical Intelligence in Real-World Pursuits: The Role of Tacit Knowledge," *Journal of Personality and Social Psychology,* 49, 1985, 436–58.

271   **why executives fail:** Morgan W. McCall and Michael M. Lombardo, "What Makes a Top Executive?," *Psychology Today*, Feb. 1983, pp. 26–31.

272   **tests of cognitive style:** Malcolm R. Westcott, *Toward a Contemporary Psychology of Intuition* (New York: Holt, Rinehart & Winston, 1968).

273   **evaluating information:** James McKenney and Peter Keen, "How Managers' Minds Work," *Harvard Business Review*, May–June 1974, pp. 79–90.

274   **twelve executives:** Isenberg, "Senior Managers."

274   **Intuitive extroverts:** Carl G. Jung, *Psychological Types* (New York: Harcourt Brace Jovanovich, 1923).

275   **other heuristics:** Herbert A. Simon, *Administrative Behavior* (New York: Free Press, 1957).

275   **For most problems:** Paul Samuelson, in Neil McK. Agnew and John L. Brown, "From Skyhooks to Walking Sticks: On the Road to Nonrational Decision Making," *Organizational Dynamics*, autumn 1982, pp. 40–58.

275   **When a physician:** Paul Cutler, *Problem Solving in Clinical Medicine* (Baltimore: Williams and Wilkins, 1985), p. 60.

275   **does and should decide:** Joseph Hutcheson, "The Judgment Intuitive: The Function of the Hunch in Judicial Decisions," *14 Cornell Law Quarterly*, 274, p. 287.

275   **intuition as a very logical:** Weston Agor, *Intuitive Management* (Englewood Cliffs, N.J.: Prentice-Hall, 1984).

275   **not the opposite:** Isenberg, "Senior Managers."

275   **The intuitive mode:** James McKenney, in David W. Ewing, "Discovering Your Problem-Solving Style," *Psychology Today*, Dec. 1979, pp. 69–73, 138.

276   **The development of expertise:** Hubert Dreyfus and Stuart Dreyfus, *Mind over Machine* (New York: Free Press, 1986).

276   **Individuals who have:** Jerome Bruner quote, in E. Raudsepp, "Can You Trust Your Hunches?," *Administrative Management*, Oct. 1981, pp. 34–49.

276   **object to be identified:** Wescott, *Psychology of Intuition.*

276   **automation:** Robert McKim, *Experiences in Visual Thinking* (Monterey, Calif.: Brooks/Cole, 1972).

277   **verbal and logical modes:** Robert Sternberg, *Intelligence Applied* (New York: Harcourt Brace Jovanovich, 1986); Suzette Elgin, *The Gentle Art of Verbal Self-Defense* (New York: Dorsett, 1980).

277   **match our levels of intuition to our jobs:** McKenney and Keen, "Managers' Minds."

277   **The opposite of active is reflective:** Jerome Kagan, *Developmental Studies of Reflection and Analysis* (Cambridge, Mass.: Harvard University Press, 1964); S. B. Messer, "Reflection-Impulsivity: A Review," *Psychological Bulletin*, 83, 1976, pp. 1026–52.

278   **equate speed of thinking:** Robert Sternberg, *Beyond IQ* (New York: Cambridge University Press, 1985), p. 301.

278   **amount of information:** Westcott, *Psychology of Intuition.*

278   **spent less time:** McKenney and Keen, "Managers' Minds."

278   **live action:** Henry Mintzberg, *The Nature of Managerial Work* (New York: Harper & Row, 1973).

279   **"efficiency orientation":** Richard Boyatzis, *The Competent Manager* (New York: Wiley, 1982).

279   **H. Ross Perot:** Eric Gelman, Richard Manning, Daniel Pedersen, and Nikki Finke Greenberg, "Wheels of the Future," *Newsweek,* June 17, 1985, pp. 64–71.

279   **bias for action:** Thomas Peters and Robert Waterman, *In Search of Excellence,* (New York: Harper & Row, 1982).

280   **process of thinking:** Isenberg quote, "Senior Managers."

280   **epistemological function:** George Gilder, *The Spirit of Enterprise* (New York: Simon & Schuster, 1984).

280   **Harding Lawrence's dramatic expansion:** John Nance, *Splash of Colors* (New York: Morrow, 1984).

281   **cognitive complexity:** Siegfried Streufert, "The Stress of Excellence," *Across the Board,* 20, Number 9, 1983, pp. 8–16; Harold M. Schroder, Michael J. Driver, and Siegfried Steufert, *Human Information Processing* (New York: Holt, Rinehart & Winston, 1967), pp. 57–58; Siegfried Streufert, *Behavior in the Complex Environment* (New York: John Wiley and Victor Winston, 1978).

283   **"perceptual objectivity":** Boyatzis, *Competent Manager,* p. 165.

283   **thirst for current information:** Mintzberg, *Managerial Work,* p. 36.

283   **Plato's description:** Plato, *Theaetetus,* in *The Dialogues of Plato, Volume II,* trans. Benjamin Jowett (London: Oxford University Press, 1871), p. 177.

284   **appear less decisive:** Streufert, "Stress of Excellence."

284   **much work:** Mintzberg, *Managerial Work,* p. 29.

284   **fluidity:** Peters and Waterman, *Excellence,* pp. 121–25.

284   **how physicians interview:** Janet Gale, "Some Cognitive Components of the Diagnostic Thinking Process," *British Journal of Educational Psychology,* 52, 1982, pp. 64–76.

284   **effective teachers:** Carol Schneider, George Klemp, and Susan Kastendiek, *The Balancing Act: Competencies of Effective Teachers and Mentors in Degree Programs for Adults* (Center for Continuing Education, University of Chicago, 1981).

285   **Inflexibility:** McCall and Lombardo, "Top Executive."

285   **long-range planning:** Geneen, *Managing,* p. 47.

285   **In making:** Isenberg, "Senior Managers."

285   **plan long into the future:** Streufert, "Stress of Excellence."

285   **Konosuke Matsushita:** Walter Kiechel III, "How Executives Think," *Fortune,* Feb. 4, 1985, pp. 127–28.

285   **Elliott Jacques:** ibid.

286   **Approximately two-thirds:** Isenberg, "Senior Managers."

286   **U-curve hypothesis:** Schroder, Driver, and Streufert, *Information Processing,* pp. 59–61.

287   **can be enhanced:** ibid., pp. 50, 123; Streufert, "Stress of Excellence."

287   **Complexity can be developed:** O. J. Harvey, D. E. Hunt, and H. M. Schroder, *Conceptual Systems and Personality Organization* (New York: Wiley, 1961); William Perry, "Cognitive and Ethical Growth," in

The Modern American College, ed. A. Chickering (San Francisco: Jossey-Bass, 1981).

288   **abstraction ladder of semanticist:** S. I. Hayakawa: McKim, *Visual Thinking,* p. 128.

288   **optimal environments:** Peters and Waterman, *Excellence,* pp. 121–25.

288   **match systems to their styles:** Larry Corman, "Cognitive Style Research and Information Systems: The Current Status," Unpublished manuscript, Department of Business Computer Information Systems, North Texas State University, 1986.

288   **mixed groups were more effective:** K. B. White, "MIS Project Teams: An Investigation of Cognitive Style Implications," *MIS Quarterly,* June 1984, pp. 95–101; McKenney and Keen, "Managers' Minds."

288   **Let styles alternate:** Nugent, "Modes of Thought."

12. Practical Creation

290   **Imagination rules:** Napoleon Bonaparte, in Robin Hogarth, *Judgment and Choice* (New York: Wiley, 1980), p. 126.

290   **"effective surprise":** Jerome Bruner, *On Knowing: Essays for the Left Hand* (Cambridge, Mass.: Harvard University Press, 1962).

290   **The Apple II:** Michael Moritz, *The Little Kingdom* (New York: Morrow, 1984).

291   **"creative imagination":** A. Z. Carr, *Business As a Game* (New York: New American Library, 1968), p. 102.

291   **air force captains:** F. Barron, "Originality in Relation to Personality and Intellect," *Journal of Personality,* 25, 1957, pp. 730–42.

291   **saleswomen:** H. R. Wallace, "Creative Thinking: A Factor in Sales Productivity," *Vocational Guidance Quarterly,* 9, 1961, pp. 223–26.

291   **government administrators:** G. A. Forehand and W. L. Libby, Jr., "Effects of Educational Programs and Perceived Organizational Climate upon Changes in Innovative Administrative Behavior," in *Innovative Behavior* (Chicago: University of Chicago Center for Programs in Government Administration, 1962).

291   **advertising and public relations:** J. M. Elliott, "Measuring Creative Abilities in Public Relations and Advertising Work," in *Widening Horizons in Creativity,* ed. W. Taylor (New York: Wiley, 1964).

291   **Peter Principle:** Lawrence Peter and Raymond Hull, *The Peter Principle* (New York: Morrow, 1969). David Ogilvy quote; *Confessions of an Advertising Man* (New York: Atheneum, 1963).

291   **John Dryden:** "Absalom and Achitophel," in Parker E. Lichtenstein, "Genius as Productive Neurosis," *The Psychological Record,* 21, 1971, pp. 151–64.

291   **Albert Einstein's line:** in Arthur Koestler, *The Act of Creation* (New York: Macmillan, 1964), p. 146.

291   **combination of ingredients:** David Perkins, *The Mind's Best Work* (Cambridge, Mass.: Harvard University Press, 1981).

291   **given even:** Hogarth, *Judgment and Choice,* p. 111.

292   **divergent production:** Joy Paul Guilford, *The Nature of Human Intelligence* (New York: McGraw-Hill, 1967), pp. 138–70.

293   **not strongly related to real-world creativity:** Nathan Kogan and E.

Pankove, "Long-Term Predictive Validity of Divergent Thinking Tests: Some Negative Evidence," *Journal of Educational Psychology*, 66, 1974, pp. 802–10.

293 **have relied on IQ:** Guilford, *Nature of Human Intelligence*, pp. 166–69; Michael Wallach, "Tests Tell Us Little About Talent," *American Scientist*, 64, 1976, pp. 57–63.

293 **threshold:** Barron, "Originality."

294 **Creative work in practical realms:** John Horn, "Trends in the Measurement of Intelligence," in *Human Intelligence: Perspectives on Its Theory and Measurement*, ed. Robert J. Sternberg and Douglas K. Detterman (Norwood, N.J.: Ablex, 1979).

294 **multiple intelligences:** Howard Gardner, *Frames of Mind* (New York: Basic Books, 1983).

294 **any normal person:** Perkins, *Mind's Best Work*, p. 287.

295 **networks of enterprise:** Howard E. Gruber, *Darwin on Man: A Psychological Study of Scientific Creativity* (New York: Dutton, 1974).

296 **AC Spark Plug Company:** J. E. Arnold, "Education for Innovation," in *A Source Book for Creative Thinking*, ed. S. J. Parnes and H. F. Harding (New York: Scribner, 1962).

296 **Henri Poincaré:** *The Psychology of Invention in the Mathematical Field*, ed. Jacques Hadamard (Princeton: Princeton University Press, 1945), pp. 45–47.

297 **brainstorming:** Alex F. Osborn, *Applied Imagination* (New York: Scribners, 1963).

297 **lateral thinking:** Edward DeBono, *Lateral Thinking* (New York: Harper & Row, 1970).

298 **The test of a first-rate:** F. Scott Fitzgerald, "The Crack-Up," in *American Literary Masters*, vol. 2, ed. Charles R. Anderson (New York: Holt, Rinehart & Winston, 1965), p. 1007.

298 **one evening:** Poincaré, in Hadamard, *Psychology of Invention*, pp. 45–47. Ramon Lull: Martin Gardner, *Science: Good, Bad, and Bogus* (New York: Avon, 1981), pp. 27–51.

299 **morphological analysis:** Fritz Zwicky, *Morphological Analysis* (Berlin: Springer, 1957).

299 **the K-J method:** Kawakita Jiro: T. Hoshino and J. H. McPherson, *The K. J. Method of Creative Problem Solving* (Menlo Park: Stanford Research Institute).

299 **morphological forced analysis:** Don Koberg and Jim Bagnall, *The Universal Traveler, A Soft-Systems Guidebook to: Creativity, Problem-solving and the Process of Design* (Los Altos, Calif.: William Kaufmann, 1974).

300 **structure of intellect model:** Guilford, *Intelligence*, p. 340.

300 **products of the kind:** Perkins, *Best Work*, p. 4.

300 **Anyone could make:** Poincaré quote, Hadamard, *Psychology of Invention*, pp. 45–47.

300 **the physics student:** Guilford, *Intelligence*, p. 148.

301 **Truly creative solutions:** James L. Adams, *Conceptual Blockbusting* (New York: Norton, 1979), pp. 24–31.

301 **"real problem":** Perkins, *Best Work*, p. 217.

301   **abstraction:** W. J. J. Gordon, *Synectics* (New York: Harper & Row, 1961).

302   **The sign of genius:** Aristotle, *De Anima,* ed. Richard McKeon (New York: Random House, 1941), pp. 535–606.

302   **metaphors:** Gardner, *Frames,* pp. 286, 292.

303   **Steven Jobs:** Tom Zito, "Steve Jobs Explains," *Access,* fall 1984, pp. 42–45.

303   **genuinely original:** Gardner, *Frames,* p. 288.

303   **extensive knowledge:** Anne Roe, "A Psychologist Examines Sixty-Four Eminent Scientists," *Scientific American,* 187, 1952, pp. 21–25.

303   **no substitute:** Perkins, *Best Work,* p. 207.

304   **interconnections:** Robert J. Sternberg, *Beyond IQ* (Cambridge, Mass.: Cambridge University Press, 1985), p. 125.

305   **I have never heard:** Charles Kettering, in J. H. Austin, "The Roots of Serendipity," *Saturday Review/World,* 2, April 1974, pp. 60–64.

305   **"In practical matters":** Aristotle, *Nichomachean Ethics,* ed. Richard McKeon (New York: Random House, 1941), pp. 935–1126.

Index

corporate culture, 104, 208
correlations, 23-25
  illusory, 228
creativity, 45, 290-304
critical thinking, 241-263
  tests of, 245-246
Cutler, Paul, 221, 239, 275

DeBono, Edward, 297-298
decisionmaking, 32, 233-237
  rational model, 32
defense mechanisms, 78-80
DeLorean, John Z., 55-56
dentists, 126, 128
depression, 58-61
desensitization, 207-208
designing, 150-151
Dewey, John, 35, 242, 259
diagnosis, 214-216, 224, 229, 230
dictation, 198
differentiation, 282
divergent production, 292-293
Dr. Fox effect, 247
drawing, 128
  maps, 176-180
Dreyfus, Hubert and Stuart, 276
Duncan Scale, 21

edges, 171
Edwards, Betty, 128, 169
ego, 81, 82
Elbow, Peter, 198-200, 204, 206-207,
  297
Elgin, Suzette, 110-111, 116, 277
Ellis, Albert, 65
Elstein, Arthur, 223
Emergency Medical Technicians, 279
empathy, 95-98
entrepreneurs, 274
Erikson, Erik, 68, 71, 75
Eskimos, 153-154
ethological approach, 37
evidence, 253-256
expert systems, 33
Eysenck, Hans, 19, 21, 26

failure, 87, 271, 285
Faraday, Michael, 147
feedback, 134, 237
feedforward, 138-139
field dependence-independence,
  268-270
Fitts, Paul, 131, 133
Flower, Linda, 199, 202
Fog Index, 203-204
Foreign Service, 89

Foutz, Jesse L. 89-90, 148
Franklin, Benjamin, 233-234
Fredericksen, Norman, 38, 92
freewriting, 199
Freud, Sigmund, 63-64, 75, 78-79
Fuller, James, 214-218, 237

g, 19-20, 27, 30, 184
Gallwey, Timothy, 137
Galton, Francis, 161, 175
Gardner, Howard, 30, 42-44, 52-53, 57,
  91, 92, 121, 127, 155-160, 180, 210,
  302, 303
Garfield, Charles, 54, 116
Geller, Uri, 254
Geneen, Harold, 9, 56, 242
General Motors, 25, 55, 279
Gergen, Kenneth, 72, 76
Geschwind, Norman, 74, 75
Ghiselli, E. E., 37
Gilder, George, 280
Girard, Joe, 113
Glaser, Edward, 245
Glaser, Robert, 222
Goleman, Daniel, ix, 56, 64-65, 70, 80, 81
Goodwin, Guy, 144
Gordon, W., 169, 301
Greenwald, Anthony, 64-65, 75-76,
  81-82
gross motor control, 127
group process, 104-110
groupthink, 25, 109-110
Guilford, J. P., 21, 30

Heidegger, Martin, 125
Hernnstein, Richard, 17, 19, 20
heuristics, 235
hierachical motor programs, 140
Hogarth, Robin, 225-227, 291
holistic style, 268-271
Holmes, Sherlock, 257
hunches, 271-277
hunting, 154-158

Iacocca, Lee, 51-52, 55, 88, 185, 271
Illitch, Ivan, 10
implications of argument, 259-261
impulsiveness, 44, 277-280
In-basket Technique, 38
incubation, 202, 296
information, 7, 31, 99
  gathering, 221-222
integration, 281
intelligence, 4, 7, 14-16, 20, 31
  body, 44, 121-144
  crystallized, 17

Nelson, Richard, 169
networks, social, 104-106
neurotic distortion, 107
nine dots problem, 295, 301
Nisbett, Richard, 229
Nizer, Louis, 88
nodes, 171
Not Guilty by Reason of Insanity plea, 255, 260

open-mindedness, 250-252
orientation, 163
Orwell, George, 205
outlining, 201
overlapping motor programs, 138

P. T. Barnum effect, 66-67, 93
Papert, Seymour, 125, 142
paths, 170
Paul, Richard, 244
Perkins, David, 245, 257, 261, 291, 296, 300, 301, 303
Perot, H. Ross, 279
Peter Principle, 291
Peters, John H., 5-7, 281
Peters, Thomas, 25, 78, 87, 185, 279, 284, 288
physicians, 96-97, 103, 214-221, 251, 275, 283, 284
Piaget, Jean, 163, 210
pilots, 127-128, 132
planning, 232-237
    long-range, 285-286
Plato, 8, 14, 88, 283-284
Plunkett, Lorne, 212
Plutchik, Robert, 22
Poincaré, Henri, 296, 298, 300
practical intelligence, 3, 29, 39-40, 42-47
presumptions in arguments, 261-262
problem-solving, 32, 210-240
proprioception, 121
psychoanalysis, 63-64
Puluwat islanders, 153
Putnam, Hilary, 17
Pygmalion effect, 24
Pylyshyn, Zenon, 165-166

Randi, James, 254
Rational Emotive Therapy, 65, 74
Raven, John, 9, 11, 26
reader-based prose, 202-204
reading, 189-197
    speed-, 191
reflective style, 277-280
regions, 171

revision, 202-206
risky shift, 107-108
Roe, Anne, 147
Rosenthal, Robert, 24
route maps, 172-173

Scarr, Sandra, 36
Schachter, Stanley, 68
Schafer, Alan, 128
Scheflen, Albert, 100, 104
schemas, 64, 94, 195, 219
    shared, 106
    spatial, 172-174
Schön, Donald, 148, 150, 230, 239
schools, 11-13
Scribner, Sylvia, 8
self, 62-82
    multiple, 71-77
    social, 68-70
    understanding, 51-82
self defense, verbal, 110-11, 115
selling, 4, 11-115
sensitivity, see empathy
sensory extension, 144-145
Shanker, Albert, 11
Shepard, Roger, 162
Simon, Herbert, 223, 235, 274-275
simulations, 38-39, 133
skiing, 129-131
skills, 46
social facilitation, 108
social intelligence, 85-119
    learnable, 93
    tests of, 91-92, 95, 99
social loafing, 108
sociogram, 105
soldiers, 186, 279
source evaluation, 247-250
spatial relations, 162-163
speaking, public, 206-209
Spearman, Charles, 18-19, 27, 29
Spock, Mr., 210-211, 246
Sternberg, Robert J., 33-34, 36, 39-40, 53, 58, 87, 99, 186, 238, 271, 277, 278, 304
Stevens, Wallace, 36, 121, 183
Streufert, Siegfried, 38, 281, 285, 286-287
success, 25
Sudnow, David, 126, 137, 139, 143, 145
Synectics, 301-303
systematic style, 271-273

teachers, 54, 57, 97-98
Terkel, Studs, 122, 189, 244
Terman, Louis, 15, 16, 17